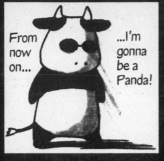

From now on... ...I'm gonna be a Panda!

I always draw ridiculous looking self-portraits for this series, so I have a really hard time when I need to draw one for other magazines. It's regrettable how they always use the "underwear" picture from volume one. Really regrettable.

—*Hiromu Arakawa, 2004*

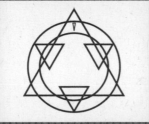

Born in Hokkaido (northern Japan), Hiromu Arakawa first attracted national attention in 1999 with her award-winning manga *Stray Dog*. Her series *Fullmetal Alchemist* debuted in 2001 in Square Enix's monthly manga anthology *Shonen Gangan*.

FULLMETAL ALCHEMIST VOL. 8

Story and Art by Hiromu Arakawa

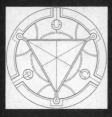

Translation/Akira Watanabe
English Adaptation/Jake Forbes
Touch-up Art & Lettering/Wayne Truman
Design/Amy Martin
Editor/Urian Brown

Editor in Chief, Books/Alvin Lu
Editor in Chief, Magazines/Marc Weidenbaum
VP, Publishing Licensing/Rika Inouye
VP, Sales & Product Marketing/Gonzalo Ferreyra
VP, Creative/Linda Espinosa
Publisher/Hyoe Narita

Printed in the U.S.A.

Published by VIZ Media, LLC
P.O. Box 77010
San Francisco, CA 94107

10 9 8 7 6 5 4 3 2
First printing, July 2006
Second printing, September 2008

www.viz.com

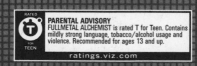

store.viz.com

鋼の錬金術師

FULLMETAL ALCHEMIST

8

荒川弘

HIROMU ARAKAWA

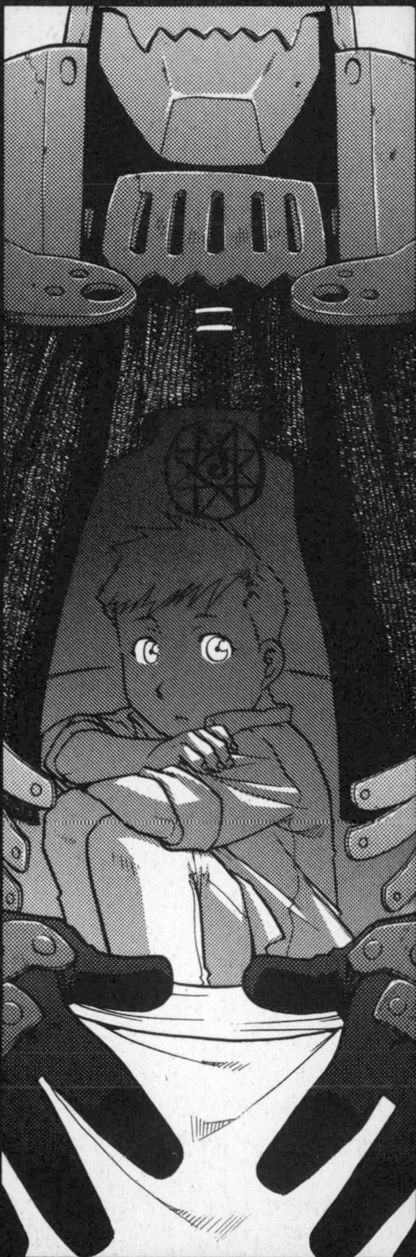

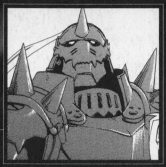

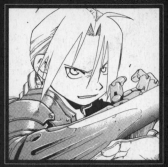

□ アルフォンス・エルリック

Alphonse Elric

□ エドワード・エルリック

Edward Elric

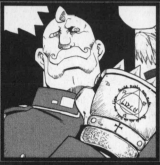

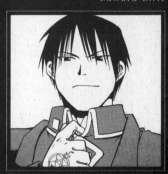

□ アレックス・ルイ・アームストロング

Alex Louis Armstrong

□ ロイ・マスタング

Roy Mustang

OUTLINE
FULLMETAL ALCHEMIST

Using a forbidden alchemical ritual, the Elric brothers attempted to bring their dead mother back to life. But the ritual went wrong, consuming Edward Elric's leg and Alphonse Elric's entire body. At the cost of his arm, Edward was able to graft his brother's soul into a suit of armor. Equipped with mechanical "auto-mail" to replace his missing limbs, Edward becomes a state alchemist, serving the military on deadly missions. Now, the two brothers roam the world in search of a way to regain what they have lost…

Having reunited with their former teacher, Izumi Curtis, the boys now seek a way to recall Al's lost memories of losing his physical body, which may be the key to changing the brothers back to normal. Little do the Elrics know that they, too, are being hunted. Greed, a homunculus who bears the Ouroboros tattoo, kidnaps Al to find the secrets of merging a soul with a suit of armor. When Ed tries to rescue his brother, the situation turns violent. Soon, chaos ensues as Führer President Bradley himself leads an assault on Greed's underground lair…

鋼の錬金術師
FULLMETAL ALCHEMIST

CHARACTERS
FULLMETAL ALCHEMIST

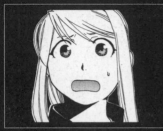

□ ウィンリィ・ロックベル

Winry Rockbell

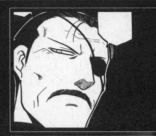

□ イズミ・カーティス

King Bradley

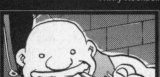

□ グラトニー

Gluttony

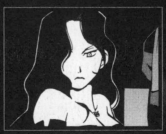

□ ラスト

Lust

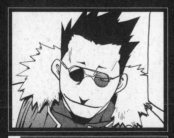

□ グリード

Greed

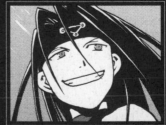

□ エンヴィー

Envy

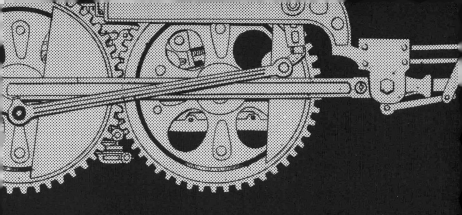

CONTENTS

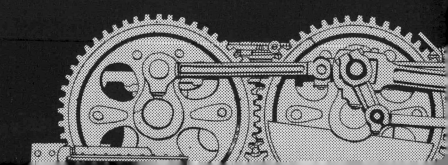

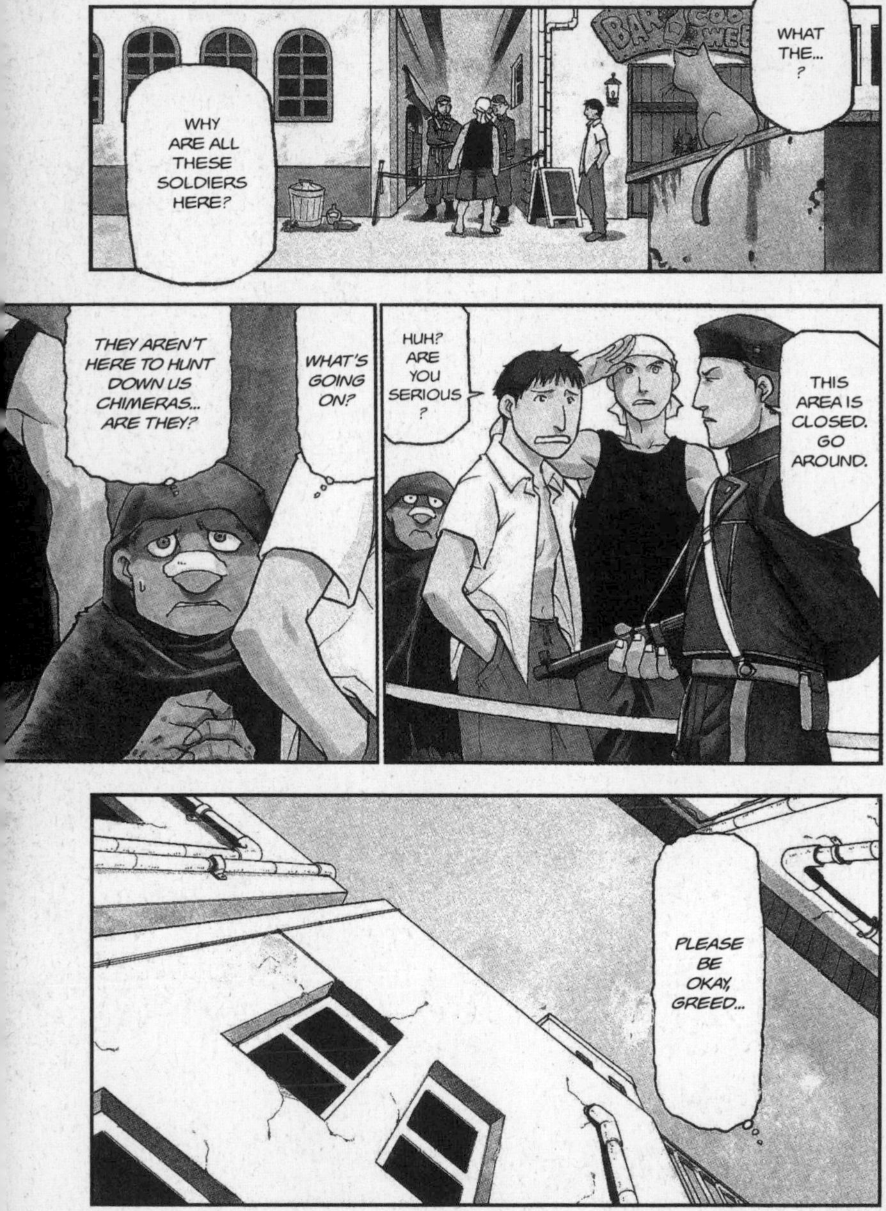
WHAT THE... ?
WHY ARE ALL THESE SOLDIERS HERE?
THIS AREA IS CLOSED. GO AROUND.
HUH? ARE YOU SERIOUS?
WHAT'S GOING ON?
THEY AREN'T HERE TO HUNT DOWN US CHIMERAS... ARE THEY?
PLEASE BE OKAY, GREED...

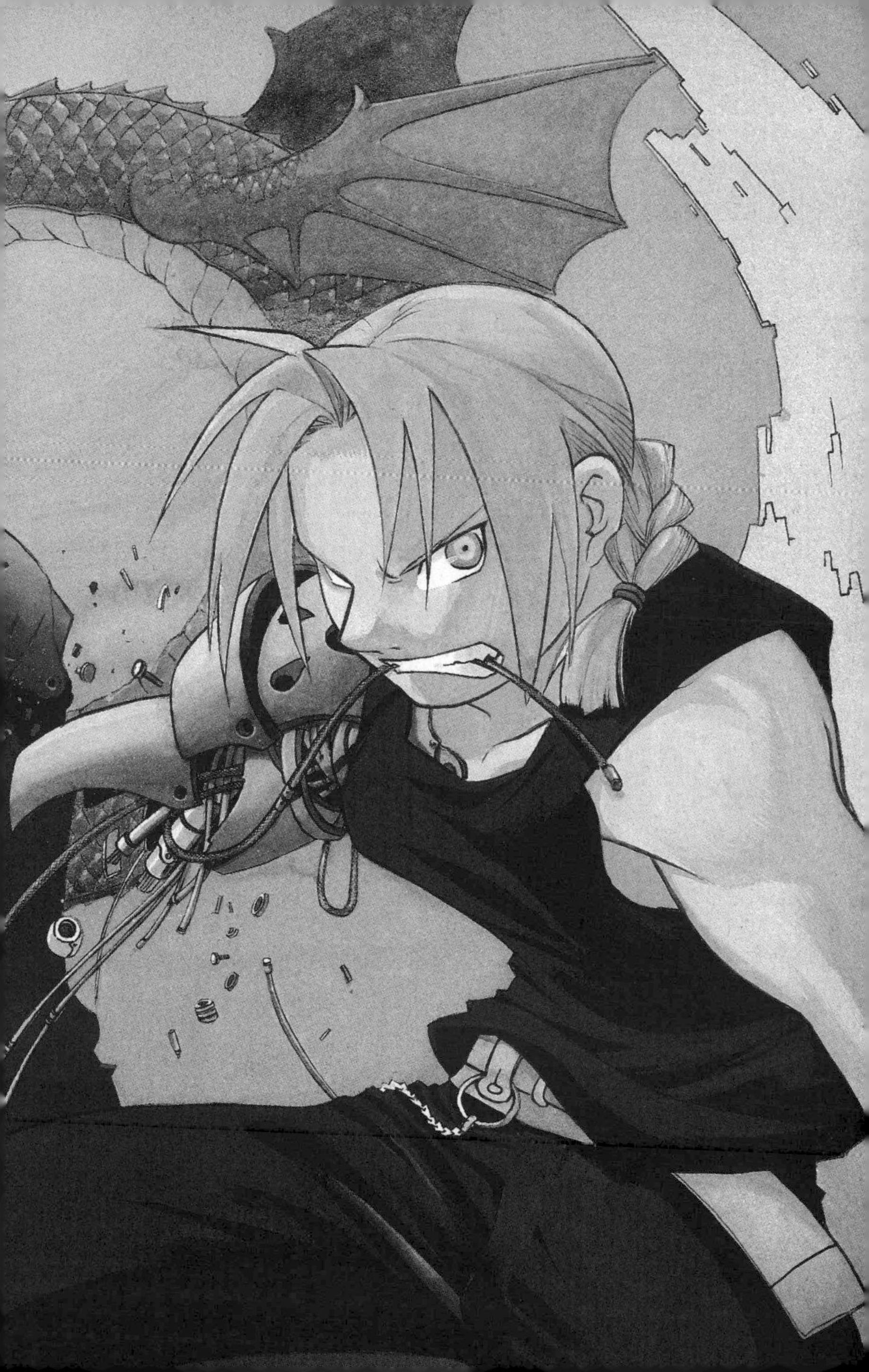

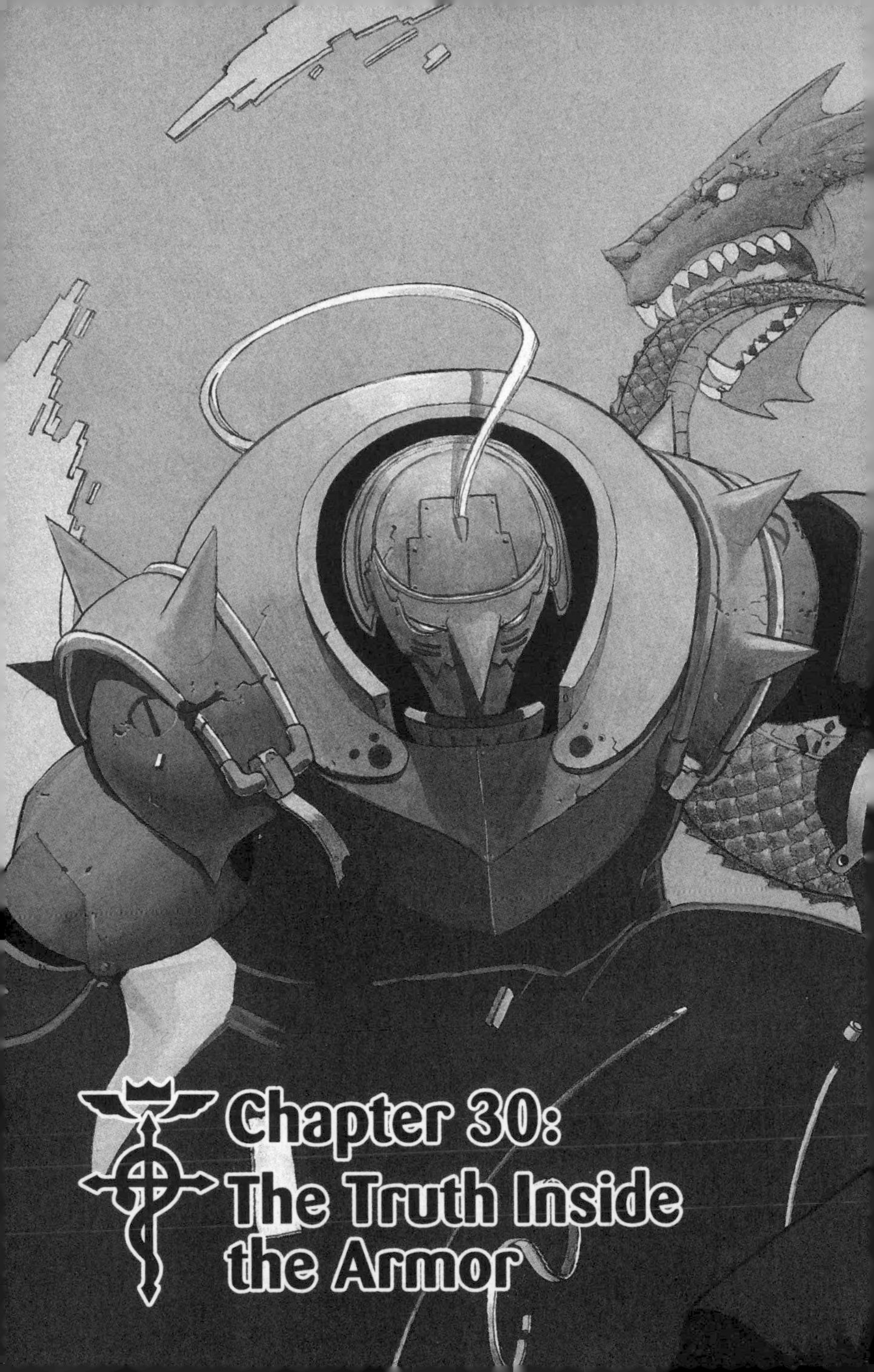
Chapter 30:
The Truth Inside the Armor

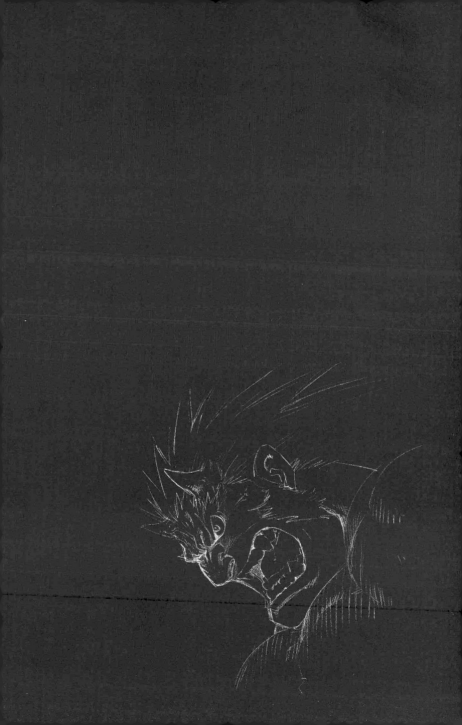

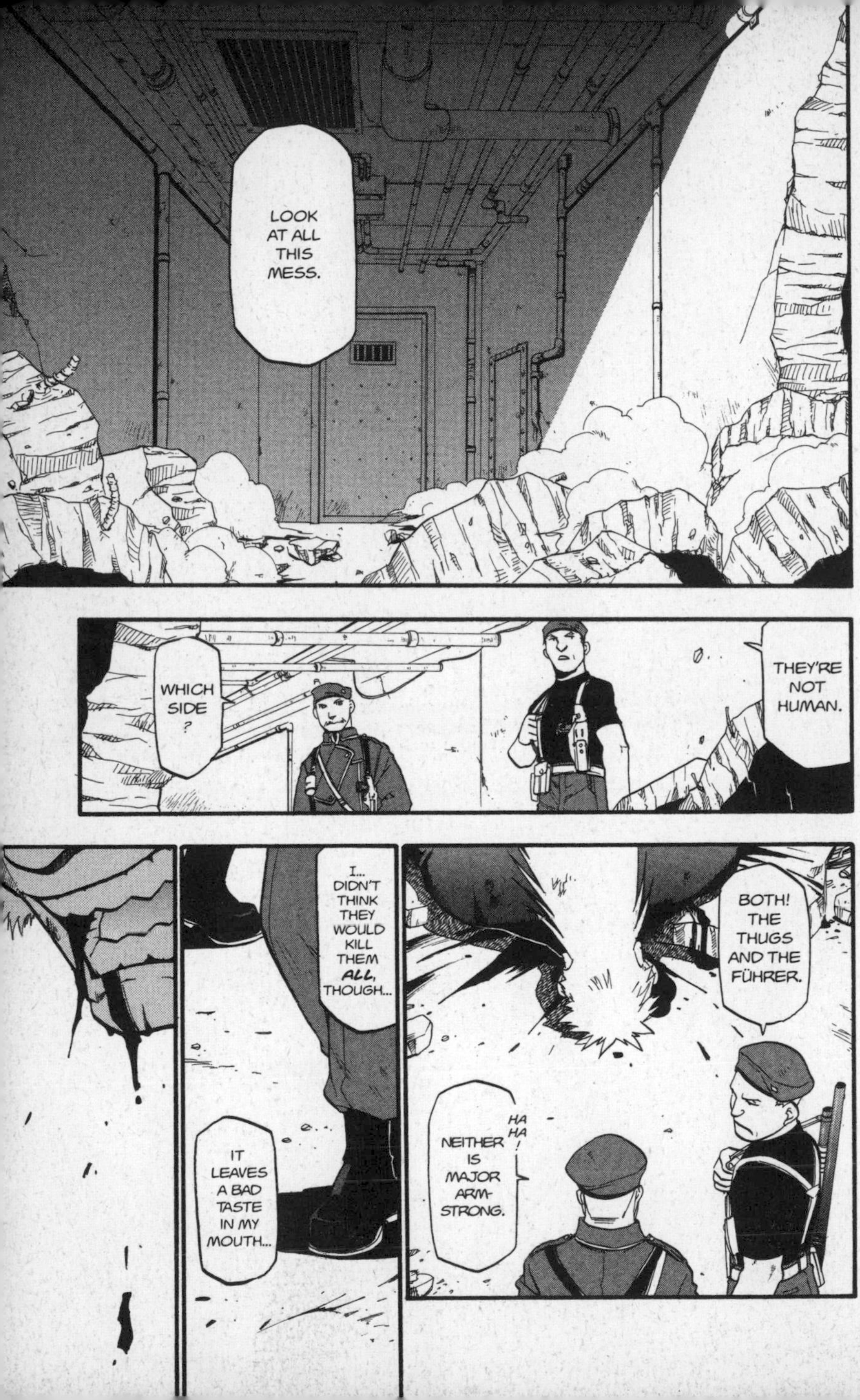
LOOK AT ALL THIS MESS.
THEY'RE NOT HUMAN.
WHICH SIDE?
BOTH! THE THUGS AND THE FÜHRER.
HA HA!
NEITHER IS MAJOR ARMSTRONG.
I... DIDN'T THINK THEY WOULD KILL THEM *ALL*, THOUGH...
IT LEAVES A BAD TASTE IN MY MOUTH...

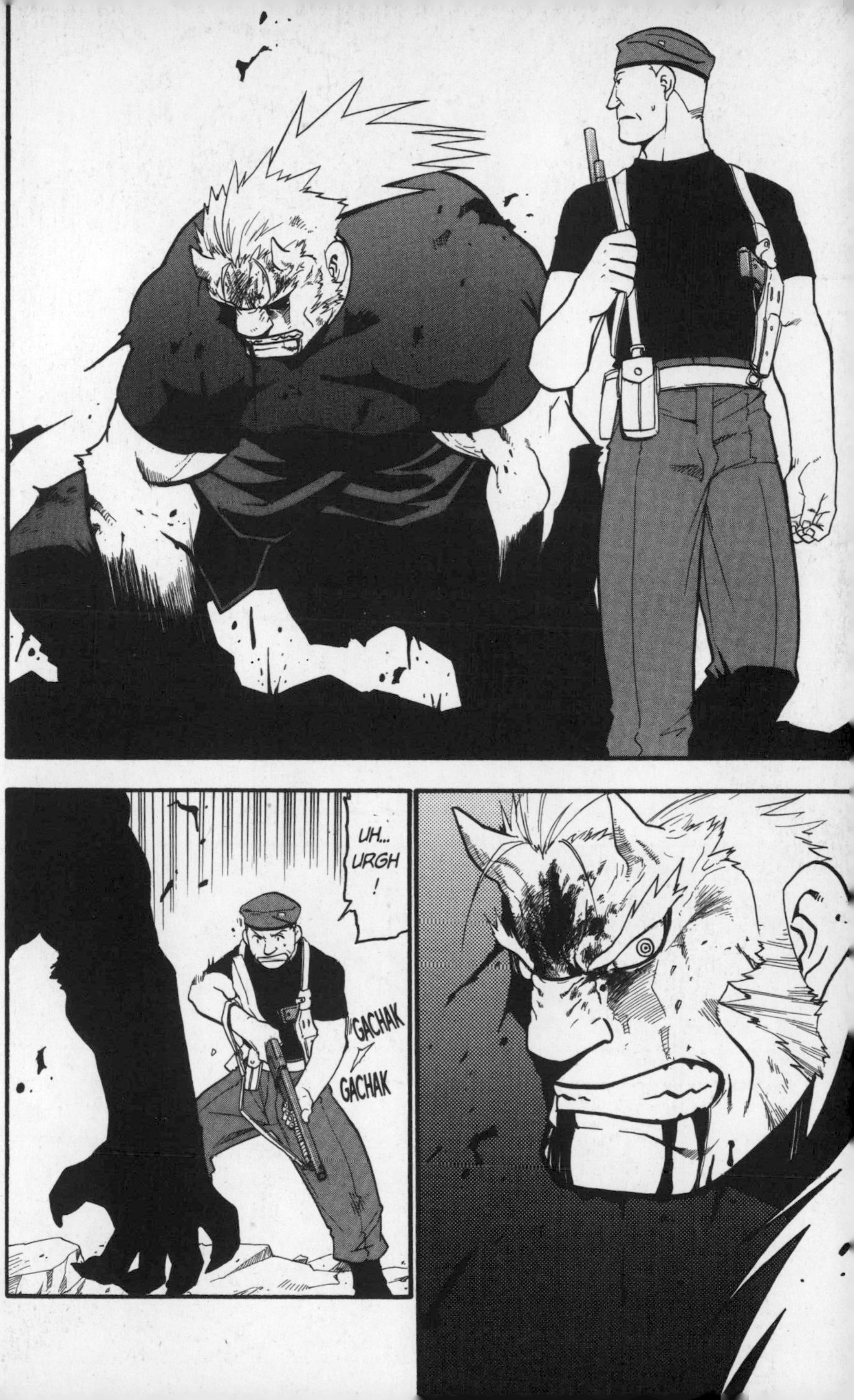
UH... URGH!
GACHAK GACHAK

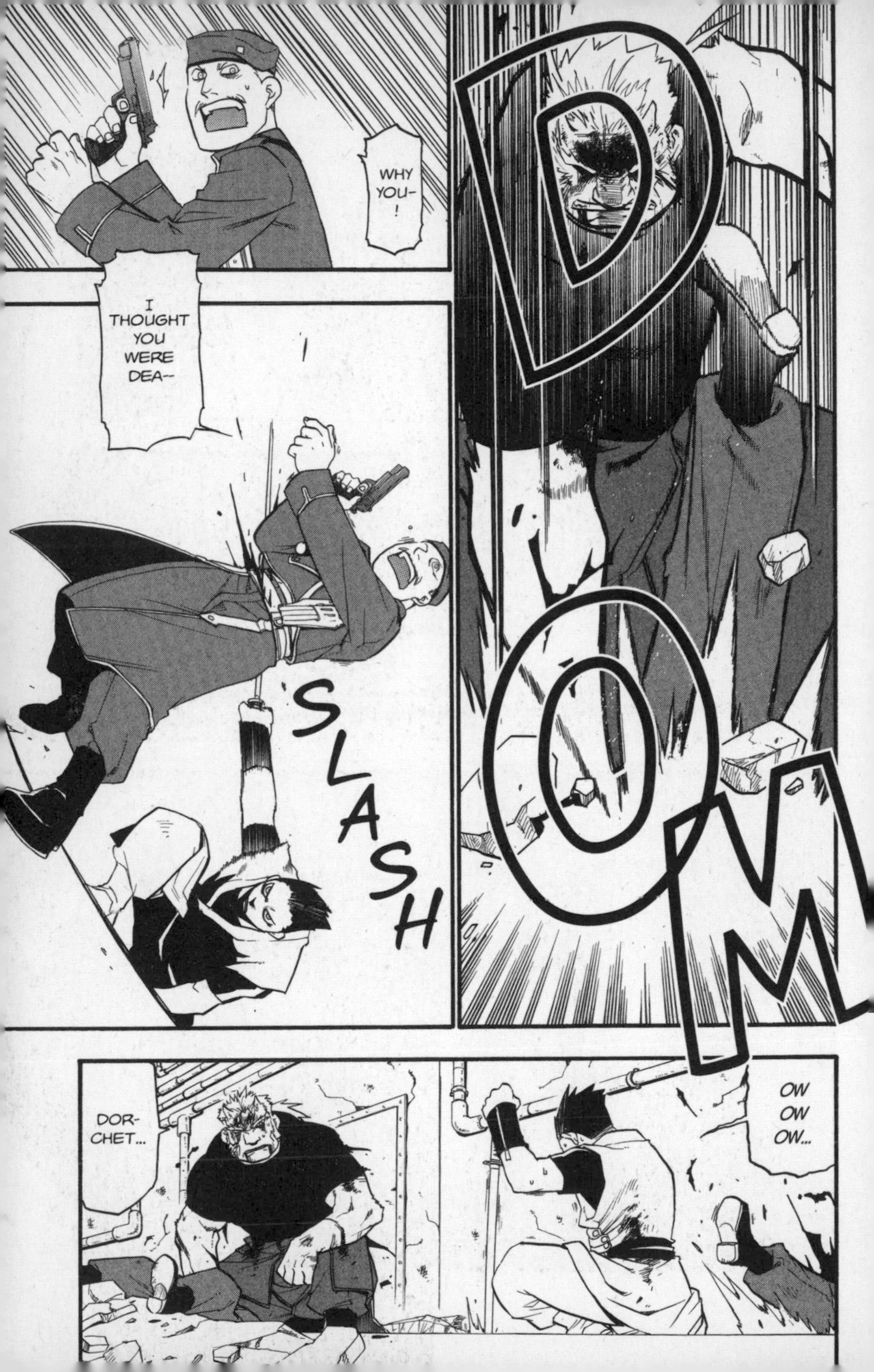
DOOM
WHY YOU-!
I THOUGHT YOU WERE DEA--
SLASH
OW OW OW...
DOR-CHET...

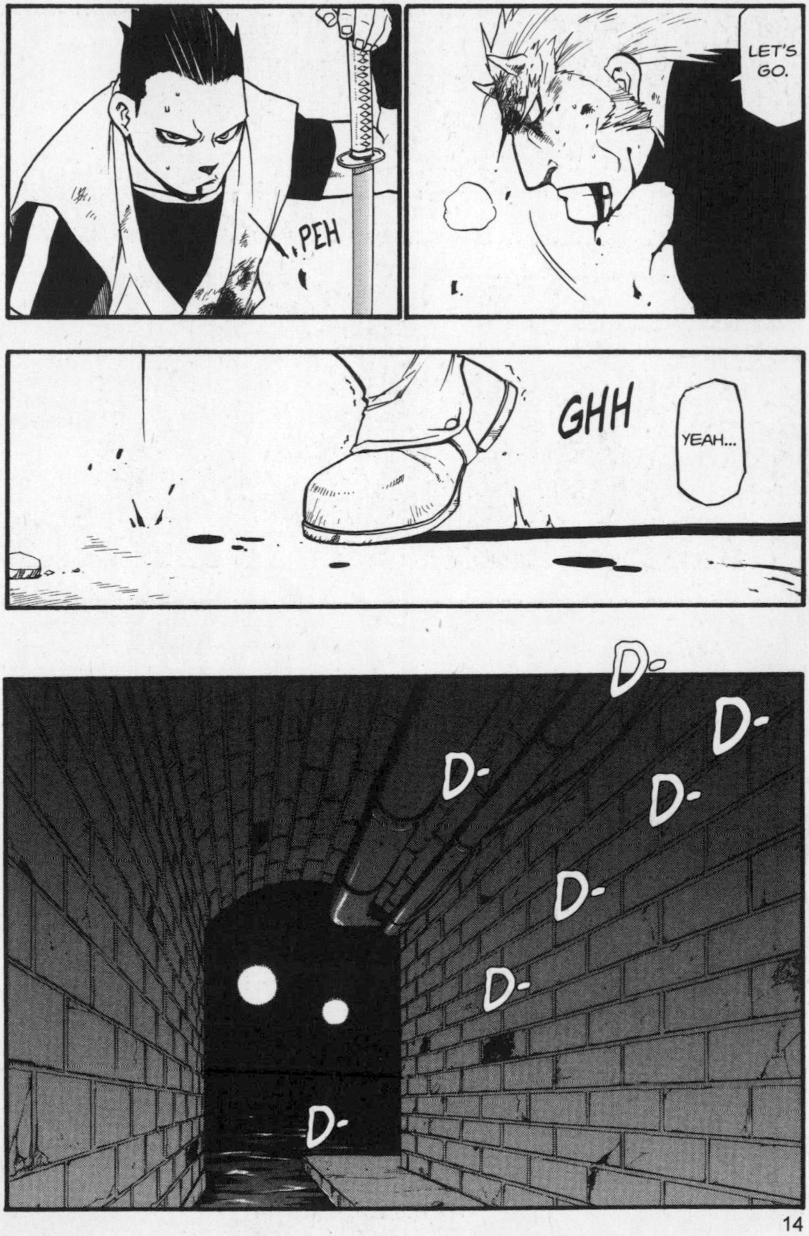
LET'S GO.
PEH
GHH
YEAH...
D-
D-
D-
D-
D-
D-
D-

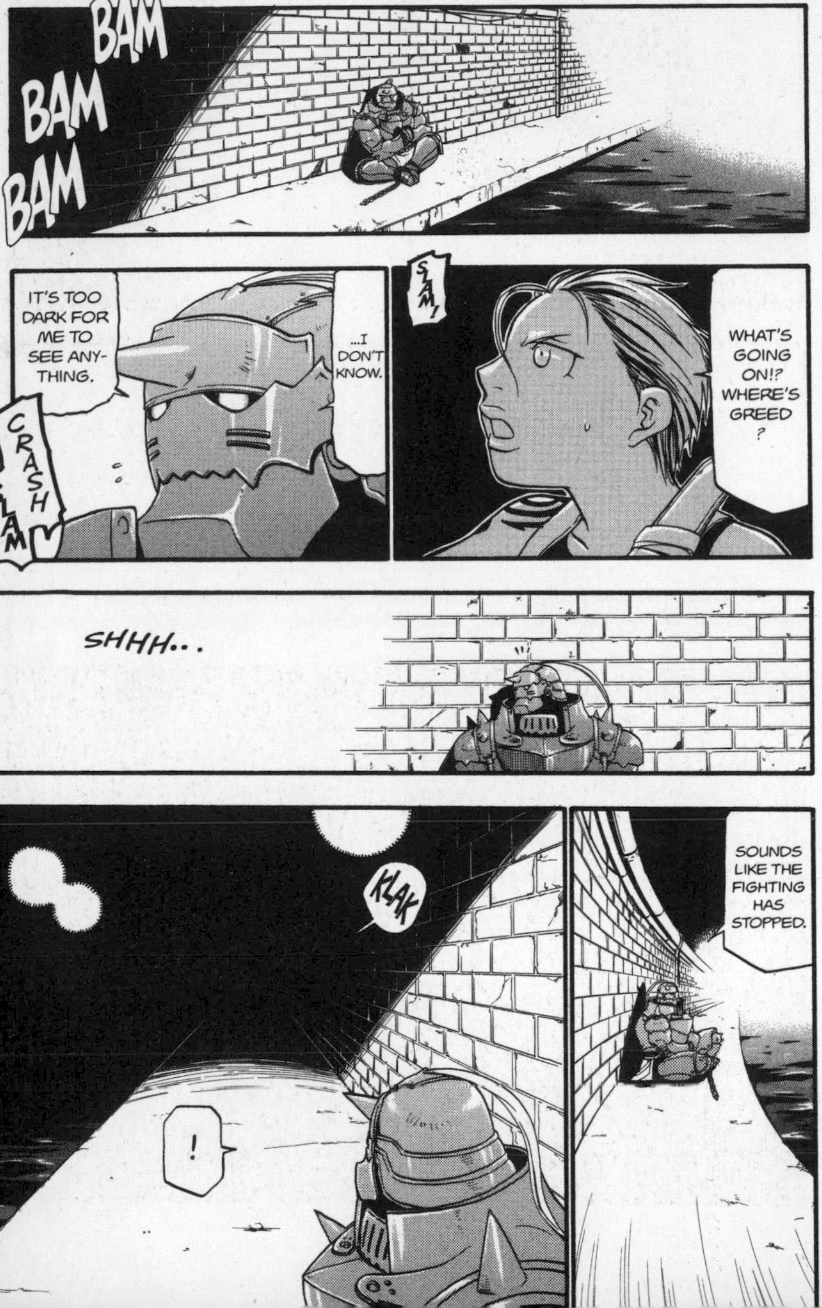
BAM
BAM
BAM
BAM
SLAM!
WHAT'S GOING ON!? WHERE'S GREED?
...I DON'T KNOW.
IT'S TOO DARK FOR ME TO SEE ANY-THING.
CRASH
SLAM
SHHH...
SOUNDS LIKE THE FIGHTING HAS STOPPED.
KLAK
!

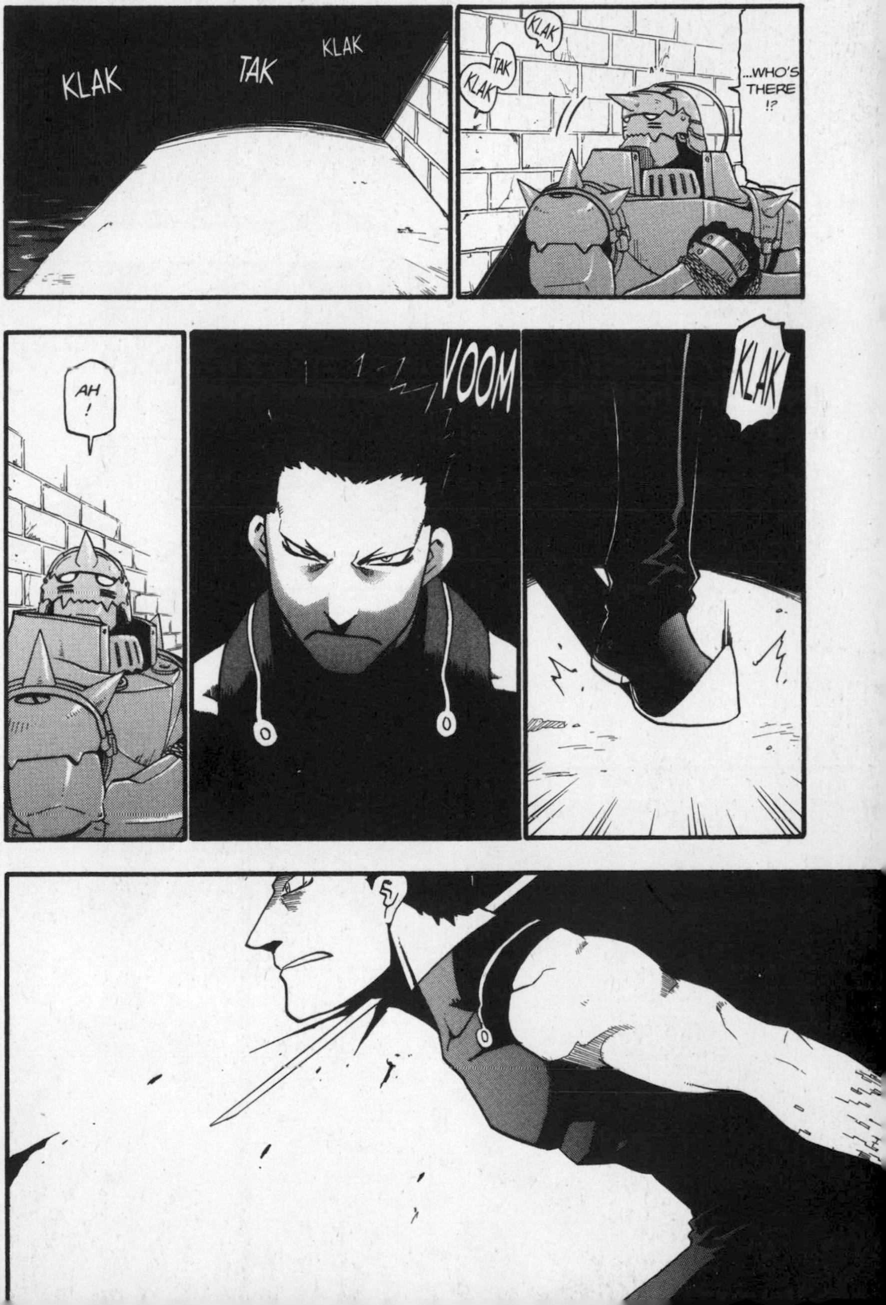
KLAK
TAK
KLAK
...WHO'S THERE !?
KLAK
TAK
KLAK
KLAK
VOOM
AH !

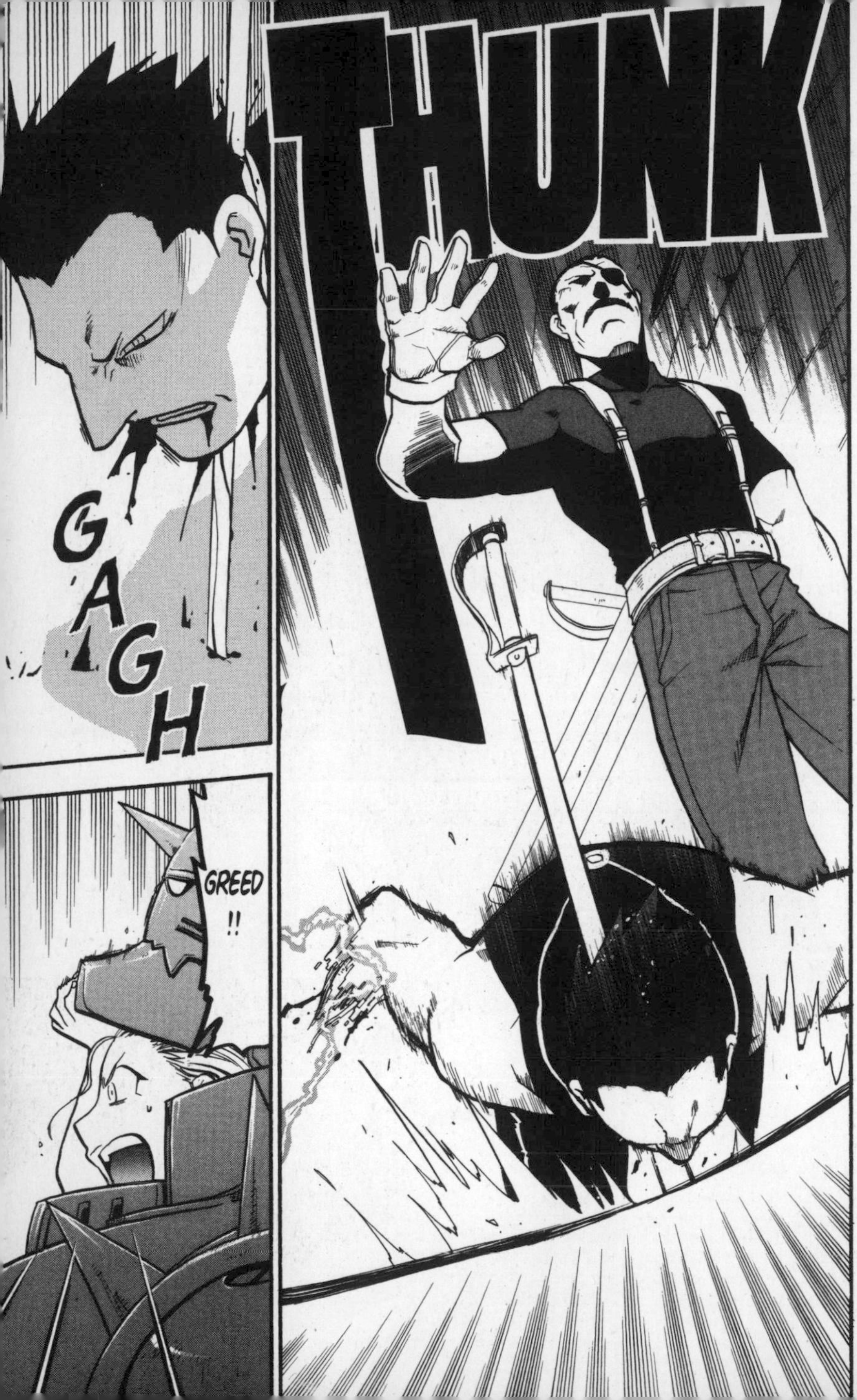
THUNK
GAGH
GREED !!

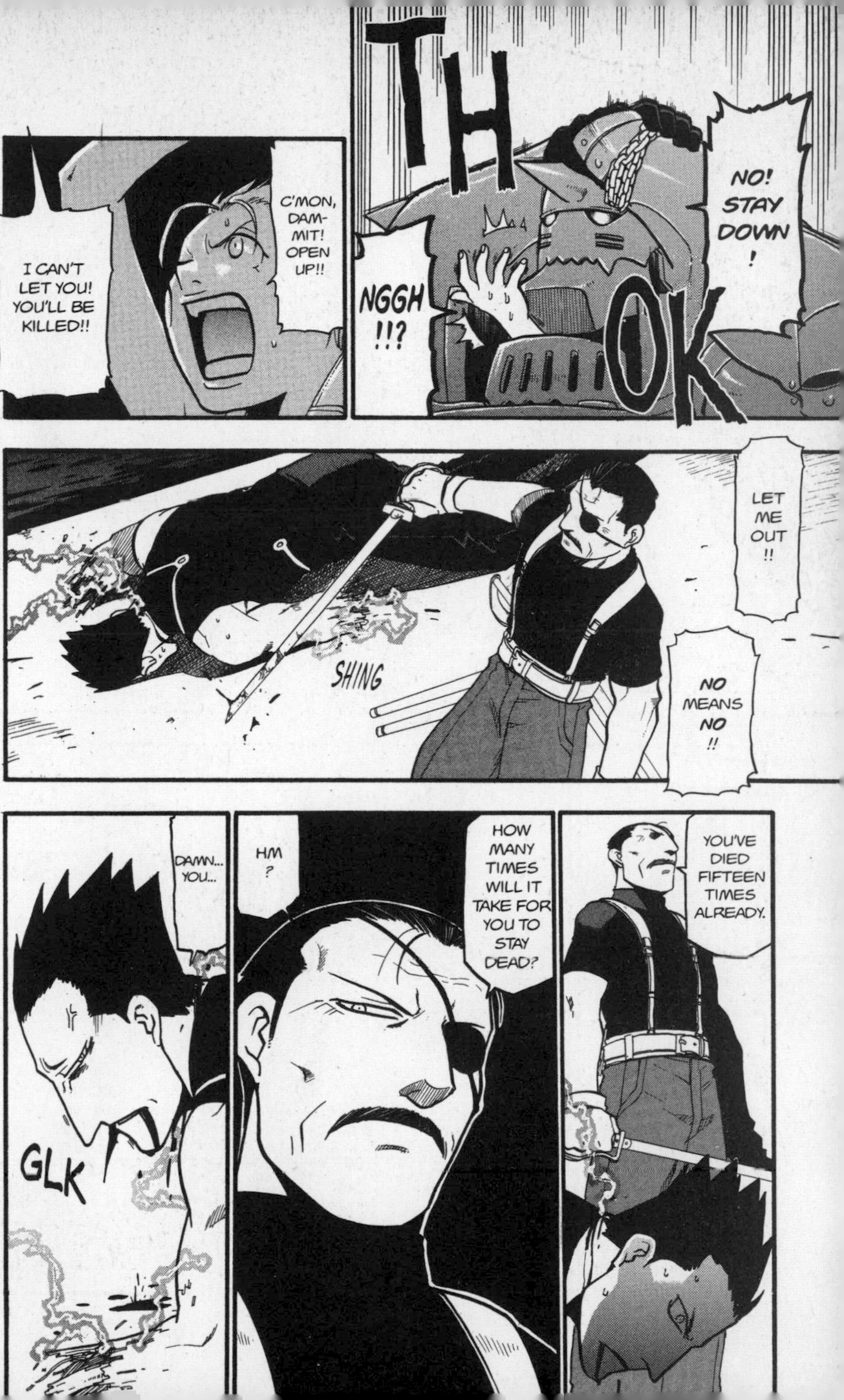

THOK
NO! STAY DOWN!
NGGH!!?
C'MON, DAM-MIT! OPEN UP!!
I CAN'T LET YOU! YOU'LL BE KILLED!!
LET ME OUT!!
NO MEANS NO!!
SHING
YOU'VE DIED FIFTEEN TIMES ALREADY.
HOW MANY TIMES WILL IT TAKE FOR YOU TO STAY DEAD?
HM?
DAMN... YOU...
GLK

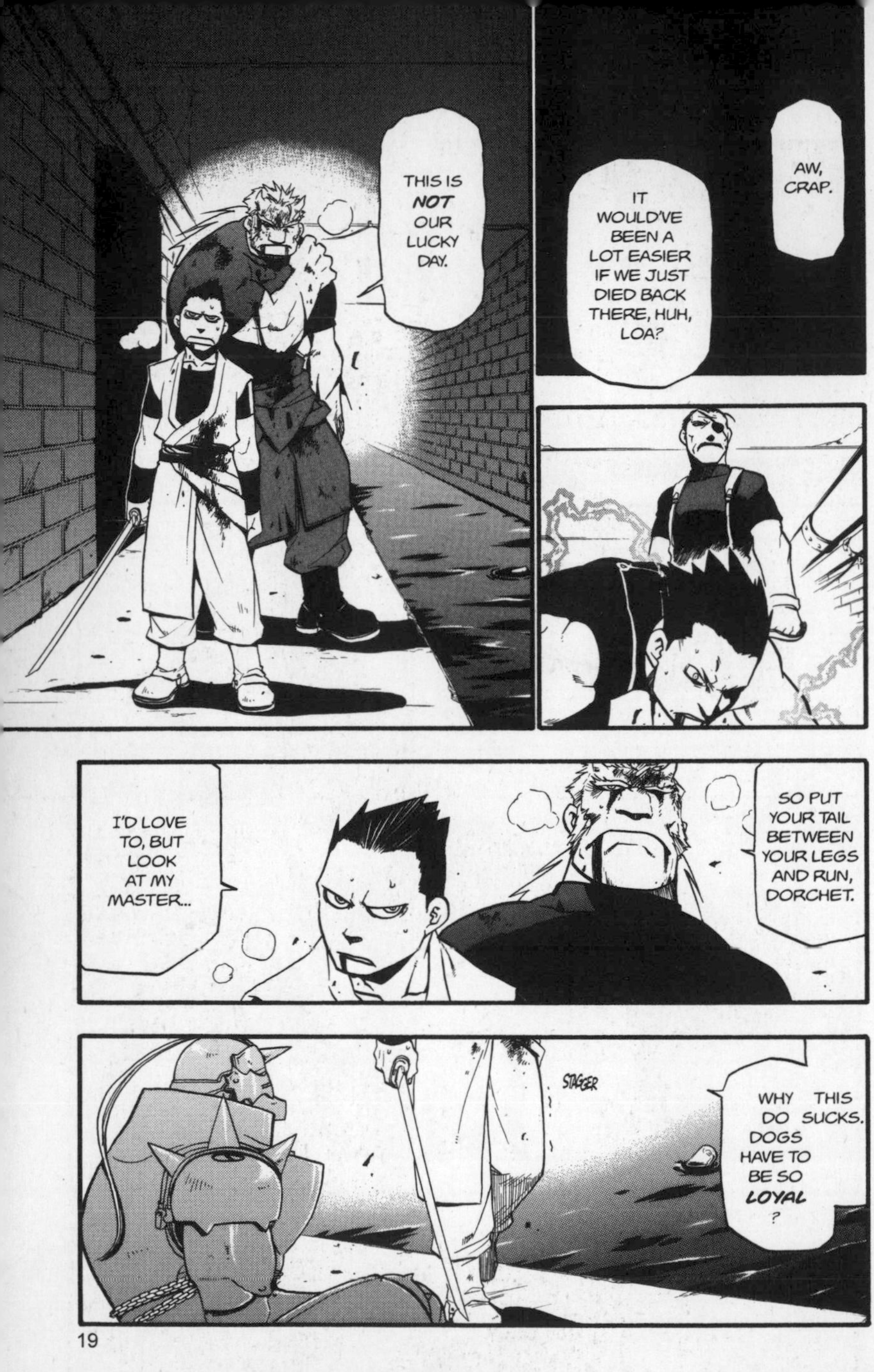
AW, CRAP.
IT WOULD'VE BEEN A LOT EASIER IF WE JUST DIED BACK THERE, HUH, LOA?
THIS IS ***NOT*** OUR LUCKY DAY.
SO PUT YOUR TAIL BETWEEN YOUR LEGS AND RUN, DORCHET.
I'D LOVE TO, BUT LOOK AT MY MASTER...
THIS SUCKS.
WHY DO DOGS HAVE TO BE SO ***LOYAL***?
STAGGER

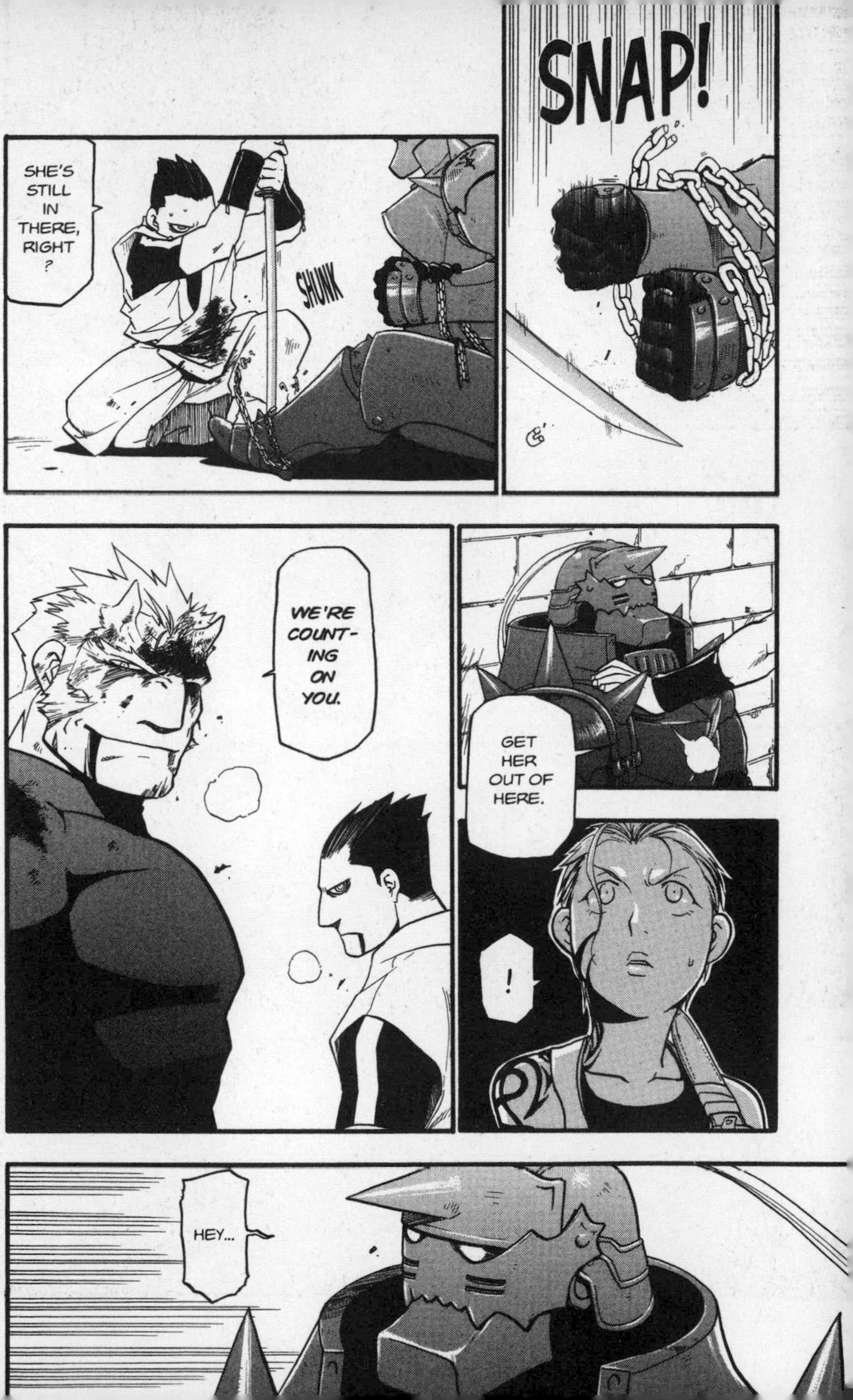
SNAP!
SHE'S STILL IN THERE, RIGHT?
SHUNK
GET HER OUT OF HERE.
!
WE'RE COUNTING ON YOU.
HEY...

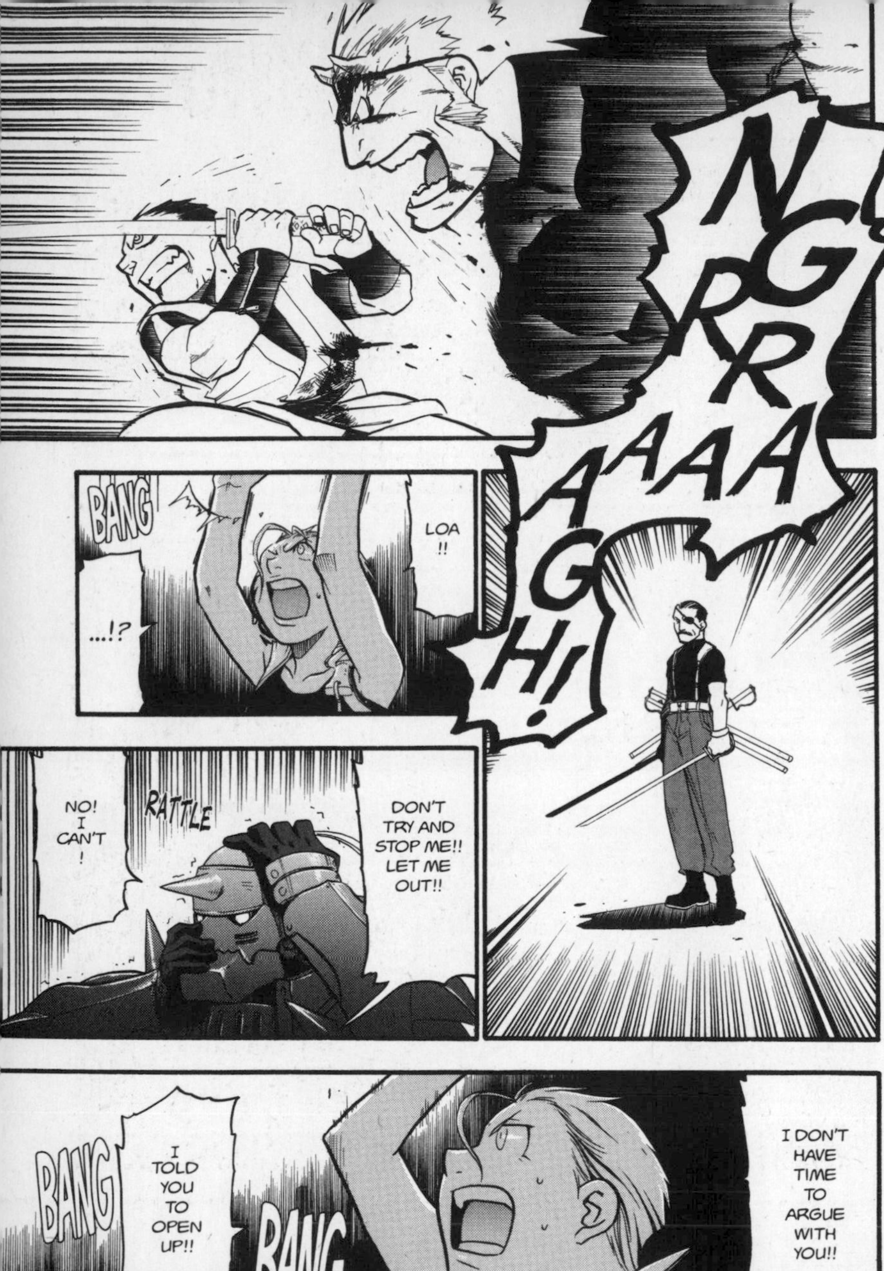
NGRRAAAAAGH!!
LOA !!
BANG
...!?
DON'T TRY AND STOP ME!! LET ME OUT!!
RATTLE
NO! I CAN'T !
I DON'T HAVE TIME TO ARGUE WITH YOU!!
BANG
I TOLD YOU TO OPEN UP!!
BANG

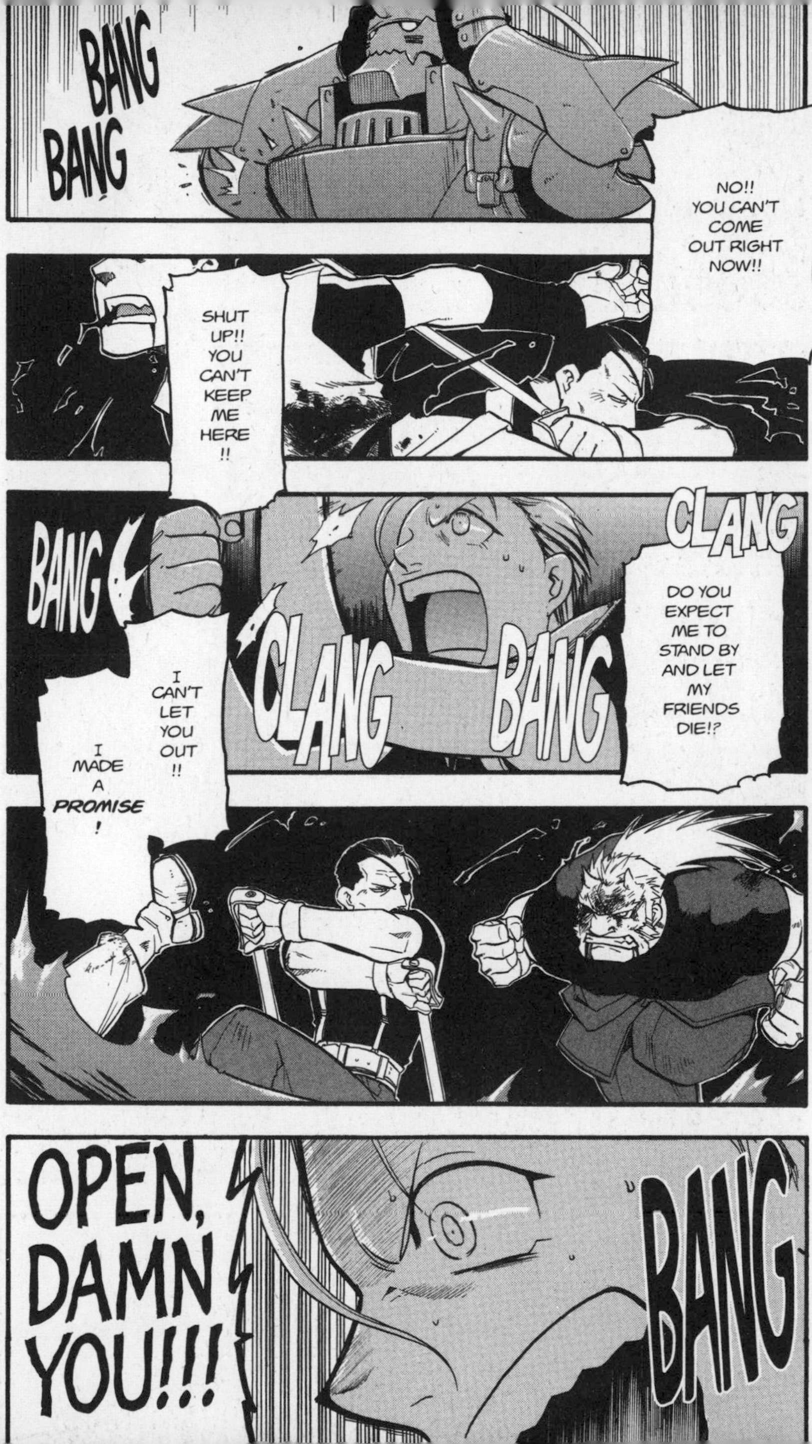
BANG BANG
NO!! YOU CAN'T COME OUT RIGHT NOW!!
SHUT UP!! YOU CAN'T KEEP ME HERE!!
CLANG
DO YOU EXPECT ME TO STAND BY AND LET MY FRIENDS DIE!?
BANG
CLANG
BANG
I CAN'T LET YOU OUT!!
I MADE A PROMISE!
BANG
OPEN, DAMN YOU!!!

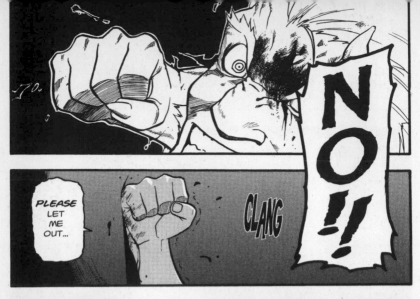

PLEASE
LET
ME
OUT...

CLANG

NO!!

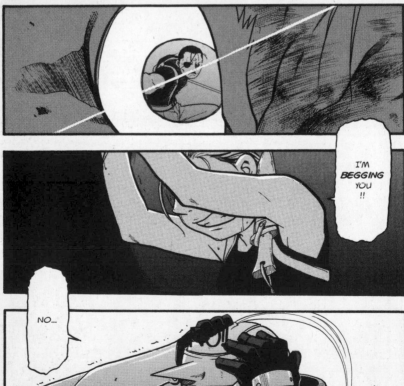

I'M
BEGGING
YOU
!!

NO...

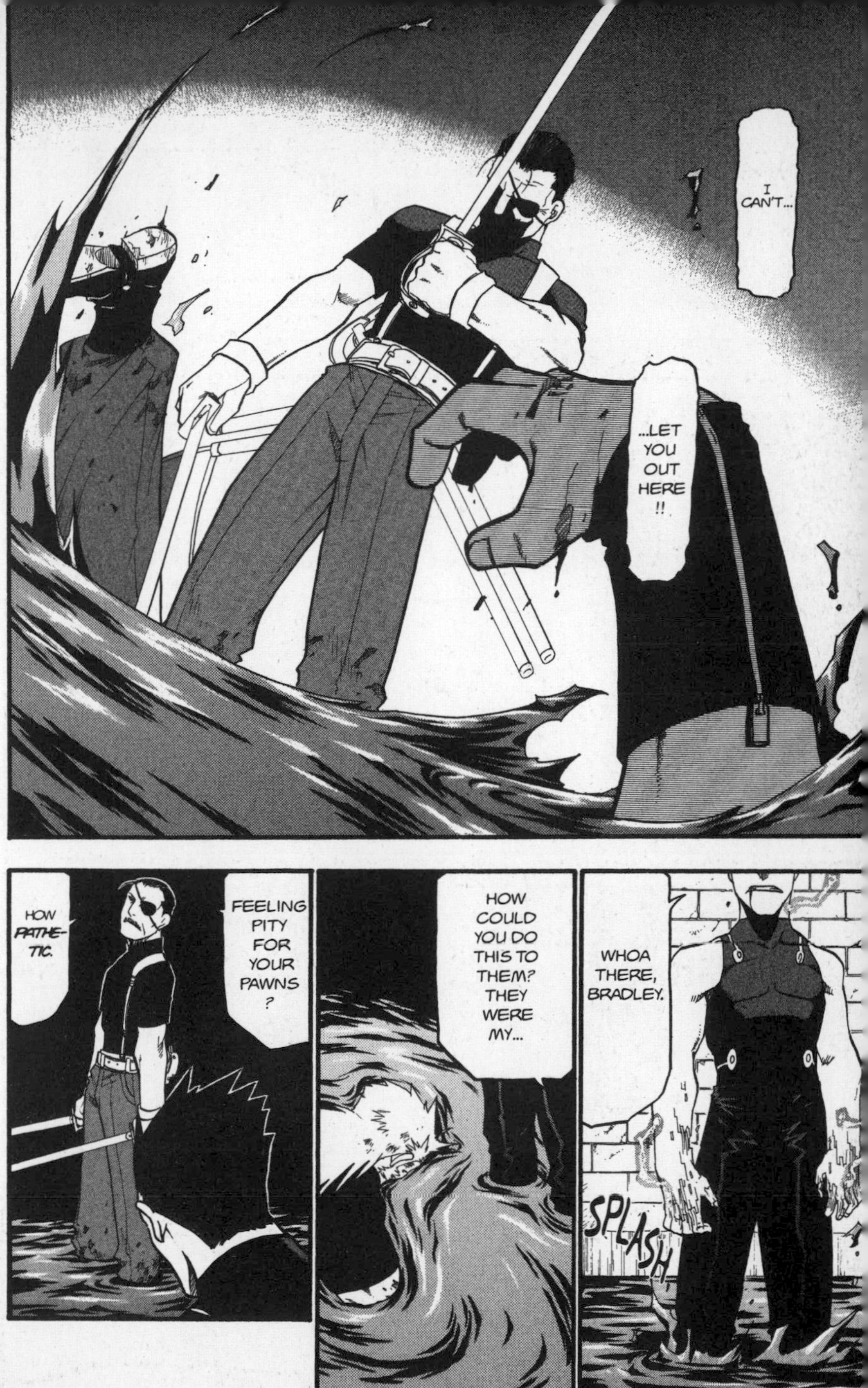
I CAN'T...
...LET YOU OUT HERE!!
WHOA THERE, BRADLEY.
SPLASH
HOW COULD YOU DO THIS TO THEM? THEY WERE MY...
FEELING PITY FOR YOUR PAWNS?
HOW PATHETIC.

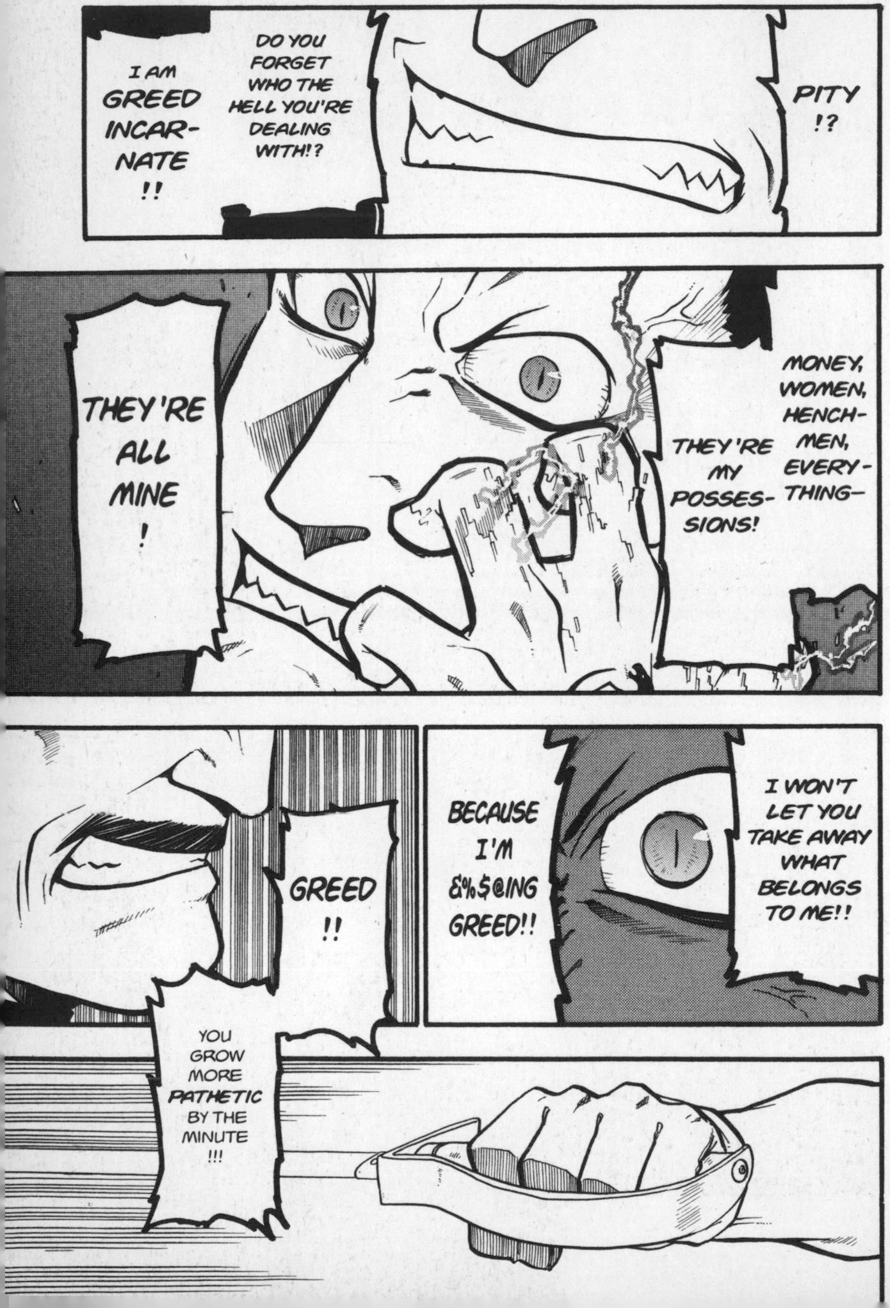
PITY !?
DO YOU FORGET WHO THE HELL YOU'RE DEALING WITH!?
I AM GREED INCARNATE !!
MONEY, WOMEN, HENCHMEN, EVERYTHING—
THEY'RE MY POSSESSIONS!
THEY'RE ALL MINE !
I WON'T LET YOU TAKE AWAY WHAT BELONGS TO ME!!
BECAUSE I'M &%$@ING GREED!!
GREED !!
YOU GROW MORE PATHETIC BY THE MINUTE !!!

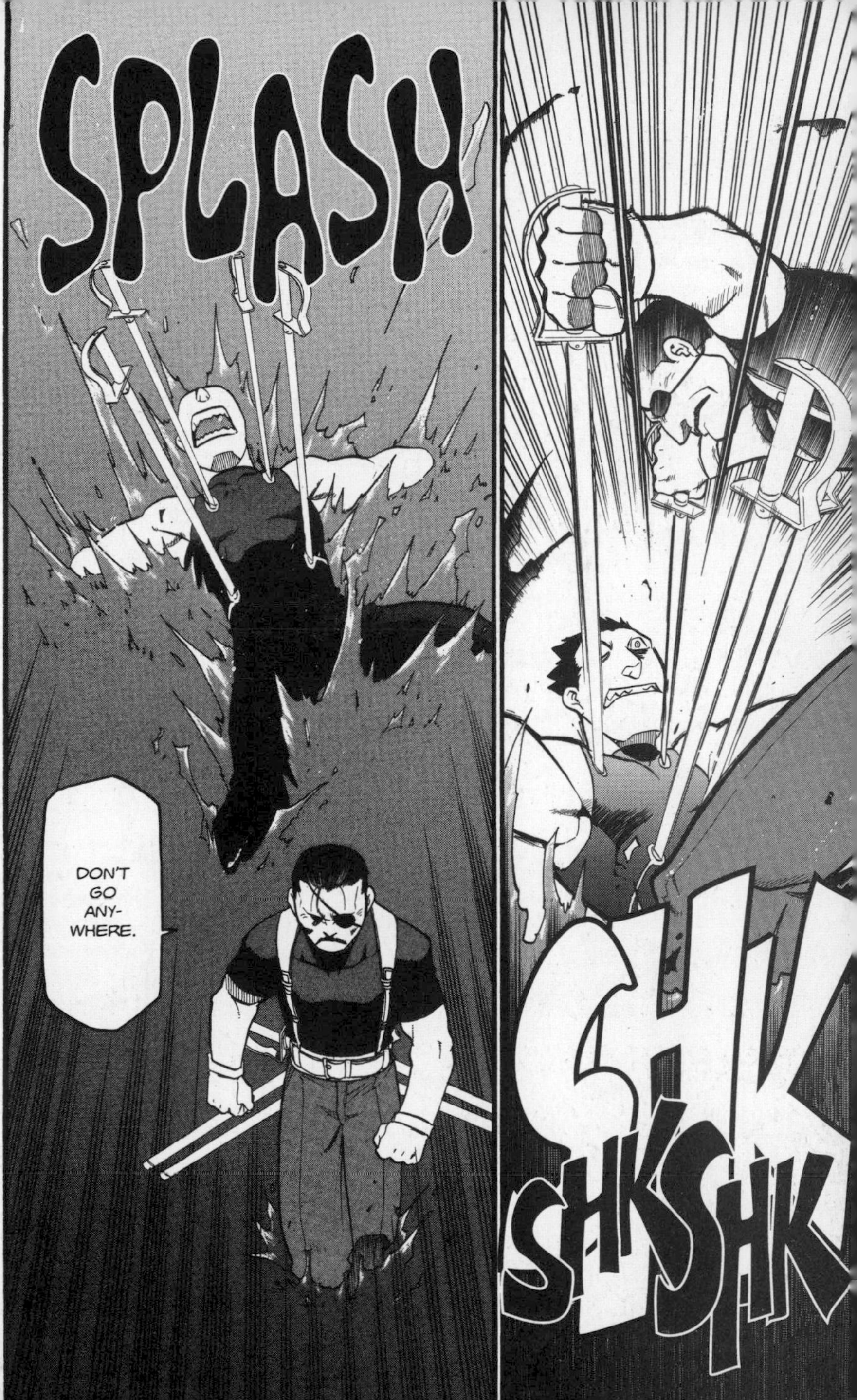
CHK
SHKSHK
SPLASH
DON'T GO ANY-WHERE.

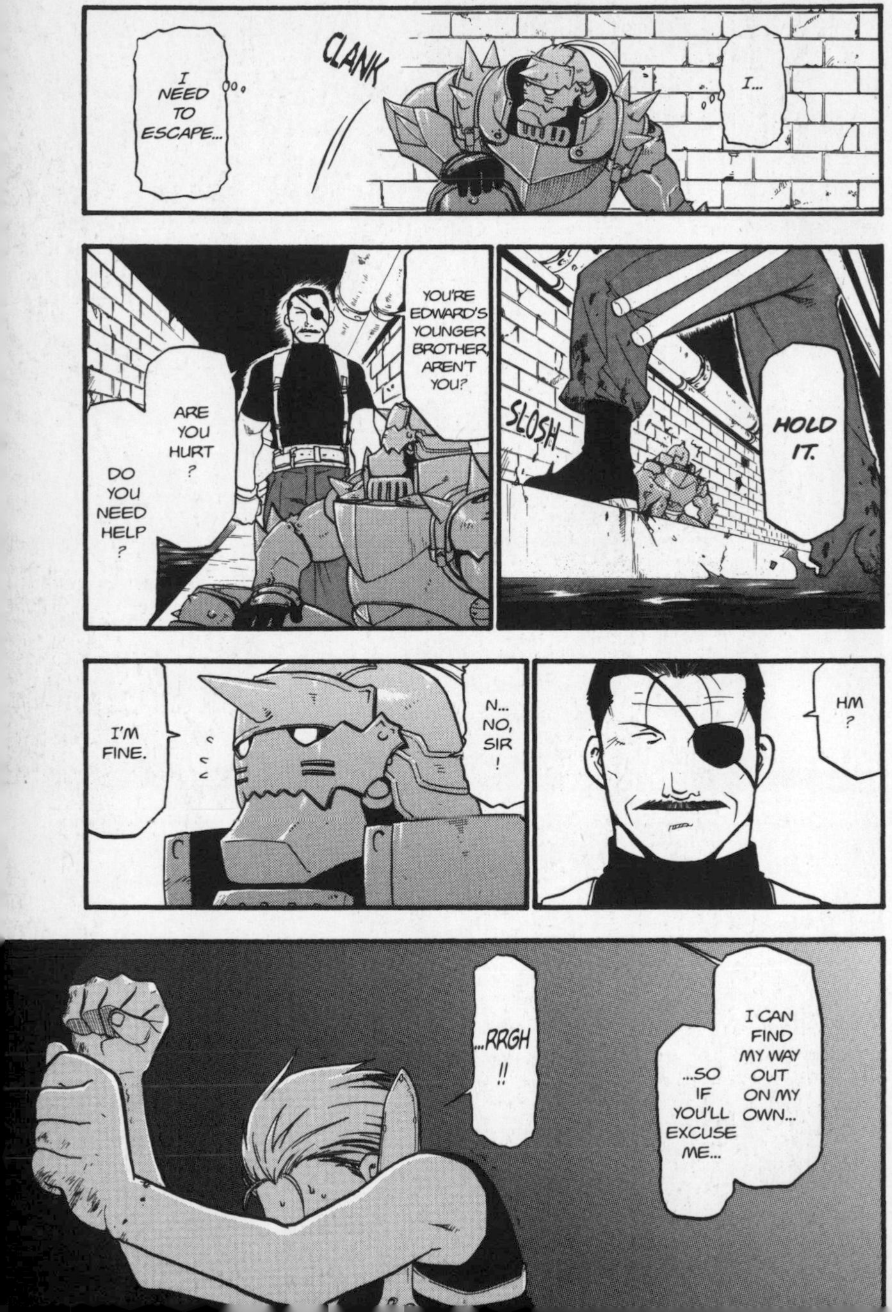
I...
CLANK
I NEED TO ESCAPE...
HOLD IT.
SLOSH
YOU'RE EDWARD'S YOUNGER BROTHER, AREN'T YOU?
ARE YOU HURT?
DO YOU NEED HELP?
HM?
N... NO, SIR!
I'M FINE.
I CAN FIND MY WAY OUT ON MY OWN...
...SO IF YOU'LL EXCUSE ME...
...RRGH!!

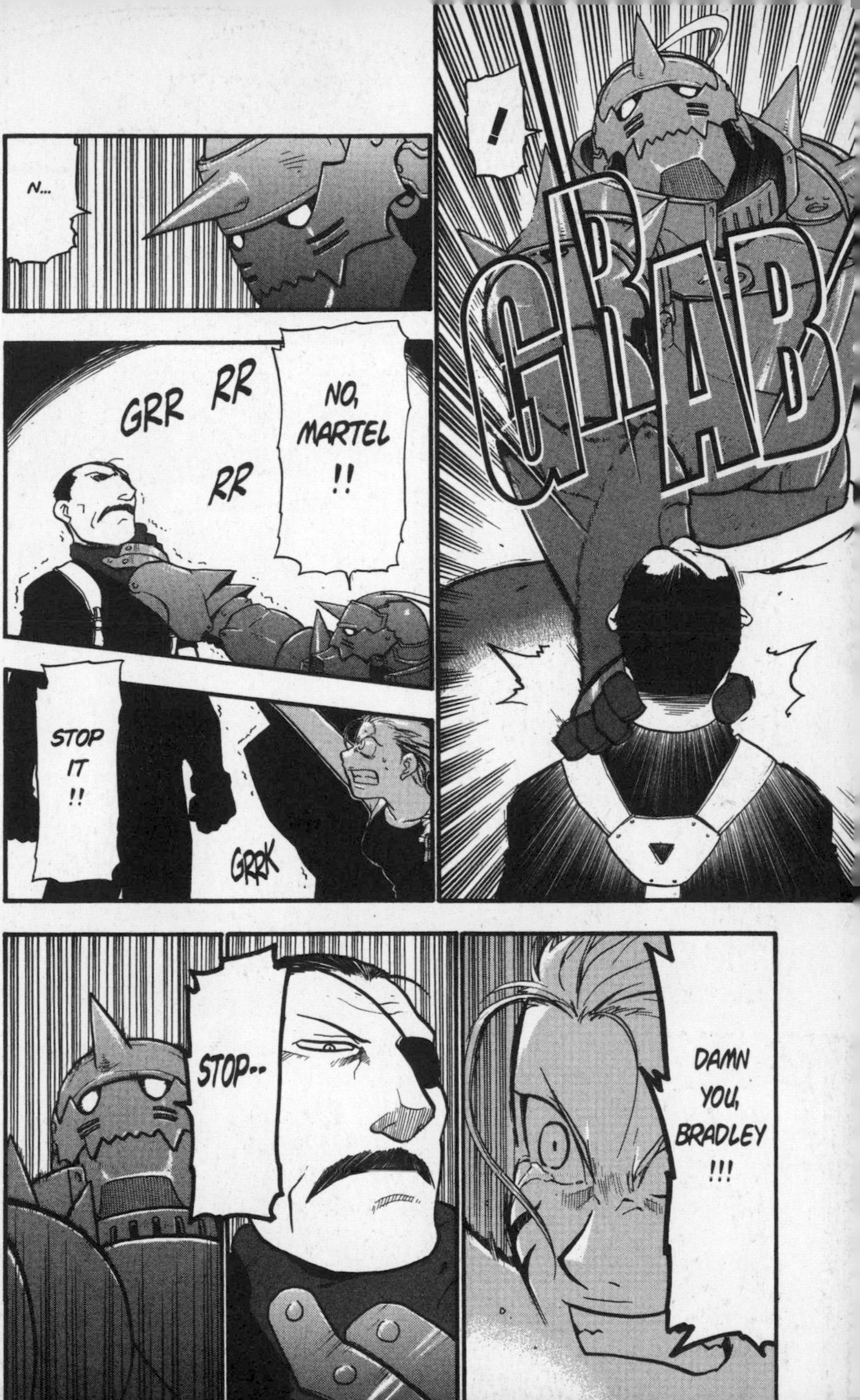
!
GRAB
N...
NO, MARTEL!!
GRR RR RR
STOP IT!!
GRRK
DAMN YOU, BRADLEY!!!
STOP..

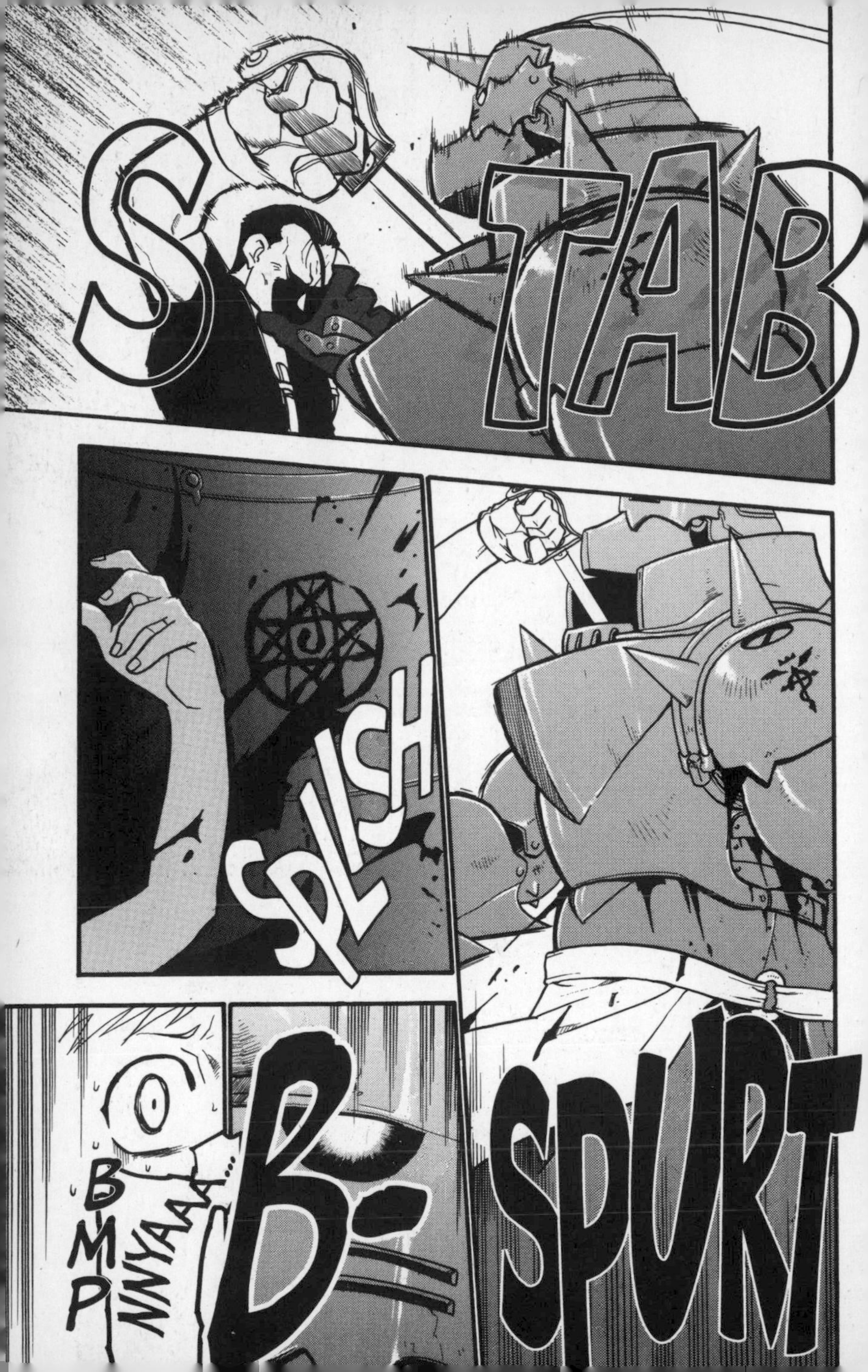
STAB
SPURT
SPLSH
B-
NNYAAA...
BMP

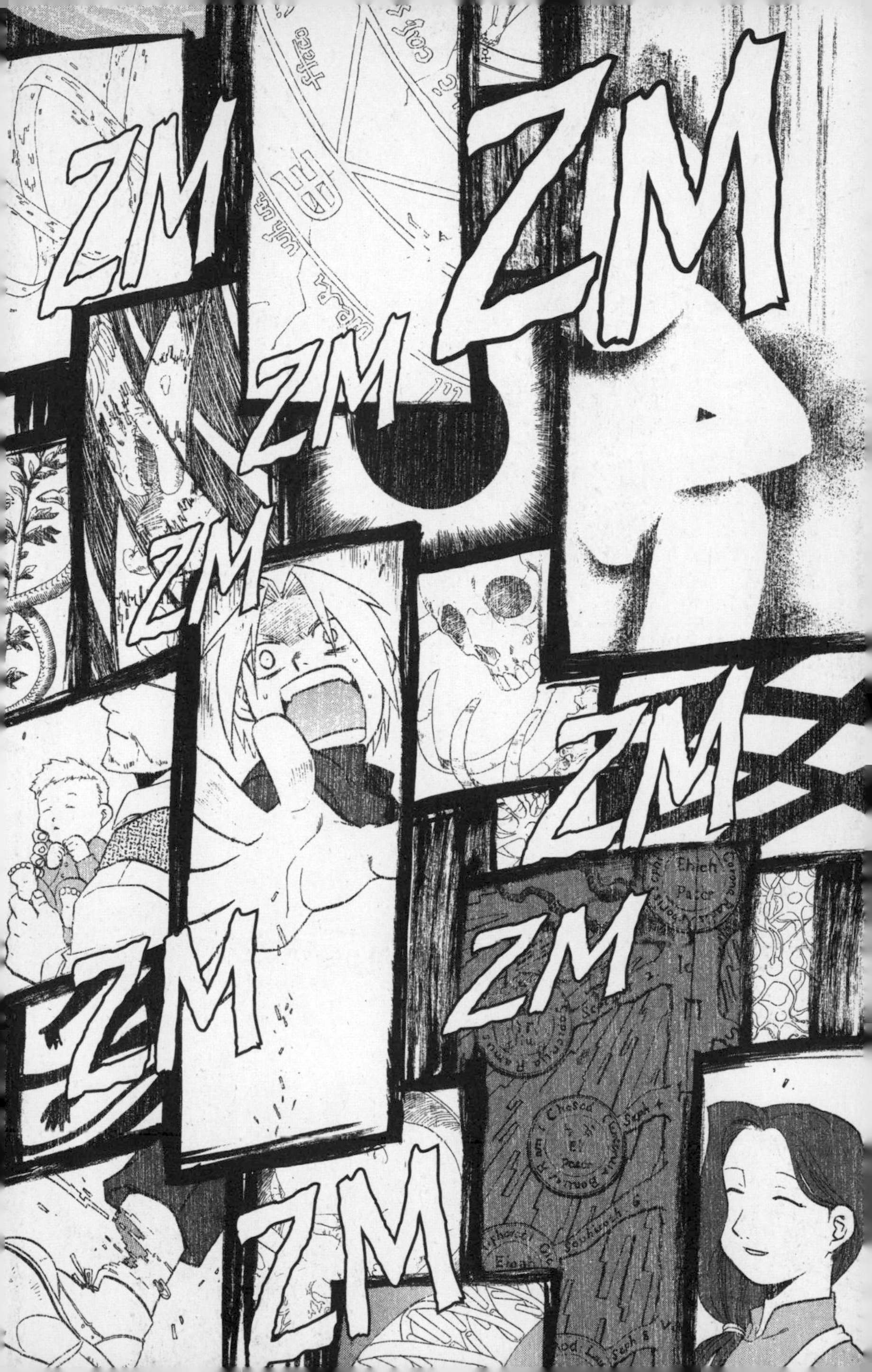
ZM
ZM
ZM
ZM
ZM
ZM
ZM
ZM

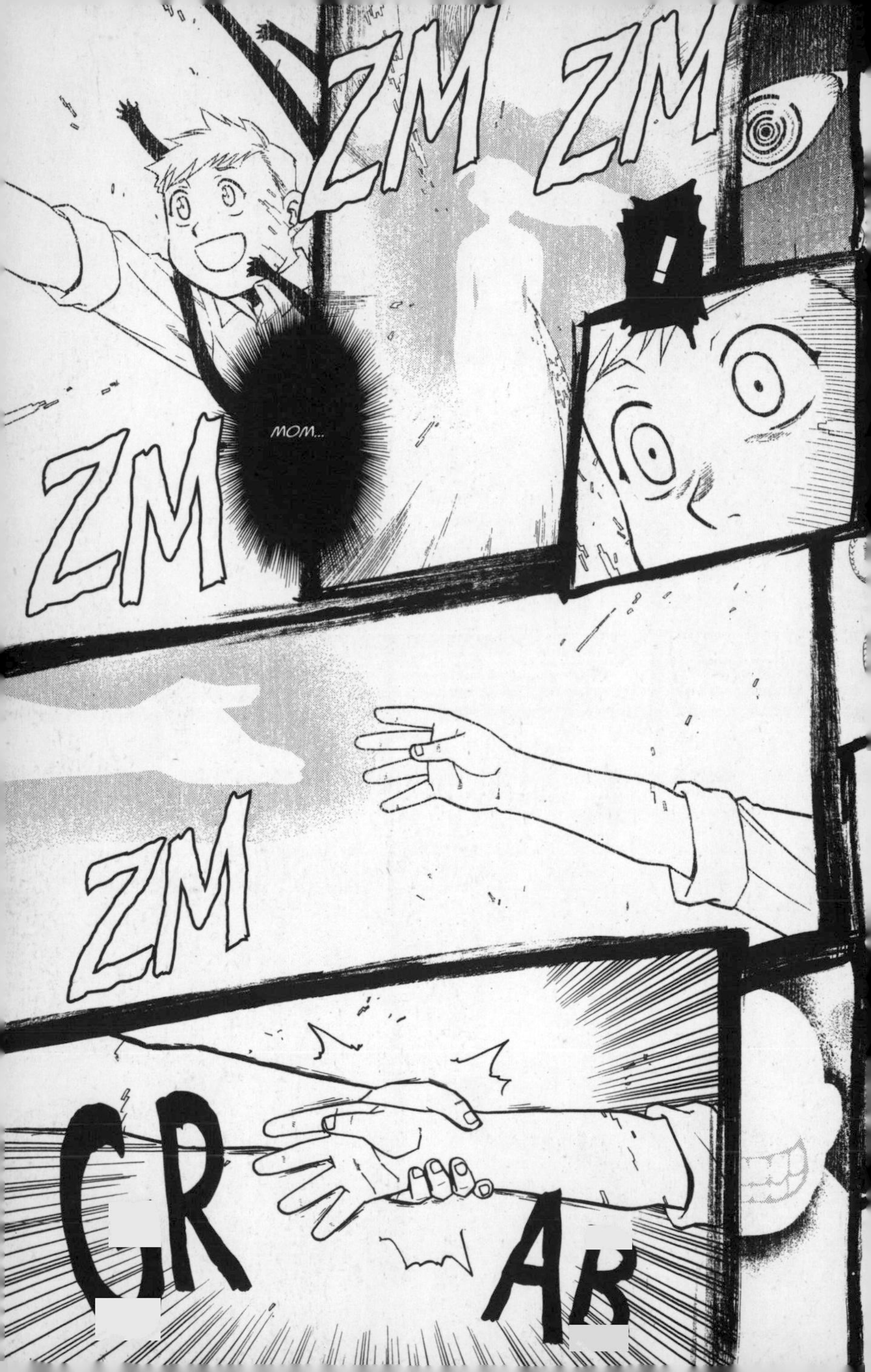
!
ZM ZM
MOM...
ZM
ZM
GR AB

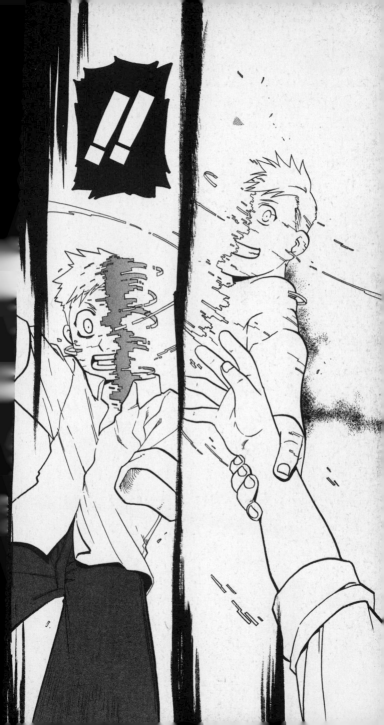

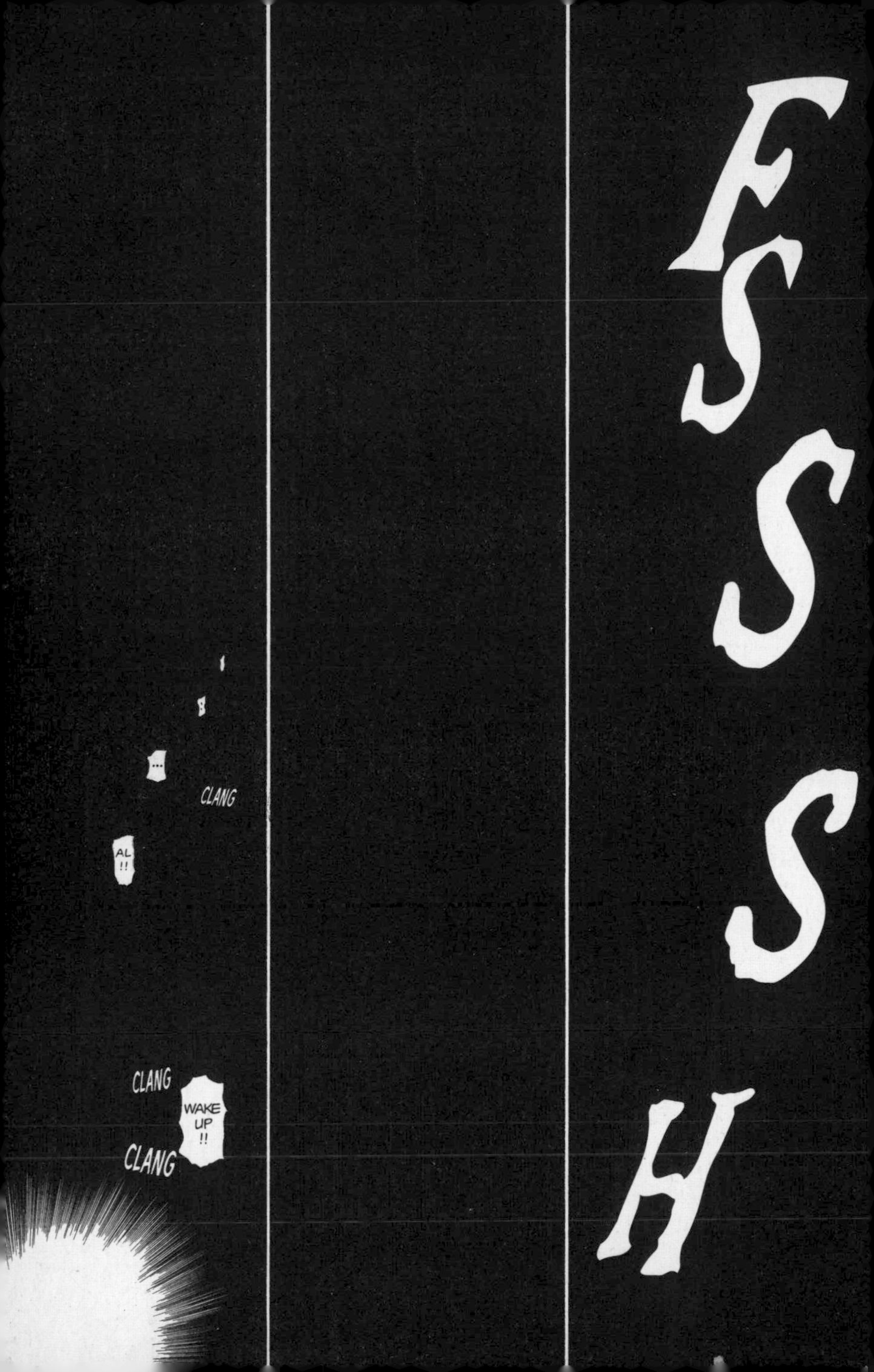
FSSSH
...
CLANG
AL !!
CLANG
WAKE UP !!
CLANG

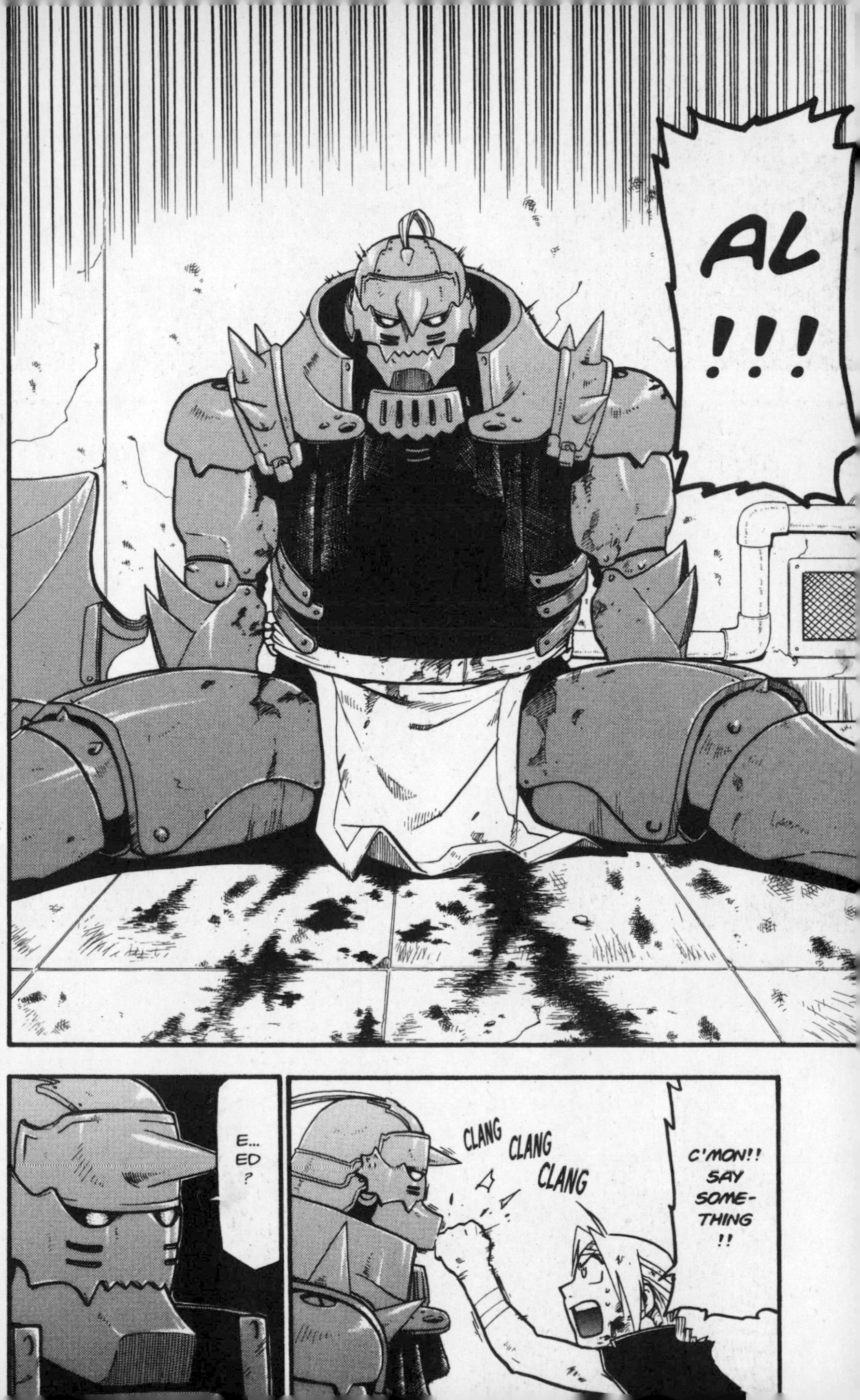
AL !!!
C'MON!! SAY SOME-THING !!
CLANG CLANG CLANG
E... ED ?

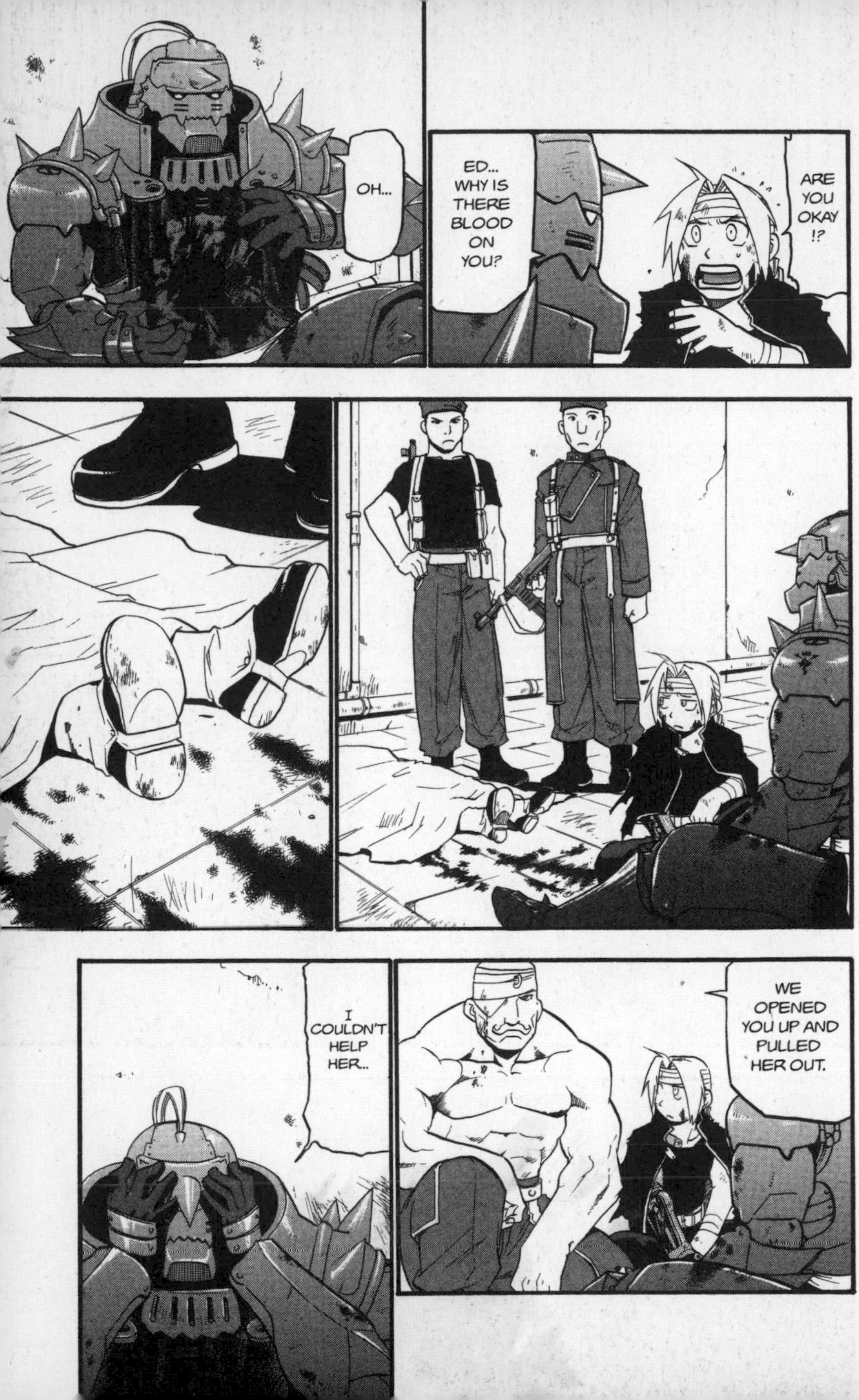
ARE YOU OKAY !?
ED... WHY IS THERE BLOOD ON YOU?
OH...
WE OPENED YOU UP AND PULLED HER OUT.
I COULDN'T HELP HER..

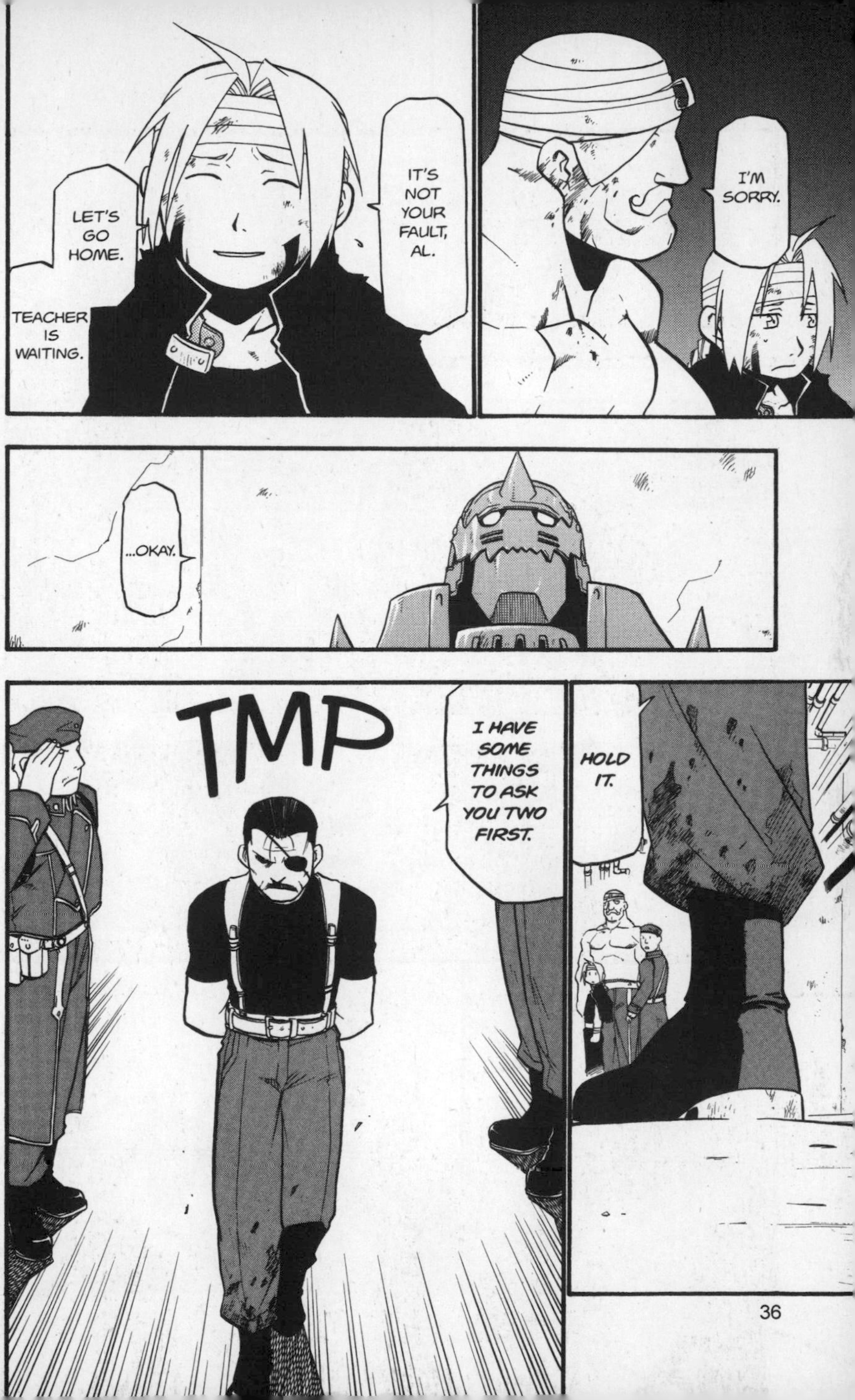
I'M SORRY.
IT'S NOT YOUR FAULT, AL.
LET'S GO HOME.
TEACHER IS WAITING.
...OKAY.
HOLD IT.
I HAVE SOME THINGS TO ASK YOU TWO FIRST.
TMP

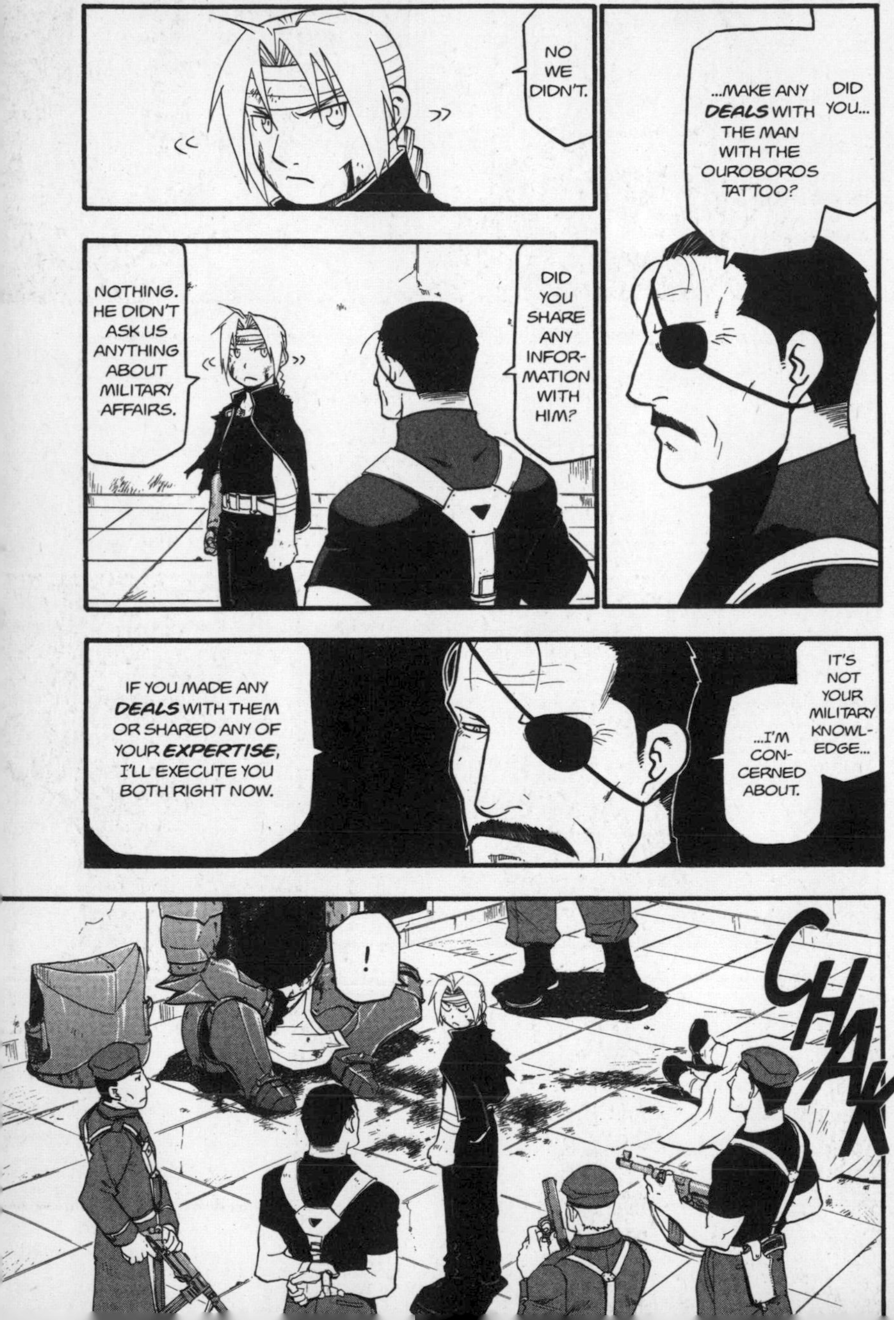
DID YOU...
...MAKE ANY DEALS WITH THE MAN WITH THE OUROBOROS TATTOO?
NO WE DIDN'T.
DID YOU SHARE ANY INFORMATION WITH HIM?
NOTHING. HE DIDN'T ASK US ANYTHING ABOUT MILITARY AFFAIRS.
IT'S NOT YOUR MILITARY KNOWLEDGE...
...I'M CONCERNED ABOUT.
IF YOU MADE ANY DEALS WITH THEM OR SHARED ANY OF YOUR EXPERTISE, I'LL EXECUTE YOU BOTH RIGHT NOW.
CHAK
!

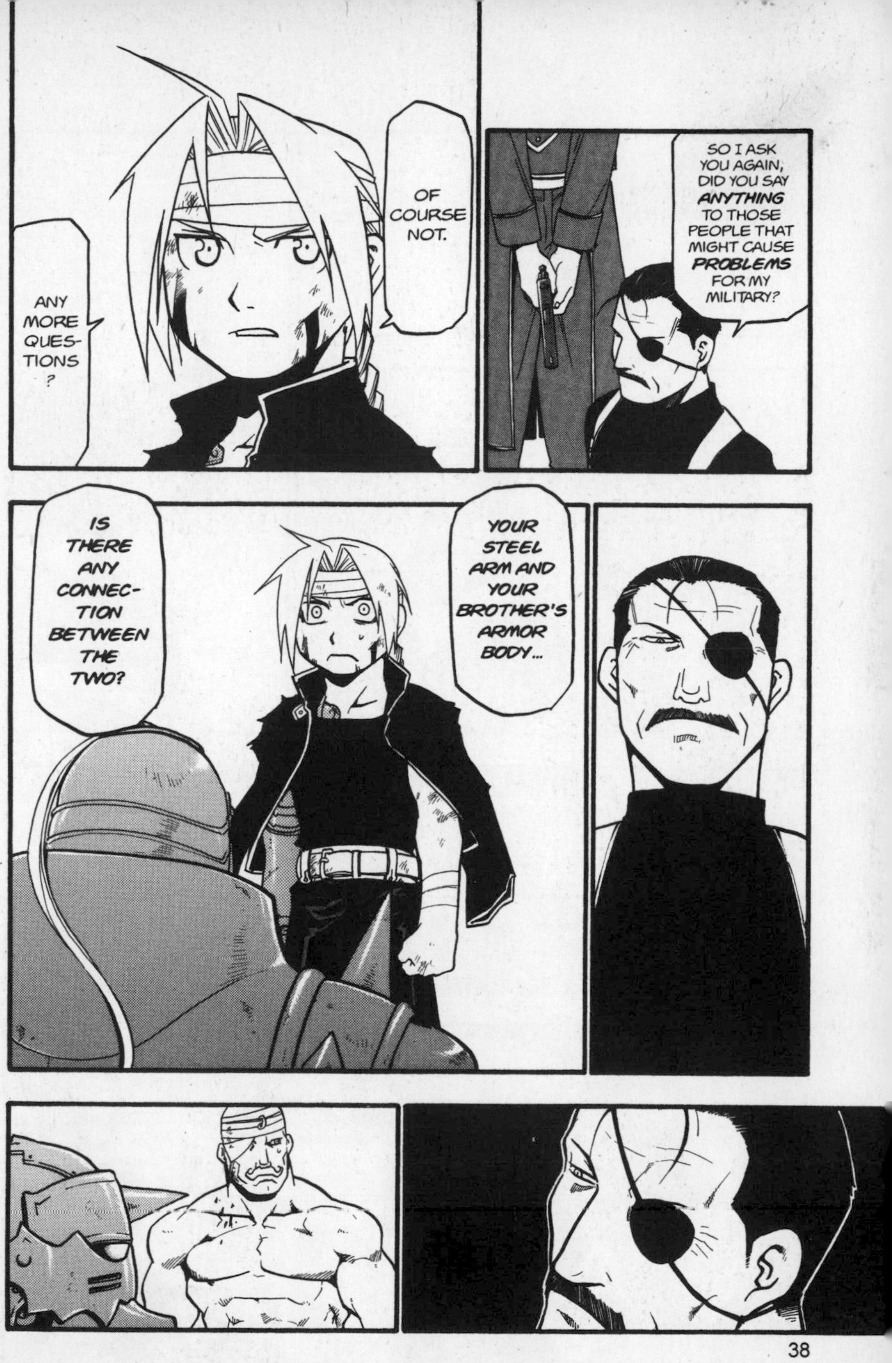
SO I ASK YOU AGAIN, DID YOU SAY ANYTHING TO THOSE PEOPLE THAT MIGHT CAUSE PROBLEMS FOR MY MILITARY?
OF COURSE NOT.
ANY MORE QUES- TIONS ?
YOUR STEEL ARM AND YOUR BROTHER'S ARMOR BODY...
IS THERE ANY CONNEC- TION BETWEEN THE TWO?

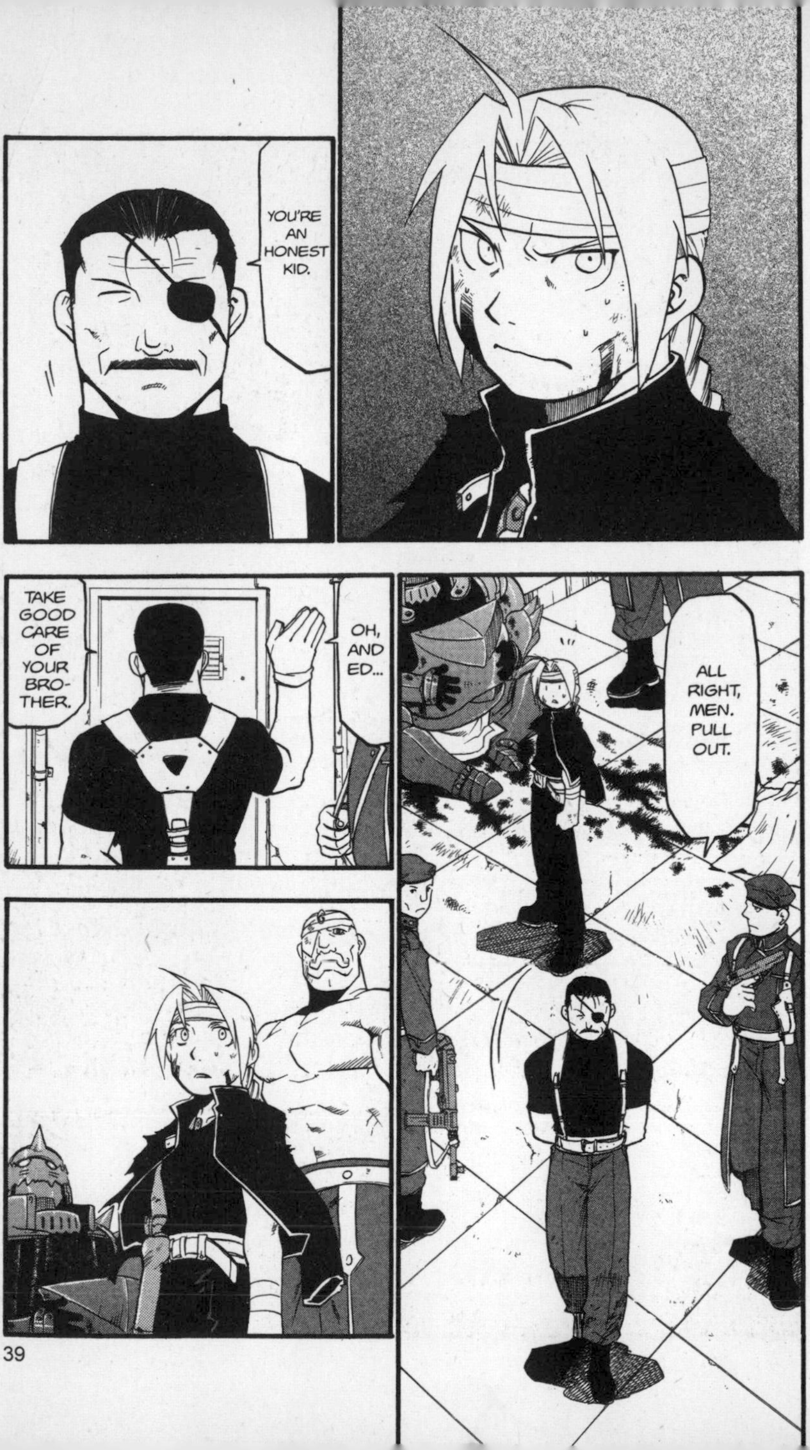
YOU'RE AN HONEST KID.
ALL RIGHT, MEN. PULL OUT.
OH, AND ED...
TAKE GOOD CARE OF YOUR BROTHER.

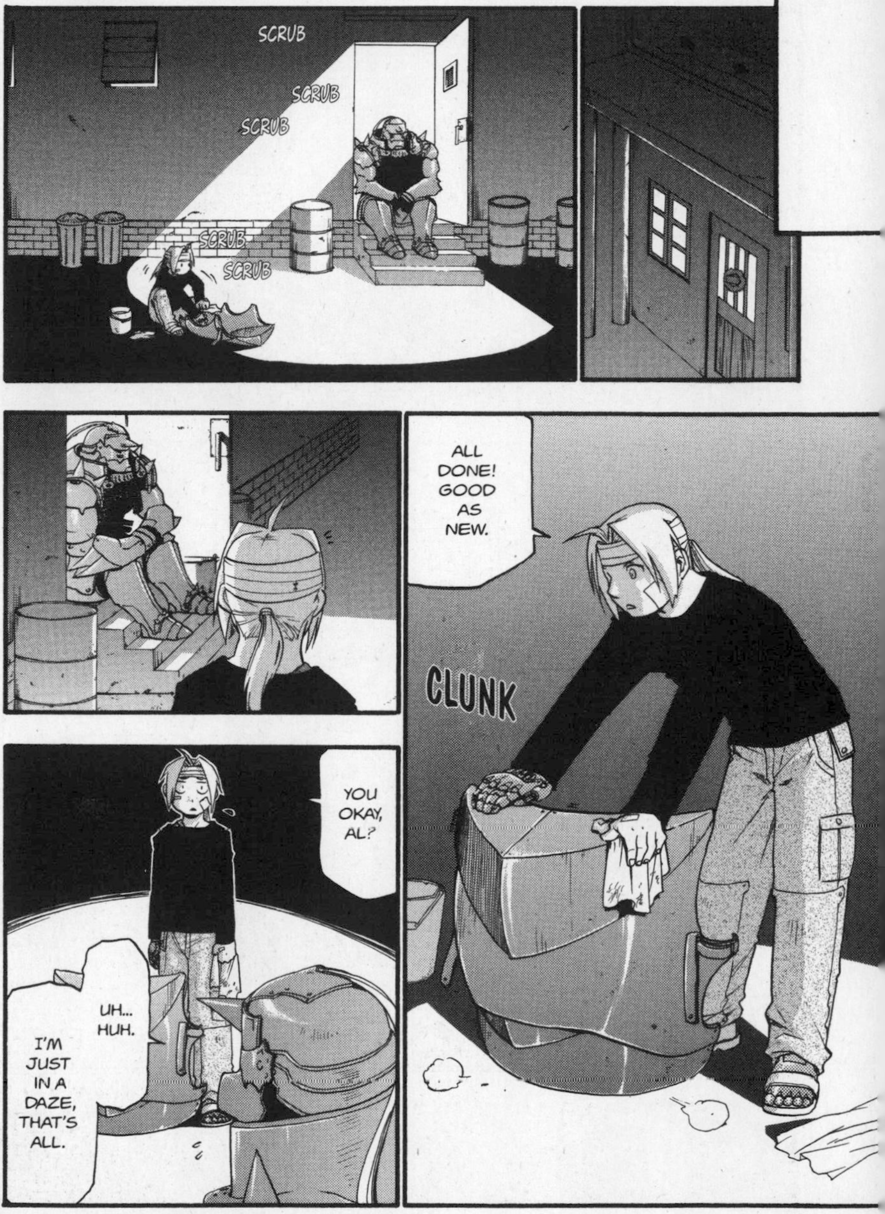
SCRUB
SCRUB
SCRUB
SCRUB
SCRUB
ALL DONE! GOOD AS NEW.
CLUNK
YOU OKAY, AL?
UH... HUH.
I'M JUST IN A DAZE, THAT'S ALL.

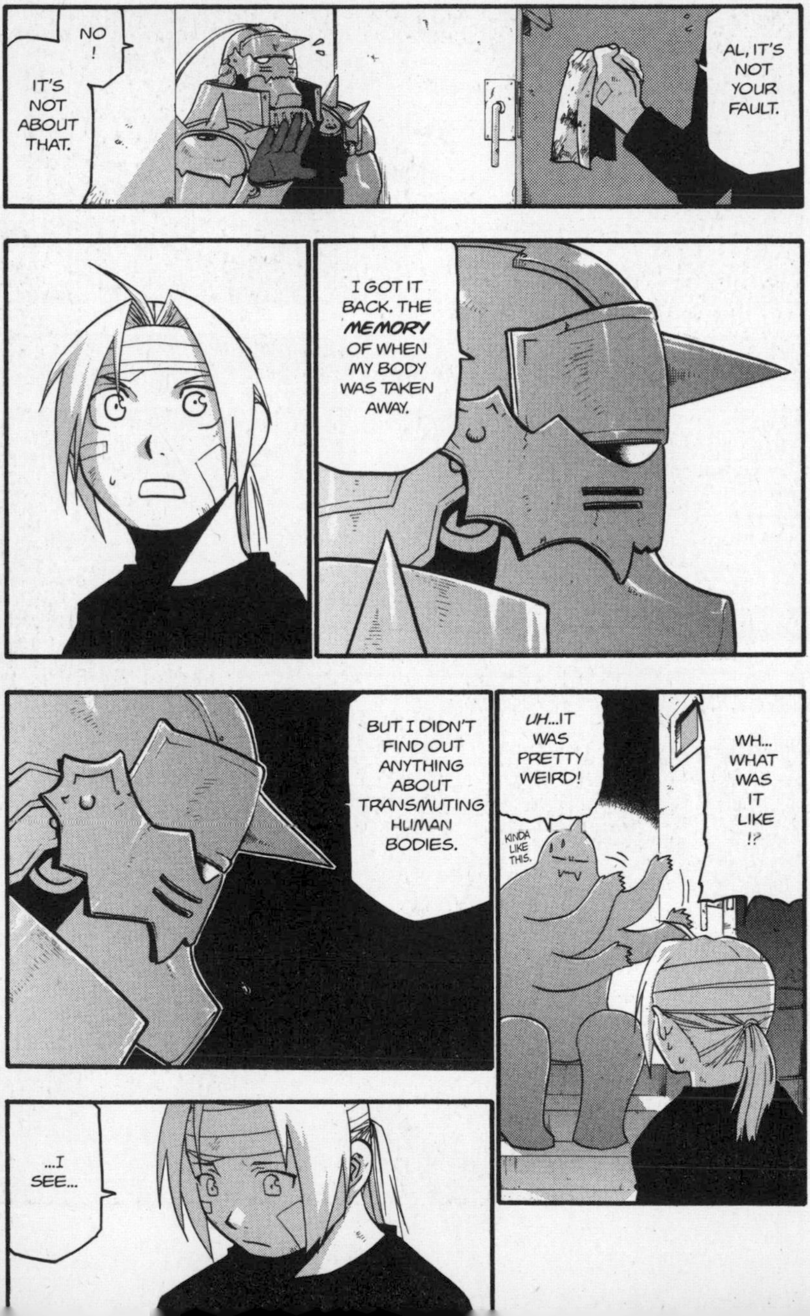
AL, IT'S NOT YOUR FAULT.
NO!
IT'S NOT ABOUT THAT.
I GOT IT BACK. THE *MEMORY* OF WHEN MY BODY WAS TAKEN AWAY.
WH... WHAT WAS IT LIKE !?
UH...IT WAS PRETTY WEIRD!
KINDA LIKE THIS.
BUT I DIDN'T FIND OUT ANYTHING ABOUT TRANSMUTING HUMAN BODIES.
...I SEE...

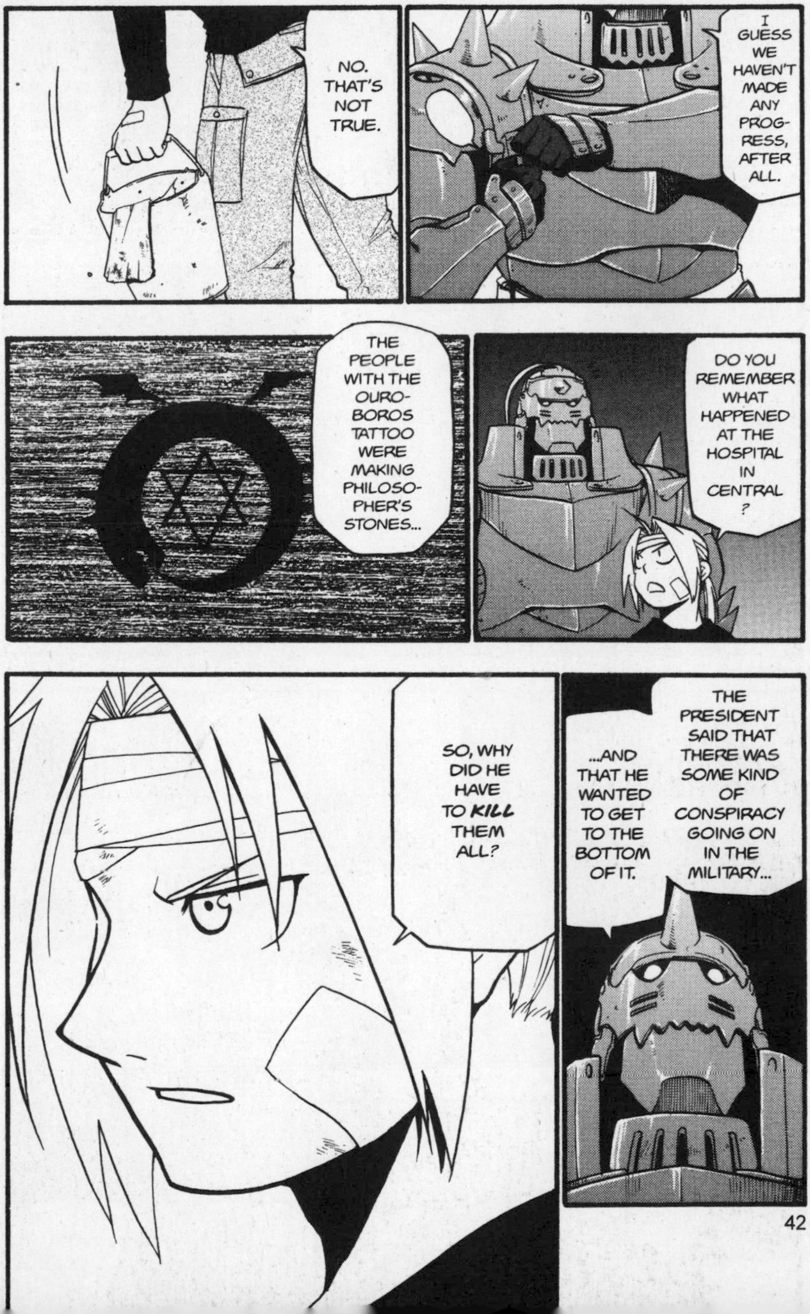
I GUESS WE HAVEN'T MADE ANY PROGRESS, AFTER ALL.
NO. THAT'S NOT TRUE.
DO YOU REMEMBER WHAT HAPPENED AT THE HOSPITAL IN CENTRAL?
THE PEOPLE WITH THE OUROBOROS TATTOO WERE MAKING PHILOSOPHER'S STONES...
THE PRESIDENT SAID THAT THERE WAS SOME KIND OF CONSPIRACY GOING ON IN THE MILITARY...
...AND THAT HE WANTED TO GET TO THE BOTTOM OF IT.
SO, WHY DID HE HAVE TO KILL THEM ALL?

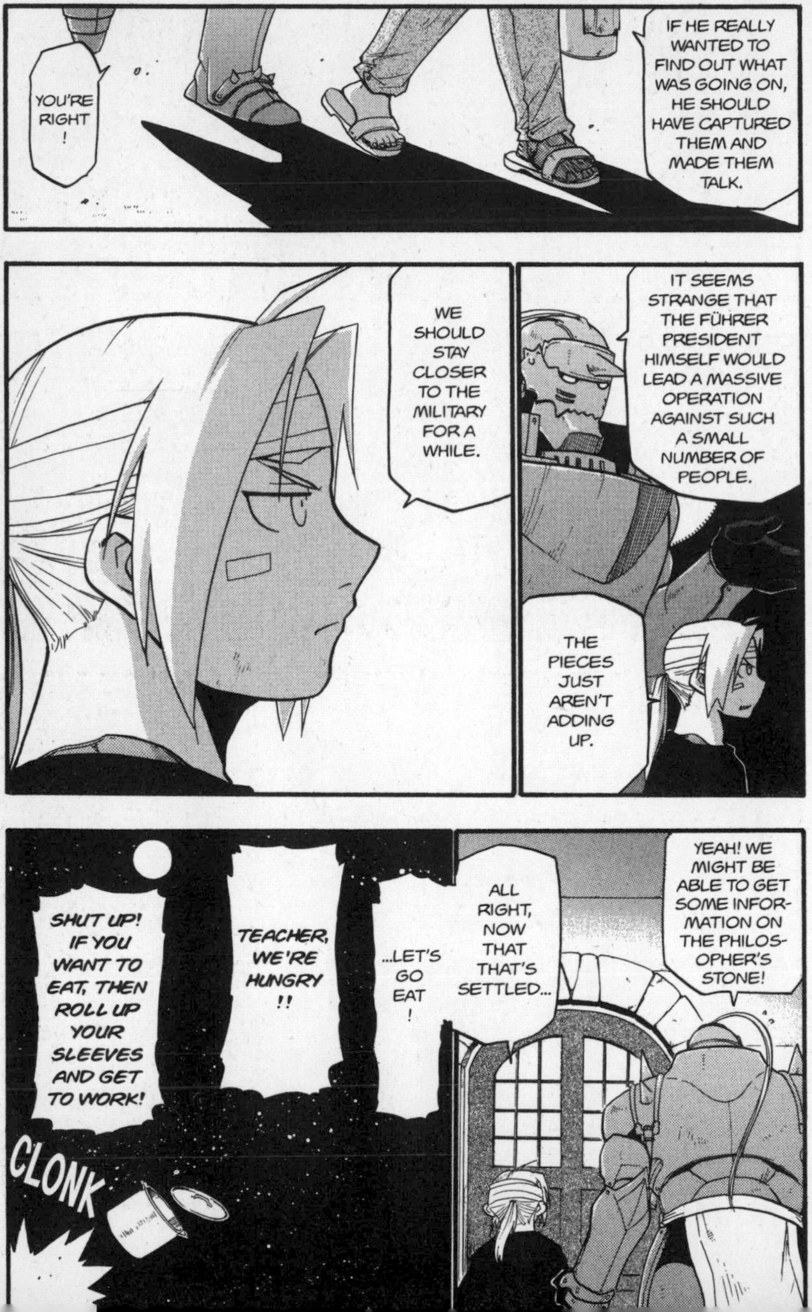
IF HE REALLY WANTED TO FIND OUT WHAT WAS GOING ON, HE SHOULD HAVE CAPTURED THEM AND MADE THEM TALK.
YOU'RE RIGHT!
IT SEEMS STRANGE THAT THE FÜHRER PRESIDENT HIMSELF WOULD LEAD A MASSIVE OPERATION AGAINST SUCH A SMALL NUMBER OF PEOPLE.
THE PIECES JUST AREN'T ADDING UP.
WE SHOULD STAY CLOSER TO THE MILITARY FOR A WHILE.
YEAH! WE MIGHT BE ABLE TO GET SOME INFOR-MATION ON THE PHILOS-OPHER'S STONE!
ALL RIGHT, NOW THAT THAT'S SETTLED...
...LET'S GO EAT!
TEACHER, WE'RE HUNGRY!!
SHUT UP! IF YOU WANT TO EAT, THEN ROLL UP YOUR SLEEVES AND GET TO WORK!
CLONK

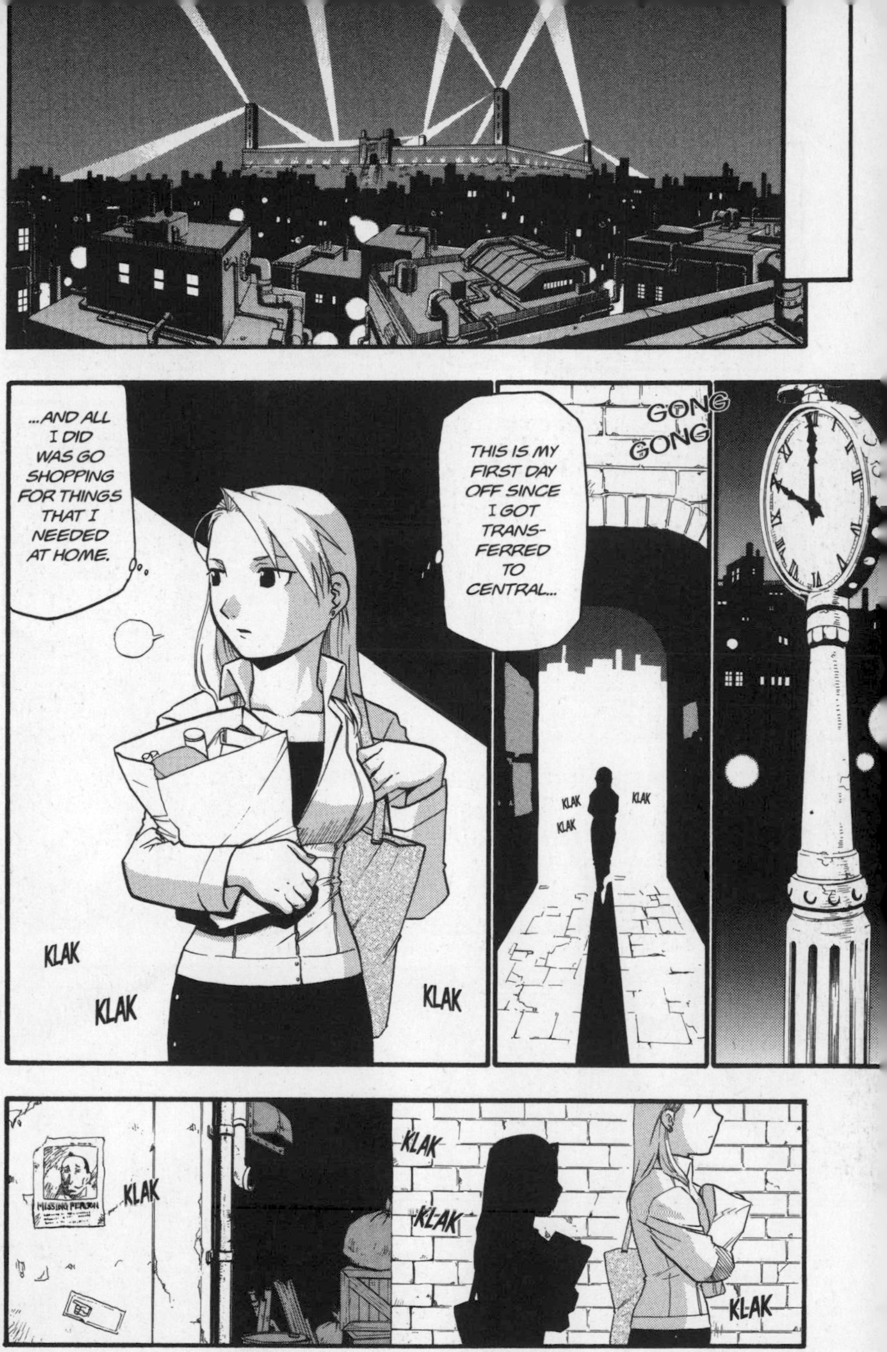
GONG
GONG
THIS IS MY FIRST DAY OFF SINCE I GOT TRANS-FERRED TO CENTRAL...
KLAK
KLAK
KLAK
...AND ALL I DID WAS GO SHOPPING FOR THINGS THAT I NEEDED AT HOME.
KLAK
KLAK
KLAK
KLAK
KLAK
KLAK
KLAK
MISSING PERSON

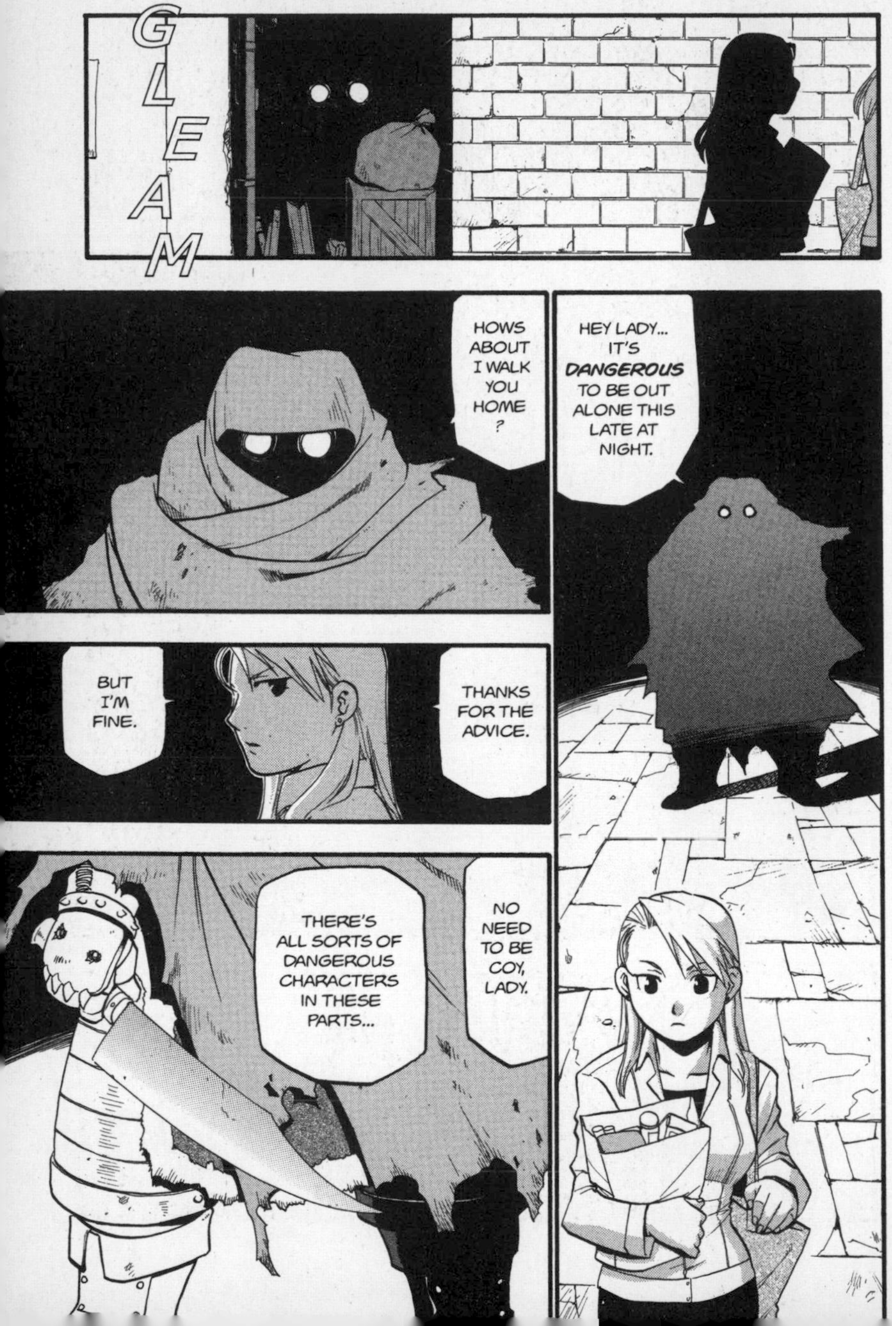
GLEAM
HEY LADY... IT'S DANGEROUS TO BE OUT ALONE THIS LATE AT NIGHT.
HOWS ABOUT I WALK YOU HOME?
THANKS FOR THE ADVICE.
BUT I'M FINE.
NO NEED TO BE COY, LADY.
THERE'S ALL SORTS OF DANGEROUS CHARACTERS IN THESE PARTS...

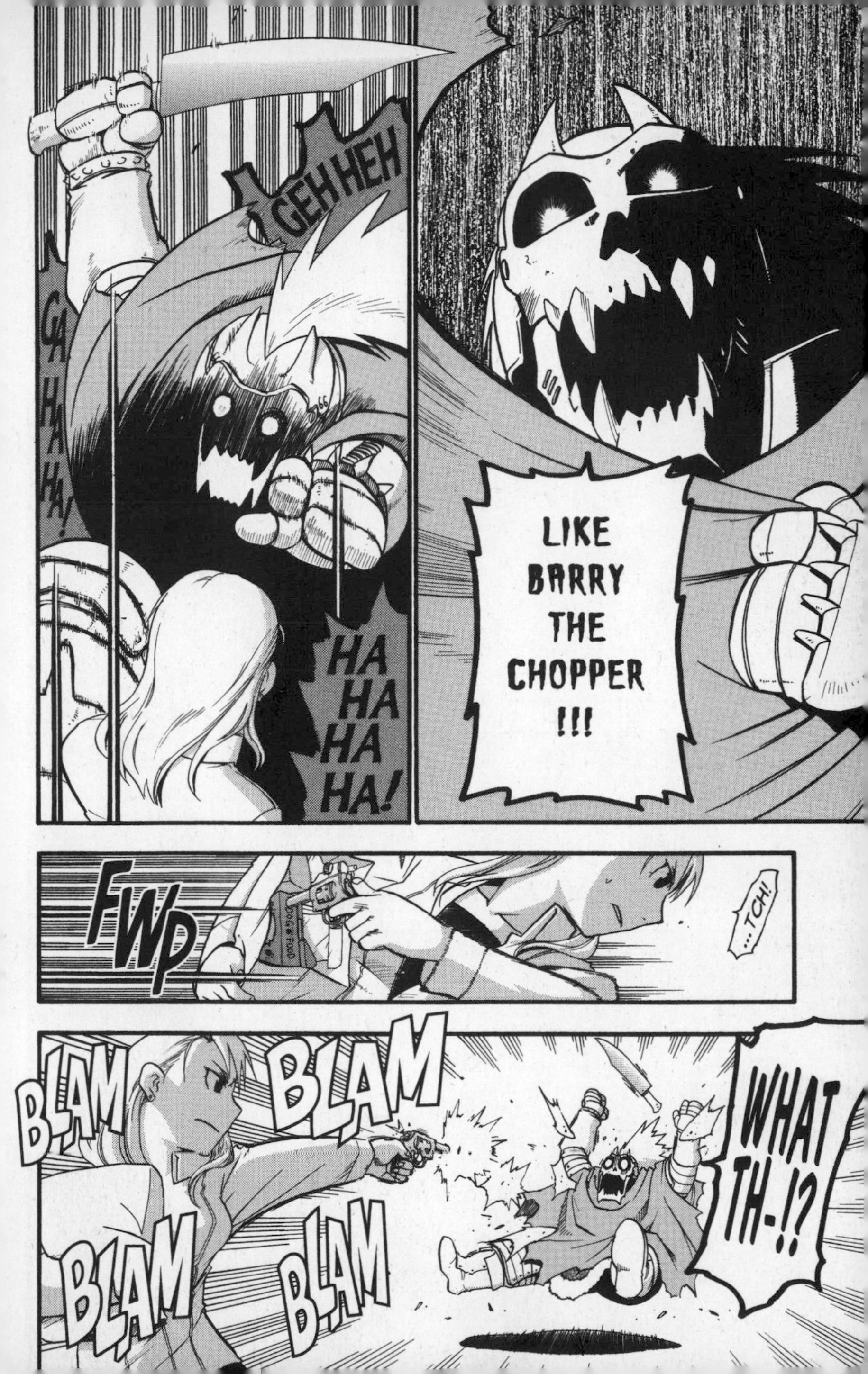
LIKE BARRY THE CHOPPER !!!
GEH HEH
GAHAHAHA!
HA HA HA HA!
...TCH!
FWP
WHAT TH-!?
BLAM
BLAM
BLAM
BLAM

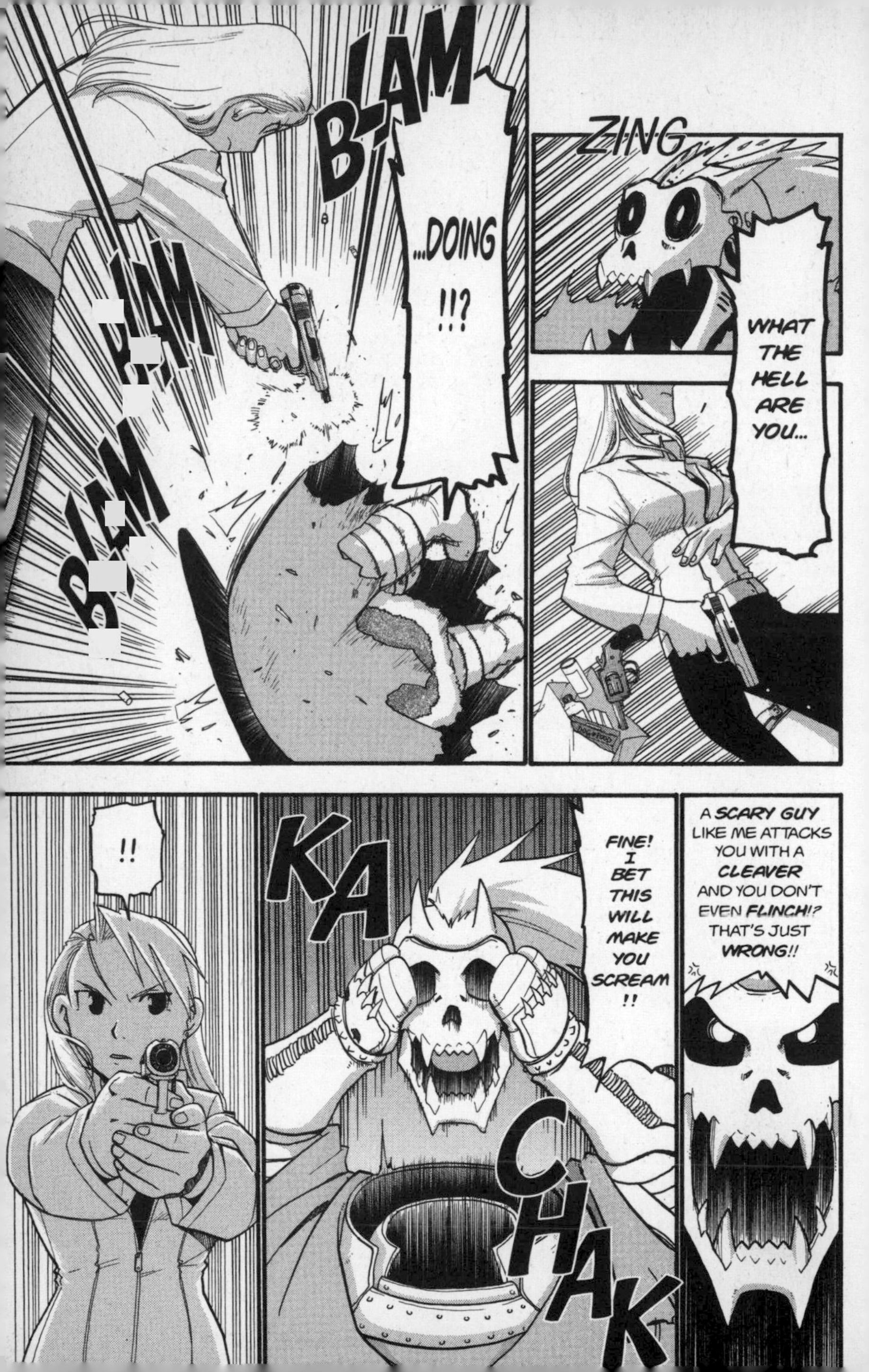
ZING
WHAT THE HELL ARE YOU...
BLAM
...DOING !!?
BLAM
BLAM
A SCARY GUY LIKE ME ATTACKS YOU WITH A CLEAVER AND YOU DON'T EVEN FLINCH!? THAT'S JUST WRONG!!
FINE! I BET THIS WILL MAKE YOU SCREAM !!
KA
CHAK
!!

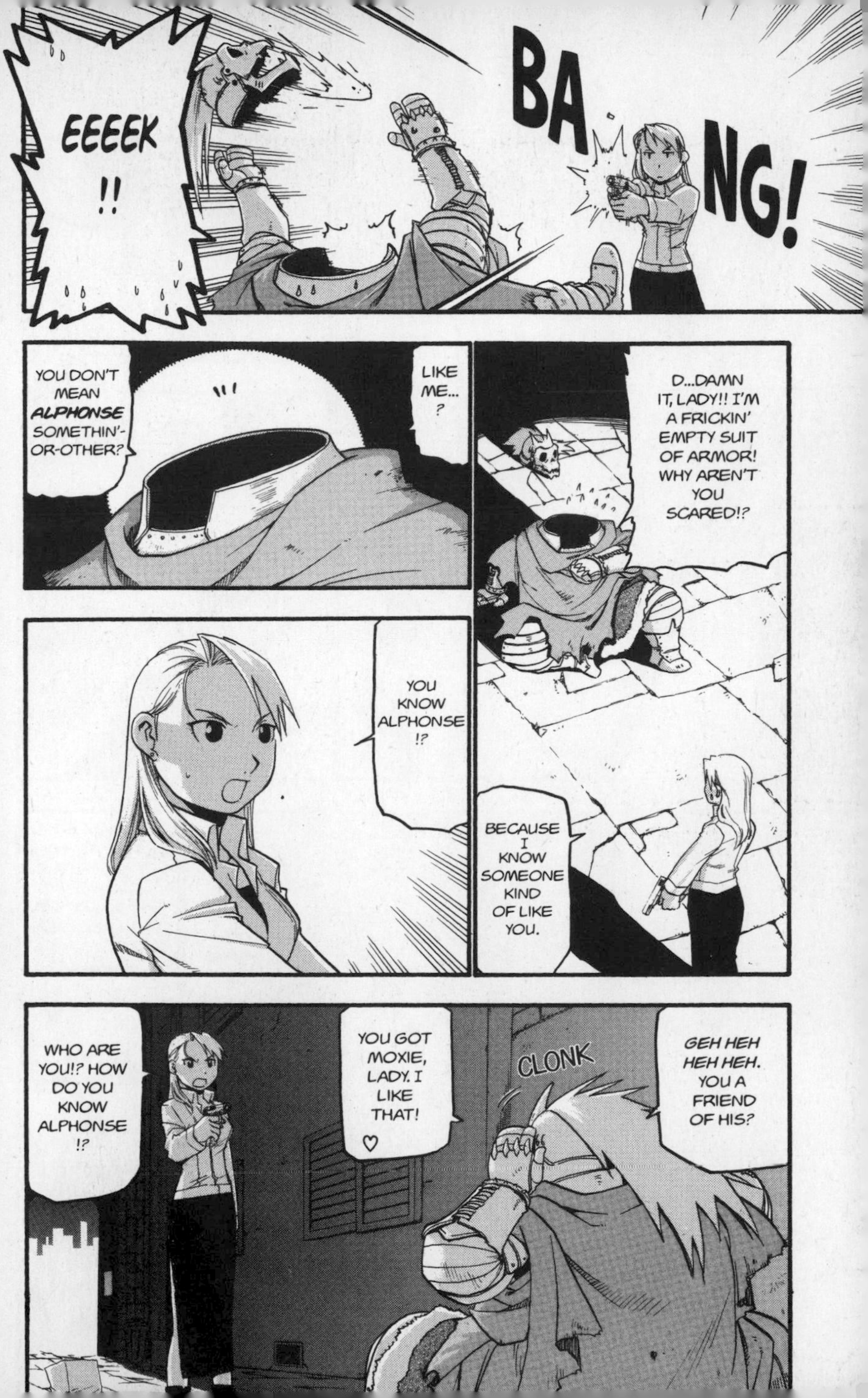
BANG!
EEEEK!!
D...DAMN IT, LADY!! I'M A FRICKIN' EMPTY SUIT OF ARMOR! WHY AREN'T YOU SCARED!?
BECAUSE I KNOW SOMEONE KIND OF LIKE YOU.
LIKE ME...?
YOU DON'T MEAN ALPHONSE SOMETHIN'-OR-OTHER?
YOU KNOW ALPHONSE!?
GEH HEH HEH HEH. YOU A FRIEND OF HIS?
CLONK
YOU GOT MOXIE, LADY. I LIKE THAT! ♡
WHO ARE YOU!? HOW DO YOU KNOW ALPHONSE!?

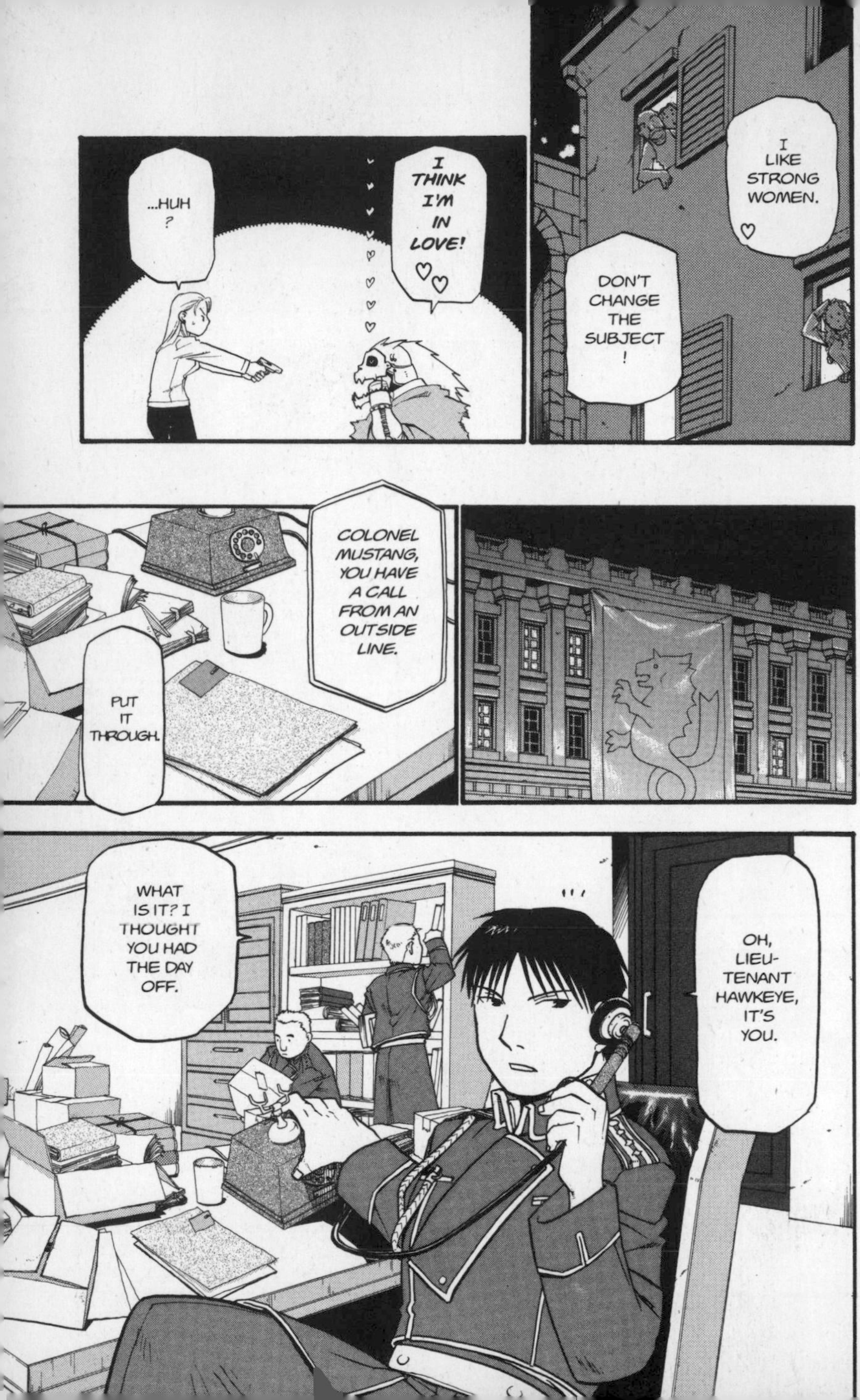
I LIKE STRONG WOMEN. ♡
DON'T CHANGE THE SUBJECT!
I THINK I'M IN LOVE! ♡ ♡
...HUH?
COLONEL MUSTANG, YOU HAVE A CALL FROM AN OUTSIDE LINE.
PUT IT THROUGH.
OH, LIEU-TENANT HAWKEYE, IT'S YOU.
WHAT IS IT? I THOUGHT YOU HAD THE DAY OFF.

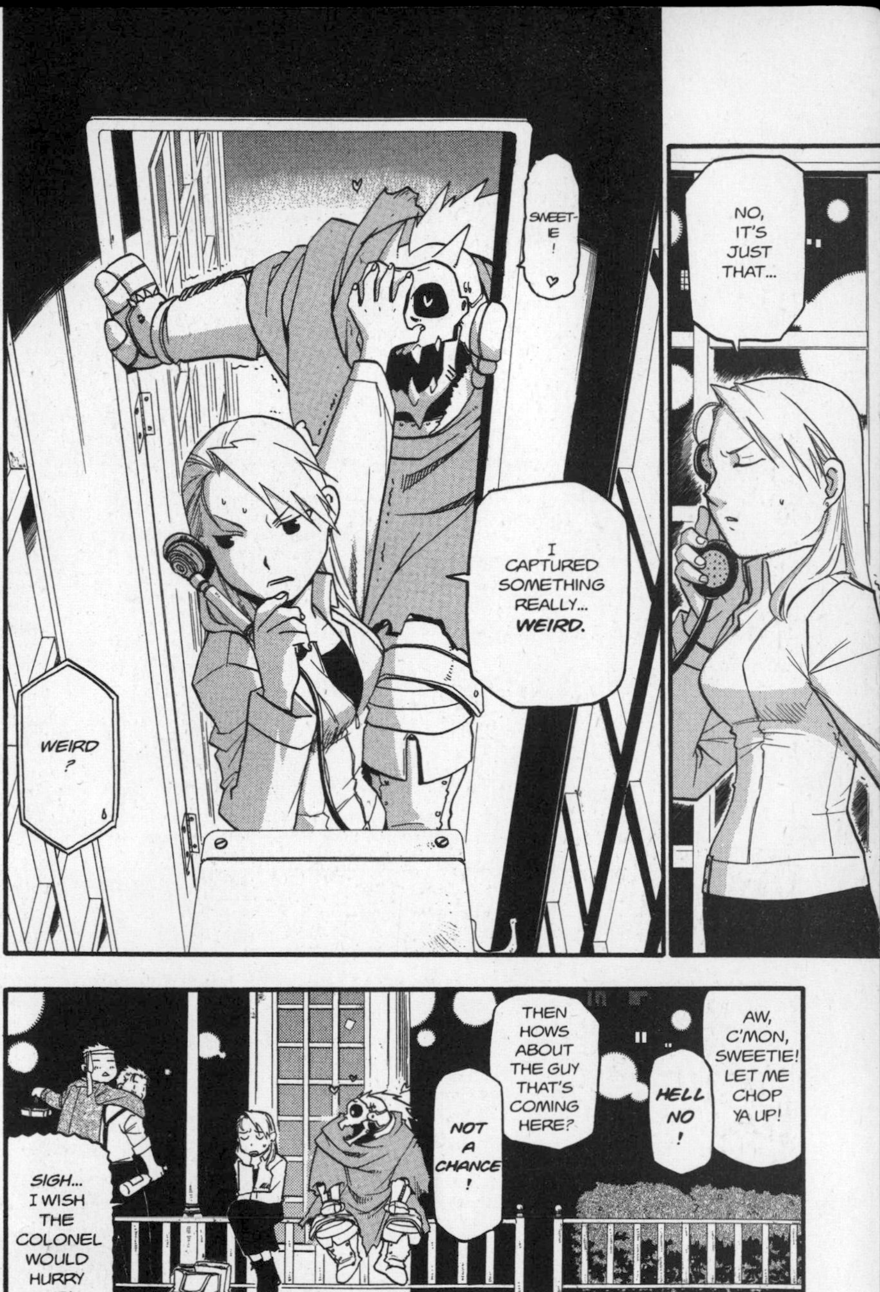
NO, IT'S JUST THAT...
SWEET-IE! ♥
I CAPTURED SOMETHING REALLY... WEIRD.
WEIRD?
AW, C'MON, SWEETIE! LET ME CHOP YA UP!
HELL NO!
THEN HOWS ABOUT THE GUY THAT'S COMING HERE?
NOT A CHANCE!
SIGH... I WISH THE COLONEL WOULD HURRY UP!

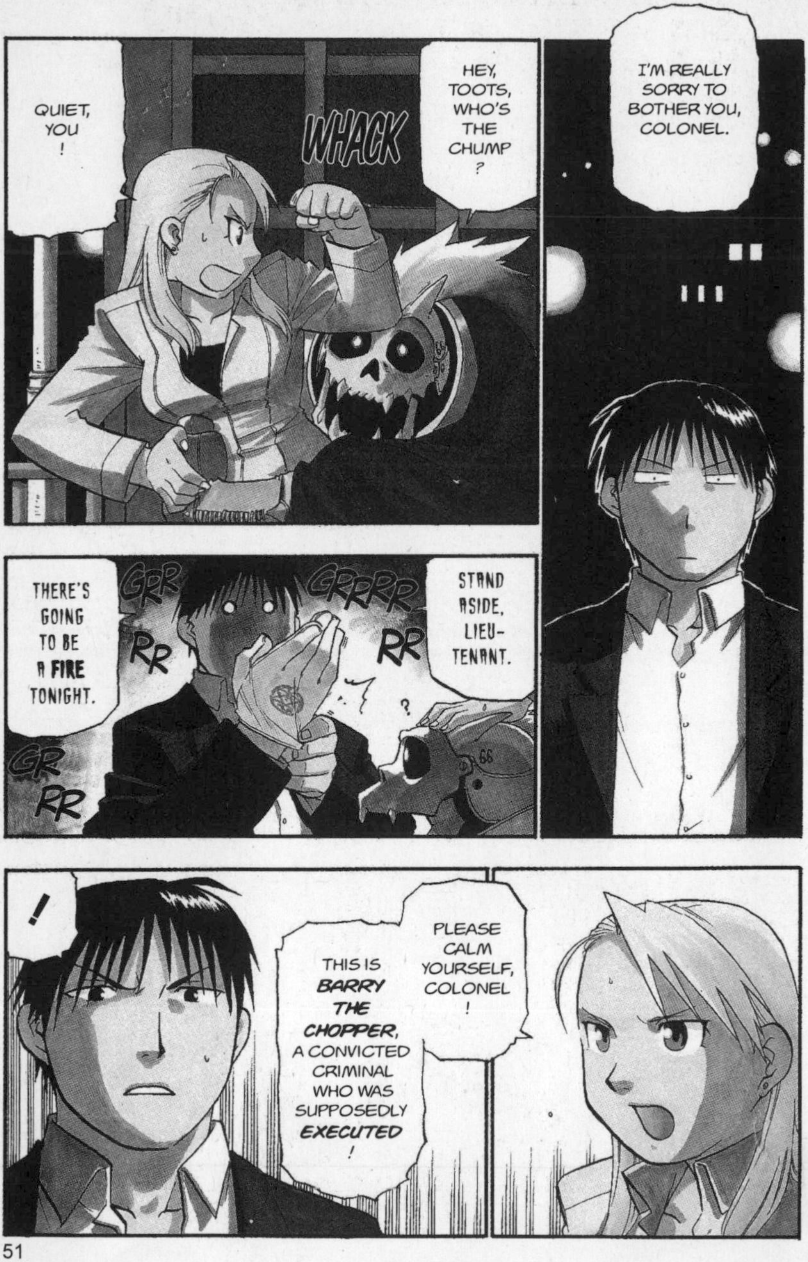

I'M REALLY SORRY TO BOTHER YOU, COLONEL.
HEY, TOOTS, WHO'S THE CHUMP?
WHACK
QUIET, YOU!
STAND ASIDE, LIEUTENANT.
GRRRRR RR
GRR RR
THERE'S GOING TO BE A FIRE TONIGHT.
GR RR
PLEASE CALM YOURSELF, COLONEL!
THIS IS BARRY THE CHOPPER, A CONVICTED CRIMINAL WHO WAS SUPPOSEDLY EXECUTED!
!

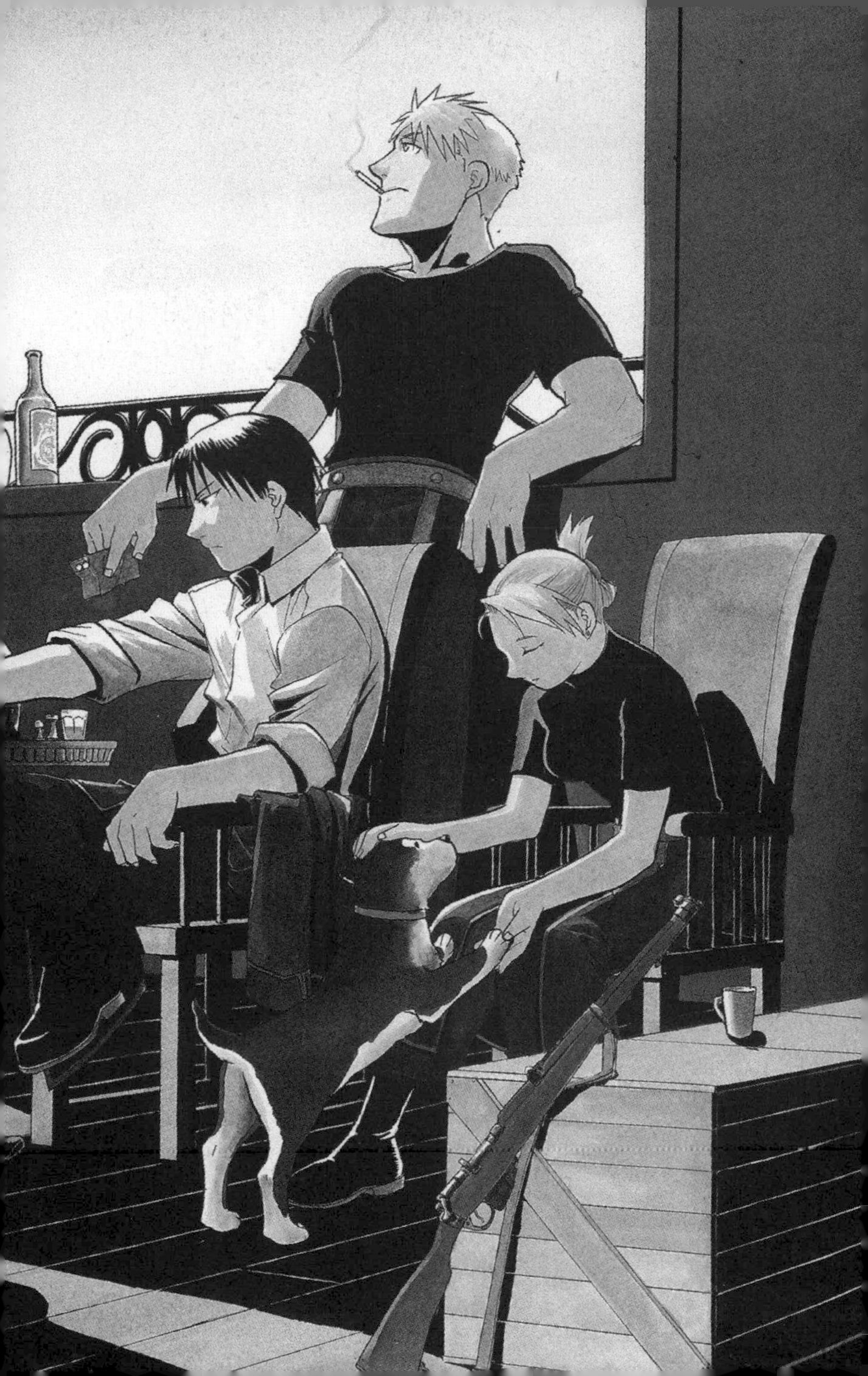

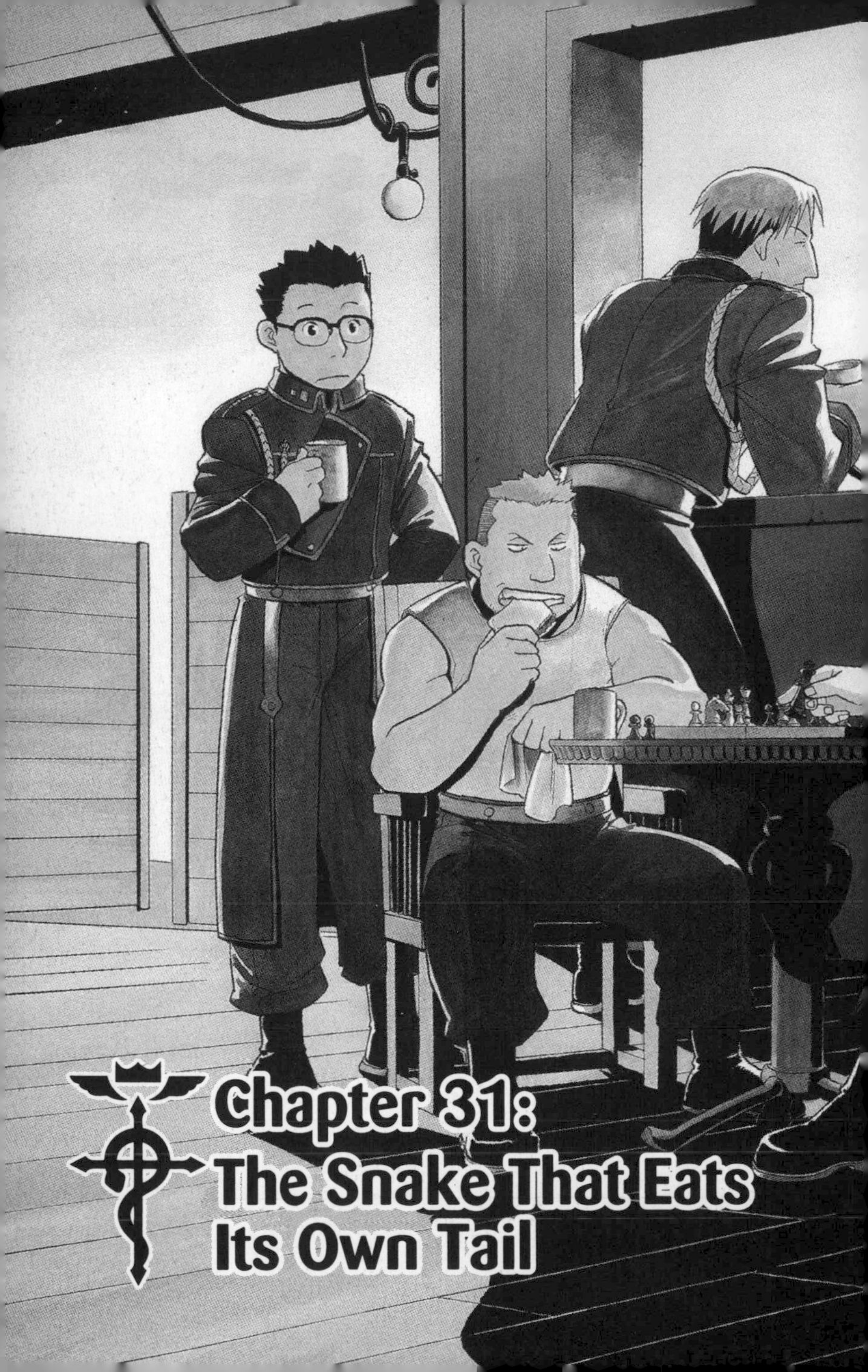
Chapter 31:
The Snake That Eats
Its Own Tail

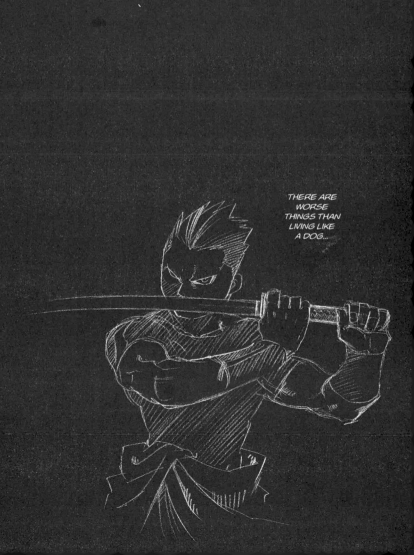

THERE ARE
WORSE
THINGS THAN
LIVING LIKE
A DOG...

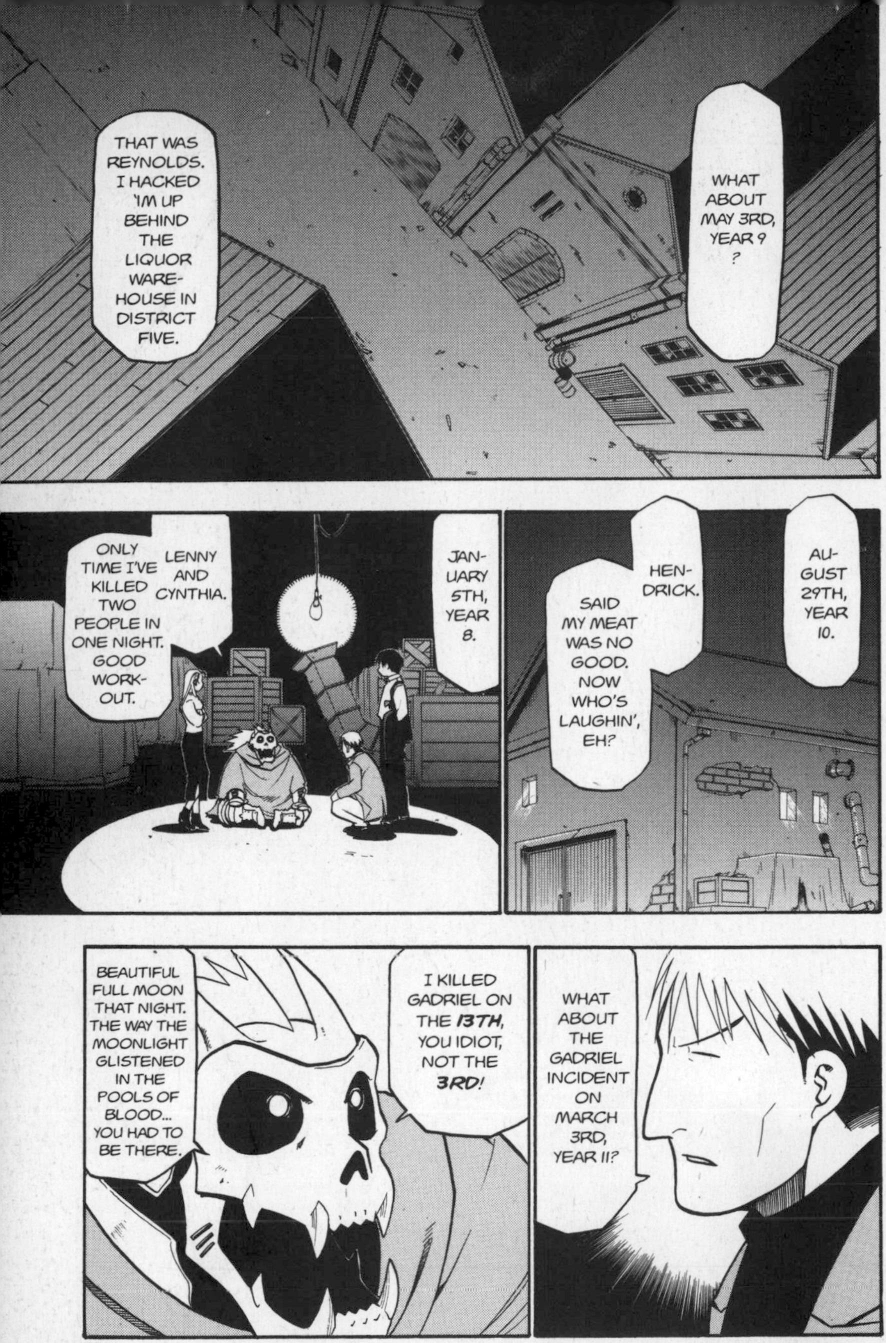
WHAT ABOUT MAY 3RD, YEAR 9?
THAT WAS REYNOLDS. I HACKED 'IM UP BEHIND THE LIQUOR WARE-HOUSE IN DISTRICT FIVE.
AU-GUST 29TH, YEAR 10.
HEN-DRICK.
SAID MY MEAT WAS NO GOOD. NOW WHO'S LAUGHIN', EH?
JAN-UARY 5TH, YEAR 8.
LENNY AND CYNTHIA.
ONLY TIME I'VE KILLED TWO PEOPLE IN ONE NIGHT. GOOD WORK-OUT.
WHAT ABOUT THE GADRIEL INCIDENT ON MARCH 3RD, YEAR 11?
I KILLED GADRIEL ON THE *13TH*, YOU IDIOT, NOT THE *3RD*!
BEAUTIFUL FULL MOON THAT NIGHT. THE WAY THE MOONLIGHT GLISTENED IN THE POOLS OF BLOOD... YOU HAD TO BE THERE.

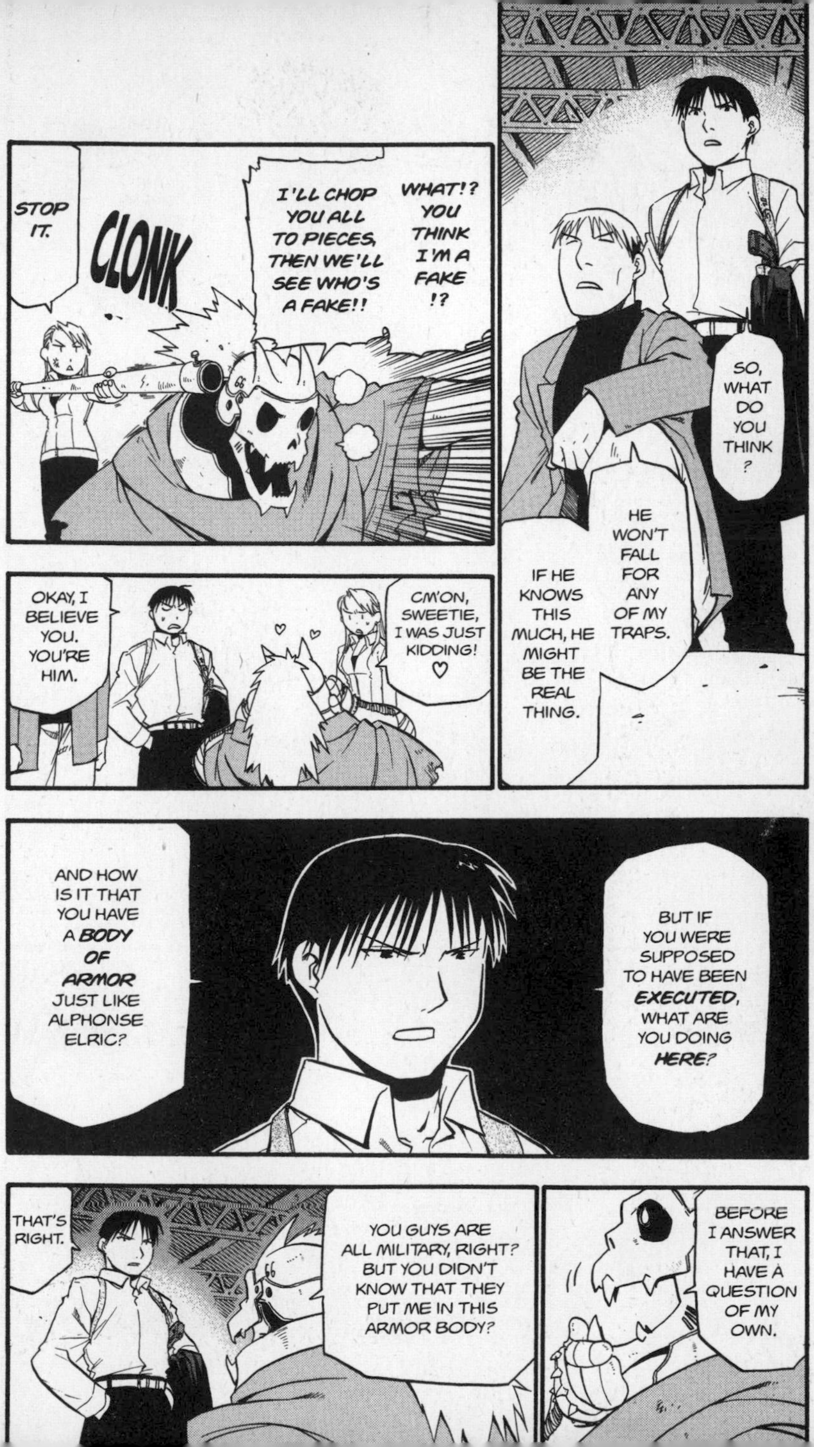
SO, WHAT DO YOU THINK?
HE WON'T FALL FOR ANY OF MY TRAPS.
IF HE KNOWS THIS MUCH, HE MIGHT BE THE REAL THING.
WHAT!? YOU THINK I'M A FAKE!?
I'LL CHOP YOU ALL TO PIECES, THEN WE'LL SEE WHO'S A FAKE!!
CLONK
STOP IT.
CM'ON, SWEETIE, I WAS JUST KIDDING! ♡
OKAY, I BELIEVE YOU. YOU'RE HIM.
BUT IF YOU WERE SUPPOSED TO HAVE BEEN EXECUTED, WHAT ARE YOU DOING HERE?
AND HOW IS IT THAT YOU HAVE A BODY OF ARMOR JUST LIKE ALPHONSE ELRIC?
BEFORE I ANSWER THAT, I HAVE A QUESTION OF MY OWN.
YOU GUYS ARE ALL MILITARY, RIGHT? BUT YOU DIDN'T KNOW THAT THEY PUT ME IN THIS ARMOR BODY?
THAT'S RIGHT.

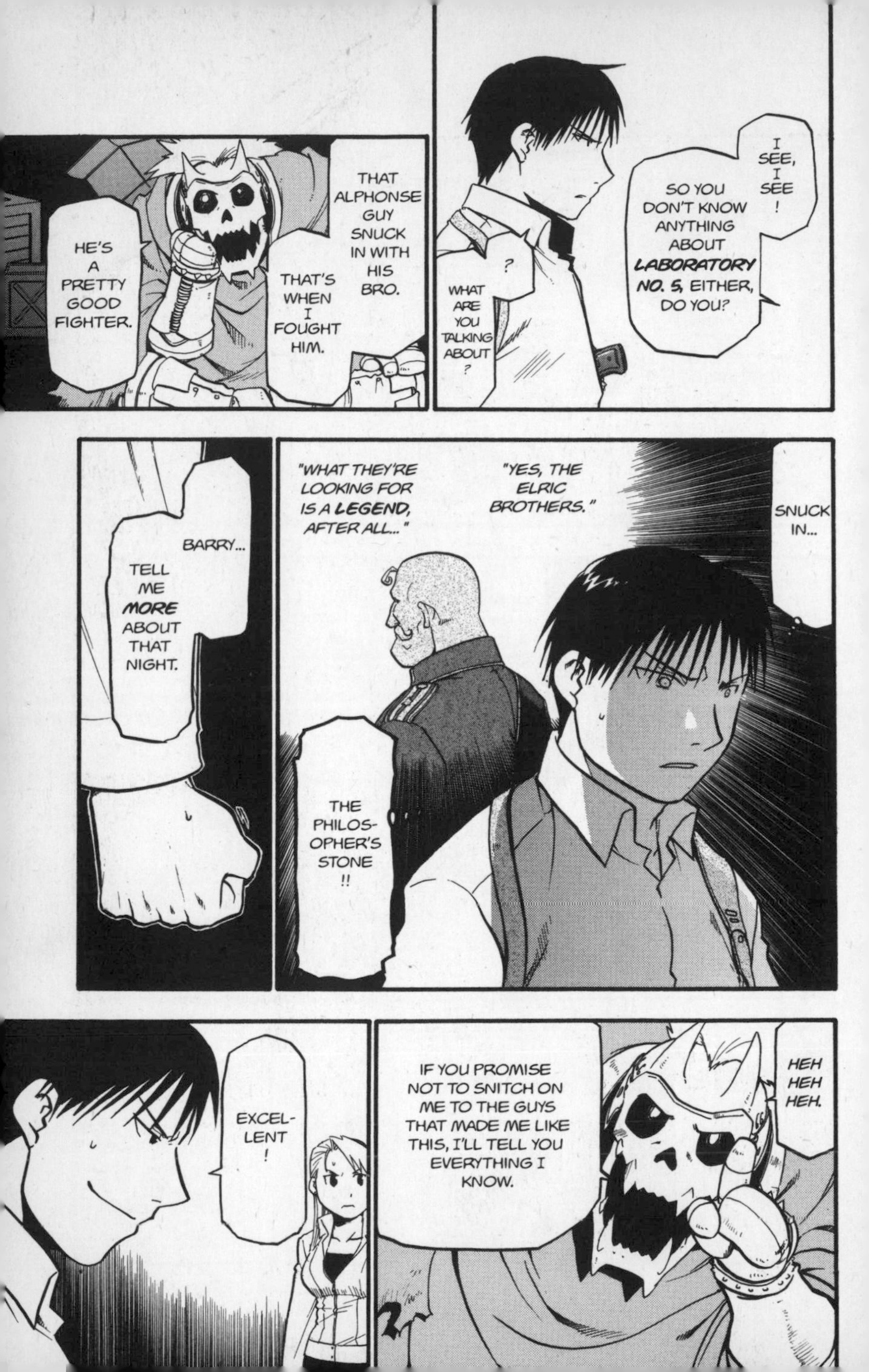
I SEE, I SEE!
SO YOU DON'T KNOW ANYTHING ABOUT LABORATORY NO. 5, EITHER, DO YOU?
? WHAT ARE YOU TALKING ABOUT ?
THAT ALPHONSE GUY SNUCK IN WITH HIS BRO.
THAT'S WHEN I FOUGHT HIM.
HE'S A PRETTY GOOD FIGHTER.
SNUCK IN...
"YES, THE ELRIC BROTHERS."
"WHAT THEY'RE LOOKING FOR IS A LEGEND, AFTER ALL..."
THE PHILOSOPHER'S STONE!!
BARRY... TELL ME MORE ABOUT THAT NIGHT.
HEH HEH HEH.
IF YOU PROMISE NOT TO SNITCH ON ME TO THE GUYS THAT MADE ME LIKE THIS, I'LL TELL YOU EVERYTHING I KNOW.
EXCELLENT!

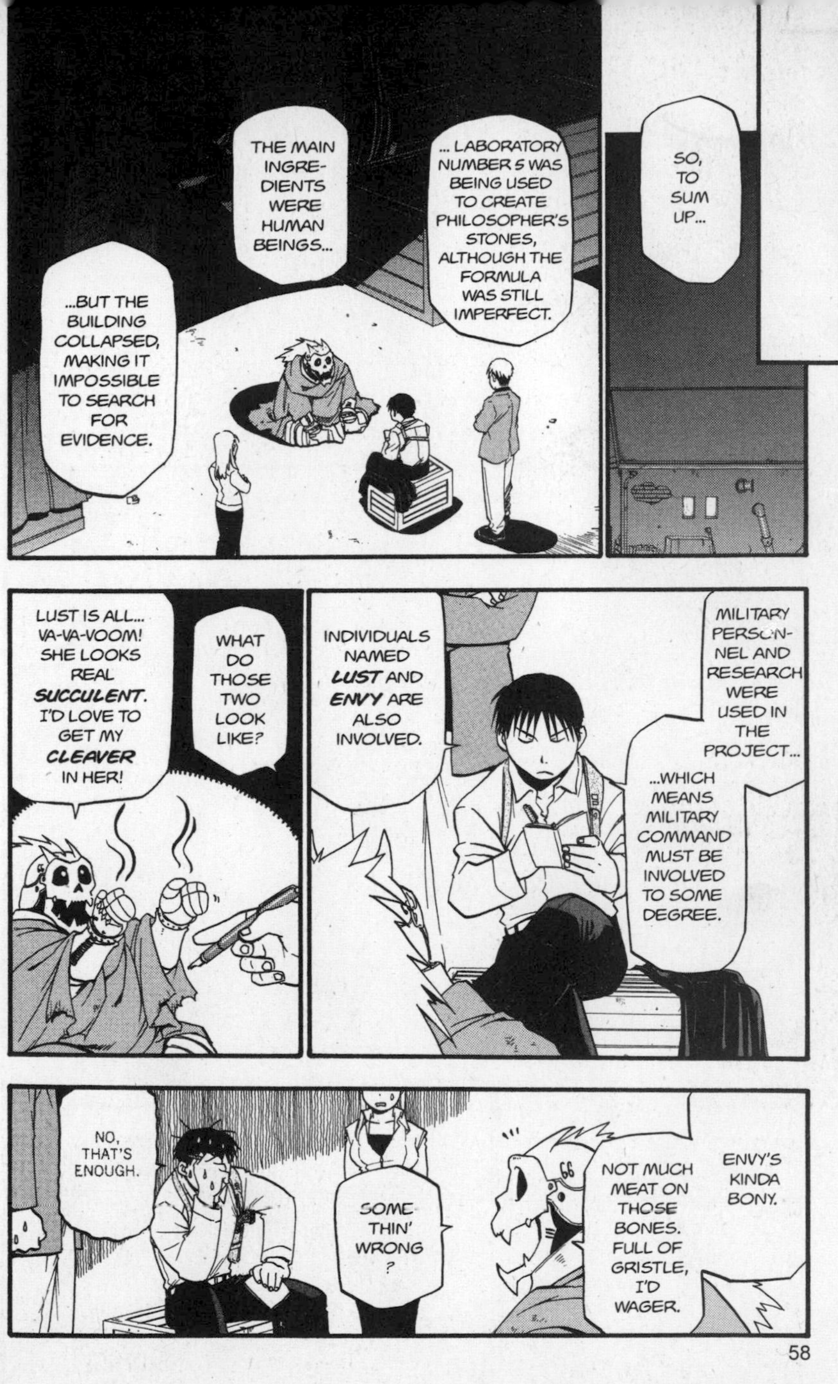
SO, TO SUM UP...
... LABORATORY NUMBER 5 WAS BEING USED TO CREATE PHILOSOPHER'S STONES, ALTHOUGH THE FORMULA WAS STILL IMPERFECT.
THE MAIN INGREDIENTS WERE HUMAN BEINGS...
...BUT THE BUILDING COLLAPSED, MAKING IT IMPOSSIBLE TO SEARCH FOR EVIDENCE.
MILITARY PERSONNEL AND RESEARCH WERE USED IN THE PROJECT...
...WHICH MEANS MILITARY COMMAND MUST BE INVOLVED TO SOME DEGREE.
INDIVIDUALS NAMED ***LUST*** AND ***ENVY*** ARE ALSO INVOLVED.
WHAT DO THOSE TWO LOOK LIKE?
LUST IS ALL... VA-VA-VOOM! SHE LOOKS REAL ***SUCCULENT***. I'D LOVE TO GET MY ***CLEAVER*** IN HER!
ENVY'S KINDA BONY.
NOT MUCH MEAT ON THOSE BONES. FULL OF GRISTLE, I'D WAGER.
SOME THIN' WRONG?
NO, THAT'S ENOUGH.

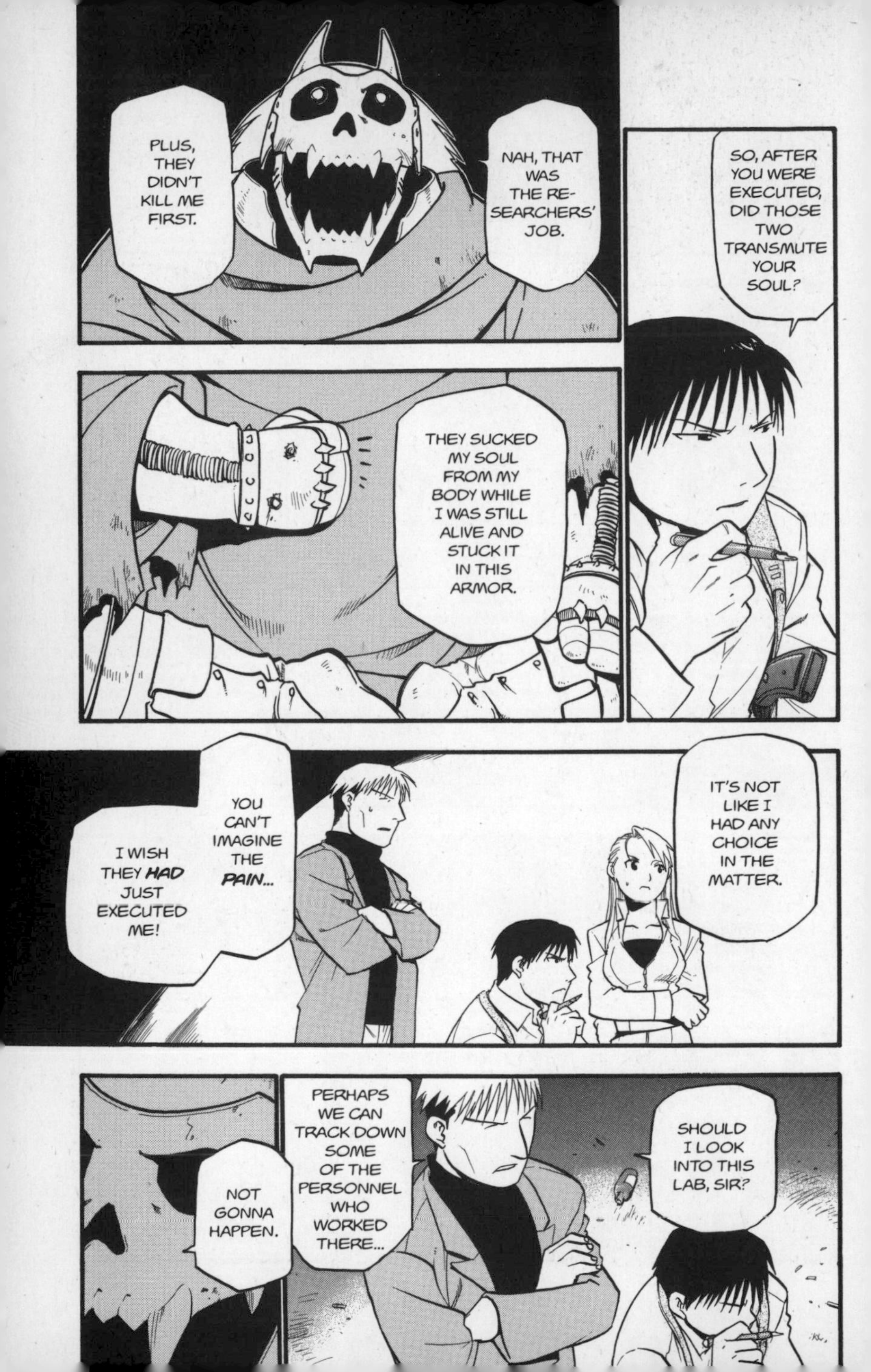
SO, AFTER YOU WERE EXECUTED, DID THOSE TWO TRANSMUTE YOUR SOUL?
NAH, THAT WAS THE RE-SEARCHERS' JOB.
PLUS, THEY DIDN'T KILL ME FIRST.
THEY SUCKED MY SOUL FROM MY BODY WHILE I WAS STILL ALIVE AND STUCK IT IN THIS ARMOR.
IT'S NOT LIKE I HAD ANY CHOICE IN THE MATTER.
YOU CAN'T IMAGINE THE ***PAIN***...
I WISH THEY ***HAD*** JUST EXECUTED ME!
SHOULD I LOOK INTO THIS LAB, SIR?
PERHAPS WE CAN TRACK DOWN SOME OF THE PERSONNEL WHO WORKED THERE...
NOT GONNA HAPPEN.

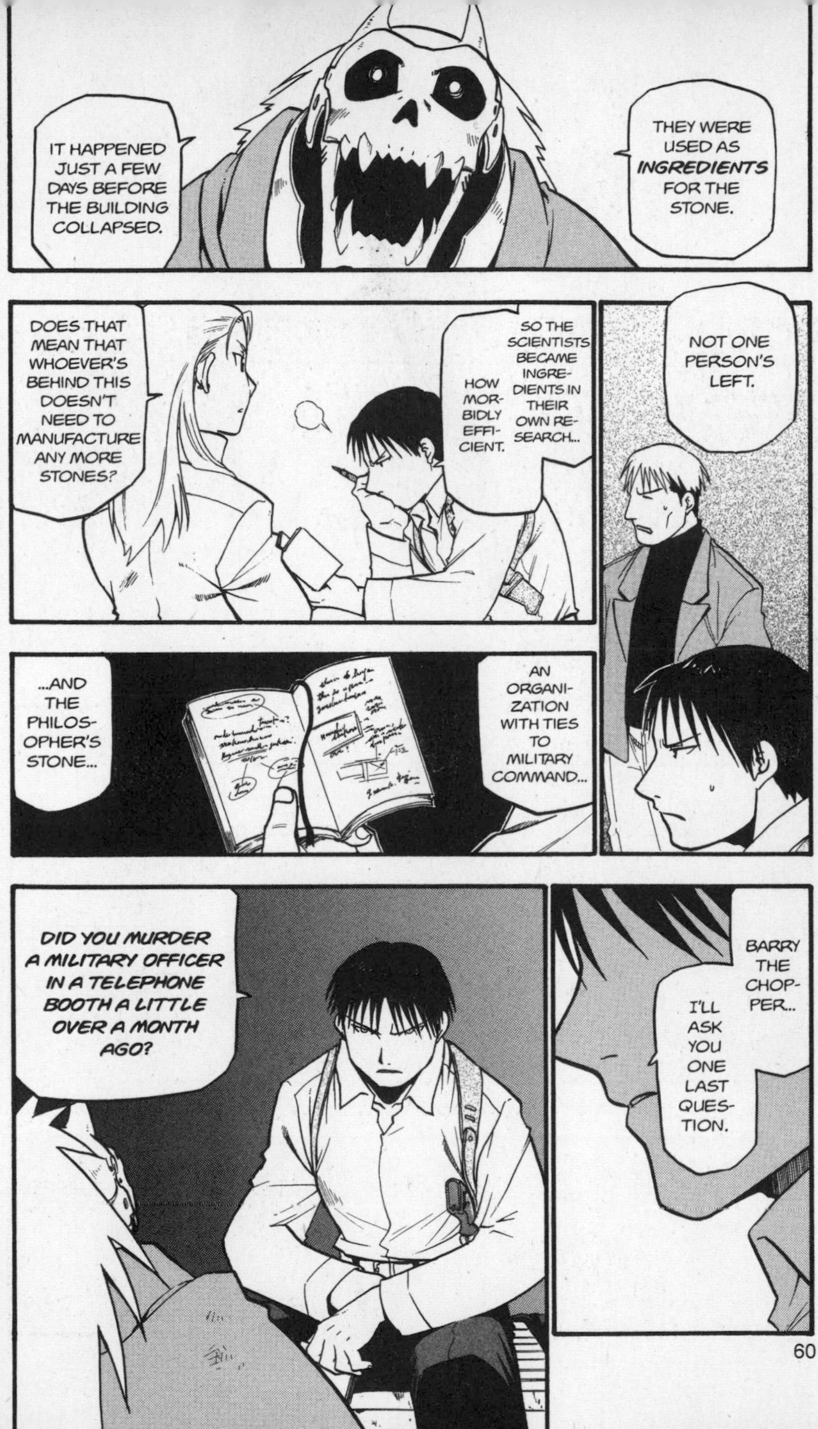
THEY WERE USED AS *INGREDIENTS* FOR THE STONE.
IT HAPPENED JUST A FEW DAYS BEFORE THE BUILDING COLLAPSED.
NOT ONE PERSON'S LEFT.
SO THE SCIENTISTS BECAME INGREDIENTS IN THEIR OWN RESEARCH...
HOW MORBIDLY EFFICIENT.
DOES THAT MEAN THAT WHOEVER'S BEHIND THIS DOESN'T NEED TO MANUFACTURE ANY MORE STONES?
AN ORGANIZATION WITH TIES TO MILITARY COMMAND...
...AND THE PHILOSOPHER'S STONE...
BARRY THE CHOPPER...
I'LL ASK YOU ONE LAST QUESTION.
DID YOU MURDER A MILITARY OFFICER IN A TELEPHONE BOOTH A LITTLE OVER A MONTH AGO?

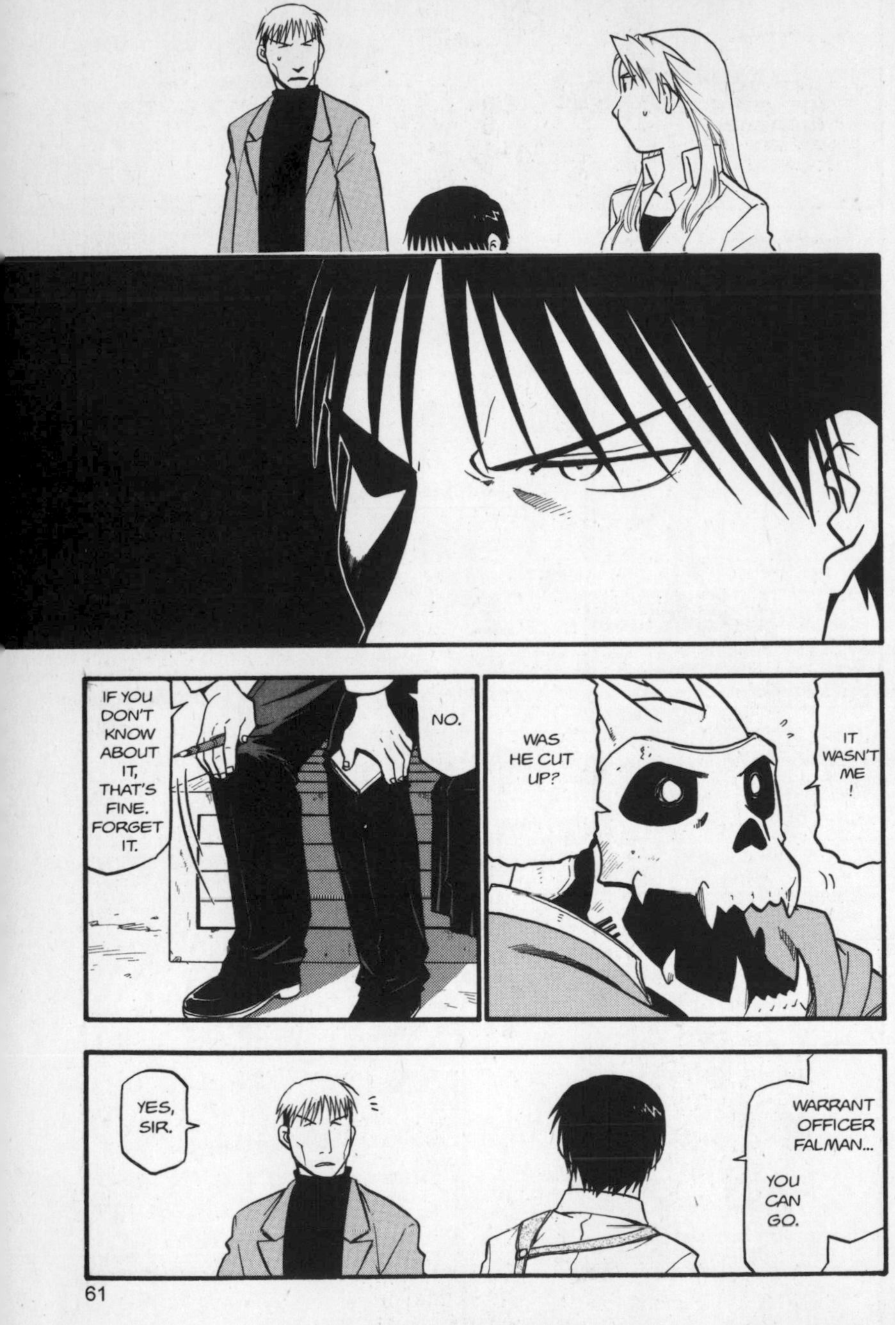
IT WASN'T ME!
WAS HE CUT UP?
NO.
IF YOU DON'T KNOW ABOUT IT, THAT'S FINE. FORGET IT.
WARRANT OFFICER FALMAN...
YOU CAN GO.
YES, SIR.

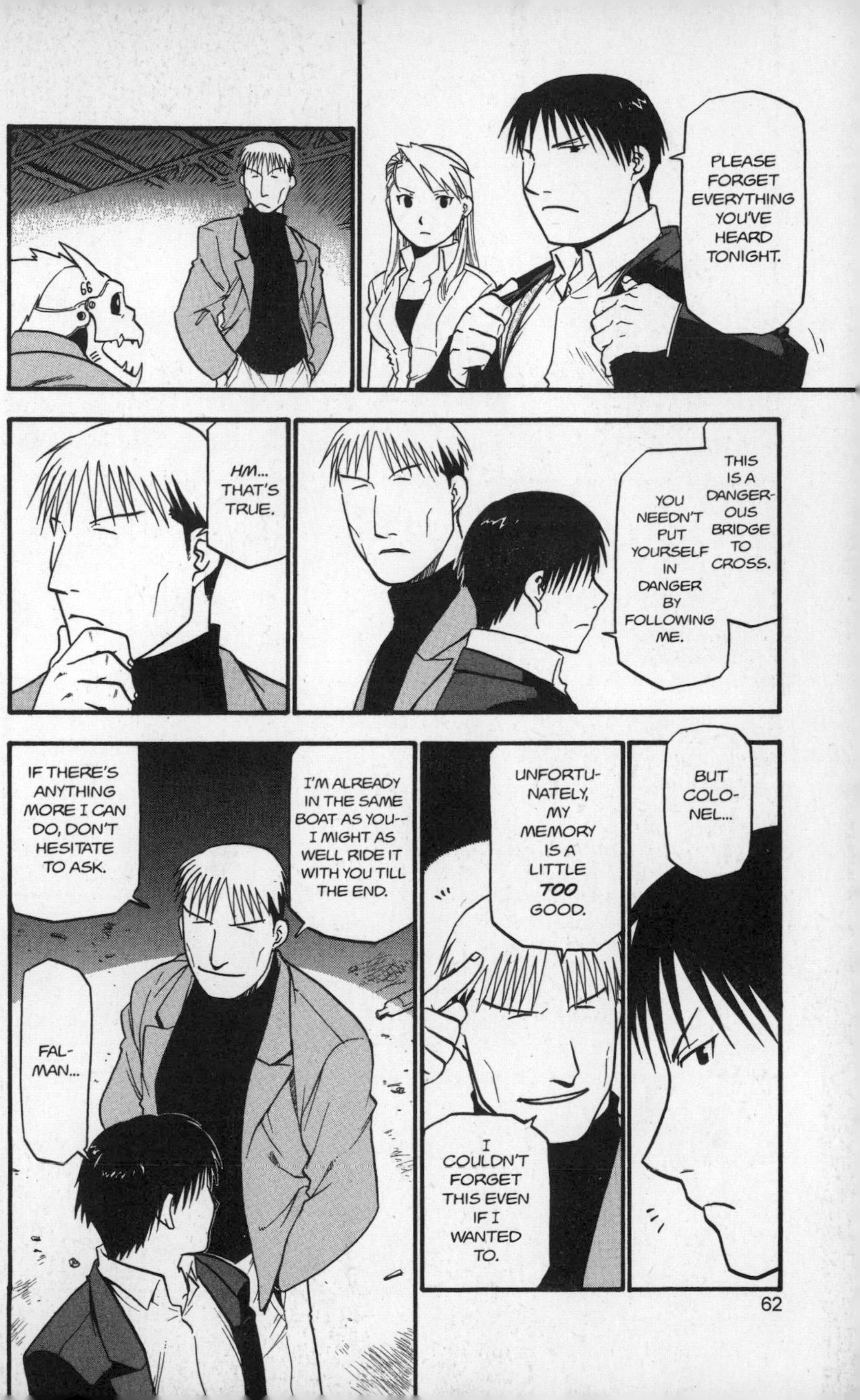
PLEASE FORGET EVERYTHING YOU'VE HEARD TONIGHT.
THIS IS A DANGER-OUS BRIDGE TO CROSS.
YOU NEEDN'T PUT YOURSELF IN DANGER BY FOLLOWING ME.
HM... THAT'S TRUE.
BUT COLO-NEL...
UNFORTU-NATELY, MY MEMORY IS A LITTLE *TOO* GOOD.
I COULDN'T FORGET THIS EVEN IF I WANTED TO.
I'M ALREADY IN THE SAME BOAT AS YOU-- I MIGHT AS WELL RIDE IT WITH YOU TILL THE END.
IF THERE'S ANYTHING MORE I CAN DO, DON'T HESITATE TO ASK.
FAL-MAN...

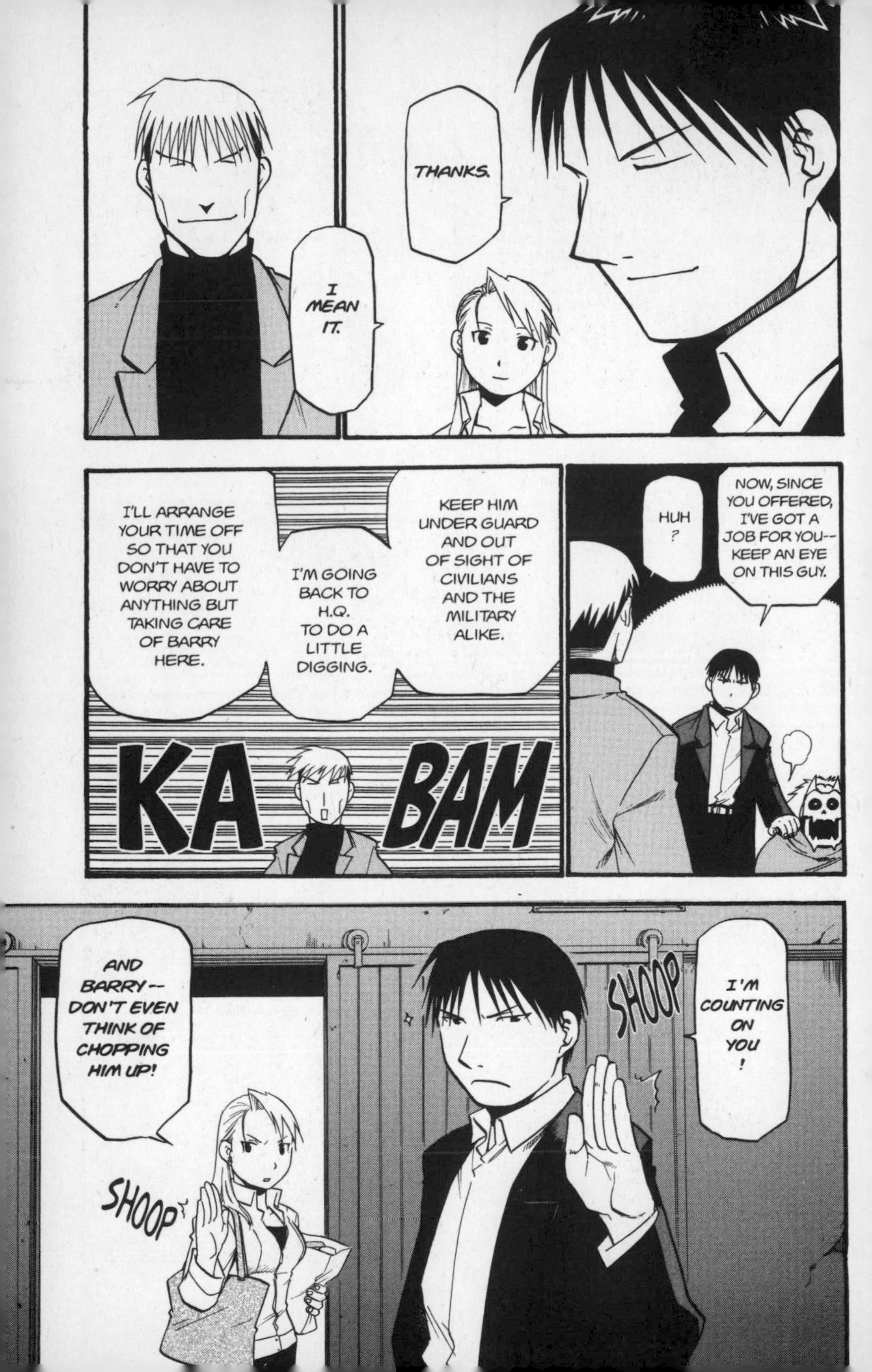
THANKS.
I MEAN IT.
NOW, SINCE YOU OFFERED, I'VE GOT A JOB FOR YOU-- KEEP AN EYE ON THIS GUY.
HUH ?
KEEP HIM UNDER GUARD AND OUT OF SIGHT OF CIVILIANS AND THE MILITARY ALIKE.
I'M GOING BACK TO H.Q. TO DO A LITTLE DIGGING.
I'LL ARRANGE YOUR TIME OFF SO THAT YOU DON'T HAVE TO WORRY ABOUT ANYTHING BUT TAKING CARE OF BARRY HERE.
KA BAM
I'M COUNTING ON YOU !
SHOOP
AND BARRY-- DON'T EVEN THINK OF CHOPPING HIM UP!
SHOOP

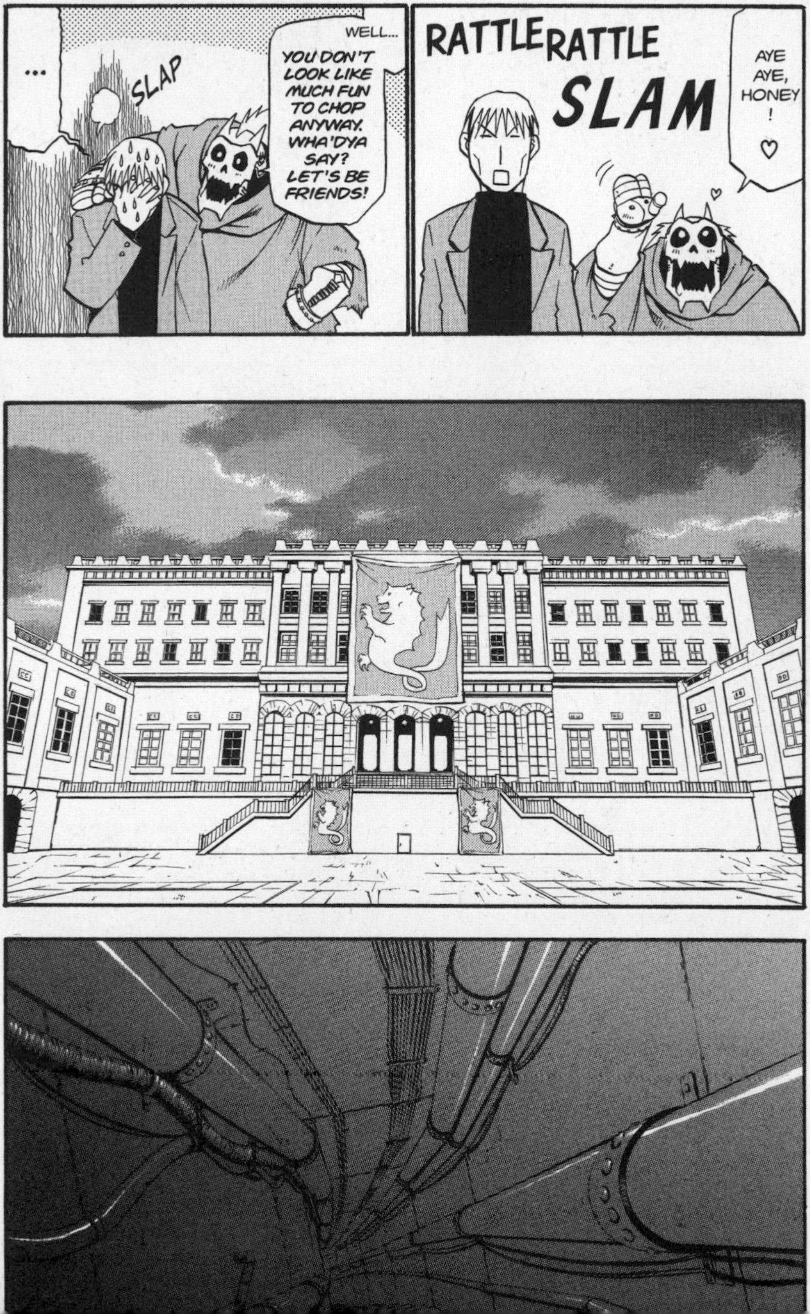
AYE AYE, HONEY ! ♡
RATTLE RATTLE
SLAM
WELL...
YOU DON'T LOOK LIKE MUCH FUN TO CHOP ANYWAY. WHA'DYA SAY? LET'S BE FRIENDS!
SLAP
...

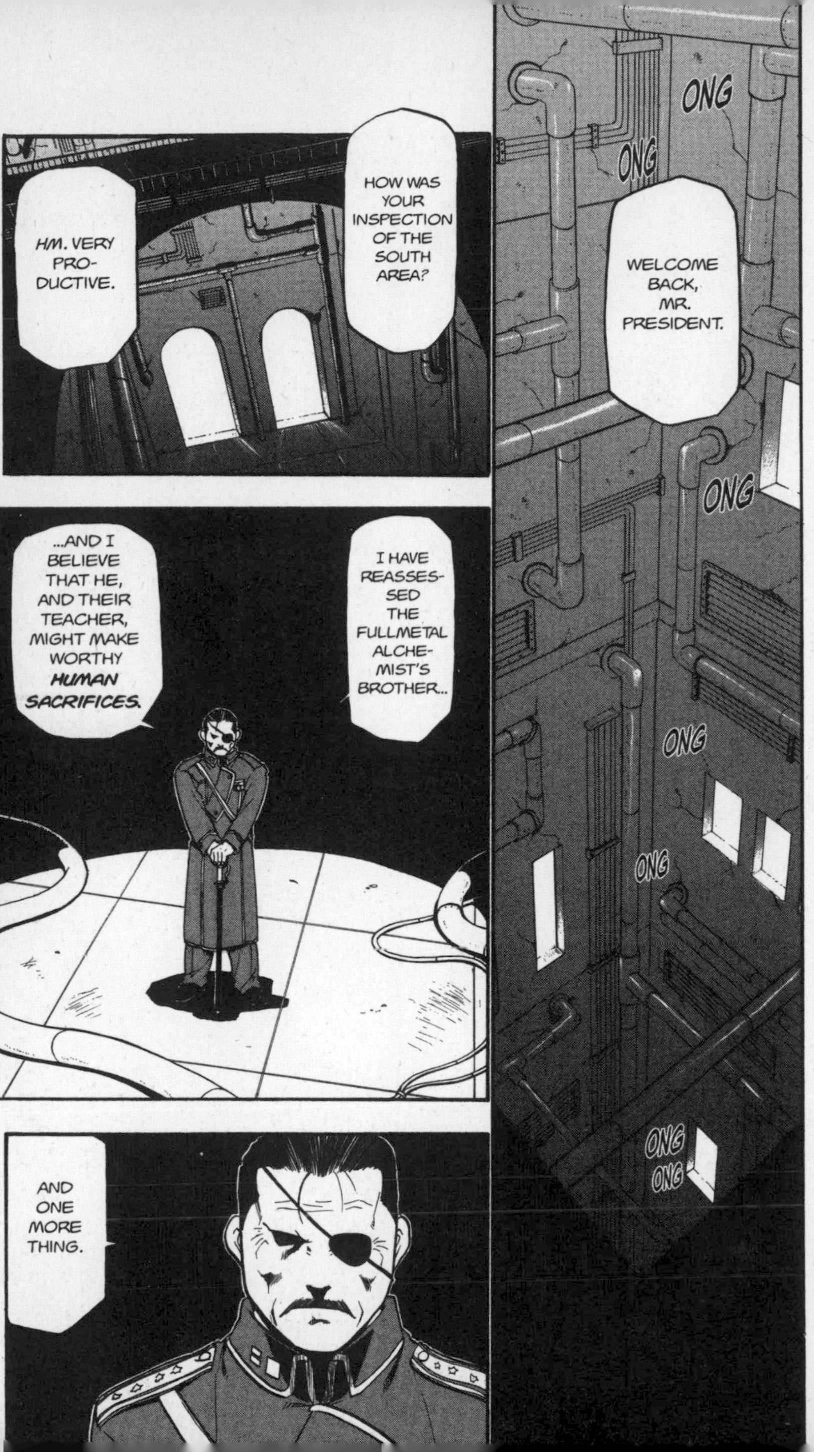
ONG
ONG
WELCOME BACK, MR. PRESIDENT.
ONG
ONG
ONG
ONG
ONG
HOW WAS YOUR INSPECTION OF THE SOUTH AREA?
HM. VERY PRO-DUCTIVE.
I HAVE REASSES-SED THE FULLMETAL ALCHE-MIST'S BROTHER...
...AND I BELIEVE THAT HE, AND THEIR TEACHER, MIGHT MAKE WORTHY **HUMAN SACRIFICES.**
AND ONE MORE THING.

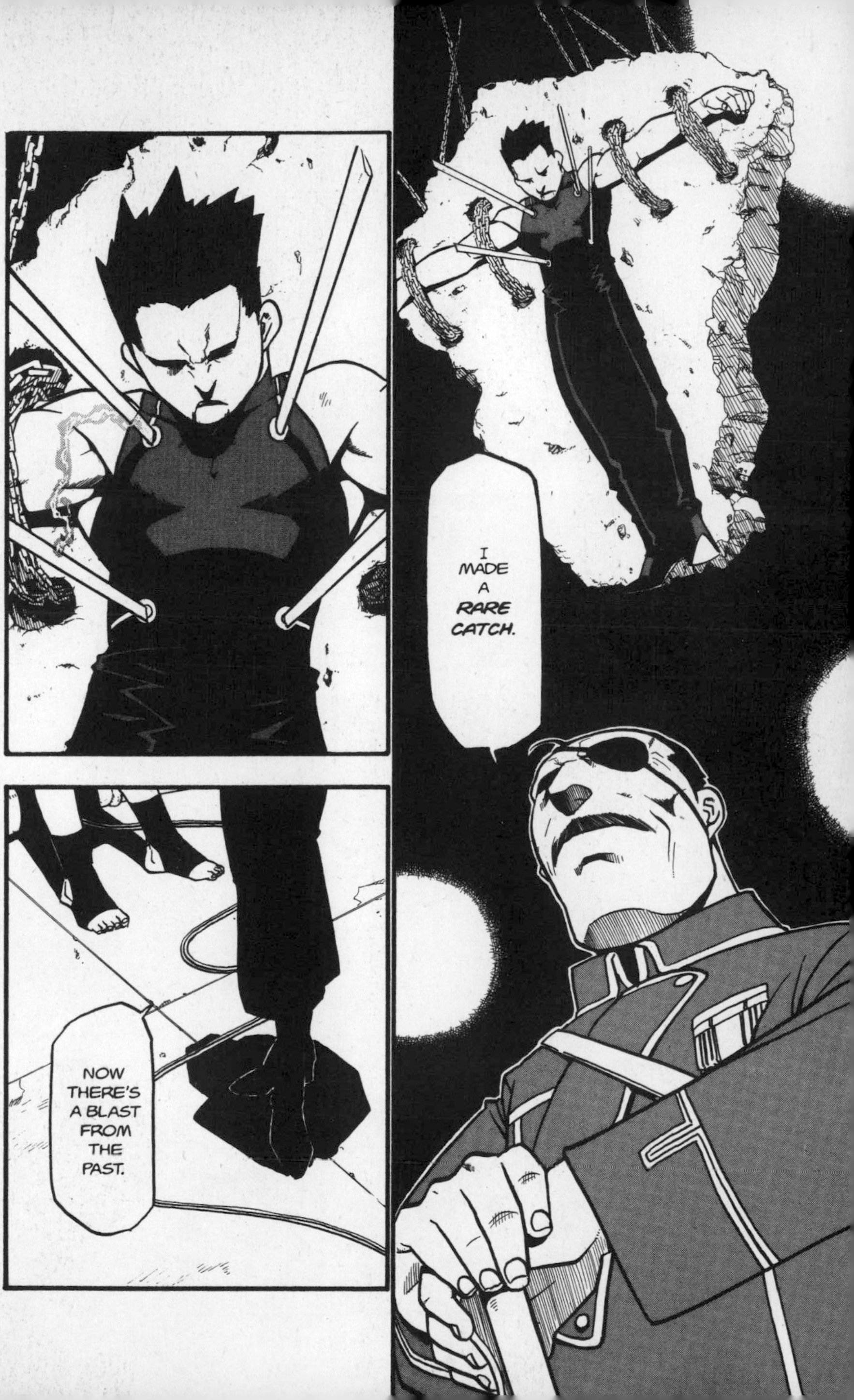
I MADE A *RARE* CATCH.
NOW THERE'S A BLAST FROM THE PAST.

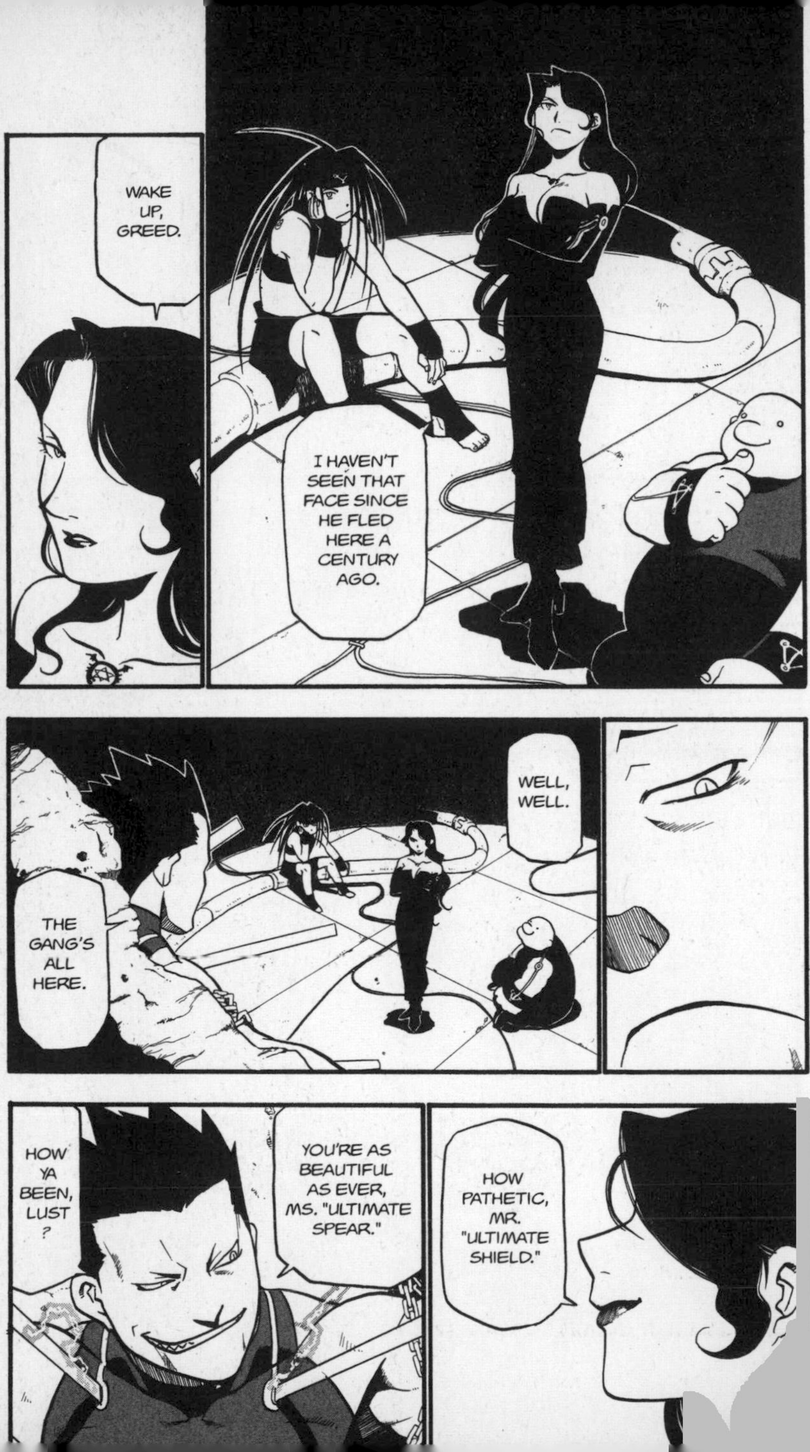
I HAVEN'T SEEN THAT FACE SINCE HE FLED HERE A CENTURY AGO.
WAKE UP, GREED.
WELL, WELL.
THE GANG'S ALL HERE.
HOW PATHETIC, MR. "ULTIMATE SHIELD."
YOU'RE AS BEAUTIFUL AS EVER, MS. "ULTIMATE SPEAR."
HOW YA BEEN, LUST?

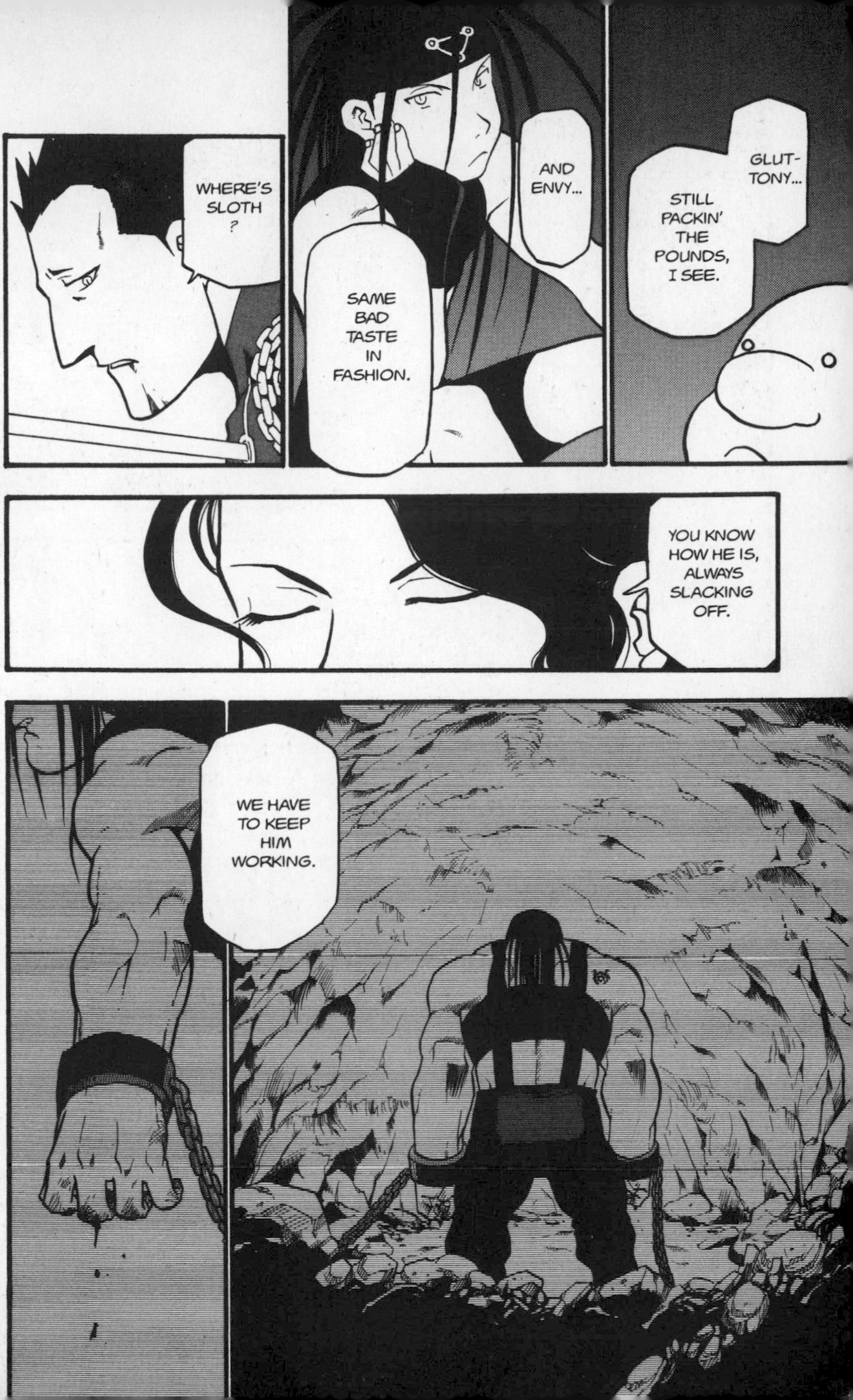
GLUT-TONY...
STILL PACKIN' THE POUNDS, I SEE.
AND ENVY...
SAME BAD TASTE IN FASHION.
WHERE'S SLOTH?
YOU KNOW HOW HE IS, ALWAYS SLACKING OFF.
WE HAVE TO KEEP HIM WORKING.

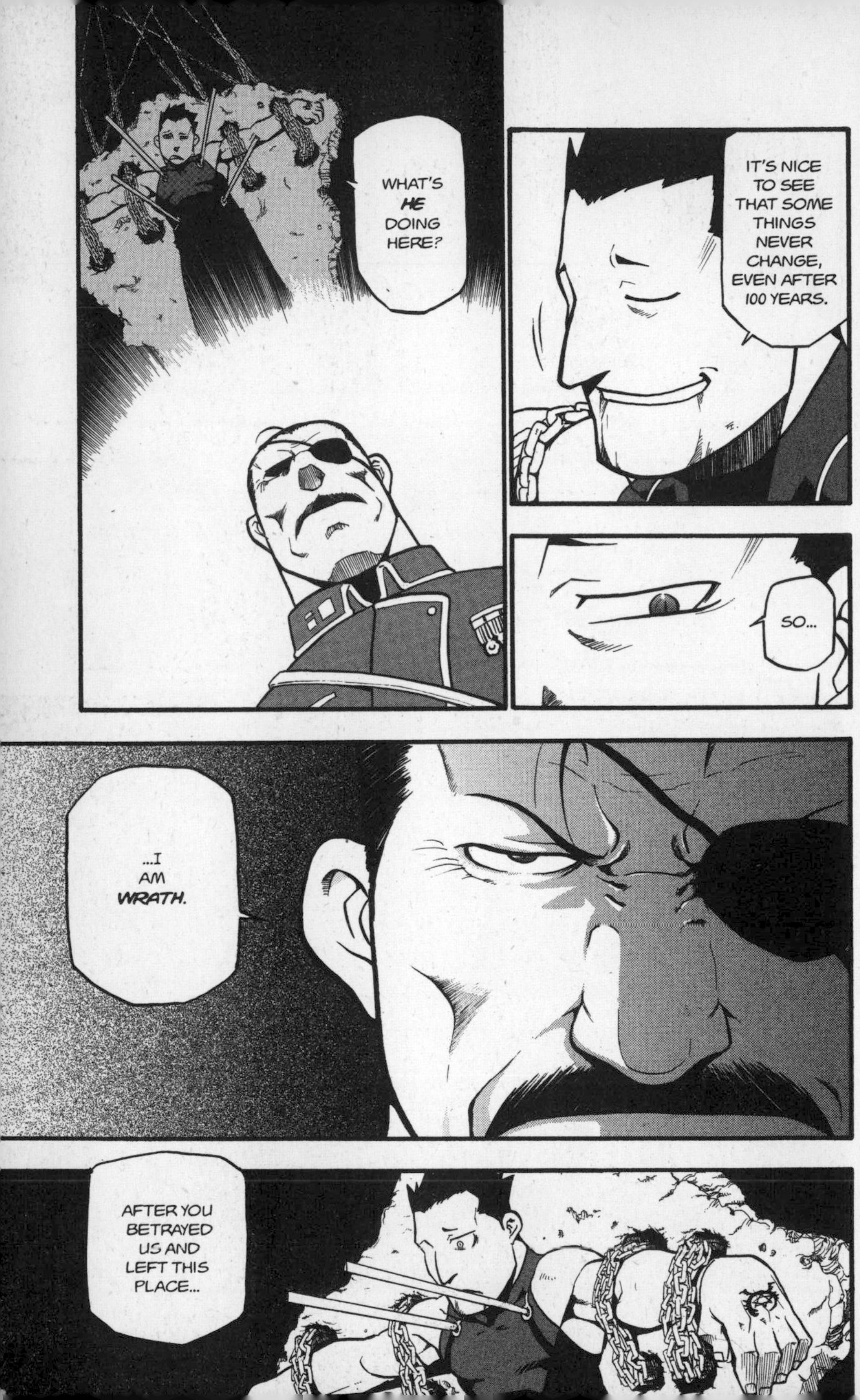
IT'S NICE TO SEE THAT SOME THINGS NEVER CHANGE, EVEN AFTER 100 YEARS.
SO...
WHAT'S *HE* DOING HERE?
...I AM *WRATH.*
AFTER YOU BETRAYED US AND LEFT THIS PLACE...

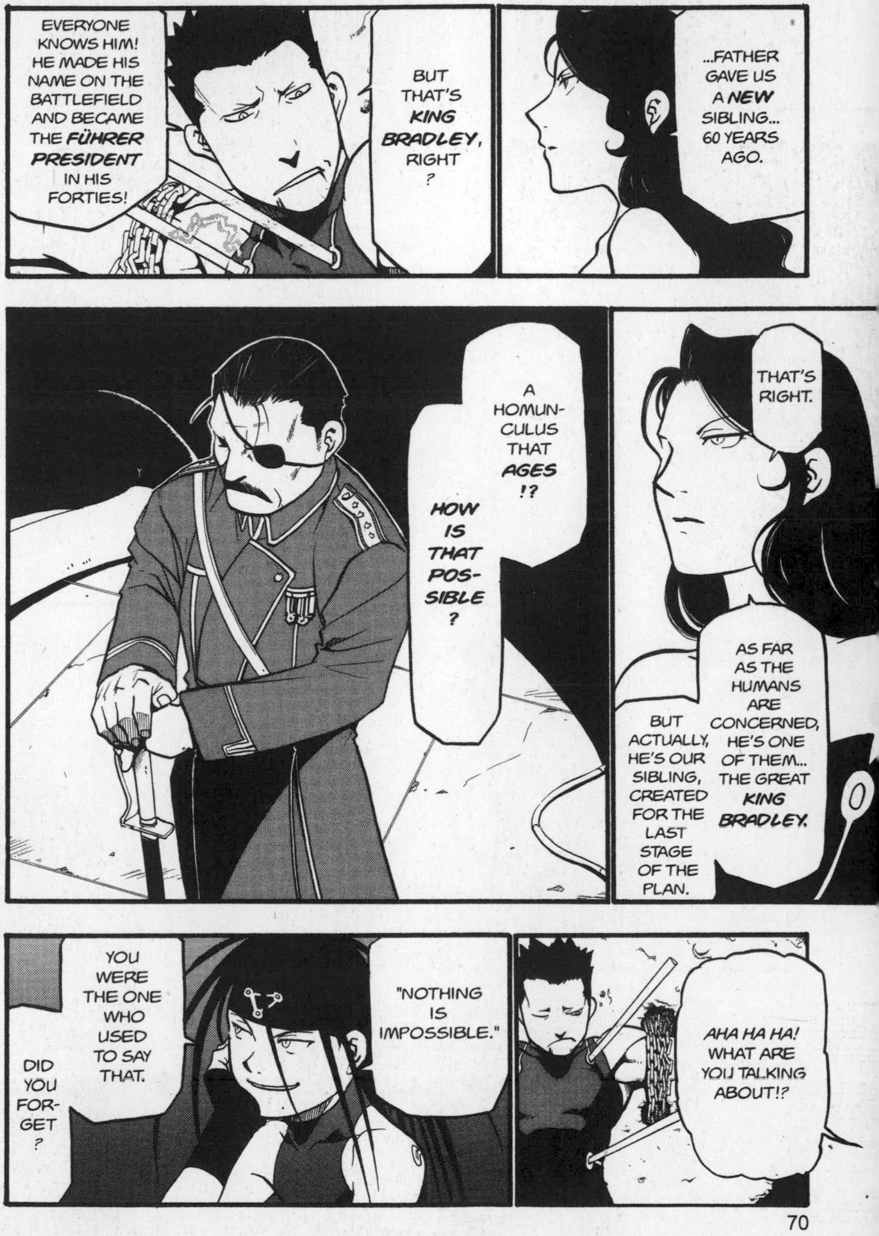
...FATHER GAVE US A NEW SIBLING... 60 YEARS AGO.
BUT THAT'S KING BRADLEY, RIGHT?
EVERYONE KNOWS HIM! HE MADE HIS NAME ON THE BATTLEFIELD AND BECAME THE FÜHRER PRESIDENT IN HIS FORTIES!
THAT'S RIGHT.
AS FAR AS THE HUMANS ARE CONCERNED, HE'S ONE OF THEM... THE GREAT KING BRADLEY.
BUT ACTUALLY, HE'S OUR SIBLING, CREATED FOR THE LAST STAGE OF THE PLAN.
A HOMUNCULUS THAT AGES!?
HOW IS THAT POSSIBLE?
AHA HA HA! WHAT ARE YOU TALKING ABOUT!?
"NOTHING IS IMPOSSIBLE."
YOU WERE THE ONE WHO USED TO SAY THAT.
DID YOU FORGET?

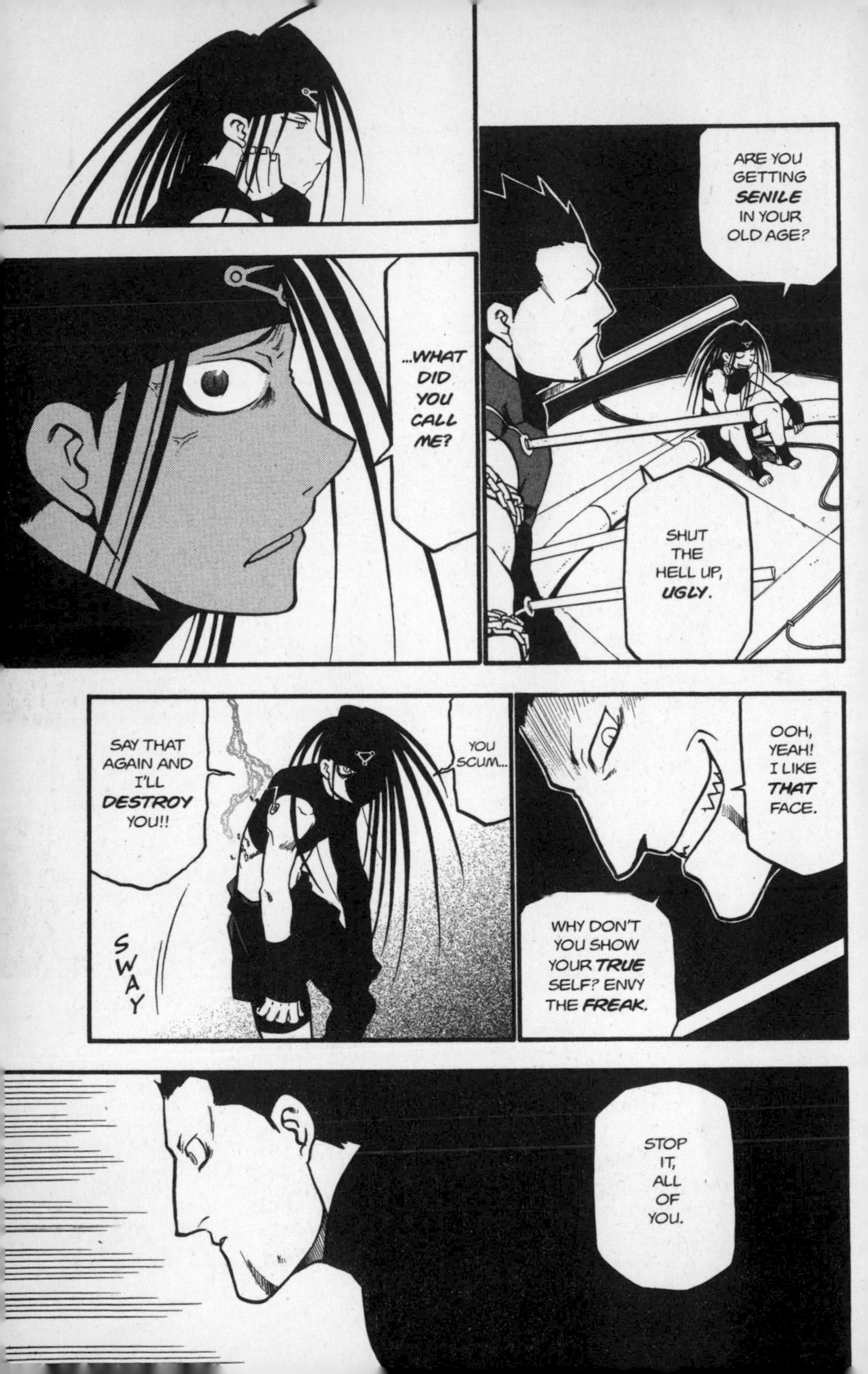
ARE YOU GETTING SENILE IN YOUR OLD AGE?
SHUT THE HELL UP, UGLY.
...WHAT DID YOU CALL ME?
OOH, YEAH! I LIKE THAT FACE.
WHY DON'T YOU SHOW YOUR TRUE SELF? ENVY THE FREAK.
YOU SCUM...
SAY THAT AGAIN AND I'LL DESTROY YOU!!
SWAY
STOP IT, ALL OF YOU.

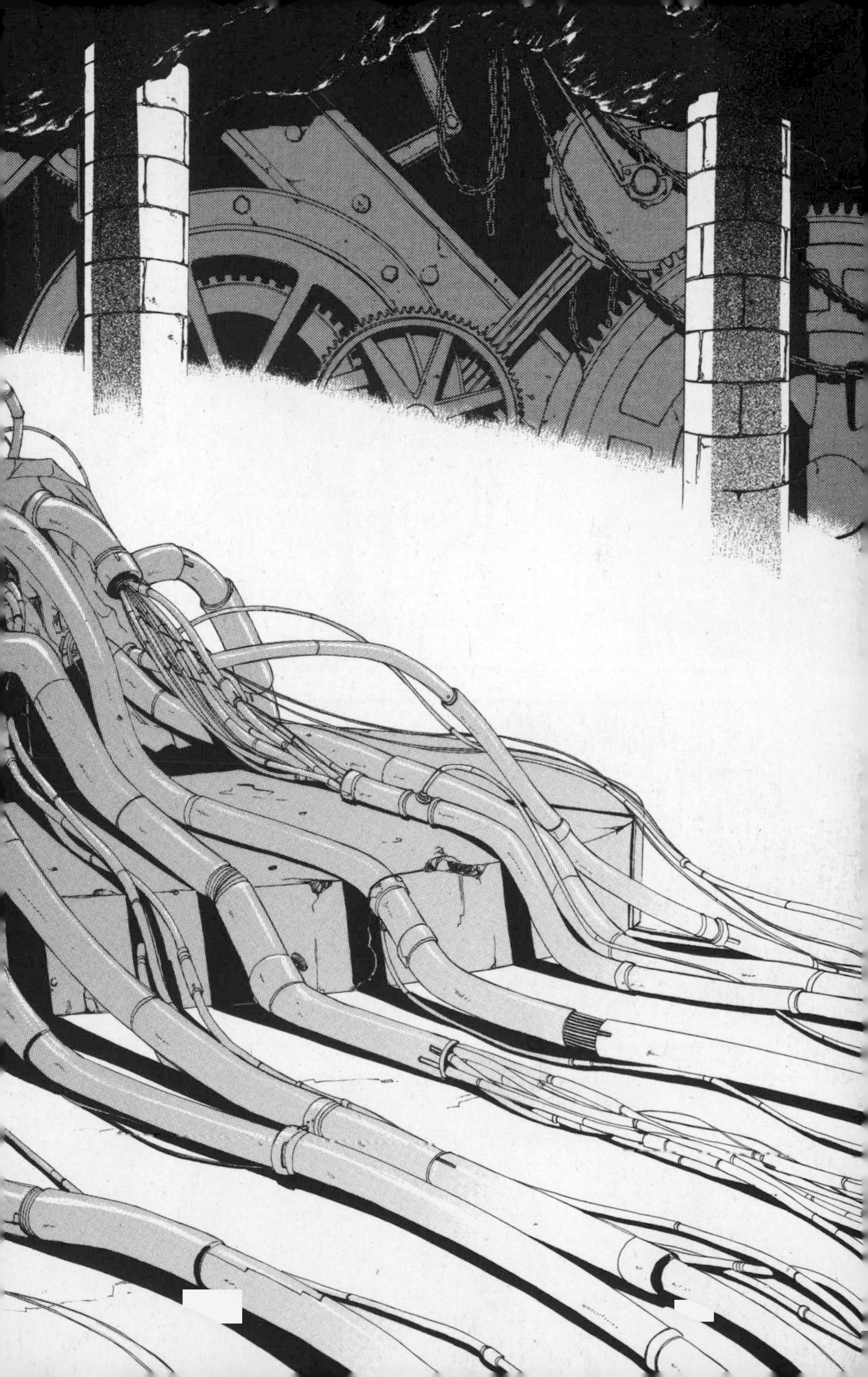

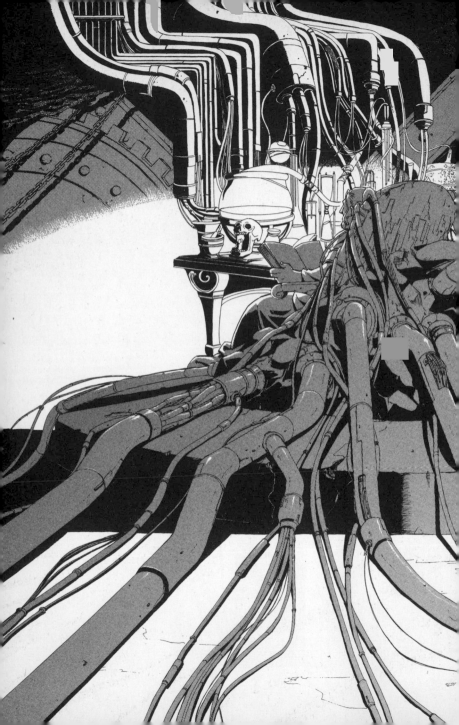

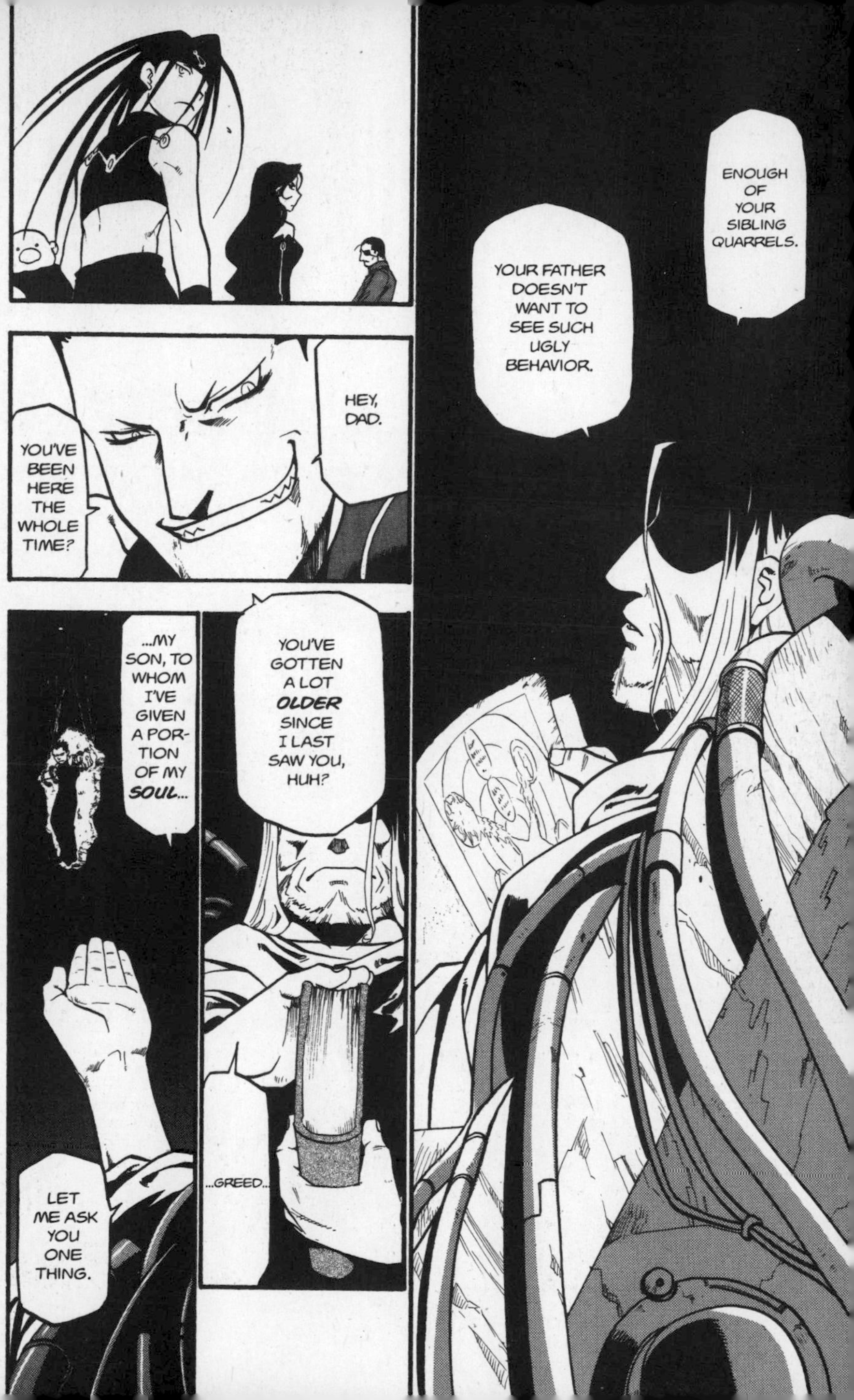
ENOUGH OF YOUR SIBLING QUARRELS.
YOUR FATHER DOESN'T WANT TO SEE SUCH UGLY BEHAVIOR.
HEY, DAD.
YOU'VE BEEN HERE THE WHOLE TIME?
YOU'VE GOTTEN A LOT OLDER SINCE I LAST SAW YOU, HUH?
...GREED...
...MY SON, TO WHOM I'VE GIVEN A PORTION OF MY SOUL...
LET ME ASK YOU ONE THING.

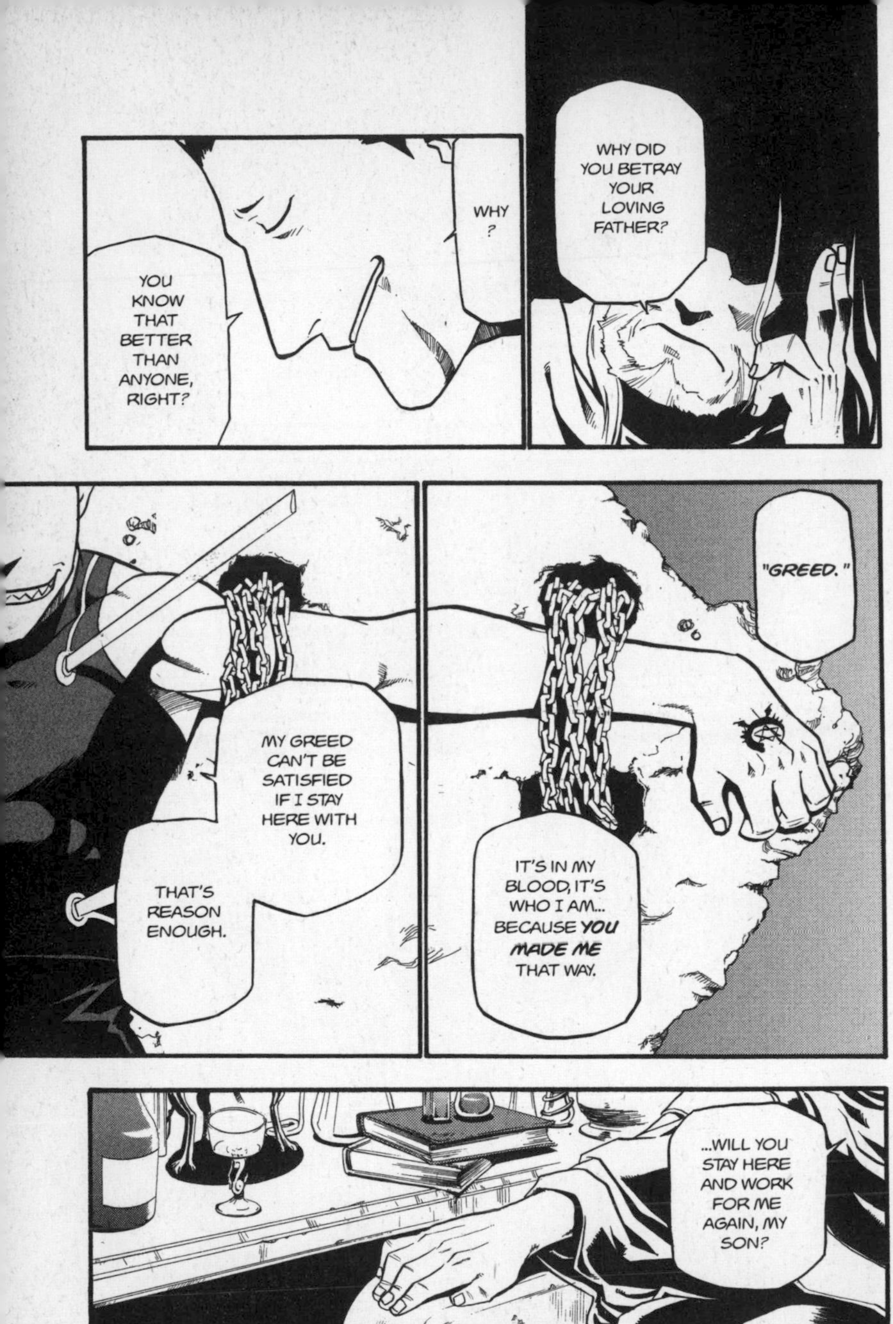
WHY DID YOU BETRAY YOUR LOVING FATHER?
WHY?
YOU KNOW THAT BETTER THAN ANYONE, RIGHT?
"GREED."
IT'S IN MY BLOOD, IT'S WHO I AM... BECAUSE YOU MADE ME THAT WAY.
MY GREED CAN'T BE SATISFIED IF I STAY HERE WITH YOU.
THAT'S REASON ENOUGH.
...WILL YOU STAY HERE AND WORK FOR ME AGAIN, MY SON?

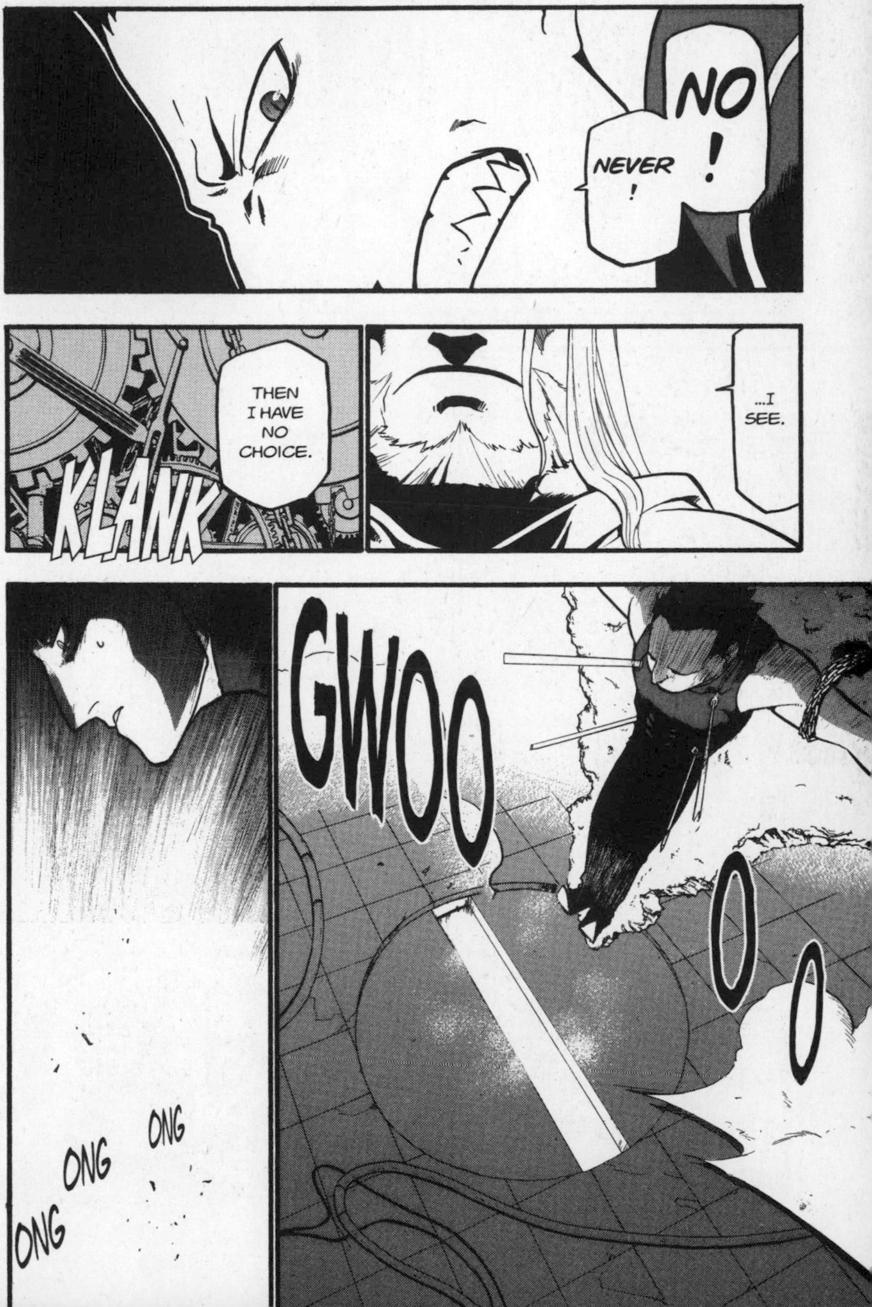
NO! NEVER!
...I SEE.
THEN I HAVE NO CHOICE.
KLANK
GWOOOO
ONG
ONG
ONG

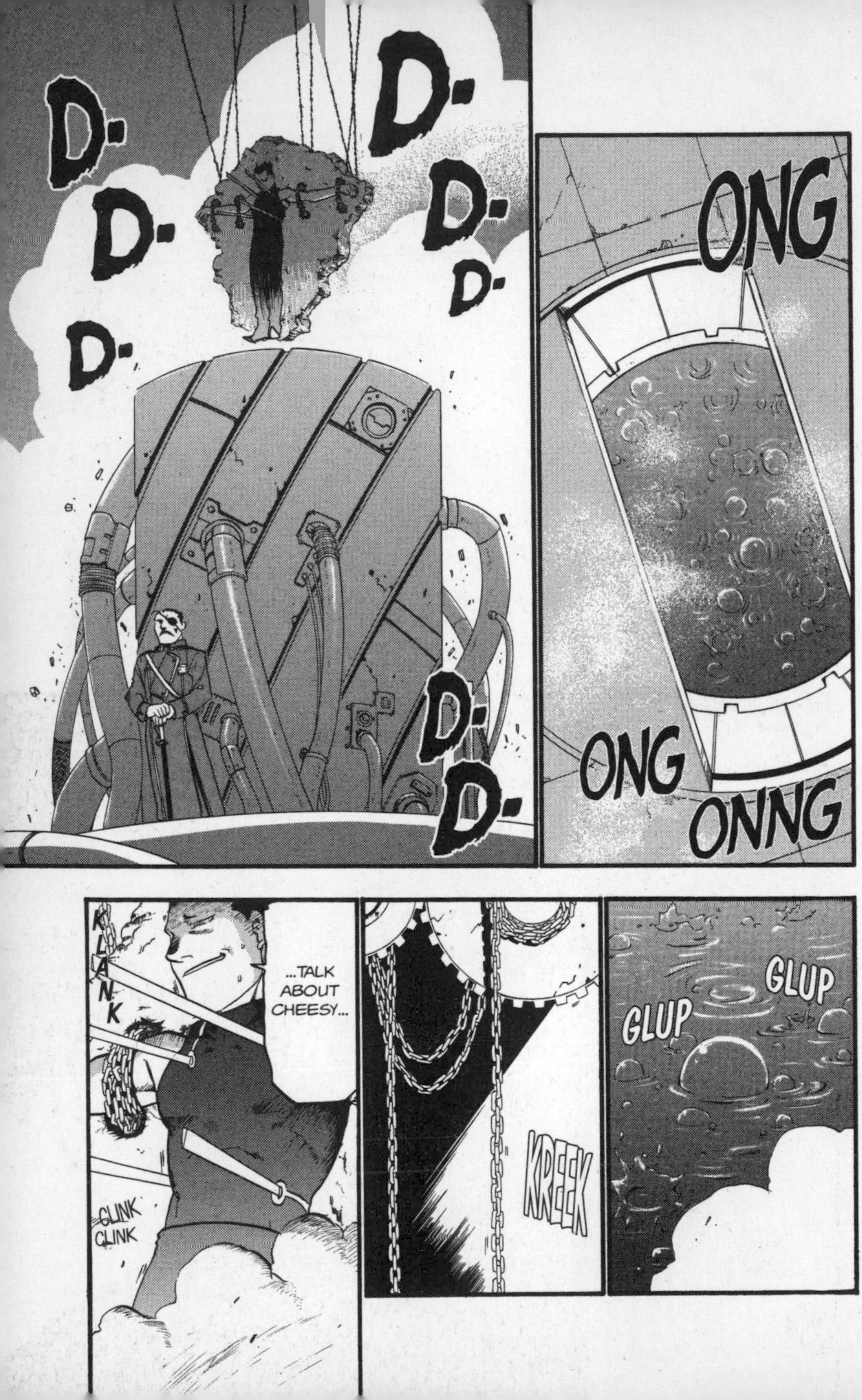
ONG
ONG
ONNG
D-
D-
D-
D-
D-
D-
D-
D-
GLUP
GLUP
KREEK
KLANK
...TALK ABOUT CHEESY...
CLINK CLINK

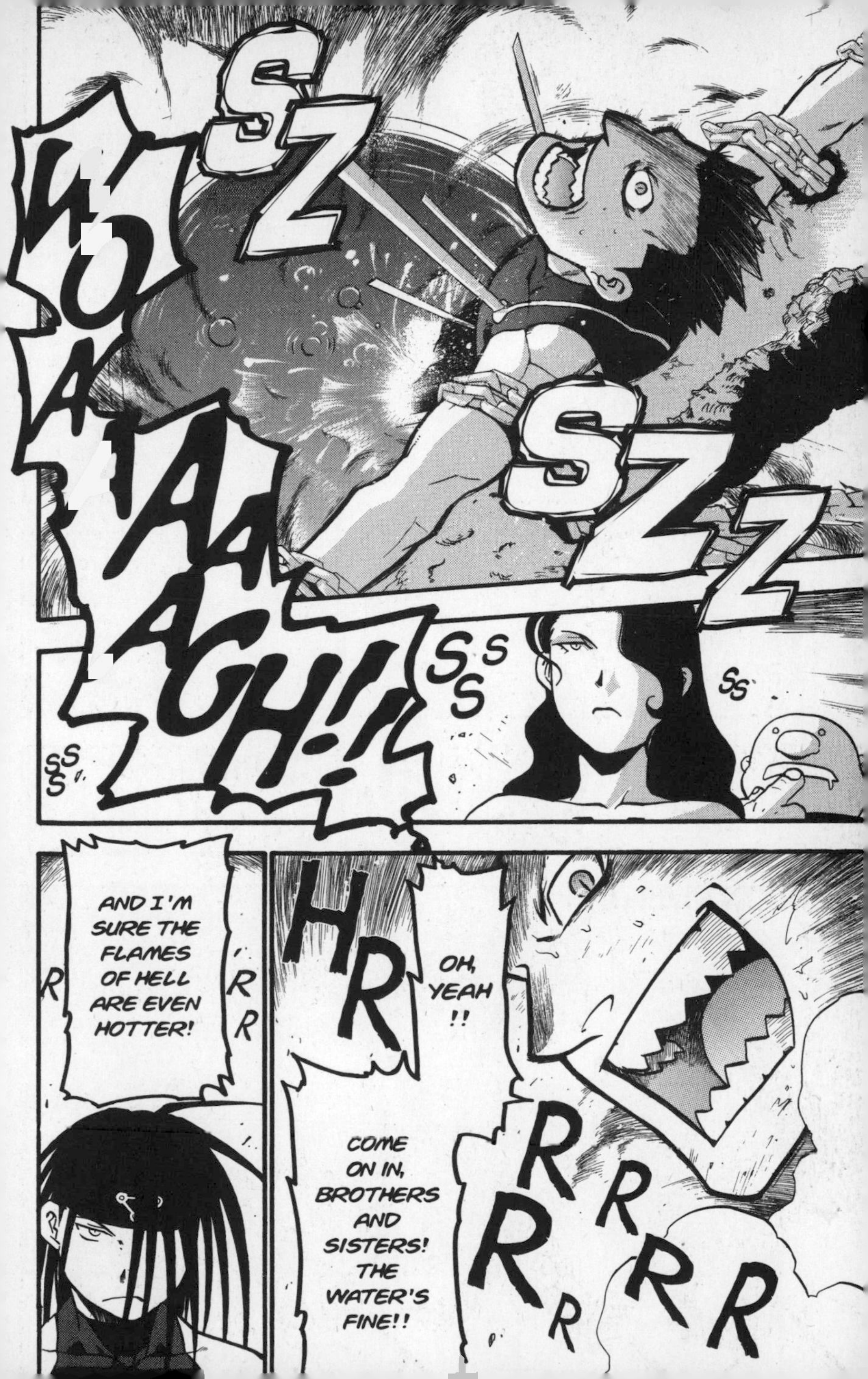
SZZ
SZZ
WOAAAAACH!!
SSS
SS
SSS
HRR
OH, YEAH!!
COME ON IN, BROTHERS AND SISTERS! THE WATER'S FINE!!
RRRRRRR
AND I'M SURE THE FLAMES OF HELL ARE EVEN HOTTER!
RRR

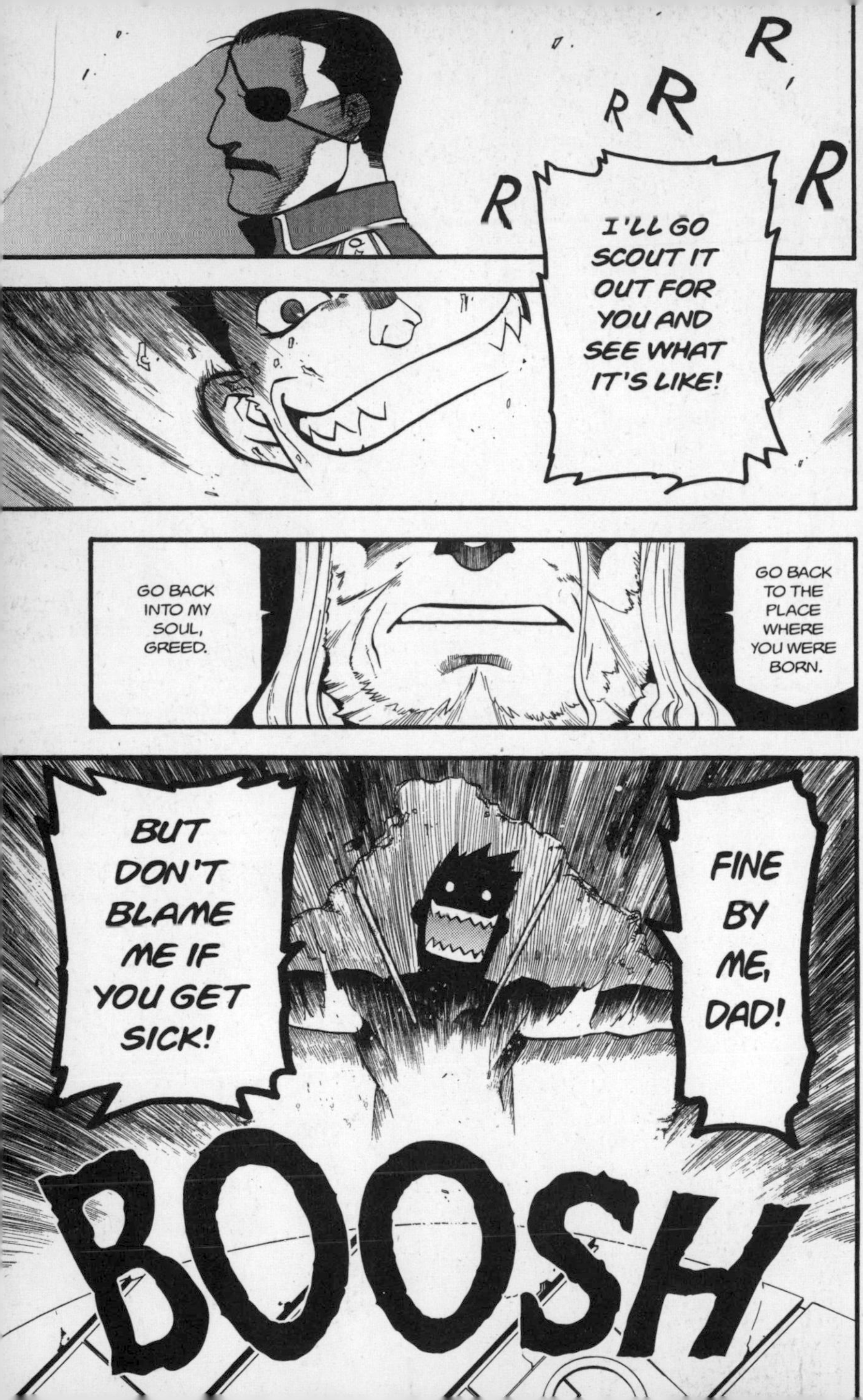
RRRRR
I'LL GO SCOUT IT OUT FOR YOU AND SEE WHAT IT'S LIKE!
GO BACK TO THE PLACE WHERE YOU WERE BORN.
GO BACK INTO MY SOUL, GREED.
FINE BY ME, DAD!
BUT DON'T BLAME ME IF YOU GET SICK!
BOOSH

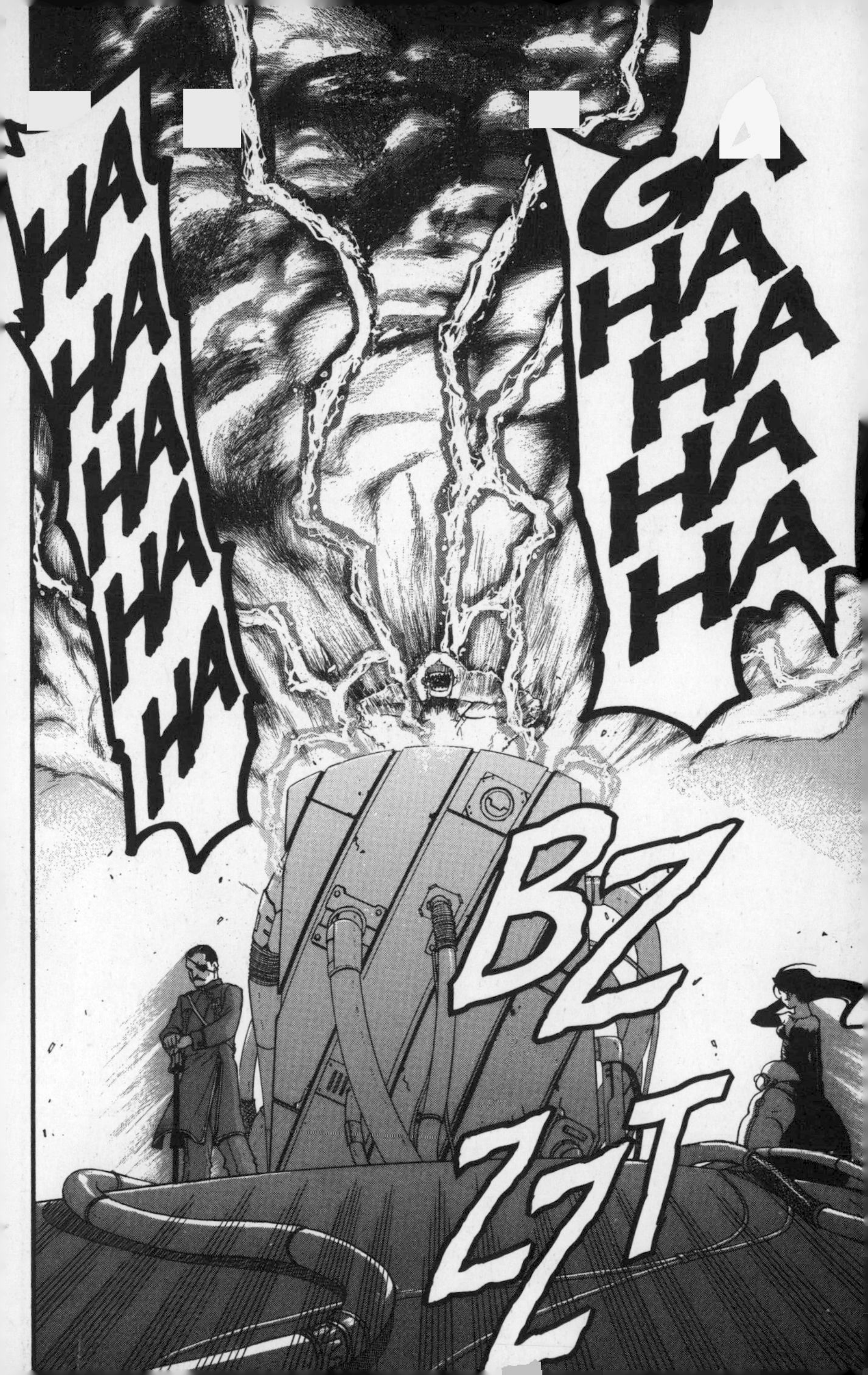
GAHAHAHAHAHA
HAHAHAHAHAHAHAHA
BZZZT

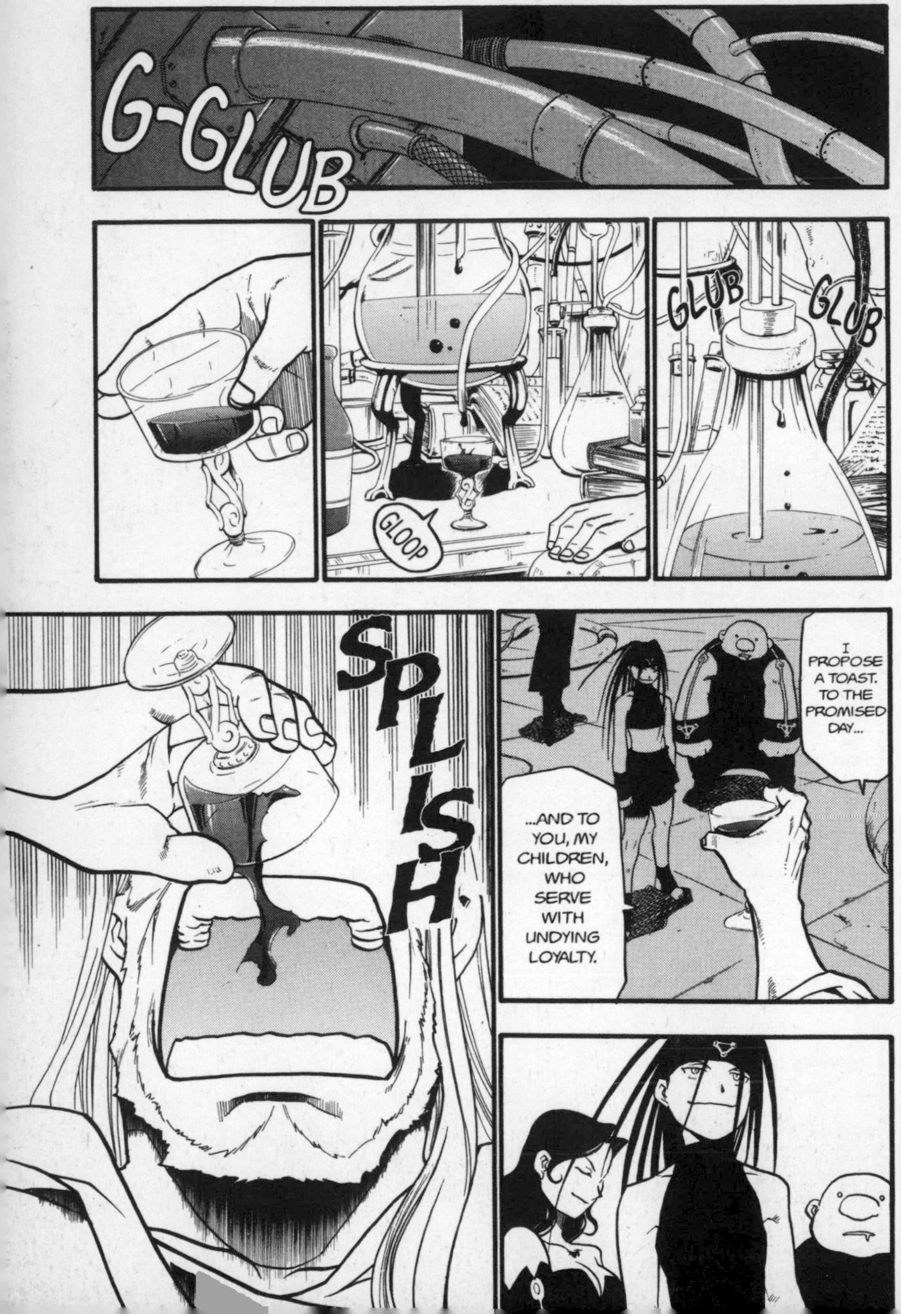
G-GLUB
GLUB GLUB
GLOOP
I PROPOSE A TOAST. TO THE PROMISED DAY...
...AND TO YOU, MY CHILDREN, WHO SERVE WITH UNDYING LOYALTY.
SPLISH

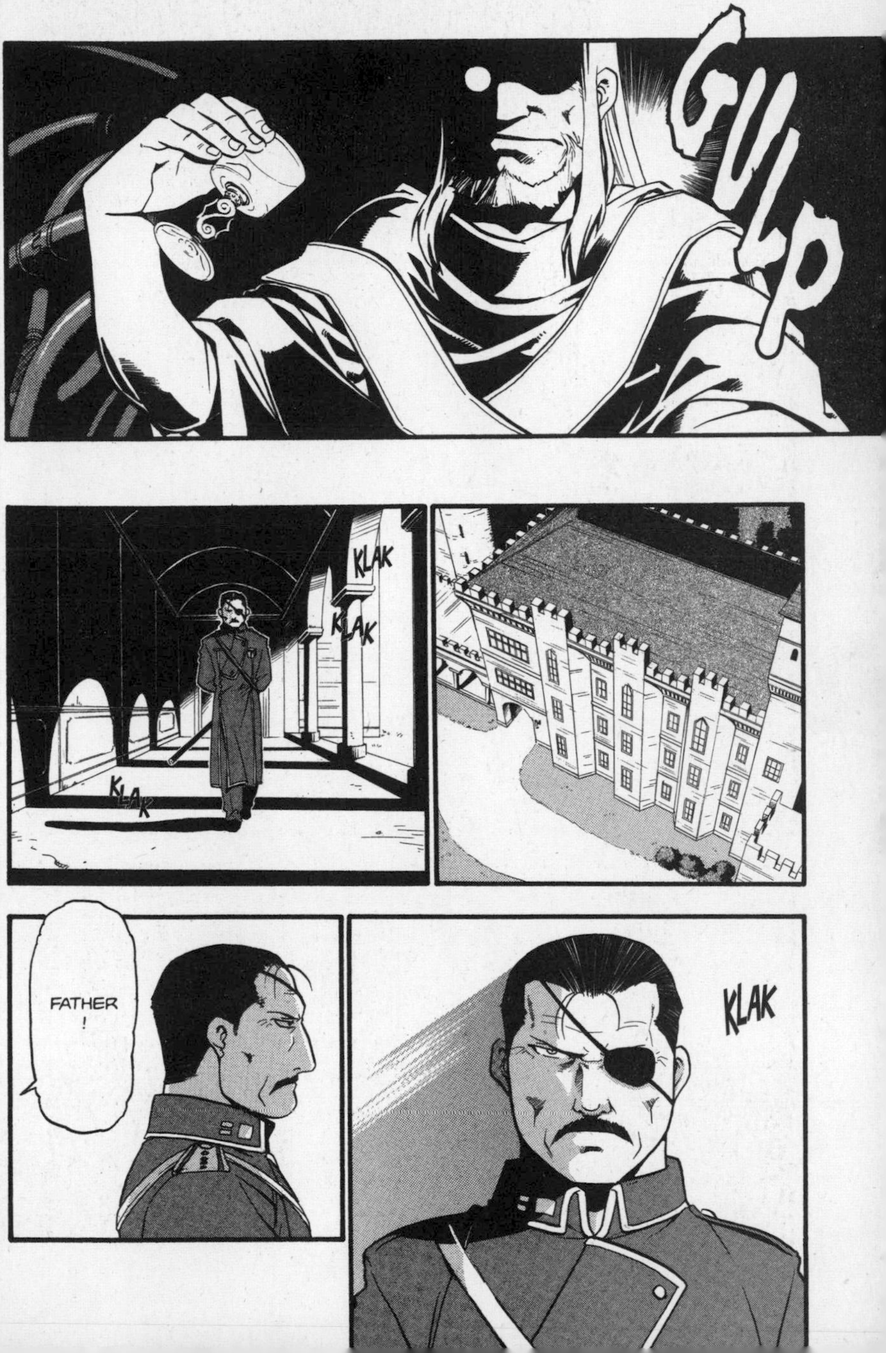
GULP
KLAK
KLAK
KLAK
KLAK
FATHER !

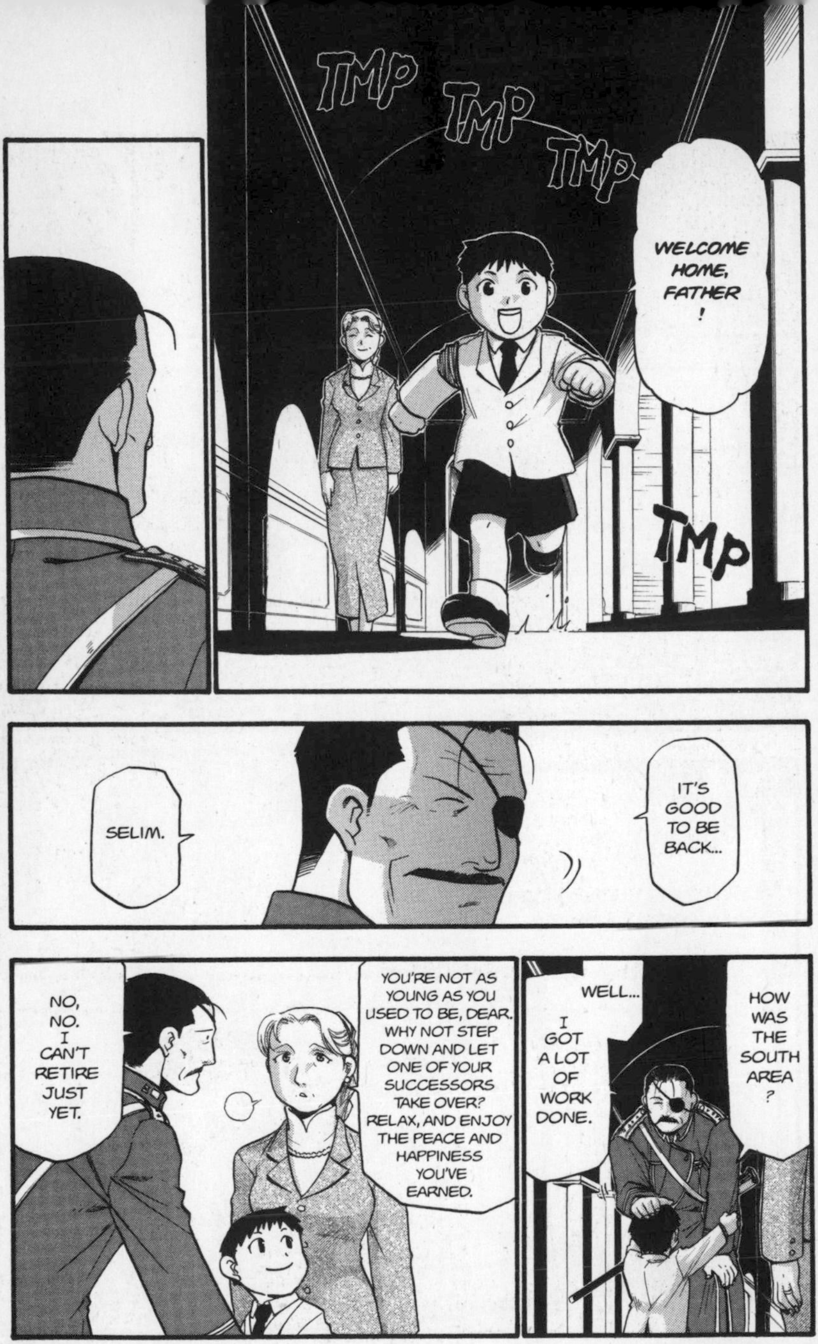
TMP
TMP
TMP
WELCOME HOME, FATHER!
TMP
IT'S GOOD TO BE BACK...
SELIM.
HOW WAS THE SOUTH AREA?
WELL...
I GOT A LOT OF WORK DONE.
YOU'RE NOT AS YOUNG AS YOU USED TO BE, DEAR. WHY NOT STEP DOWN AND LET ONE OF YOUR SUCCESSORS TAKE OVER? RELAX, AND ENJOY THE PEACE AND HAPPINESS YOU'VE EARNED.
NO, NO. I CAN'T RETIRE JUST YET.

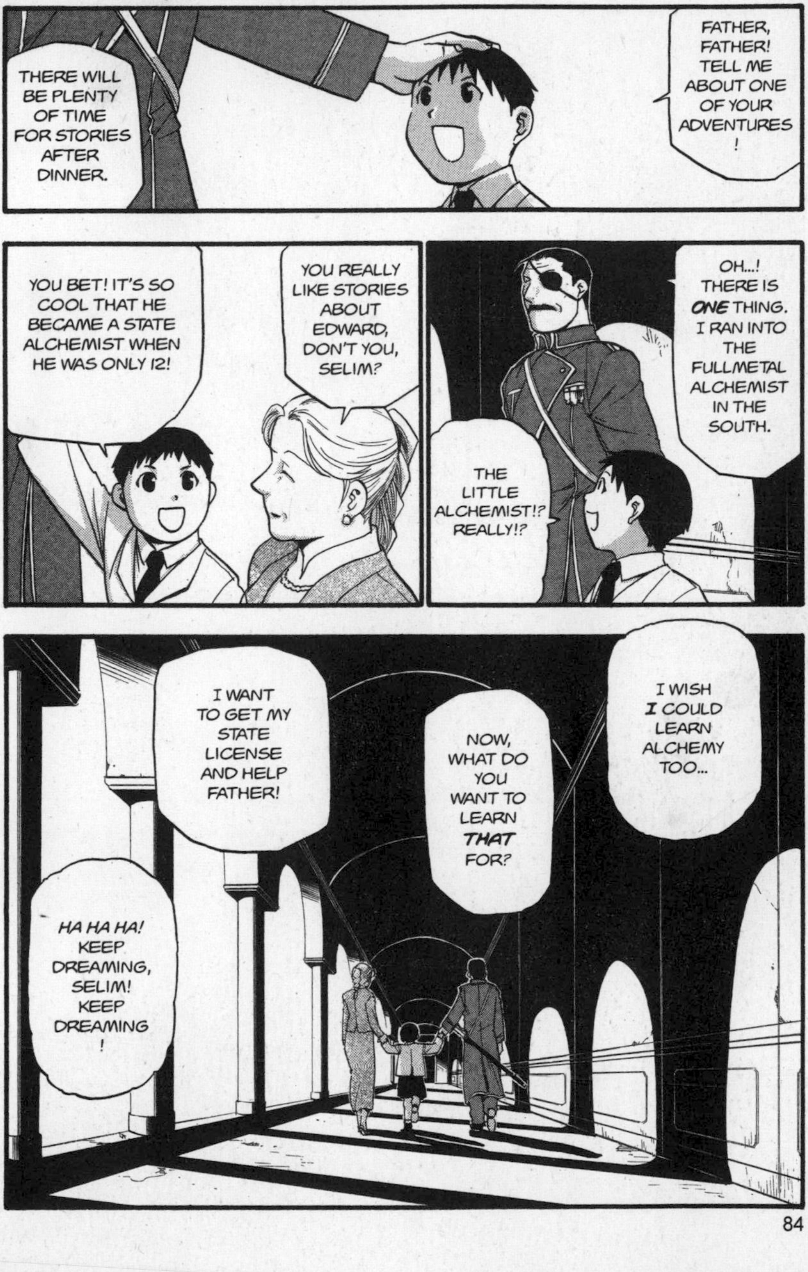
FATHER, FATHER! TELL ME ABOUT ONE OF YOUR ADVENTURES!
THERE WILL BE PLENTY OF TIME FOR STORIES AFTER DINNER.
OH...! THERE IS ONE THING. I RAN INTO THE FULLMETAL ALCHEMIST IN THE SOUTH.
THE LITTLE ALCHEMIST!? REALLY!?
YOU REALLY LIKE STORIES ABOUT EDWARD, DON'T YOU, SELIM?
YOU BET! IT'S SO COOL THAT HE BECAME A STATE ALCHEMIST WHEN HE WAS ONLY 12!
I WISH I COULD LEARN ALCHEMY TOO...
NOW, WHAT DO YOU WANT TO LEARN THAT FOR?
I WANT TO GET MY STATE LICENSE AND HELP FATHER!
HA HA HA! KEEP DREAMING, SELIM! KEEP DREAMING!

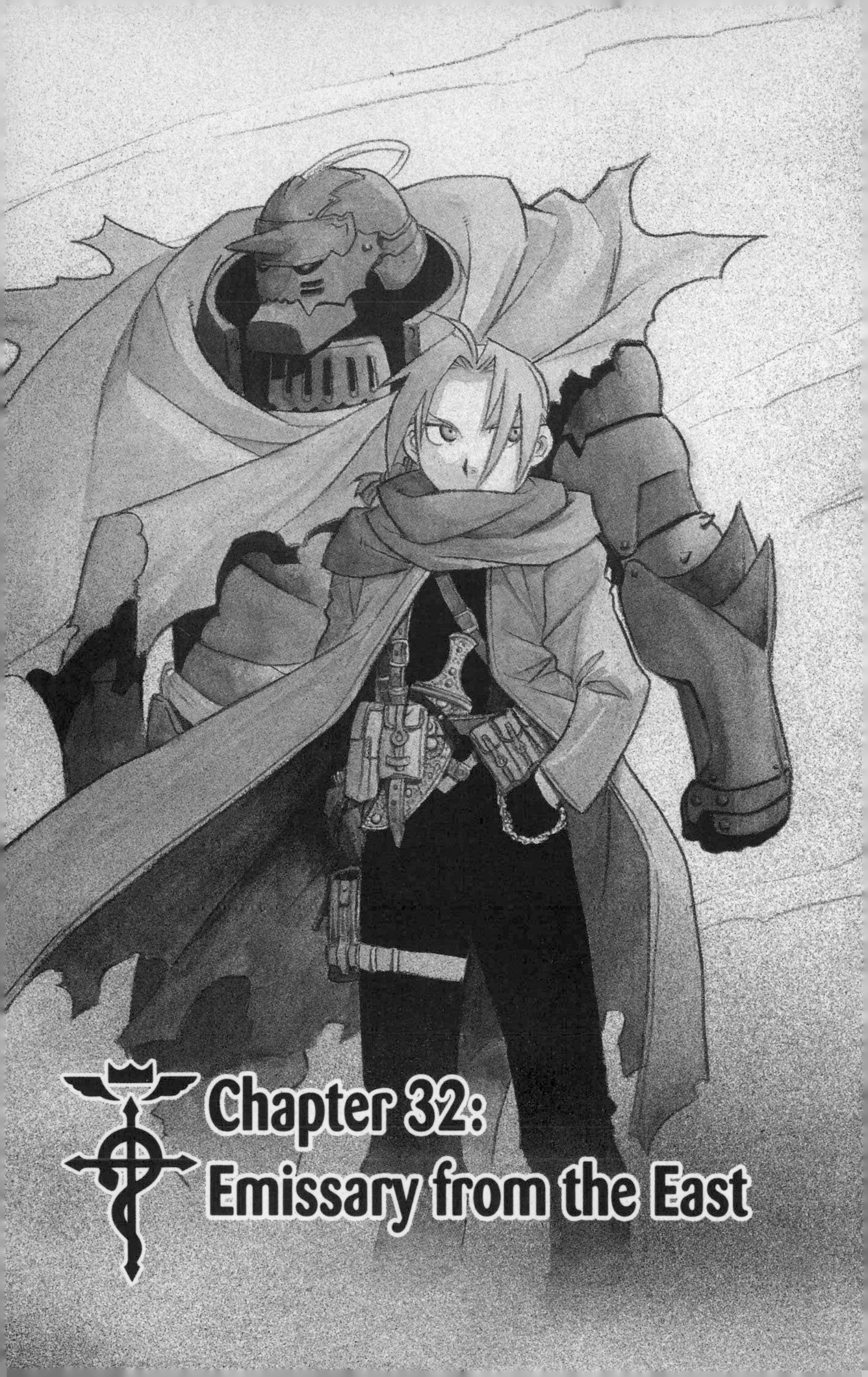

Chapter 32: Emissary from the East

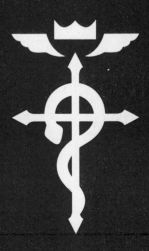

FULLMETAL
ALCHEMIST

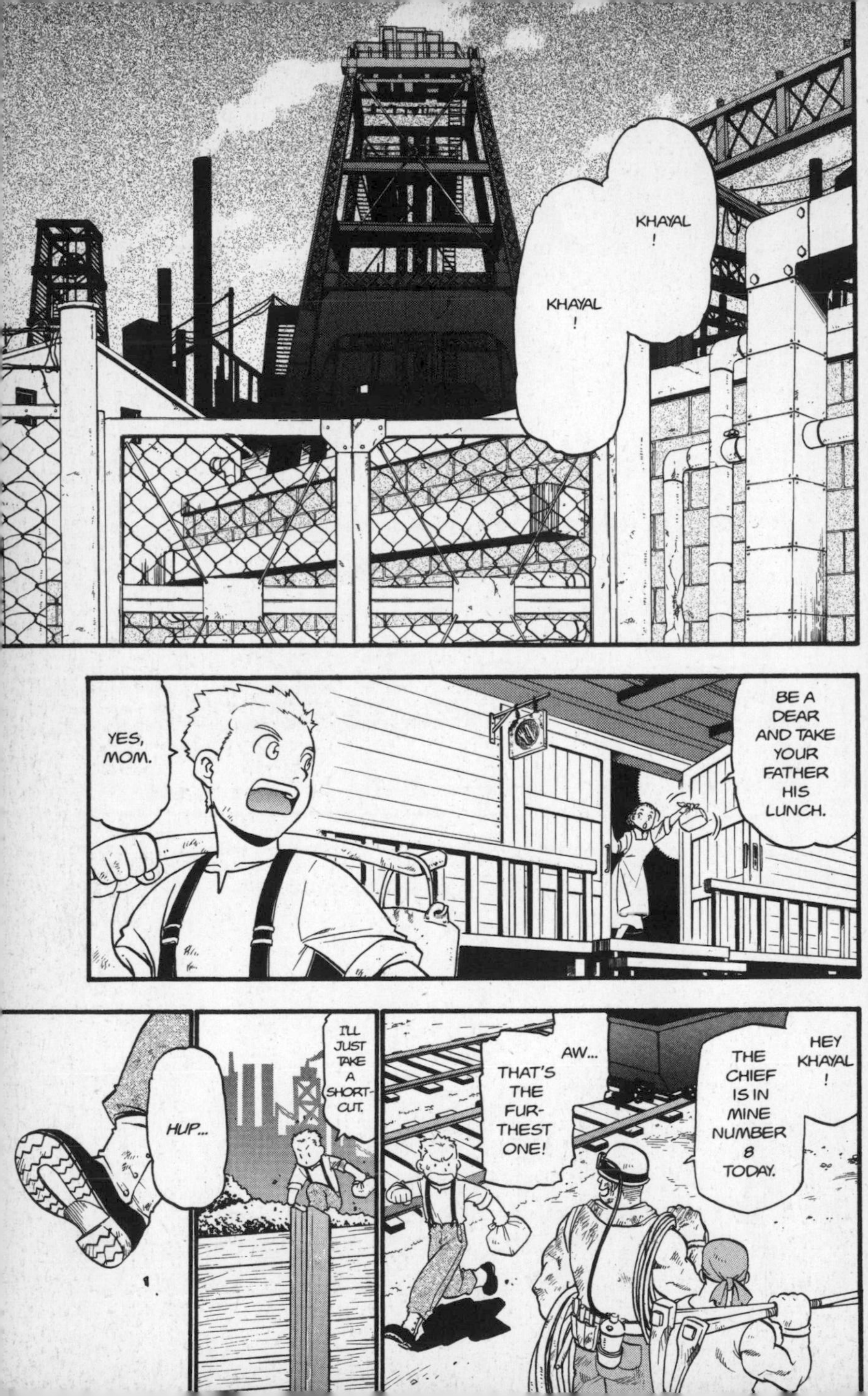
KHAYAL!
KHAYAL!
BE A DEAR AND TAKE YOUR FATHER HIS LUNCH.
YES, MOM.
HEY KHAYAL!
THE CHIEF IS IN MINE NUMBER 8 TODAY.
AW... THAT'S THE FUR-THEST ONE!
I'LL JUST TAKE A SHORT-CUT.
HUP...

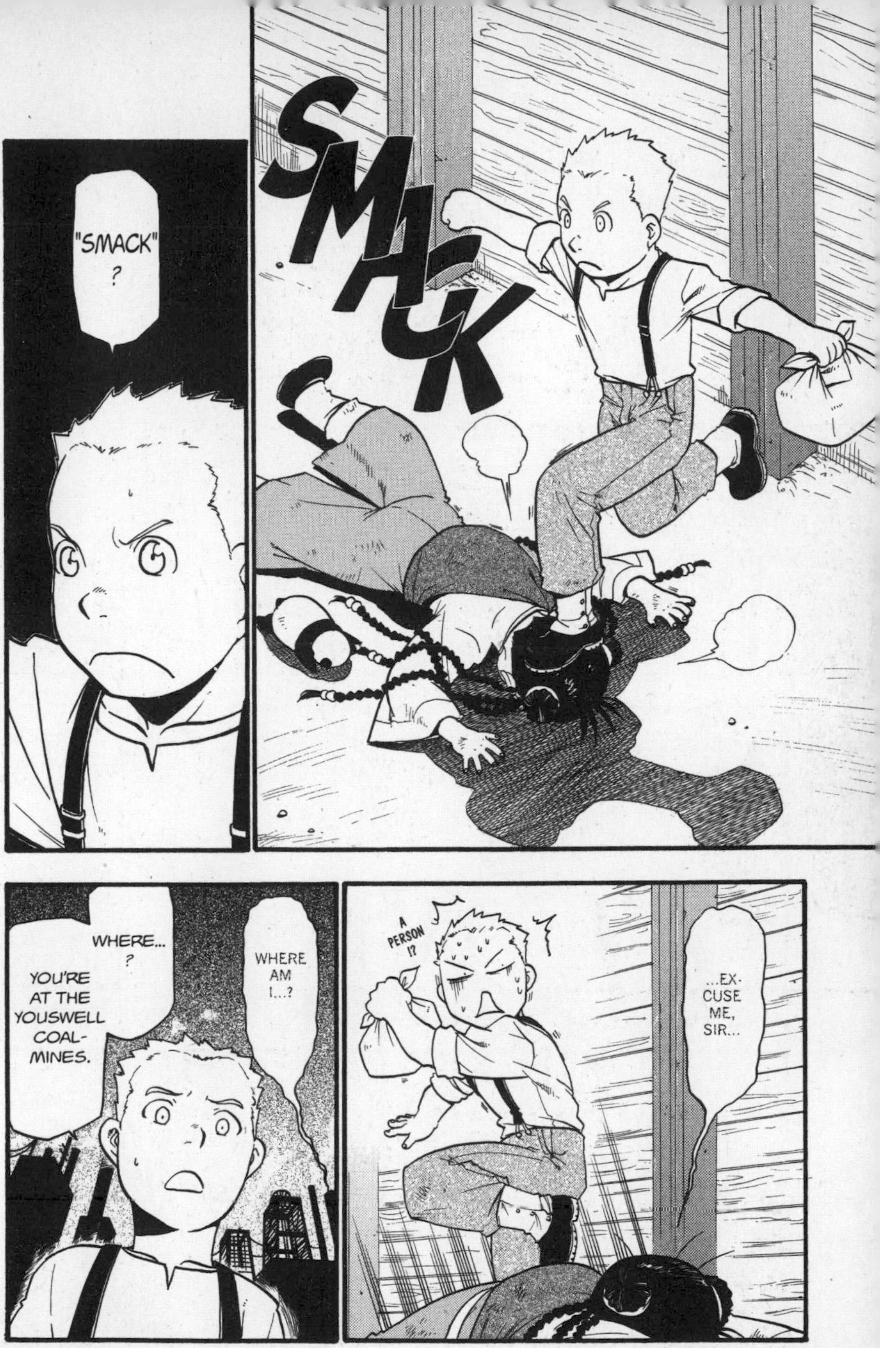
SMACK
"SMACK"?
...EXCUSE ME, SIR...
A PERSON!?
WHERE AM I...?
WHERE...?
YOU'RE AT THE YOUSWELL COAL-MINES.

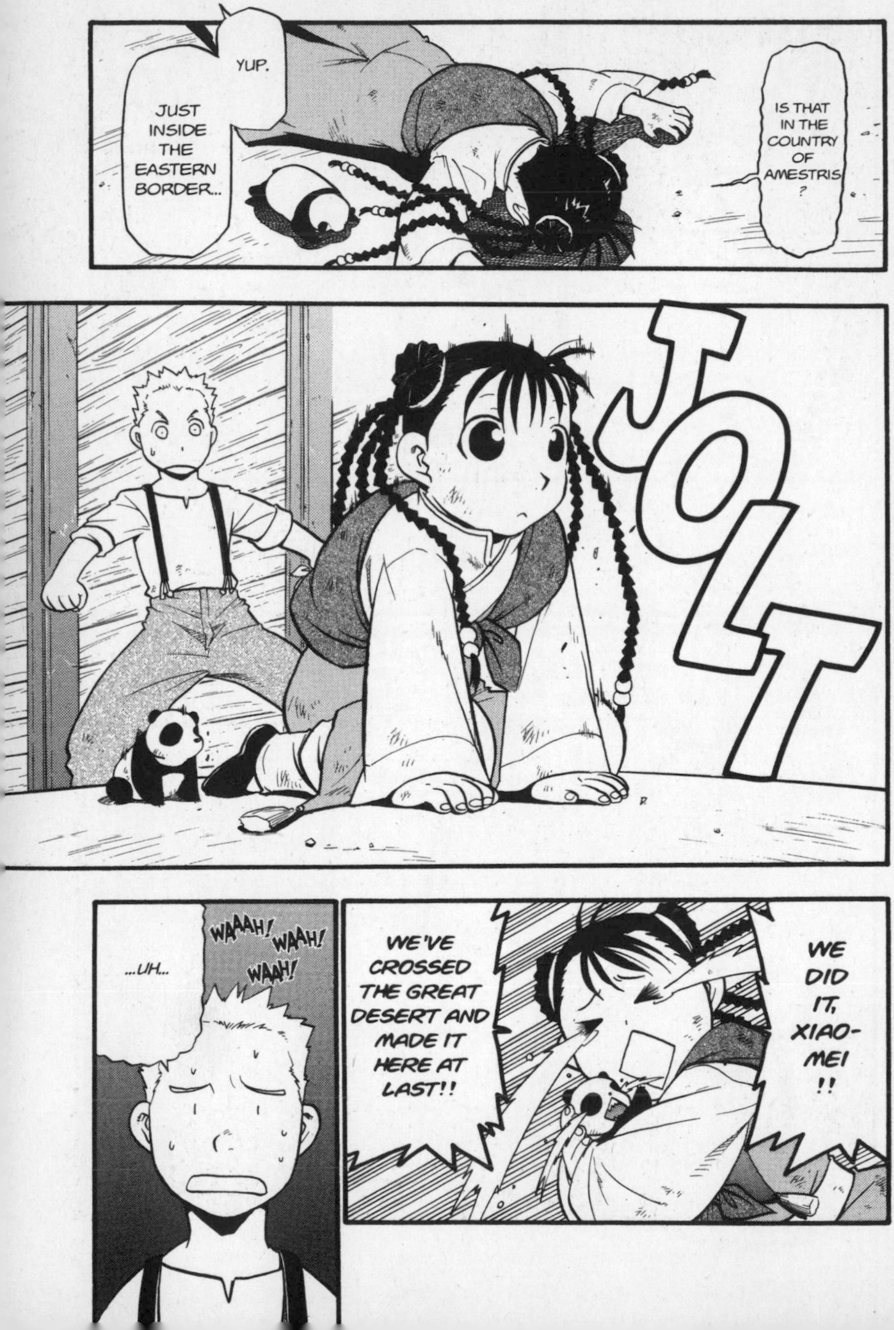
IS THAT IN THE COUNTRY OF AMESTRIS?
YUP.
JUST INSIDE THE EASTERN BORDER...
JOLT
WE DID IT, XIAO-MEI!!
WE'VE CROSSED THE GREAT DESERT AND MADE IT HERE AT LAST!!
WAAAH! WAAH! WAAH!
...UH...

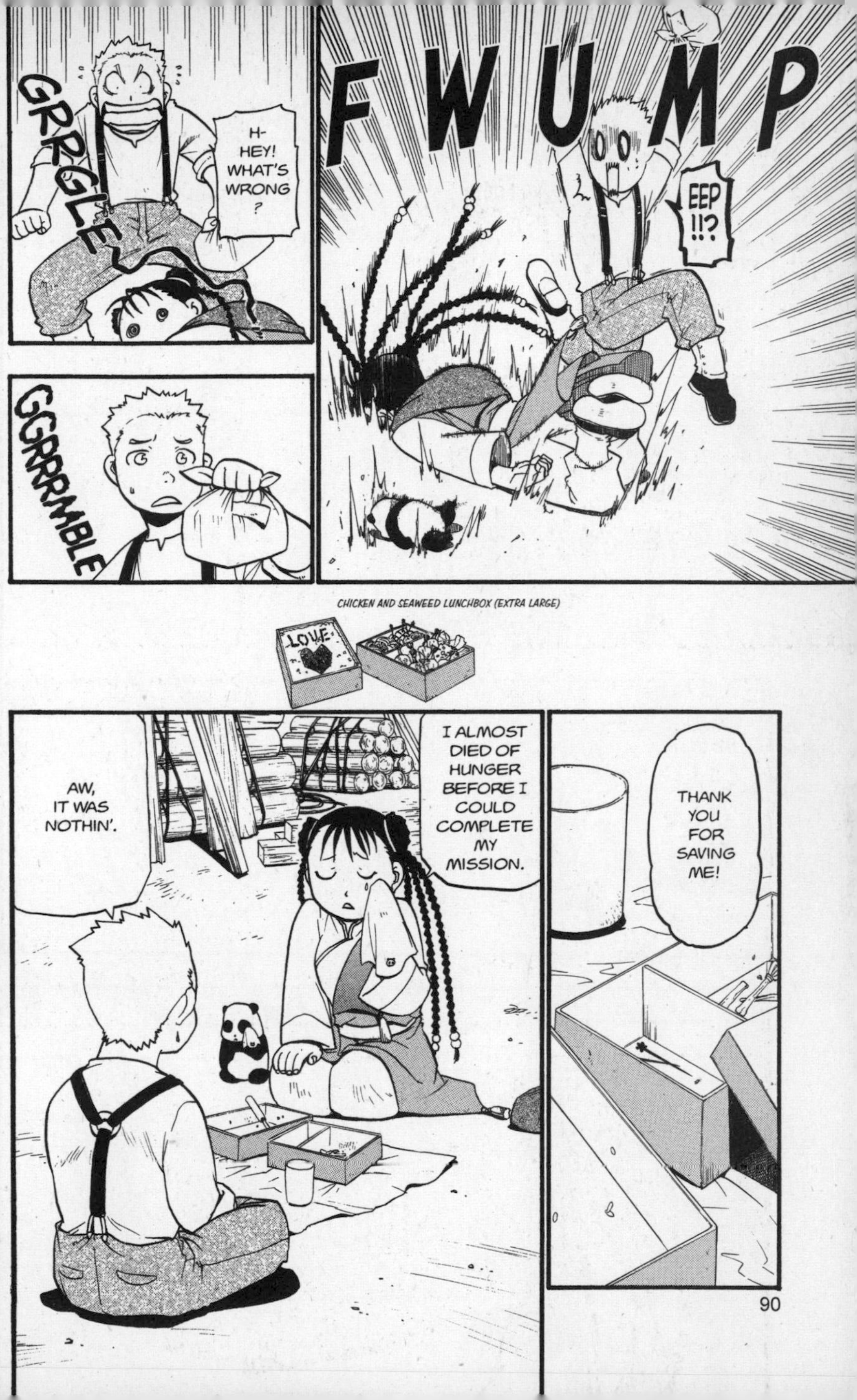
FWUMP
EEP!!?
GRRGLE
H-HEY! WHAT'S WRONG?
GGRRRMBLE
CHICKEN AND SEAWEED LUNCHBOX (EXTRA LARGE)
LOVE
THANK YOU FOR SAVING ME!
I ALMOST DIED OF HUNGER BEFORE I COULD COMPLETE MY MISSION.
AW, IT WAS NOTHIN'.

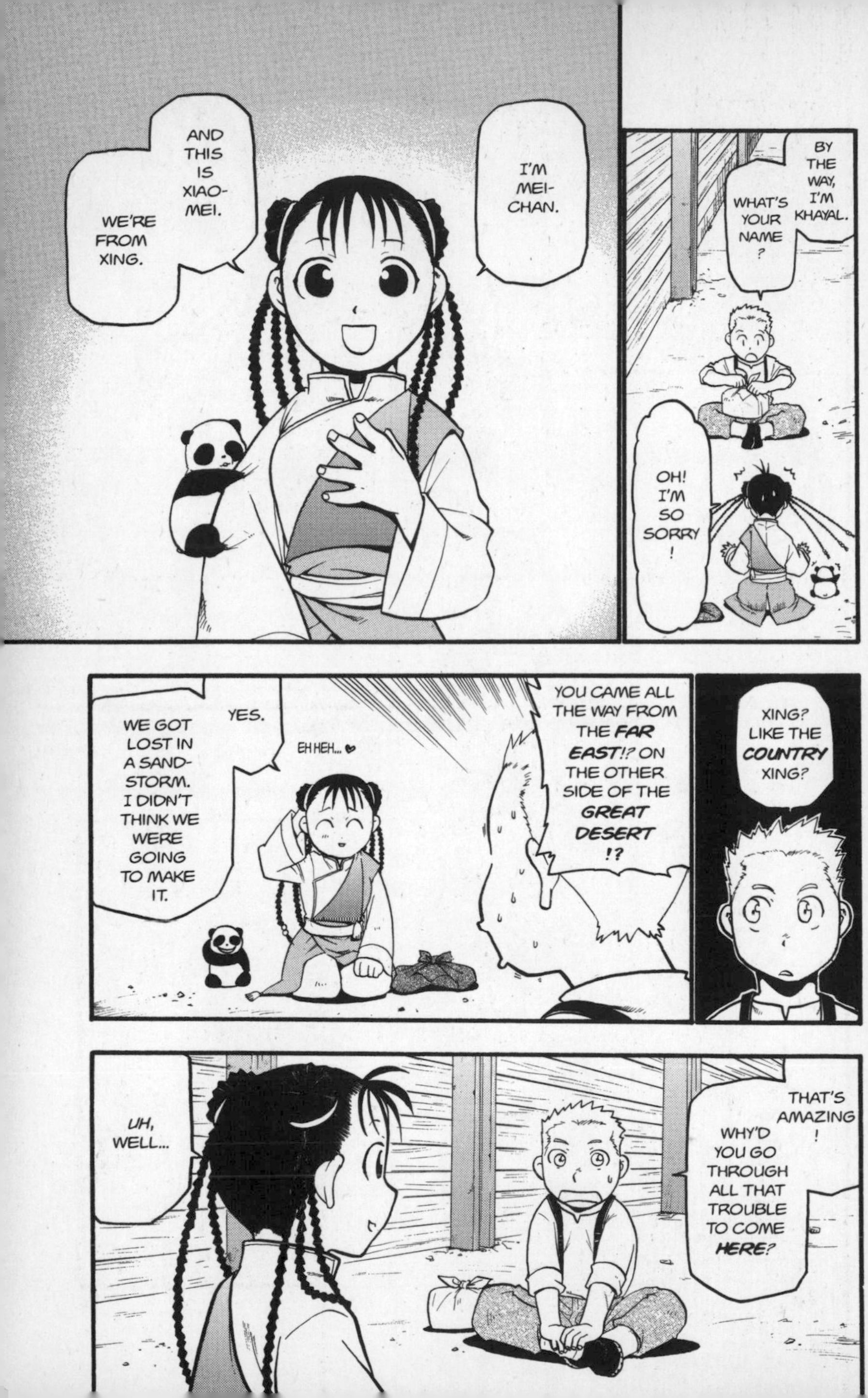
BY THE WAY, I'M KHAYAL.
WHAT'S YOUR NAME?
OH! I'M SO SORRY!
I'M MEI-CHAN.
AND THIS IS XIAO-MEI.
WE'RE FROM XING.
XING? LIKE THE COUNTRY XING?
YOU CAME ALL THE WAY FROM THE FAR EAST!? ON THE OTHER SIDE OF THE GREAT DESERT!?
YES.
EH HEH...
WE GOT LOST IN A SANDSTORM. I DIDN'T THINK WE WERE GOING TO MAKE IT.
THAT'S AMAZING!
WHY'D YOU GO THROUGH ALL THAT TROUBLE TO COME HERE?
UH, WELL...

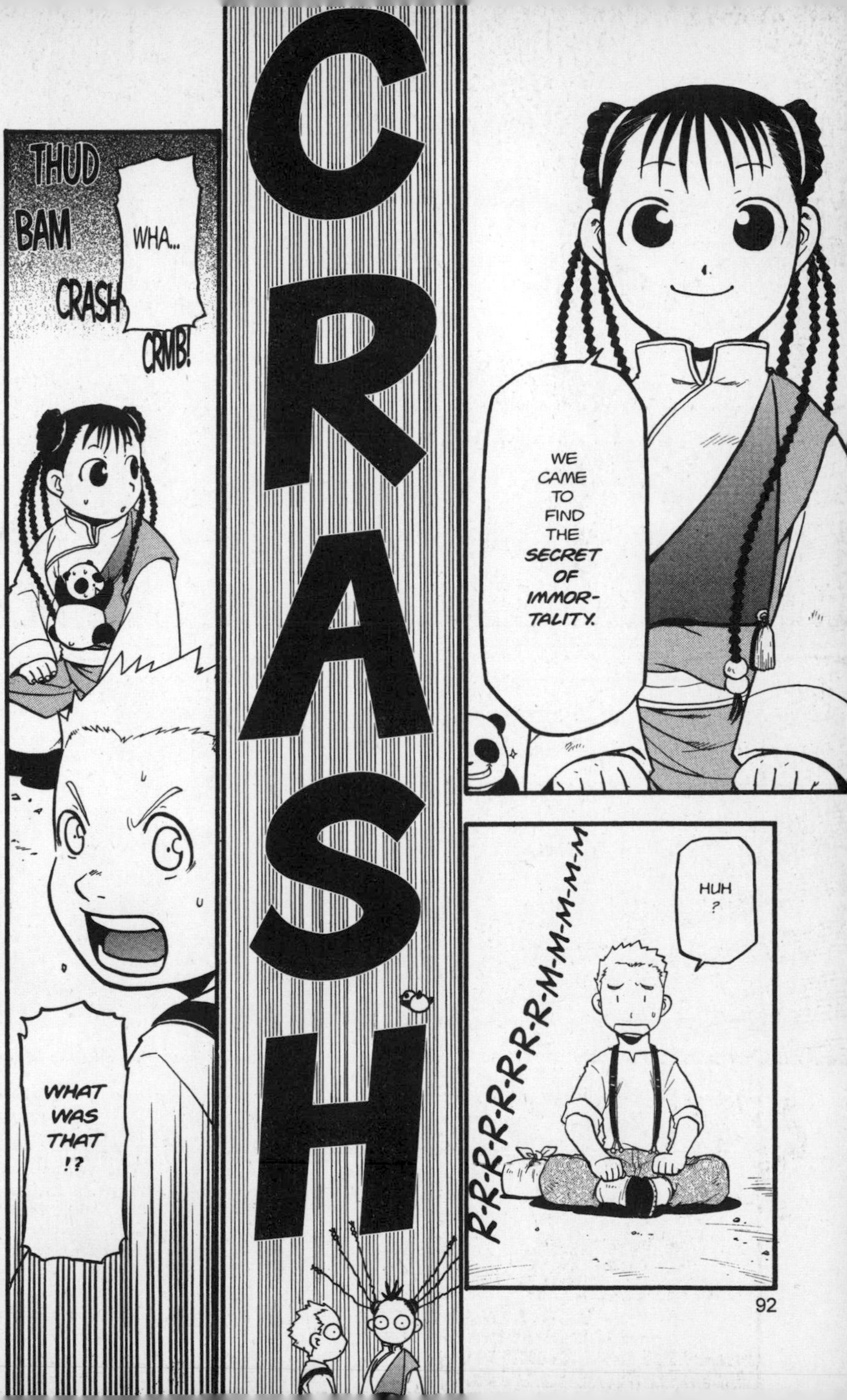
WE CAME TO FIND THE SECRET OF IMMORTALITY.
HUH ?
R-R-R-R-R-R-R-M-M-M-M-M-M
CRASH
THUD
BAM
CRASH
WHA...
CRMB!
WHAT WAS THAT !?

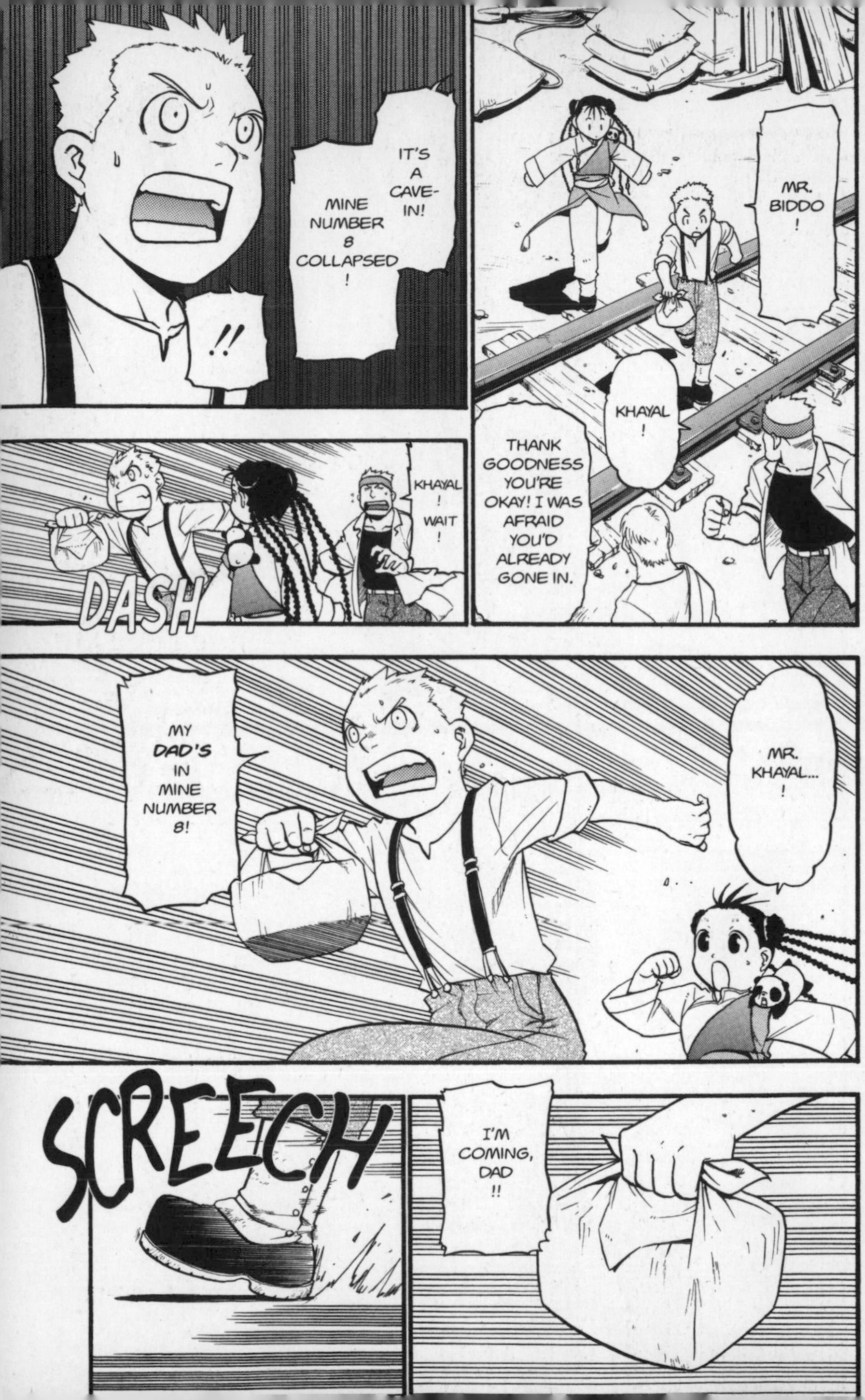
MR. BIDDO!
KHAYAL!
THANK GOODNESS YOU'RE OKAY! I WAS AFRAID YOU'D ALREADY GONE IN.
IT'S A CAVE-IN!
MINE NUMBER 8 COLLAPSED!
!!
KHAYAL! WAIT!
DASH
MR. KHAYAL...!
MY DAD'S IN MINE NUMBER 8!
I'M COMING, DAD!!
SCREECH

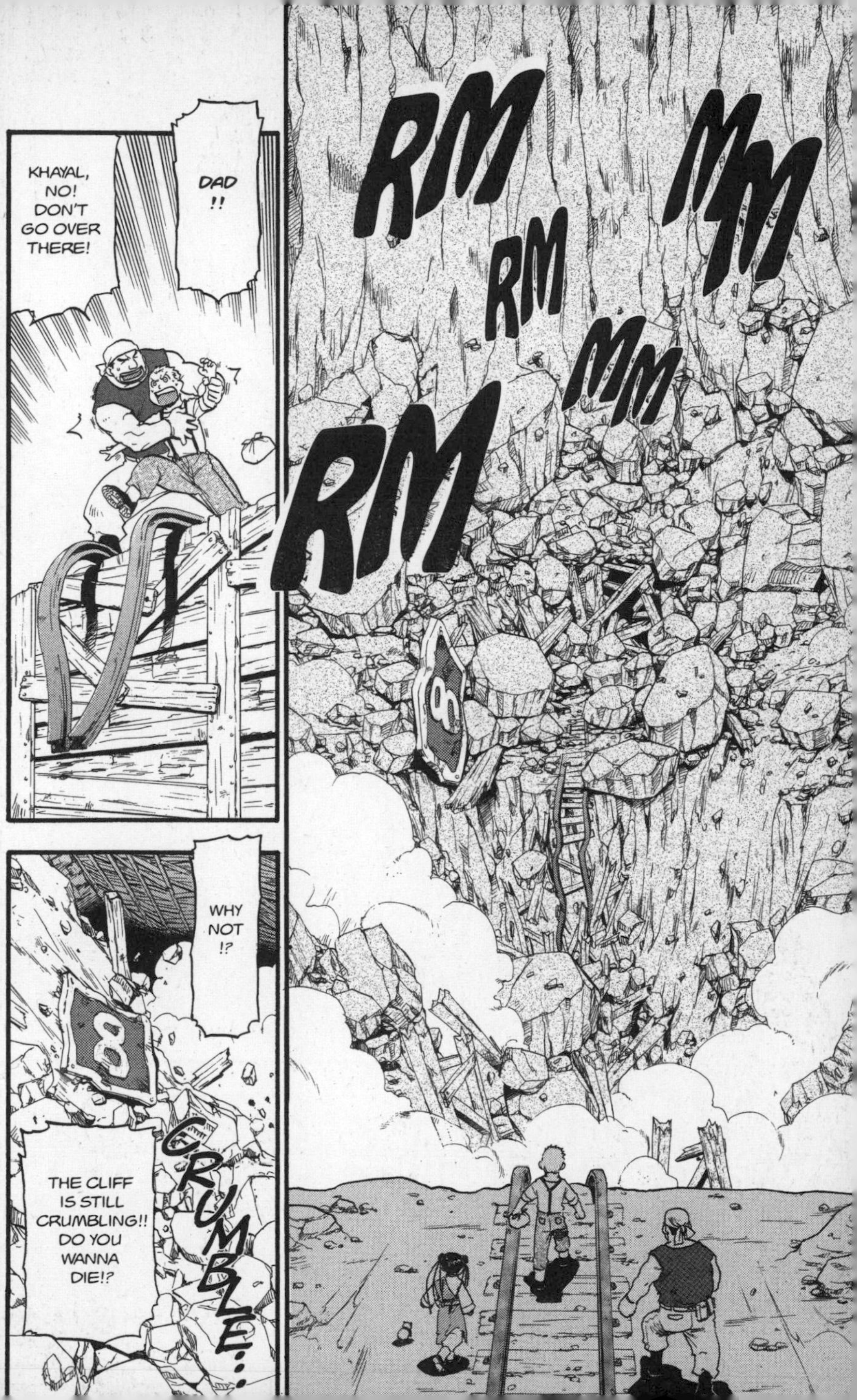
RM
RM
RM
MM
MM
DAD!!
KHAYAL, NO! DON'T GO OVER THERE!
WHY NOT!?
THE CLIFF IS STILL CRUMBLING!! DO YOU WANNA DIE!?
CRUMBLE...

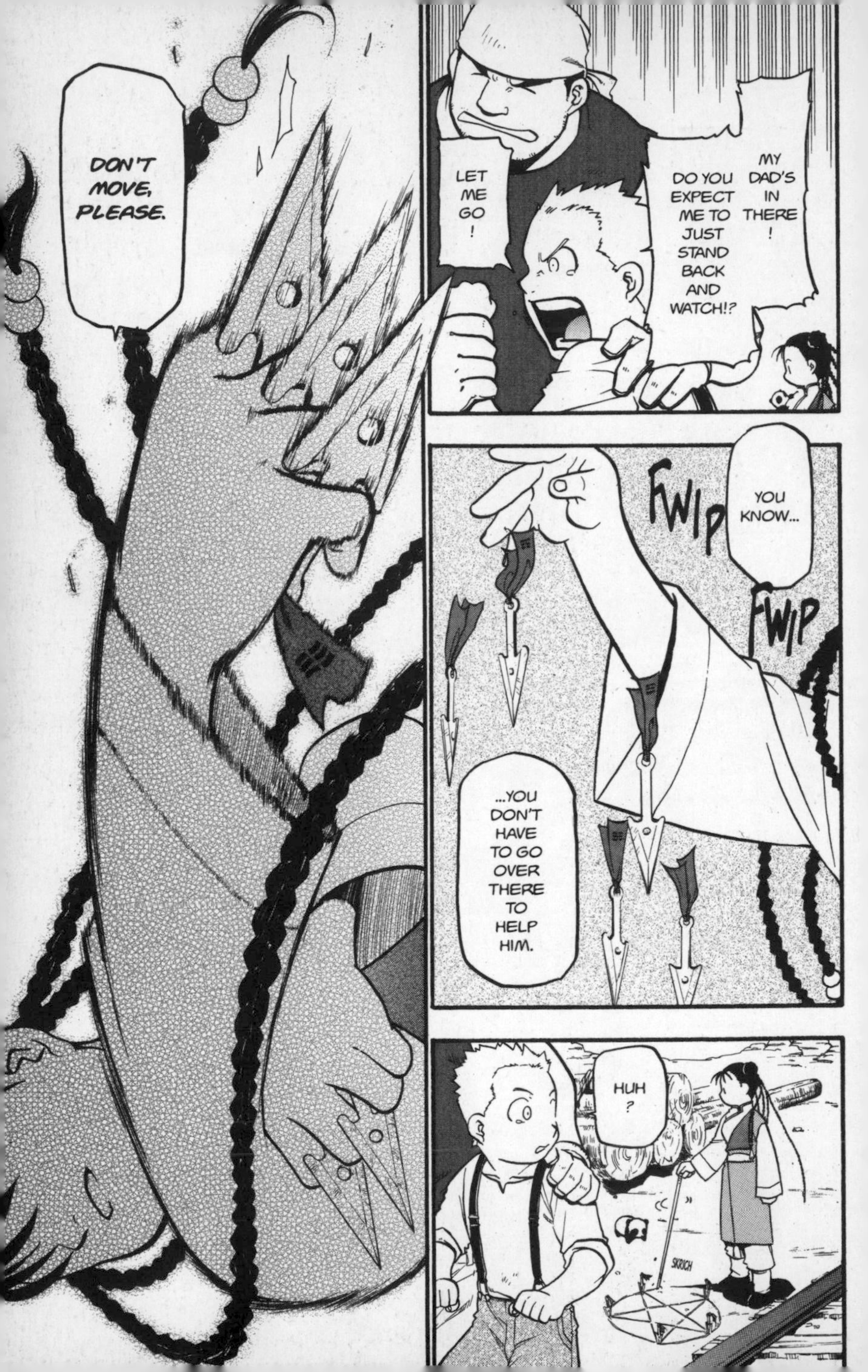
MY DAD'S IN THERE!
DO YOU EXPECT ME TO JUST STAND BACK AND WATCH!?
LET ME GO!
FWIP
YOU KNOW...
FWIP
...YOU DON'T HAVE TO GO OVER THERE TO HELP HIM.
HUH?
SKRUCH
DON'T MOVE, PLEASE.

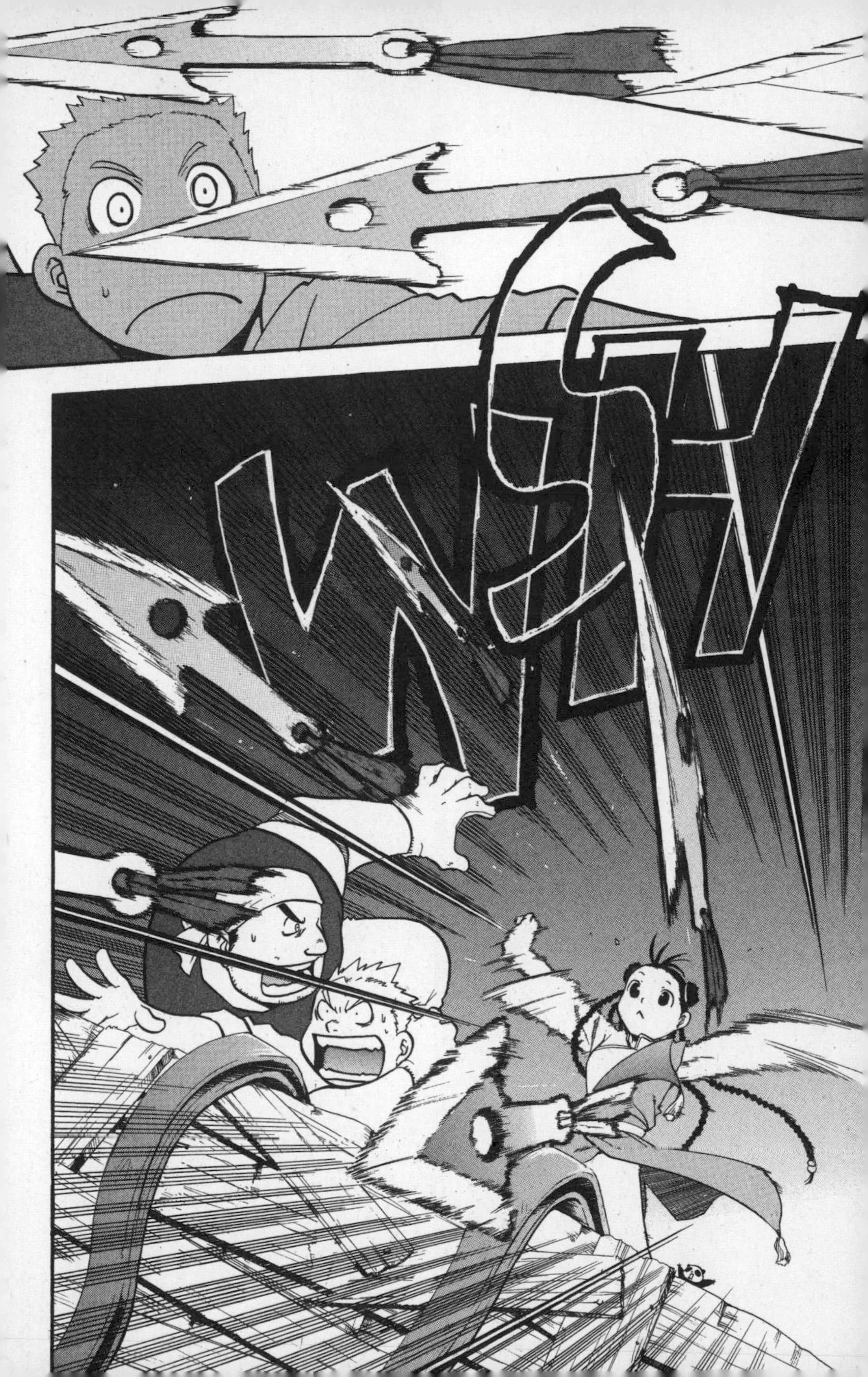
WSHH

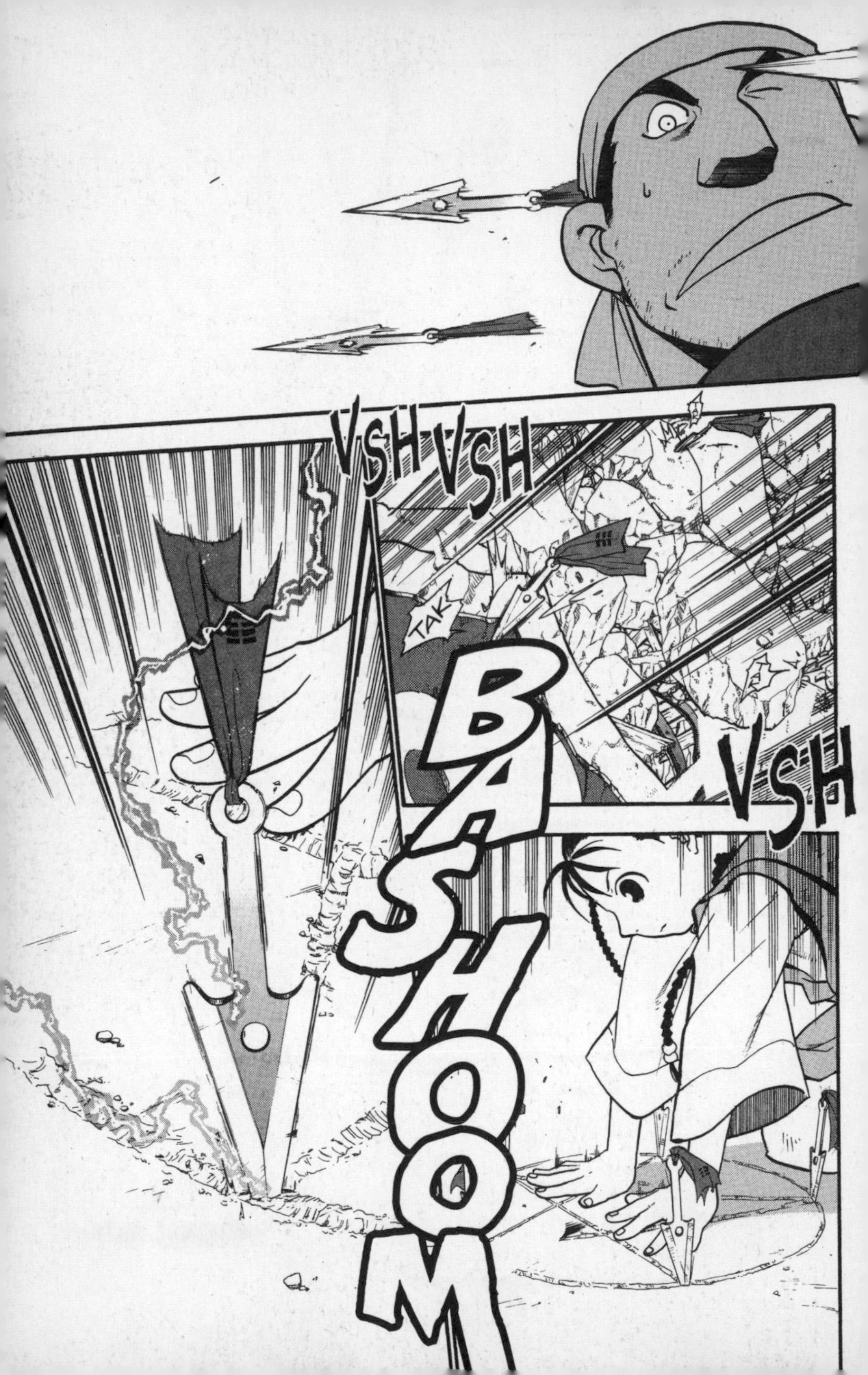
VSH VSH
TAK
VSH
BASHOOM

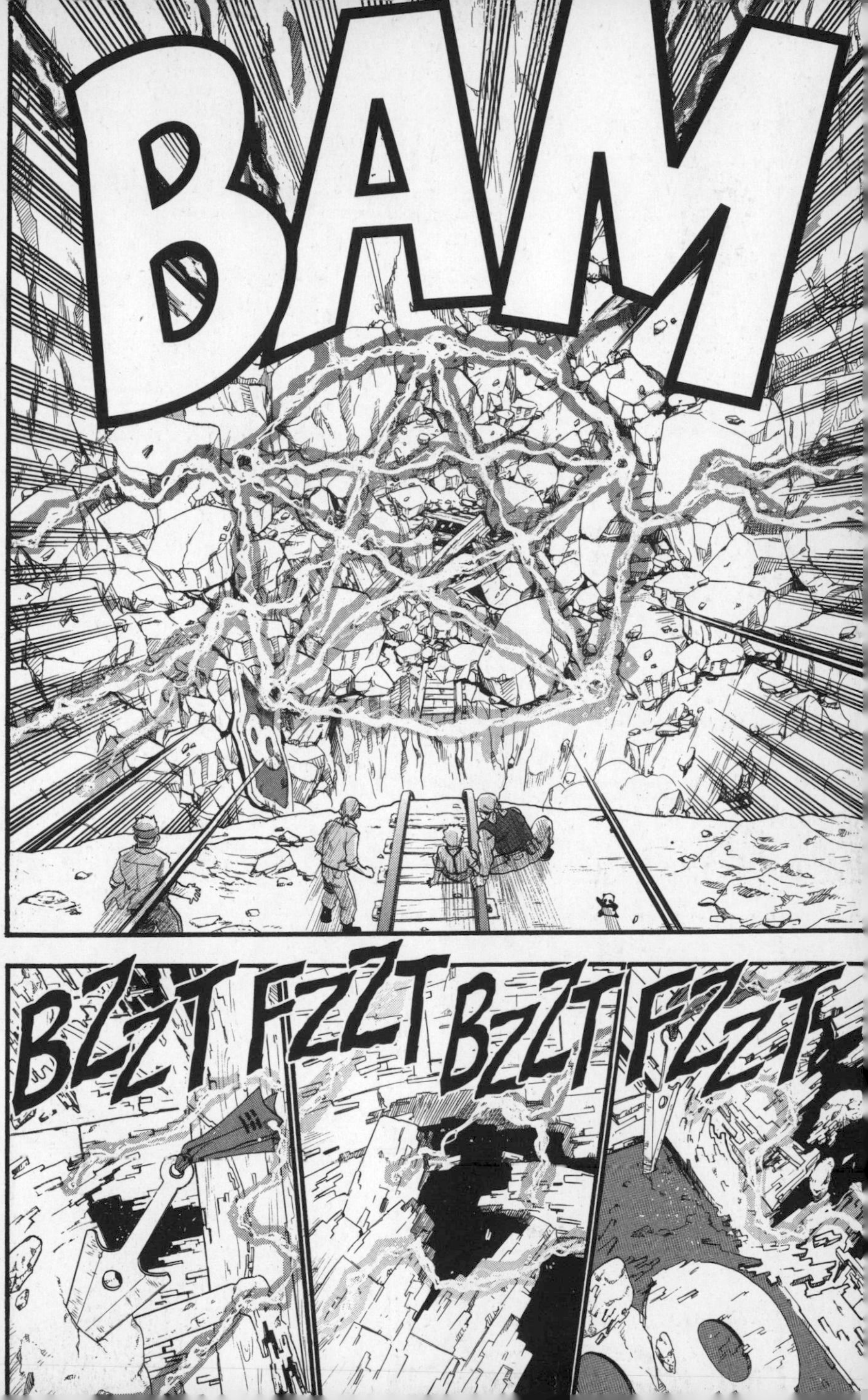
BAM
BZZT FZZT BZZT FZZT

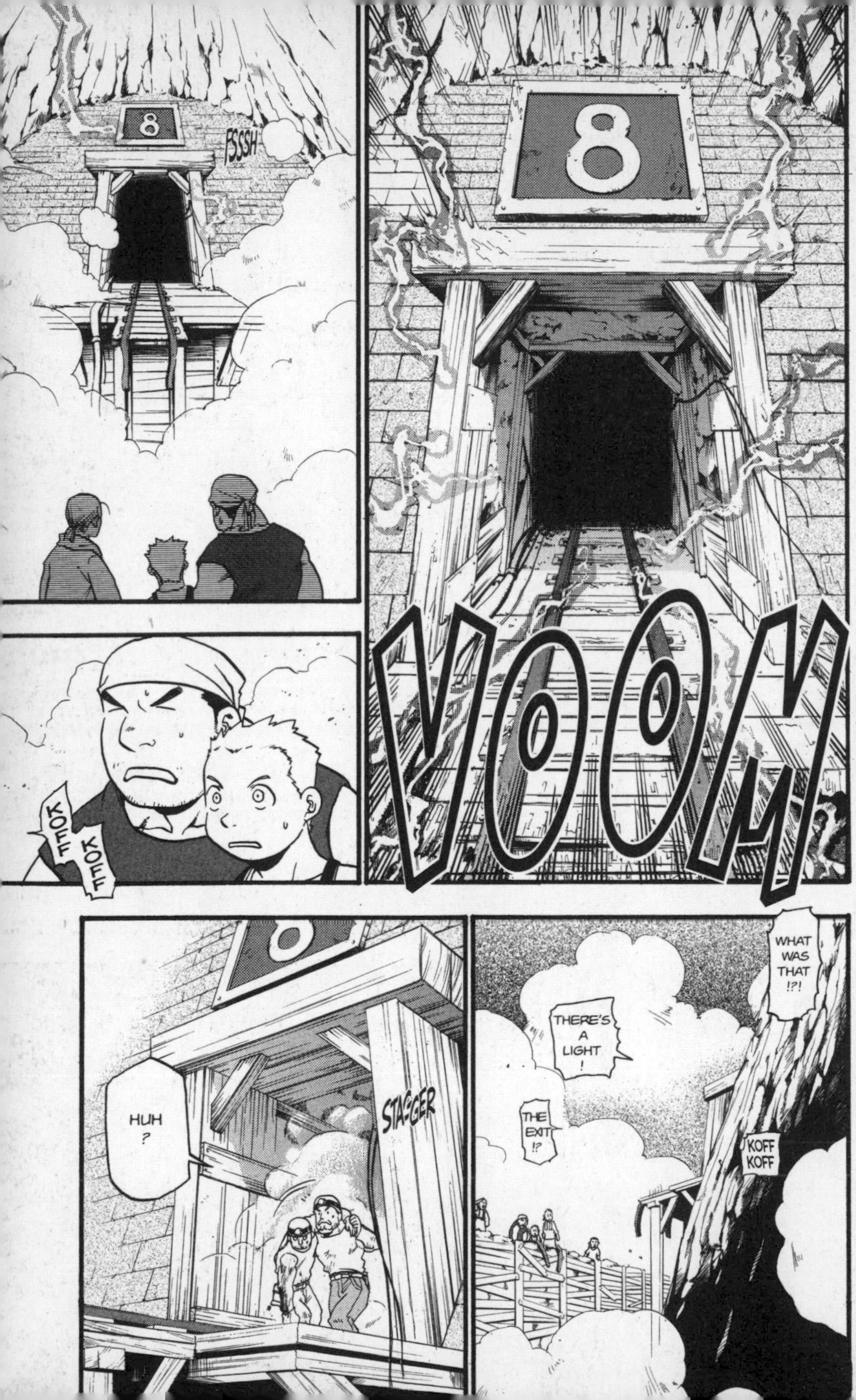
VOOM
FSSSH
KOFF KOFF
WHAT WAS THAT !?!
THERE'S A LIGHT !
THE EXIT !?
KOFF KOFF
STAGGER
HUH ?

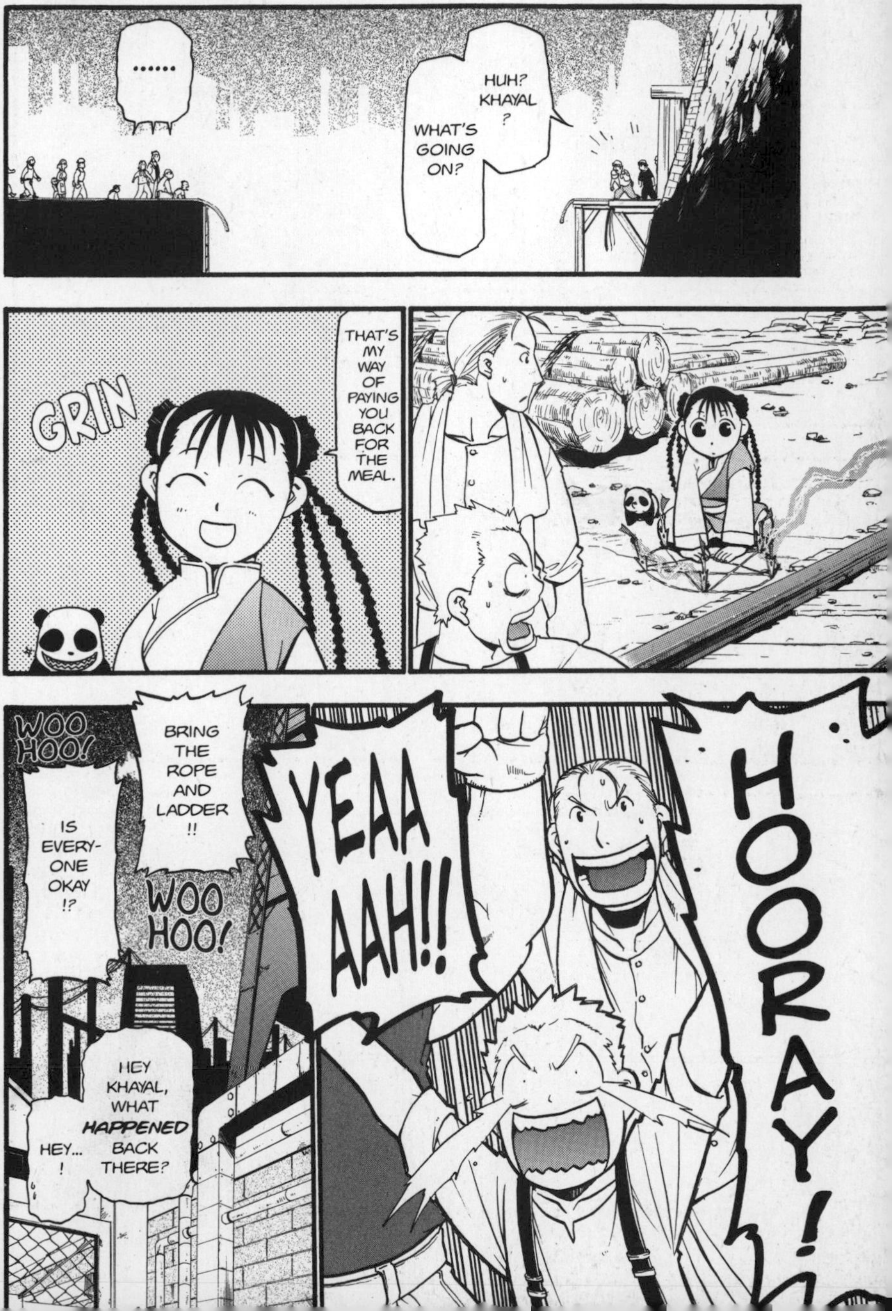
HUH? KHAYAL? WHAT'S GOING ON?
......
THAT'S MY WAY OF PAYING YOU BACK FOR THE MEAL.
GRIN
HOORAY!!
YEAAAAH!!
BRING THE ROPE AND LADDER!!
WOO HOO!
IS EVERYONE OKAY!?
WOO HOO!
HEY KHAYAL, WHAT HAPPENED BACK THERE?
HEY...!

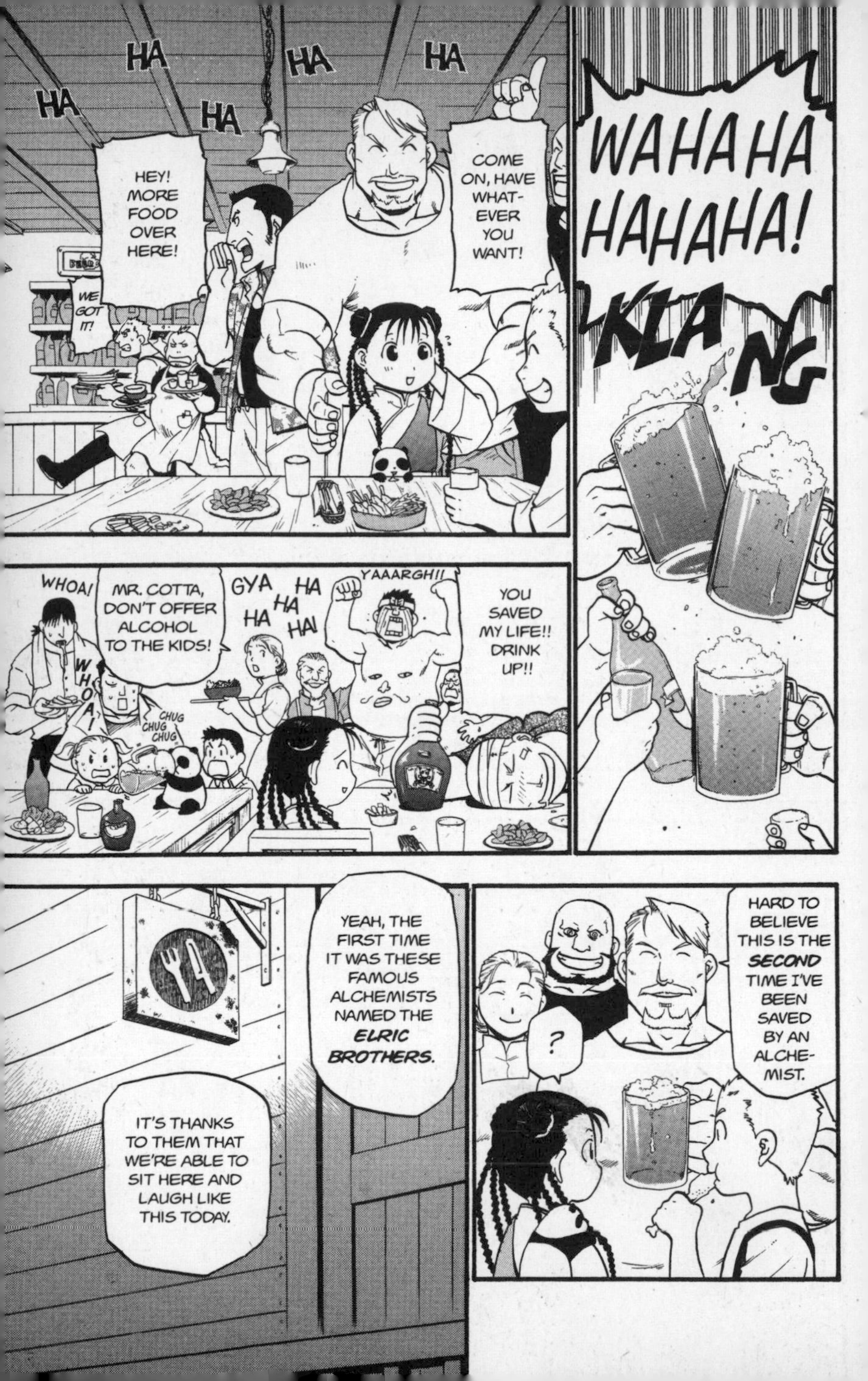
WAHAHA HAHAHAHA!
KLANG
HA HA HA HA HA
COME ON, HAVE WHATEVER YOU WANT!
HEY! MORE FOOD OVER HERE!
WE GOT IT!
YOU SAVED MY LIFE!! DRINK UP!!
YAAARGH!!
GYA HA HA HA HA!
MR. COTTA, DON'T OFFER ALCOHOL TO THE KIDS!
WHOA!
WHOA!
CHUG CHUG CHUG
HARD TO BELIEVE THIS IS THE SECOND TIME I'VE BEEN SAVED BY AN ALCHEMIST.
?
YEAH, THE FIRST TIME IT WAS THESE FAMOUS ALCHEMISTS NAMED THE ELRIC BROTHERS.
IT'S THANKS TO THEM THAT WE'RE ABLE TO SIT HERE AND LAUGH LIKE THIS TODAY.

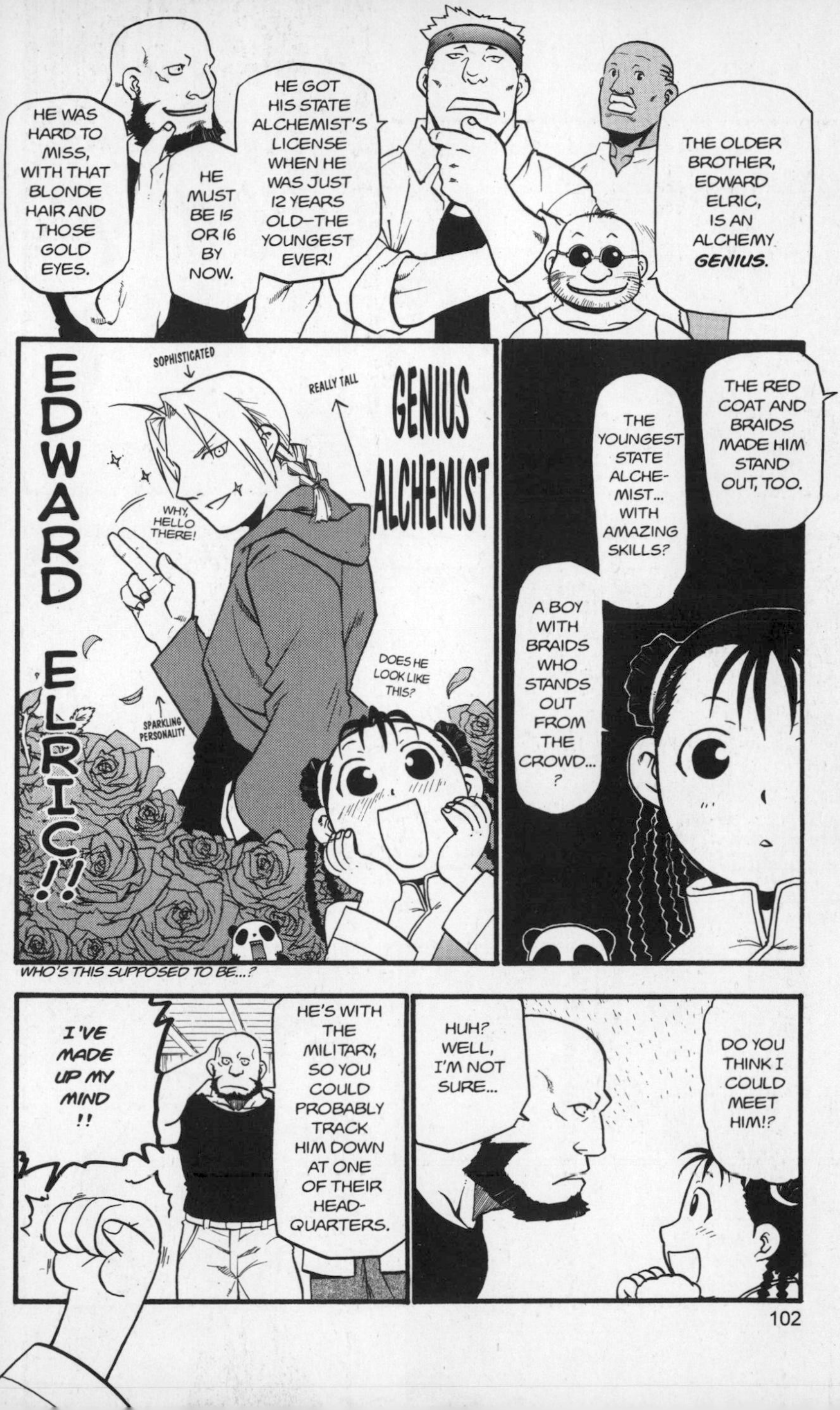
THE OLDER BROTHER, EDWARD ELRIC, IS AN ALCHEMY **GENIUS.**
HE GOT HIS STATE ALCHEMIST'S LICENSE WHEN HE WAS JUST 12 YEARS OLD—THE YOUNGEST EVER!
HE MUST BE 15 OR 16 BY NOW.
HE WAS HARD TO MISS, WITH THAT BLONDE HAIR AND THOSE GOLD EYES.
THE RED COAT AND BRAIDS MADE HIM STAND OUT, TOO.
THE YOUNGEST STATE ALCHEMIST... WITH AMAZING SKILLS?
A BOY WITH BRAIDS WHO STANDS OUT FROM THE CROWD...?
GENIUS ALCHEMIST
REALLY TALL
SOPHISTICATED
EDWARD ELRIC!!
WHY, HELLO THERE!
SPARKLING PERSONALITY
DOES HE LOOK LIKE THIS?
WHO'S THIS SUPPOSED TO BE...?
DO YOU THINK I COULD MEET HIM!?
HUH? WELL, I'M NOT SURE...
HE'S WITH THE MILITARY, SO YOU COULD PROBABLY TRACK HIM DOWN AT ONE OF THEIR HEAD-QUARTERS.
I'VE MADE UP MY MIND!!

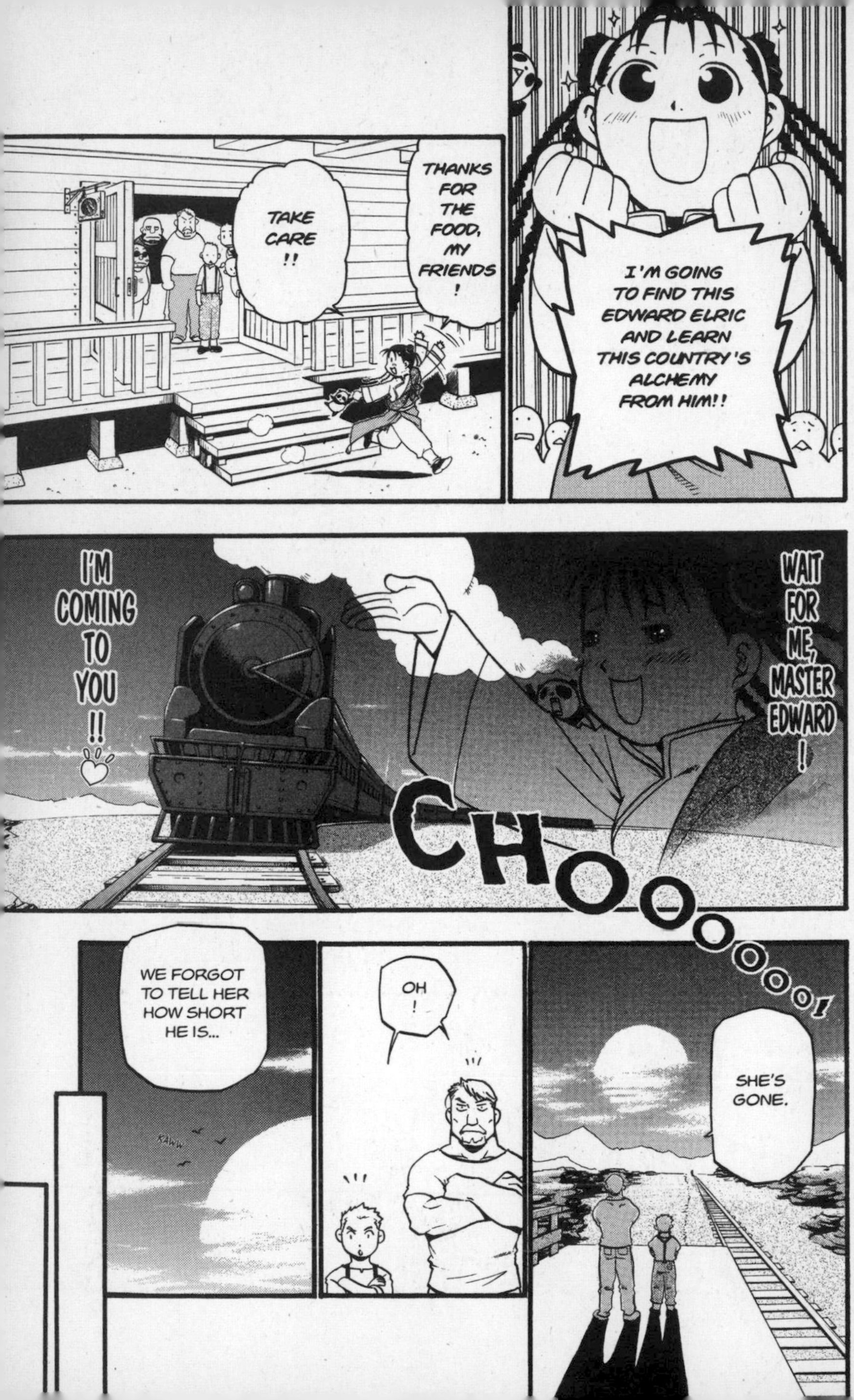
I'M GOING TO FIND THIS EDWARD ELRIC AND LEARN THIS COUNTRY'S ALCHEMY FROM HIM!!
THANKS FOR THE FOOD, MY FRIENDS!
TAKE CARE!!
WAIT FOR ME, MASTER EDWARD!
I'M COMING TO YOU!!
CHOOOOOOO!
SHE'S GONE.
OH!
WE FORGOT TO TELL HER HOW SHORT HE IS...

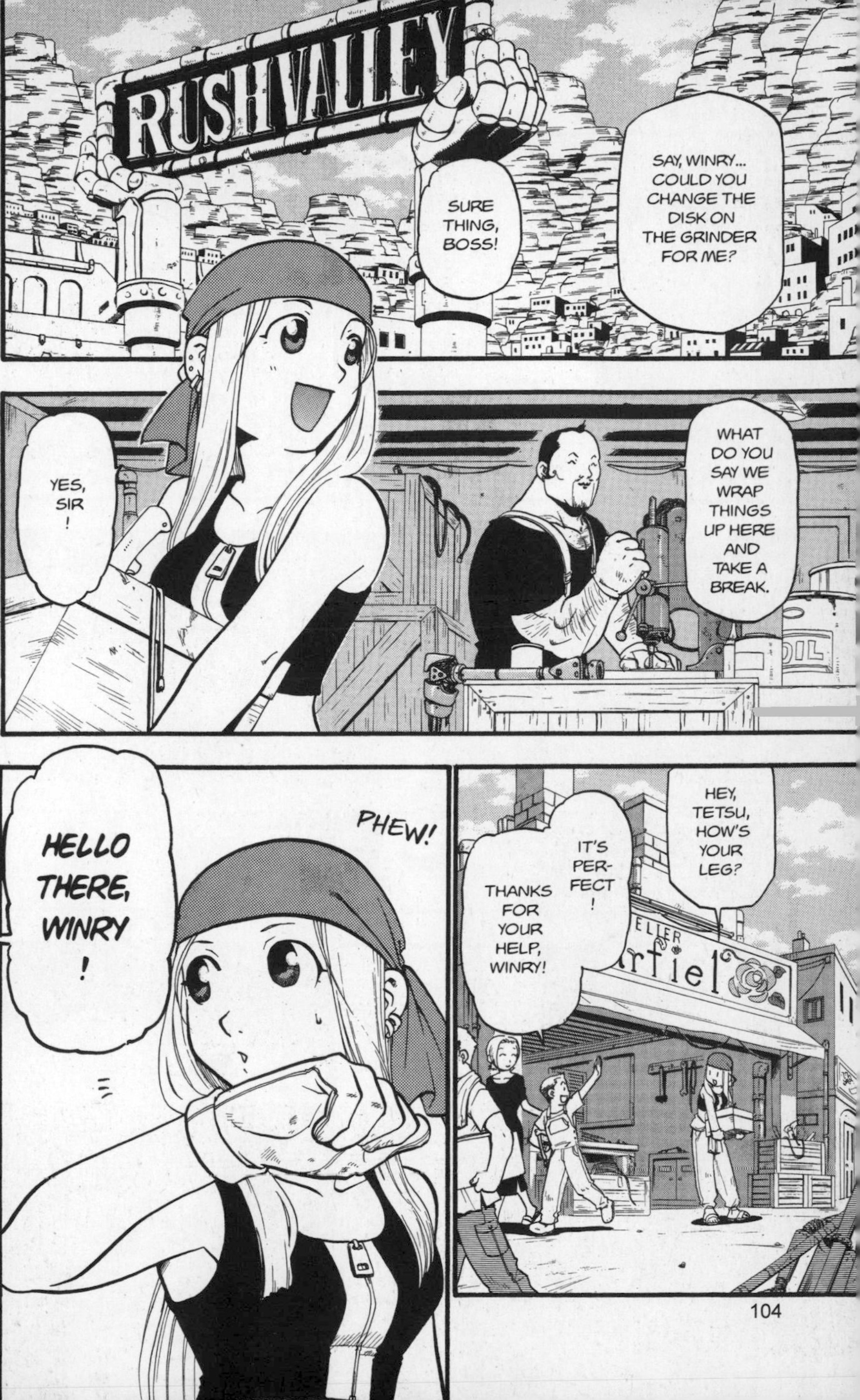
RUSH VALLEY
SAY, WINRY... COULD YOU CHANGE THE DISK ON THE GRINDER FOR ME?
SURE THING, BOSS!
WHAT DO YOU SAY WE WRAP THINGS UP HERE AND TAKE A BREAK.
YES, SIR!
OIL
HEY, TETSU, HOW'S YOUR LEG?
IT'S PERFECT!
THANKS FOR YOUR HELP, WINRY!
PHEW!
HELLO THERE, WINRY!

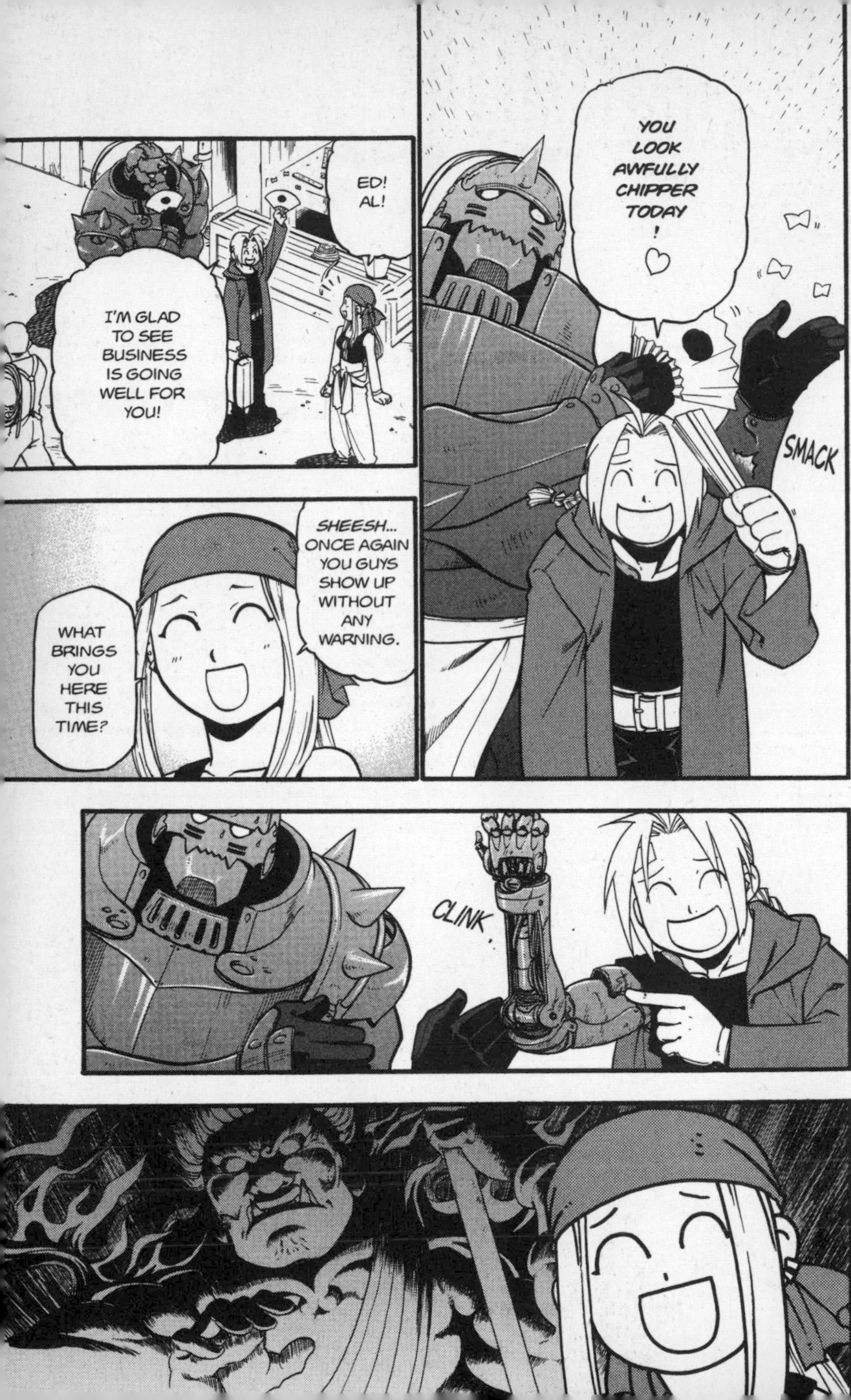
YOU LOOK AWFULLY CHIPPER TODAY ! ♡
SMACK
ED! AL!
I'M GLAD TO SEE BUSINESS IS GOING WELL FOR YOU!
SHEESH... ONCE AGAIN YOU GUYS SHOW UP WITHOUT ANY WARNING.
WHAT BRINGS YOU HERE THIS TIME?
CLINK

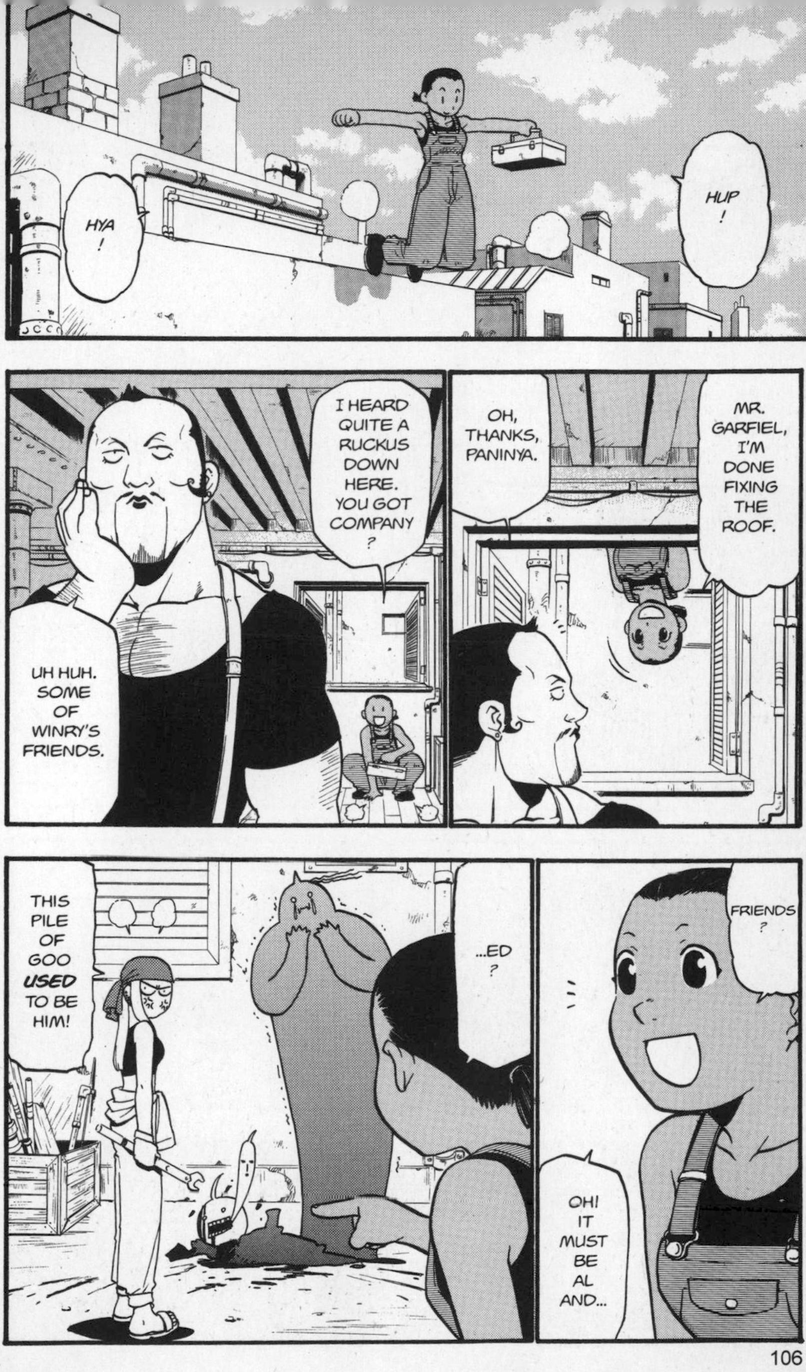
HUP!
HYA!
MR. GARFIEL, I'M DONE FIXING THE ROOF.
OH, THANKS, PANINYA.
I HEARD QUITE A RUCKUS DOWN HERE. YOU GOT COMPANY?
UH HUH. SOME OF WINRY'S FRIENDS.
FRIENDS?
OH! IT MUST BE AL AND...
...ED?
THIS PILE OF GOO USED TO BE HIM!

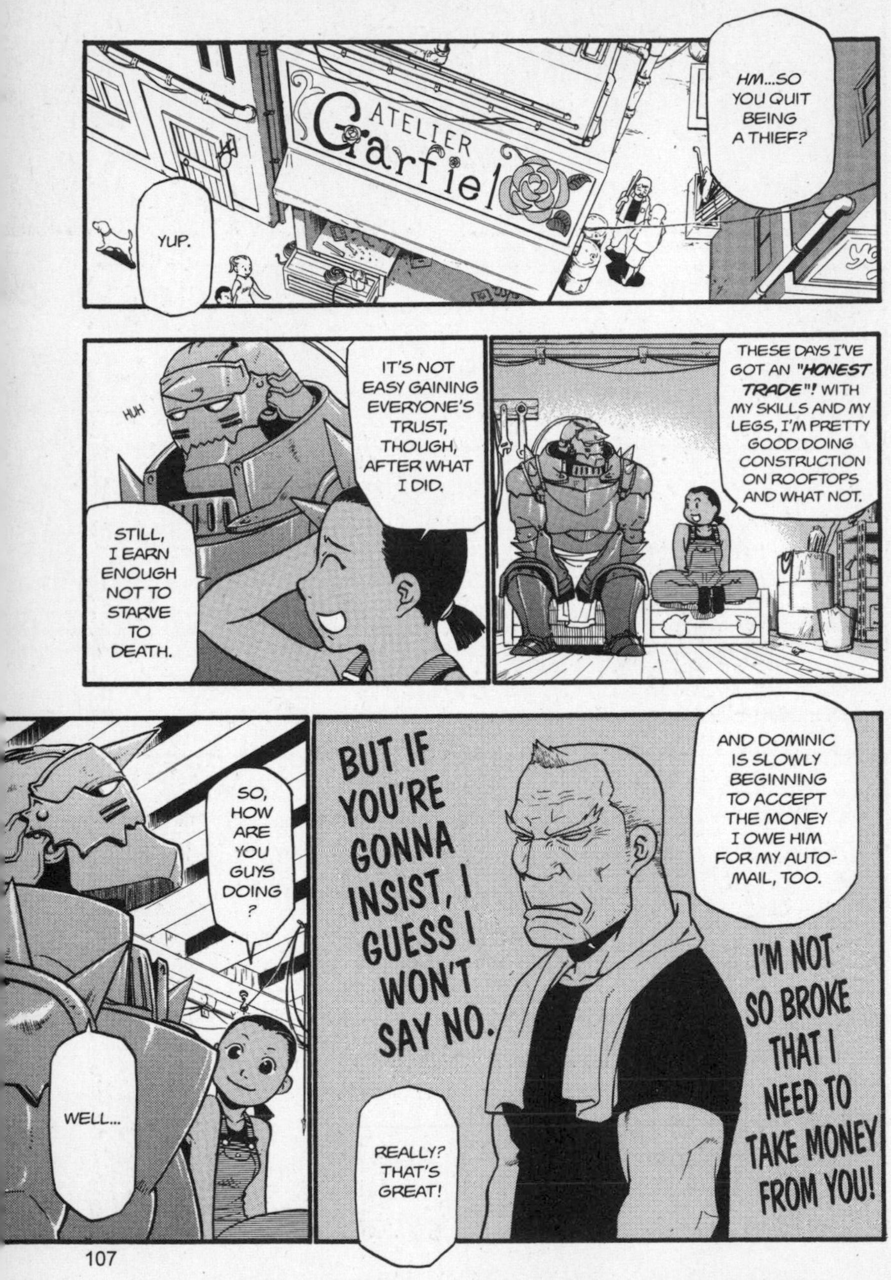
HM...SO YOU QUIT BEING A THIEF?
ATELIER Garfiel
YUP.
THESE DAYS I'VE GOT AN "HONEST TRADE"! WITH MY SKILLS AND MY LEGS, I'M PRETTY GOOD DOING CONSTRUCTION ON ROOFTOPS AND WHAT NOT.
IT'S NOT EASY GAINING EVERYONE'S TRUST, THOUGH, AFTER WHAT I DID.
HUH
STILL, I EARN ENOUGH NOT TO STARVE TO DEATH.
AND DOMINIC IS SLOWLY BEGINNING TO ACCEPT THE MONEY I OWE HIM FOR MY AUTO-MAIL, TOO.
I'M NOT SO BROKE THAT I NEED TO TAKE MONEY FROM YOU!
BUT IF YOU'RE GONNA INSIST, I GUESS I WON'T SAY NO.
REALLY? THAT'S GREAT!
SO, HOW ARE YOU GUYS DOING?
WELL...

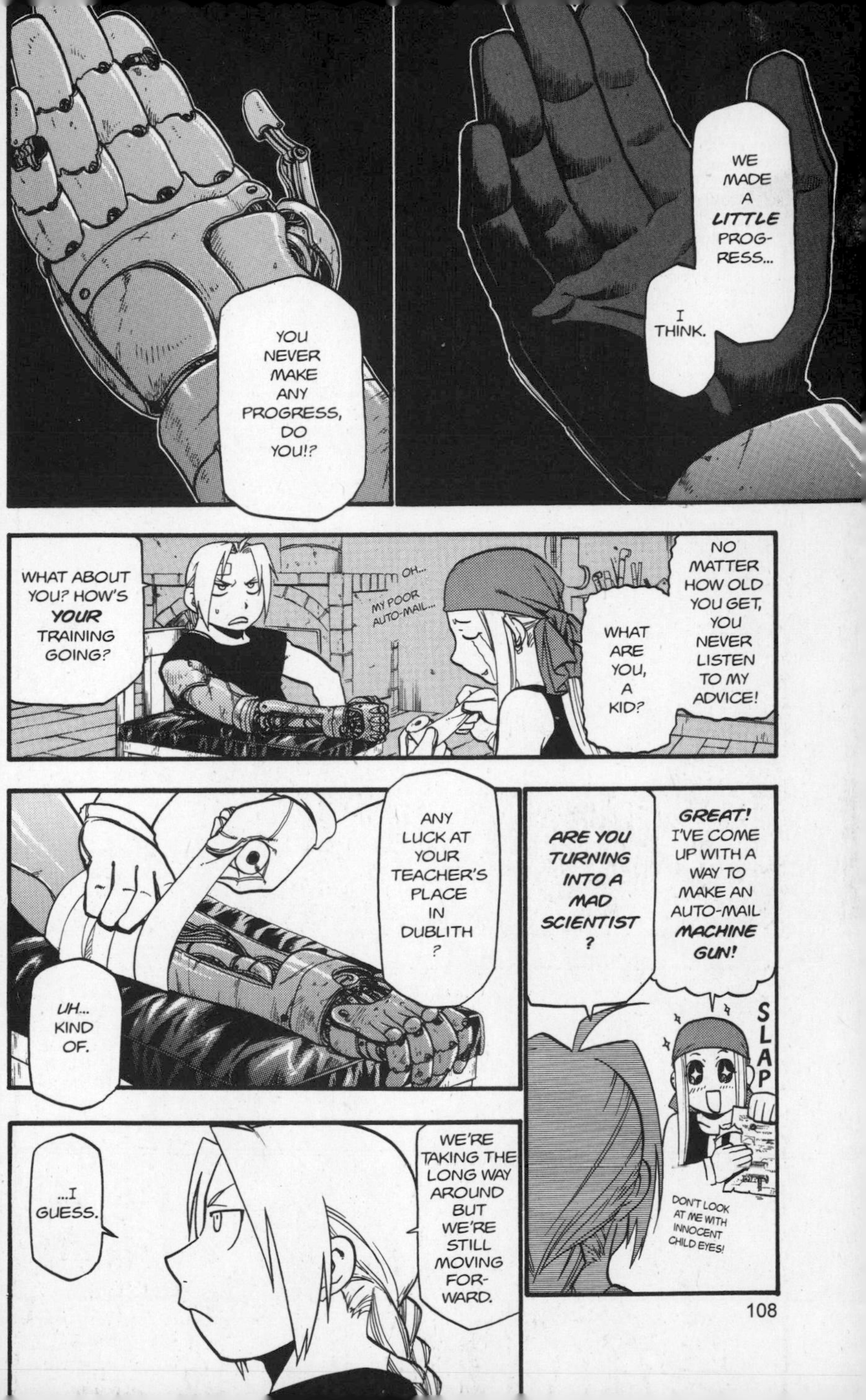
WE MADE A LITTLE PROGRESS...
I THINK.
YOU NEVER MAKE ANY PROGRESS, DO YOU!?
NO MATTER HOW OLD YOU GET, YOU NEVER LISTEN TO MY ADVICE!
WHAT ARE YOU, A KID?
OH... MY POOR AUTO-MAIL...
WHAT ABOUT YOU? HOW'S YOUR TRAINING GOING?
GREAT! I'VE COME UP WITH A WAY TO MAKE AN AUTO-MAIL MACHINE GUN!
ARE YOU TURNING INTO A MAD SCIENTIST?
SLAP
DON'T LOOK AT ME WITH INNOCENT CHILD EYES!
ANY LUCK AT YOUR TEACHER'S PLACE IN DUBLITH?
UH... KIND OF.
WE'RE TAKING THE LONG WAY AROUND BUT WE'RE STILL MOVING FORWARD.
...I GUESS.

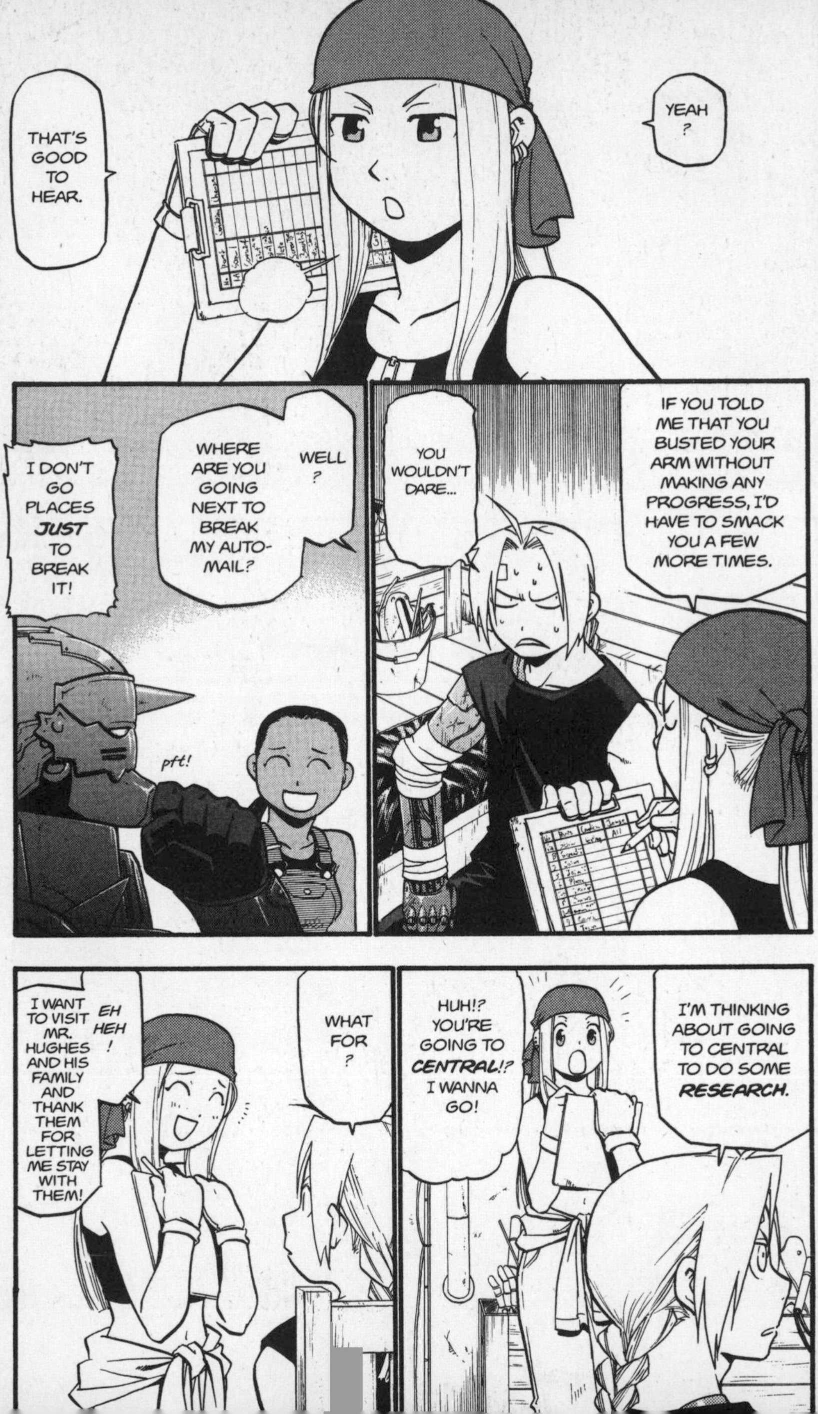
YEAH?
THAT'S GOOD TO HEAR.
IF YOU TOLD ME THAT YOU BUSTED YOUR ARM WITHOUT MAKING ANY PROGRESS, I'D HAVE TO SMACK YOU A FEW MORE TIMES.
YOU WOULDN'T DARE...
WELL?
WHERE ARE YOU GOING NEXT TO BREAK MY AUTO-MAIL?
I DON'T GO PLACES JUST TO BREAK IT!
pft!
I'M THINKING ABOUT GOING TO CENTRAL TO DO SOME RESEARCH.
HUH!? YOU'RE GOING TO CENTRAL!? I WANNA GO!
WHAT FOR?
EH HEH!
I WANT TO VISIT MR. HUGHES AND HIS FAMILY AND THANK THEM FOR LETTING ME STAY WITH THEM!

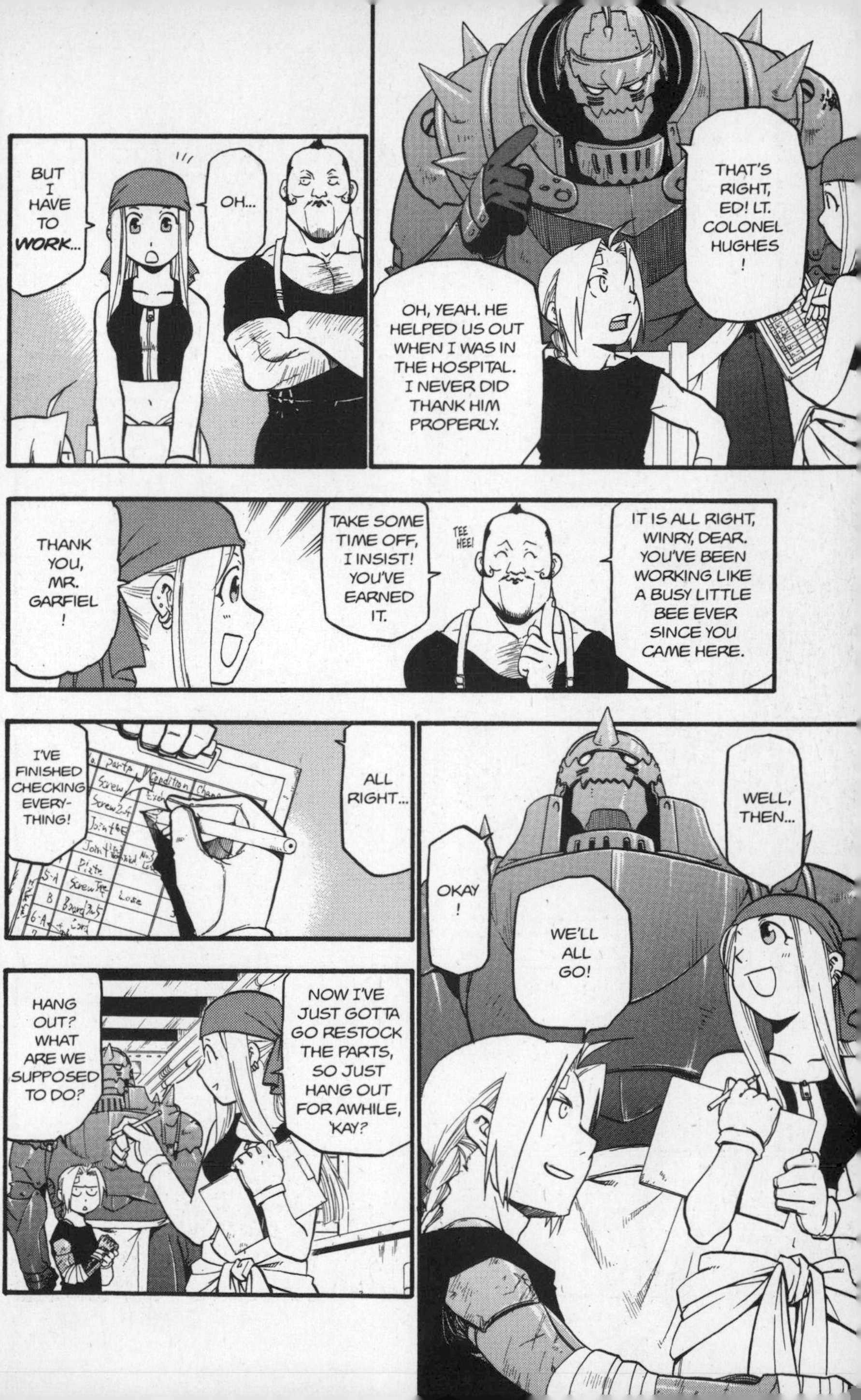
THAT'S RIGHT, ED! LT. COLONEL HUGHES!
OH, YEAH. HE HELPED US OUT WHEN I WAS IN THE HOSPITAL. I NEVER DID THANK HIM PROPERLY.
OH...
BUT I HAVE TO *WORK*...
IT IS ALL RIGHT, WINRY, DEAR. YOU'VE BEEN WORKING LIKE A BUSY LITTLE BEE EVER SINCE YOU CAME HERE.
TEE HEE!
TAKE SOME TIME OFF, I INSIST! YOU'VE EARNED IT.
THANK YOU, MR. GARFIEL!
WELL, THEN...
OKAY!
WE'LL ALL GO!
ALL RIGHT...
I'VE FINISHED CHECKING EVERY-THING!
NOW I'VE JUST GOTTA GO RESTOCK THE PARTS, SO JUST HANG OUT FOR AWHILE, 'KAY?
HANG OUT? WHAT ARE WE SUPPOSED TO DO?

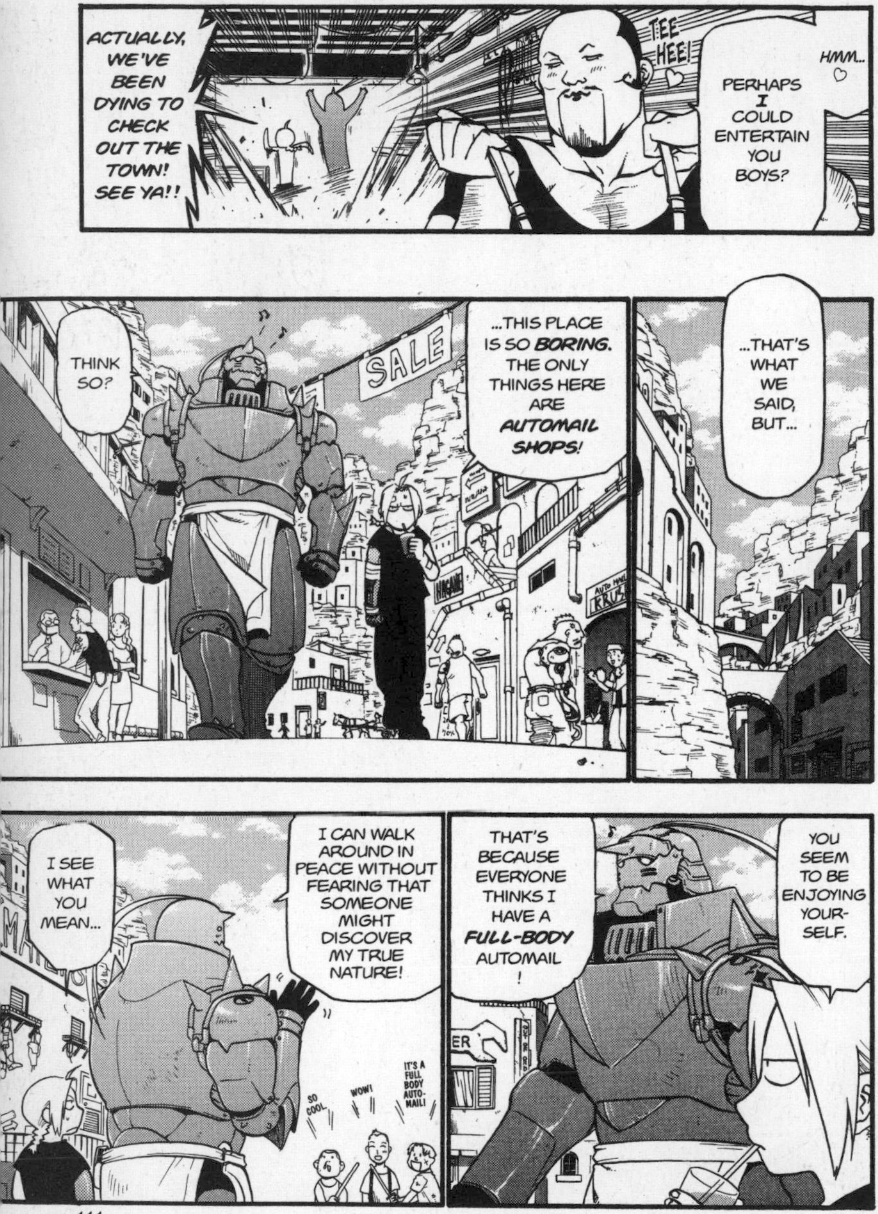
TEE HEE!
HMM... ♡
PERHAPS I COULD ENTERTAIN YOU BOYS?
ACTUALLY, WE'VE BEEN DYING TO CHECK OUT THE TOWN! SEE YA!!
...THAT'S WHAT WE SAID, BUT...
...THIS PLACE IS SO BORING. THE ONLY THINGS HERE ARE AUTOMAIL SHOPS!
SALE
THINK SO?
YOU SEEM TO BE ENJOYING YOURSELF.
THAT'S BECAUSE EVERYONE THINKS I HAVE A FULL-BODY AUTOMAIL!
I CAN WALK AROUND IN PEACE WITHOUT FEARING THAT SOMEONE MIGHT DISCOVER MY TRUE NATURE!
IT'S A FULL BODY AUTO-MAIL!
WOW!
SO COOL.
I SEE WHAT YOU MEAN...

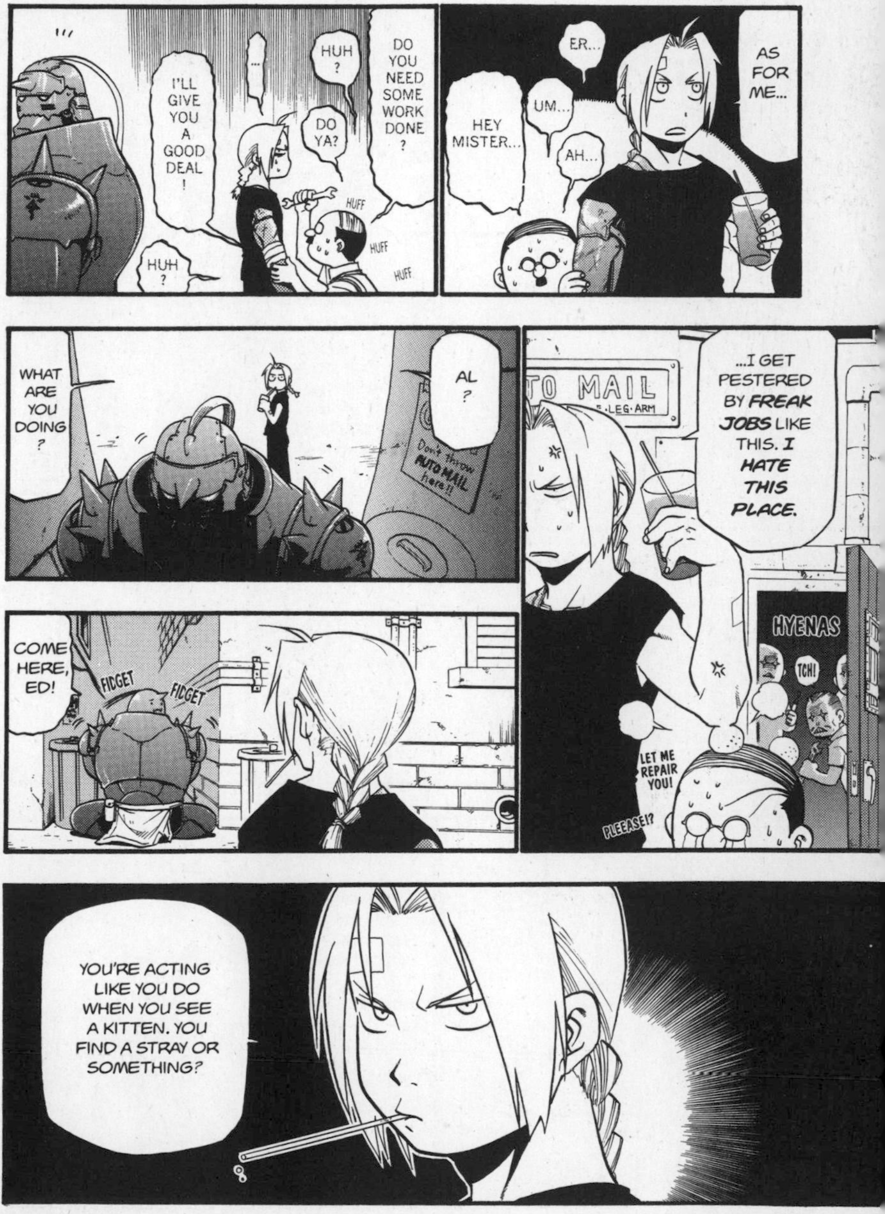
AS FOR ME...
ER...
UM...
AH...
HEY MISTER...
DO YOU NEED SOME WORK DONE?
HUH?
DO YA?
...
I'LL GIVE YOU A GOOD DEAL!
HUFF
HUFF
HUFF
HUH?
...I GET PESTERED BY **FREAK JOBS** LIKE THIS. ***I HATE THIS PLACE.***
TO MAIL
E·LEG·ARM
HYENAS
TCH!
LET ME REPAIR YOU!
PLEASE!?
AL?
WHAT ARE YOU DOING?
Don't throw AUTO MAIL here!!
COME HERE, ED!
FIDGET
FIDGET
YOU'RE ACTING LIKE YOU DO WHEN YOU SEE A KITTEN. YOU FIND A STRAY OR SOMETHING?

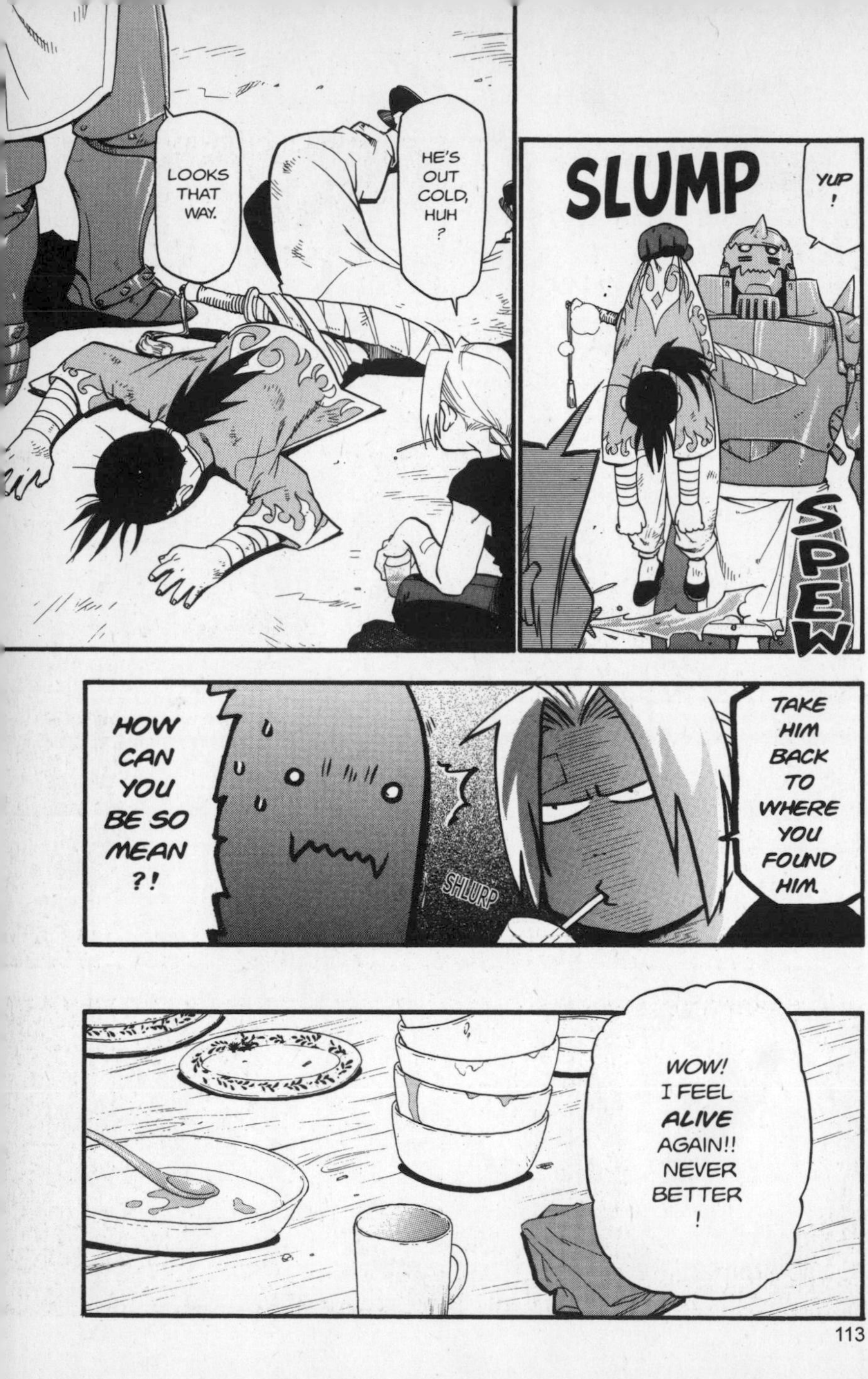
YUP!
SLUMP
SPEW
HE'S OUT COLD, HUH?
LOOKS THAT WAY.
TAKE HIM BACK TO WHERE YOU FOUND HIM.
SHLURP
HOW CAN YOU BE SO MEAN?!
WOW! I FEEL ALIVE AGAIN!! NEVER BETTER!

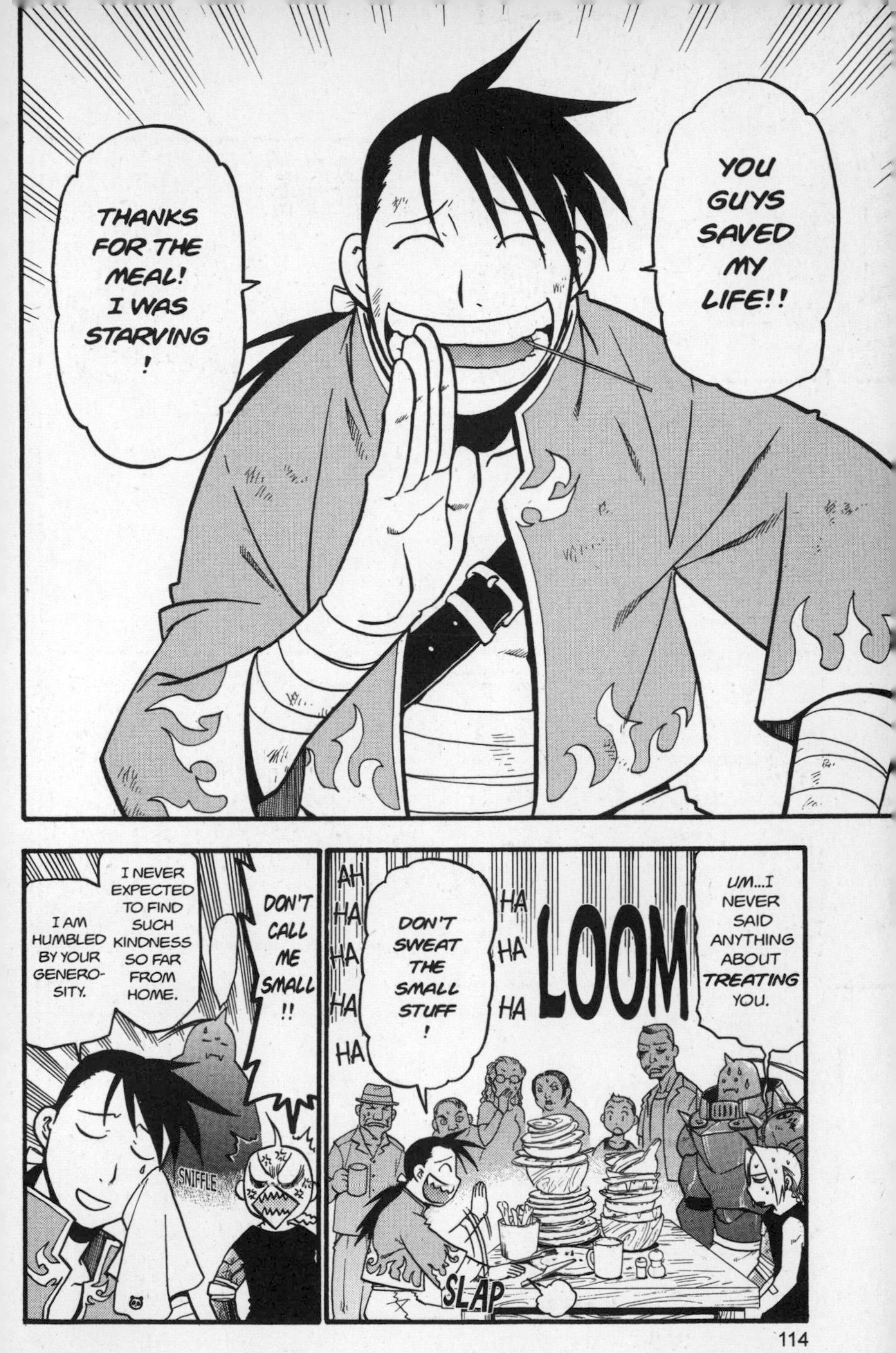
YOU GUYS SAVED MY LIFE!!
THANKS FOR THE MEAL! I WAS STARVING!
UM...I NEVER SAID ANYTHING ABOUT TREATING YOU.
LOOM
HA HA HA HA
DON'T SWEAT THE SMALL STUFF!
AH HA HA HA HA HA
SLAP
DON'T CALL ME SMALL!!
I NEVER EXPECTED TO FIND SUCH KINDNESS SO FAR FROM HOME.
I AM HUMBLED BY YOUR GENEROSITY.
SNIFFLE

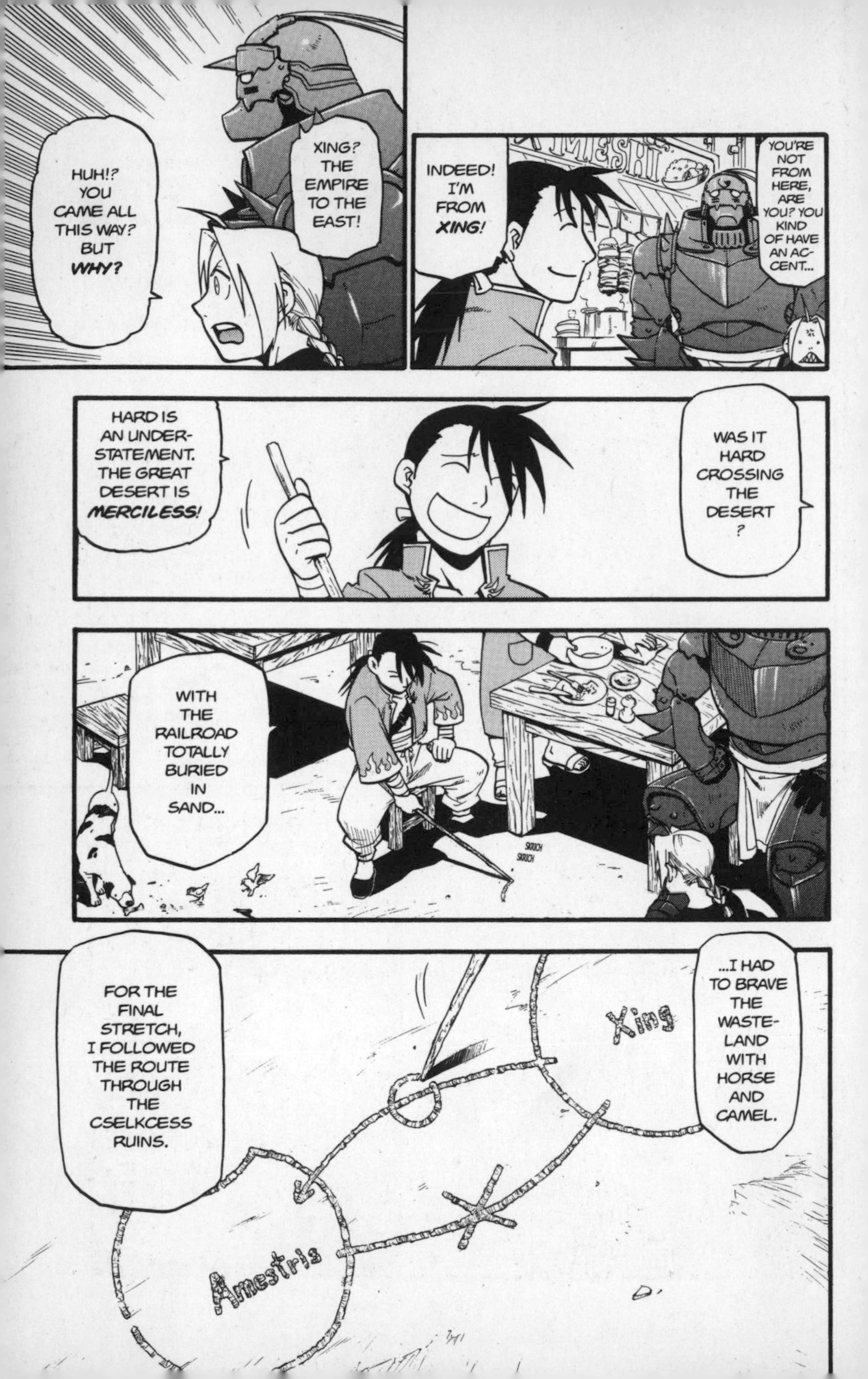
YOU'RE NOT FROM HERE, ARE YOU? YOU KIND OF HAVE AN ACCENT...
INDEED! I'M FROM *XING!*
XING? THE EMPIRE TO THE EAST!
HUH!? YOU CAME ALL THIS WAY? BUT *WHY?*
WAS IT HARD CROSSING THE DESERT?
HARD IS AN UNDERSTATEMENT. THE GREAT DESERT IS *MERCILESS!*
WITH THE RAILROAD TOTALLY BURIED IN SAND...
SKRICH SKRICH
...I HAD TO BRAVE THE WASTELAND WITH HORSE AND CAMEL.
FOR THE FINAL STRETCH, I FOLLOWED THE ROUTE THROUGH THE CSELKCESS RUINS.
Xing
Amestris

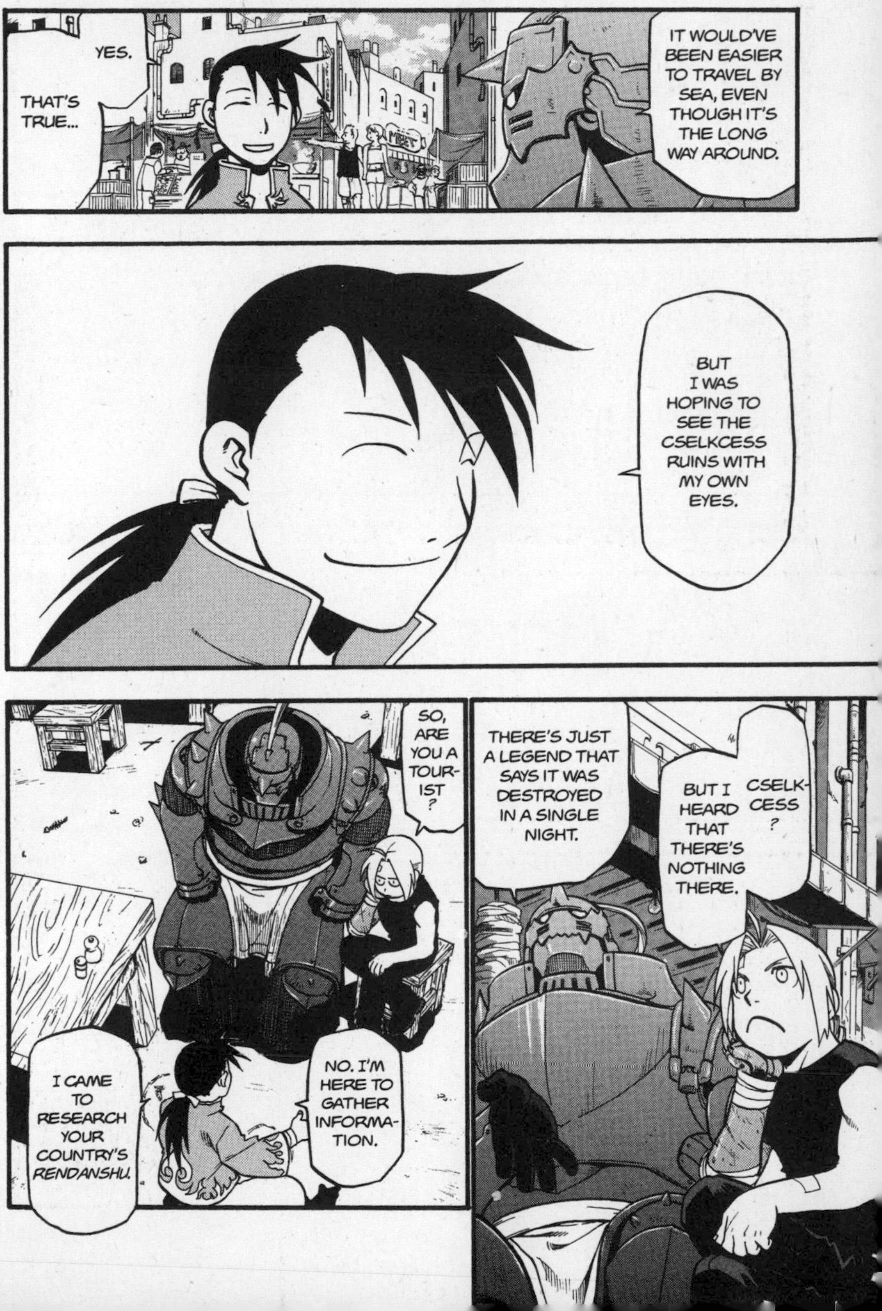
IT WOULD'VE BEEN EASIER TO TRAVEL BY SEA, EVEN THOUGH IT'S THE LONG WAY AROUND.
YES.
THAT'S TRUE...
BUT I WAS HOPING TO SEE THE CSELKCESS RUINS WITH MY OWN EYES.
CSELK-CESS?
BUT I HEARD THAT THERE'S NOTHING THERE.
THERE'S JUST A LEGEND THAT SAYS IT WAS DESTROYED IN A SINGLE NIGHT.
SO, ARE YOU A TOUR-IST?
NO. I'M HERE TO GATHER INFORMA-TION.
I CAME TO RESEARCH YOUR COUNTRY'S RENDANSHU.

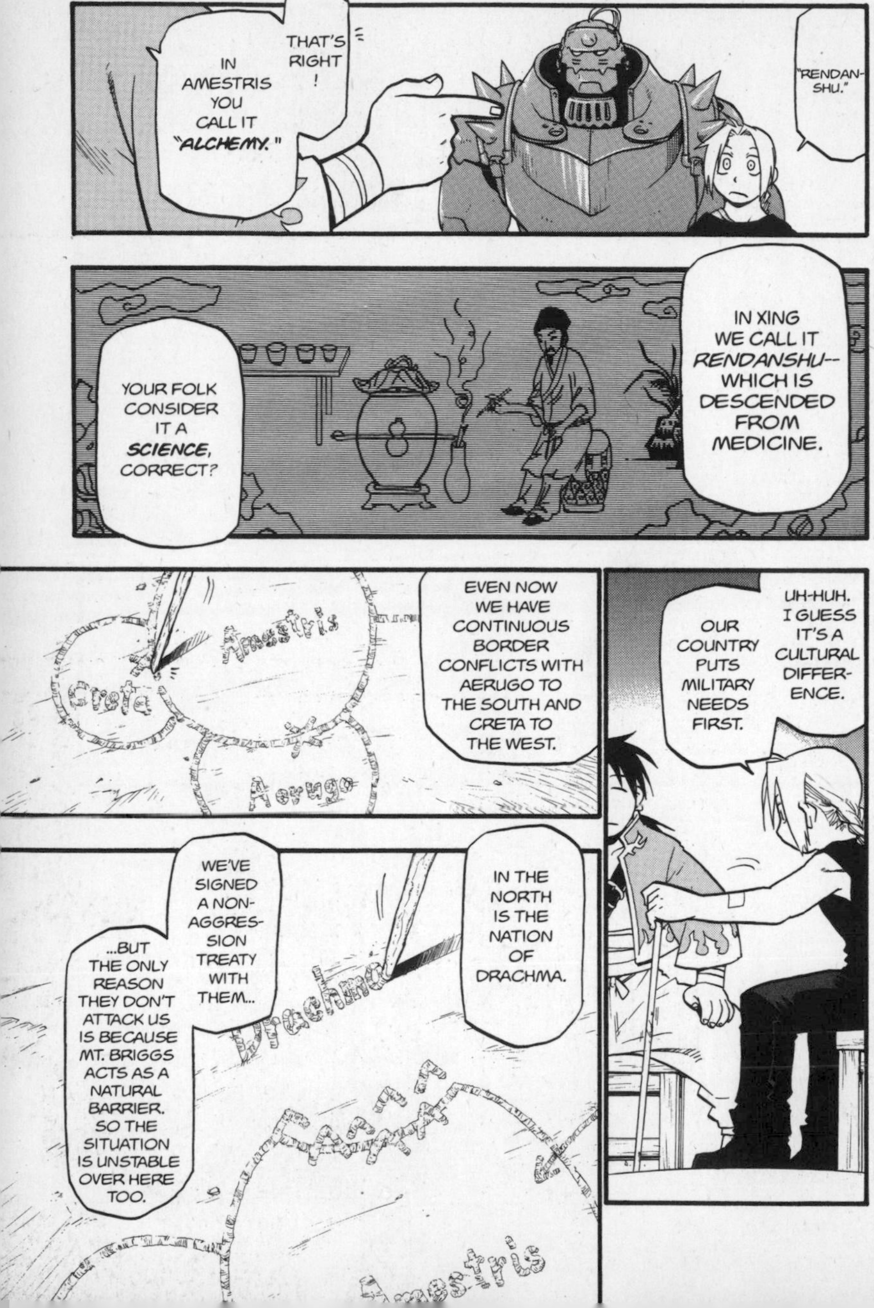
"RENDANSHU."
THAT'S RIGHT!
IN AMESTRIS YOU CALL IT "ALCHEMY."
IN XING WE CALL IT RENDANSHU--WHICH IS DESCENDED FROM MEDICINE.
YOUR FOLK CONSIDER IT A SCIENCE, CORRECT?
UH-HUH. I GUESS IT'S A CULTURAL DIFFERENCE.
OUR COUNTRY PUTS MILITARY NEEDS FIRST.
EVEN NOW WE HAVE CONTINUOUS BORDER CONFLICTS WITH AERUGO TO THE SOUTH AND CRETA TO THE WEST.
Amestris
Creta
Aerugo
IN THE NORTH IS THE NATION OF DRACHMA.
WE'VE SIGNED A NON-AGGRESSION TREATY WITH THEM...
...BUT THE ONLY REASON THEY DON'T ATTACK US IS BECAUSE MT. BRIGGS ACTS AS A NATURAL BARRIER. SO THE SITUATION IS UNSTABLE OVER HERE TOO.
Drachma
Amestris

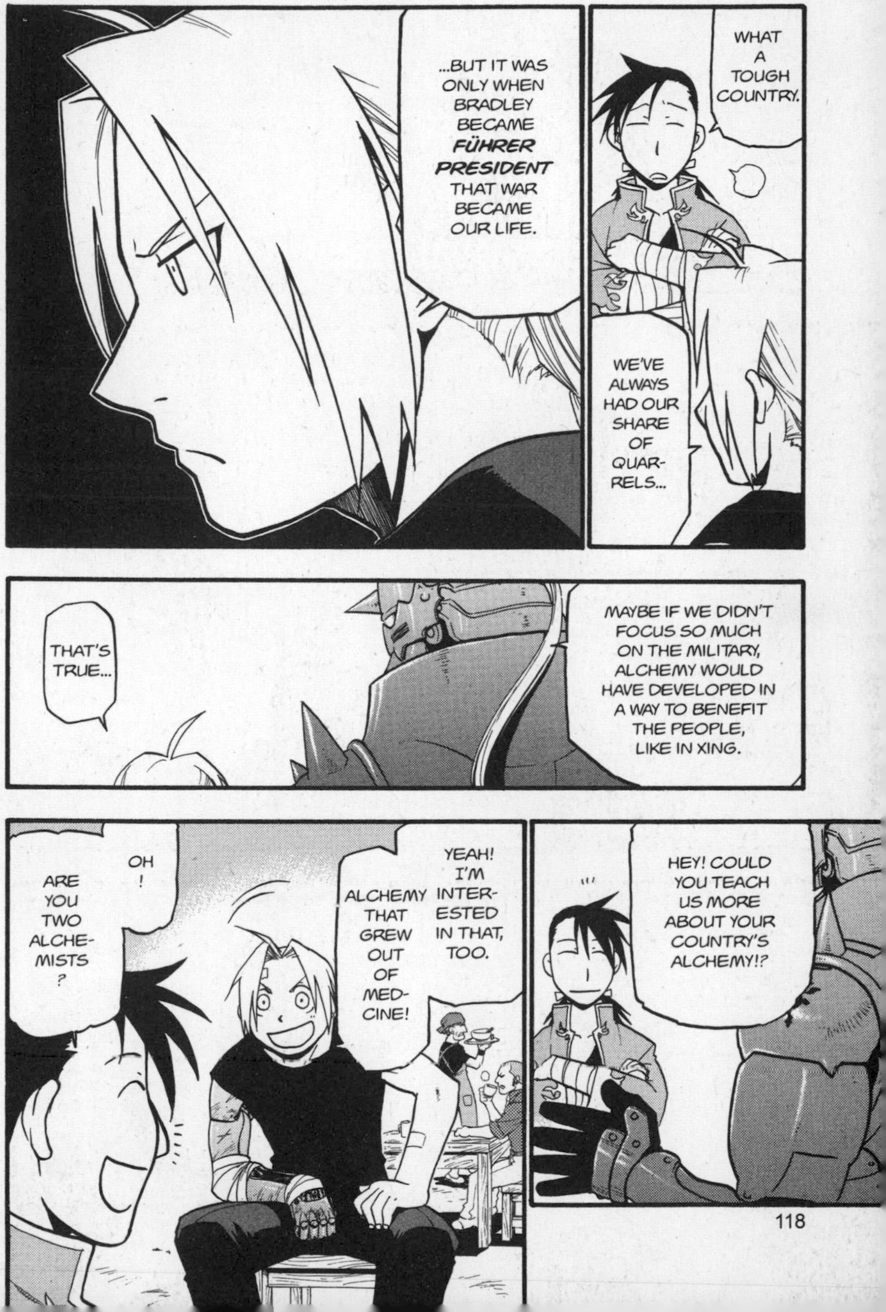
WHAT A TOUGH COUNTRY.
WE'VE ALWAYS HAD OUR SHARE OF QUARRELS...
...BUT IT WAS ONLY WHEN BRADLEY BECAME **FÜHRER PRESIDENT** THAT WAR BECAME OUR LIFE.
MAYBE IF WE DIDN'T FOCUS SO MUCH ON THE MILITARY, ALCHEMY WOULD HAVE DEVELOPED IN A WAY TO BENEFIT THE PEOPLE, LIKE IN XING.
THAT'S TRUE...
HEY! COULD YOU TEACH US MORE ABOUT YOUR COUNTRY'S ALCHEMY!?
YEAH! I'M INTERESTED IN THAT, TOO.
ALCHEMY THAT GREW OUT OF MEDICINE!
OH!
ARE YOU TWO ALCHEMISTS?

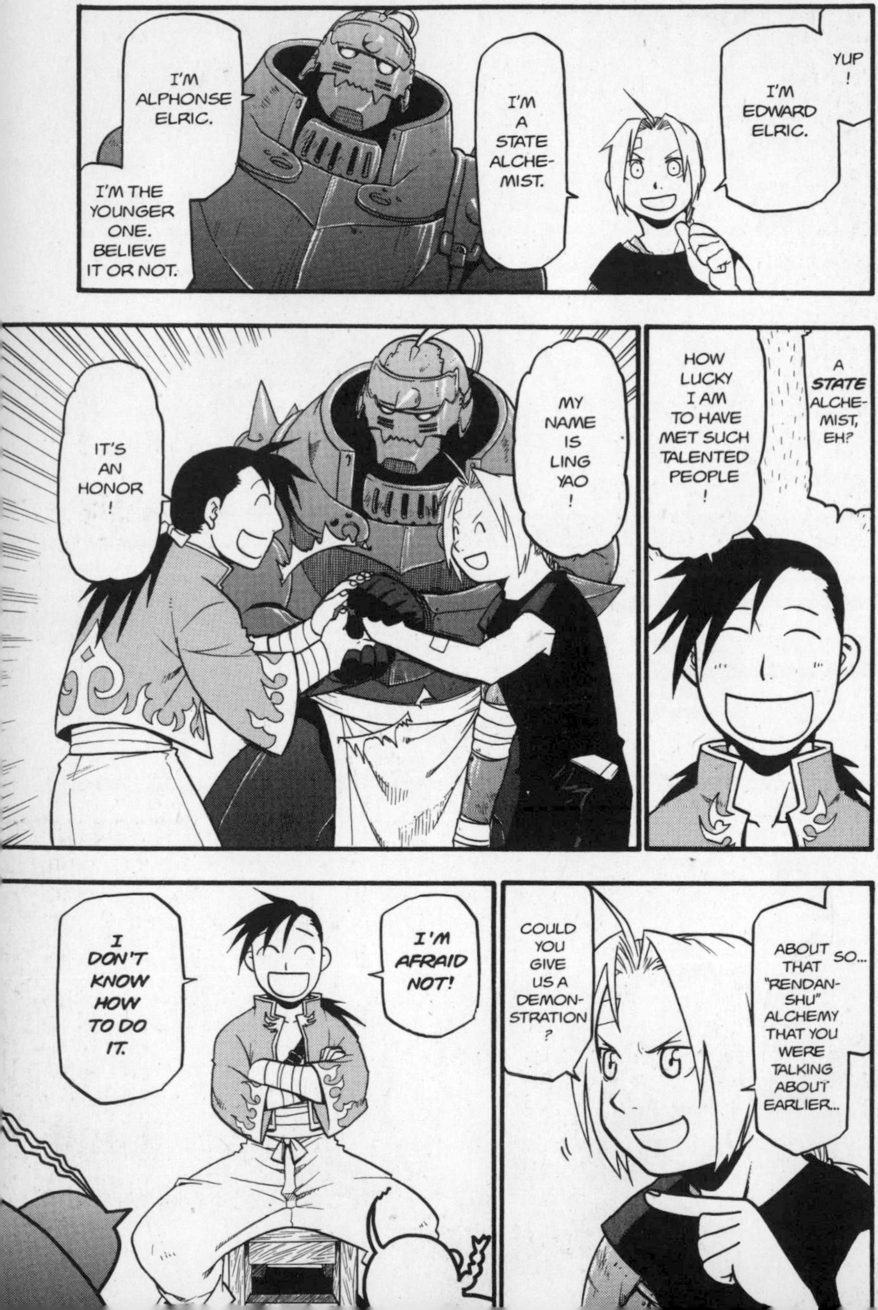
YUP!
I'M EDWARD ELRIC.
I'M A STATE ALCHEMIST.
I'M ALPHONSE ELRIC.
I'M THE YOUNGER ONE. BELIEVE IT OR NOT.
A *STATE* ALCHEMIST, EH?
HOW LUCKY I AM TO HAVE MET SUCH TALENTED PEOPLE!
MY NAME IS LING YAO!
IT'S AN HONOR!
SO...
ABOUT THAT "RENDAN-SHU" ALCHEMY THAT YOU WERE TALKING ABOUT EARLIER...
COULD YOU GIVE US A DEMONSTRATION?
I'M AFRAID NOT!
I DON'T KNOW HOW TO DO IT.

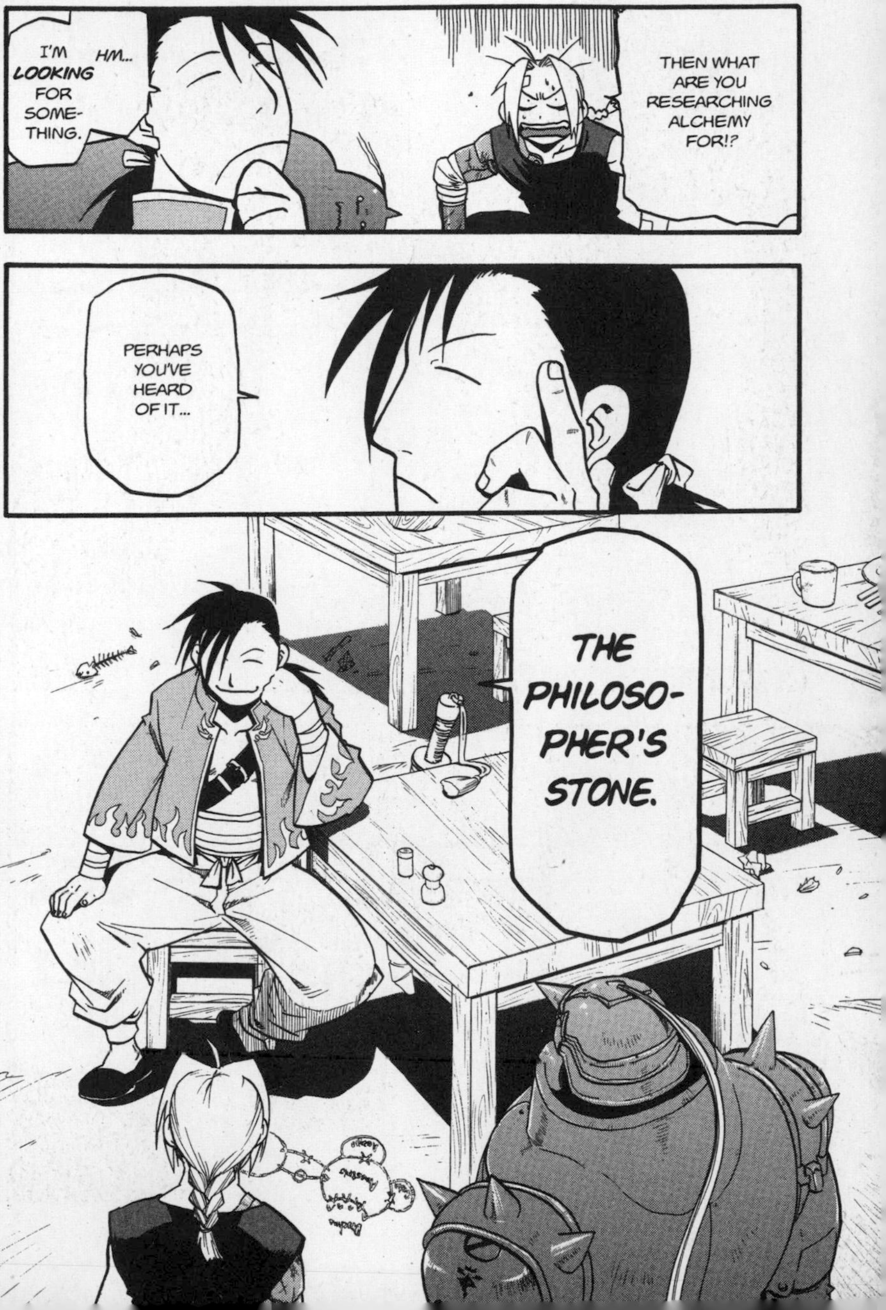
THEN WHAT ARE YOU RESEARCHING ALCHEMY FOR!?
HM...
I'M **LOOKING** FOR SOME-THING.
PERHAPS YOU'VE HEARD OF IT...
THE PHILOSO-PHER'S STONE.

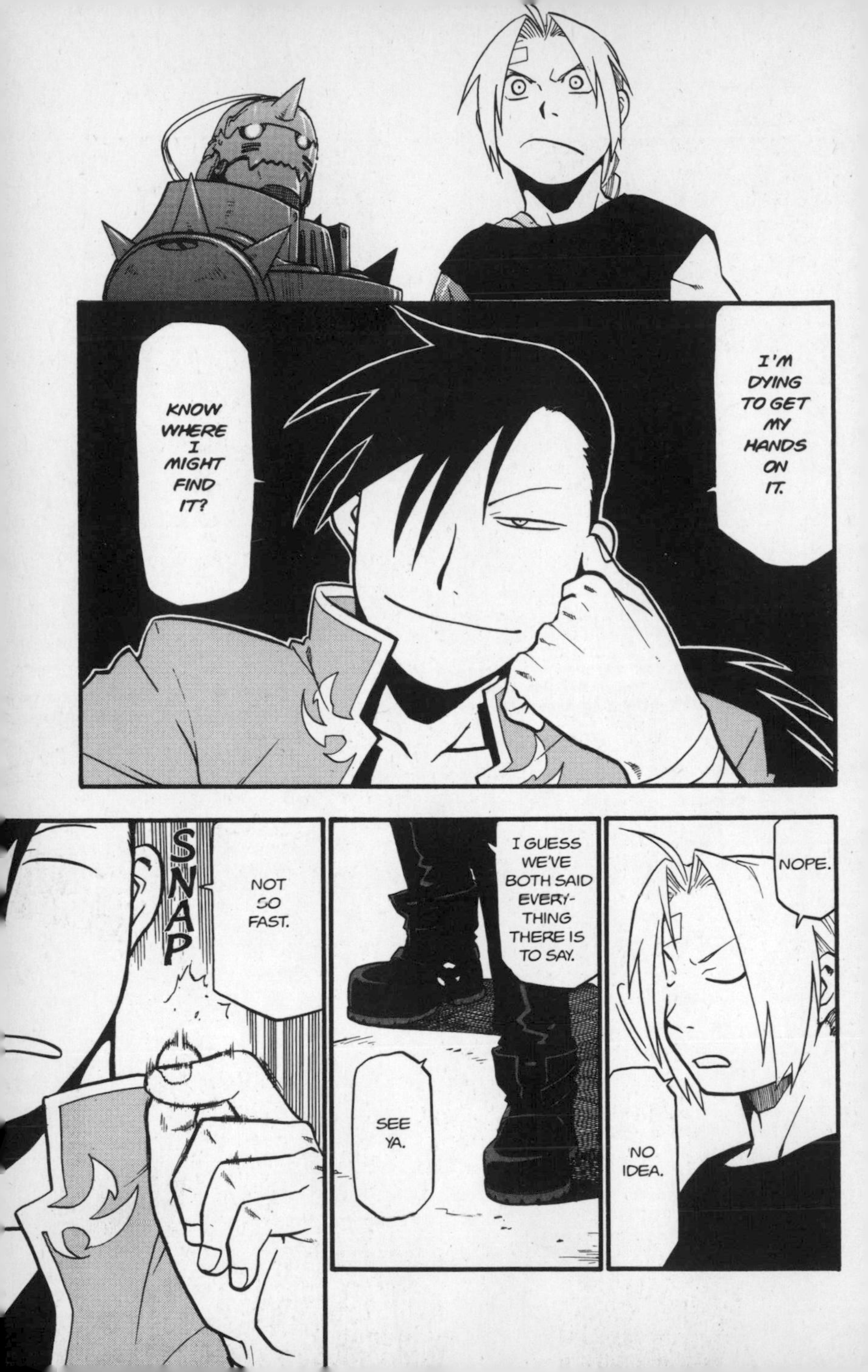
I'M DYING TO GET MY HANDS ON IT.
KNOW WHERE I MIGHT FIND IT?
NOPE.
NO IDEA.
I GUESS WE'VE BOTH SAID EVERY-THING THERE IS TO SAY.
SEE YA.
SNAP
NOT SO FAST.

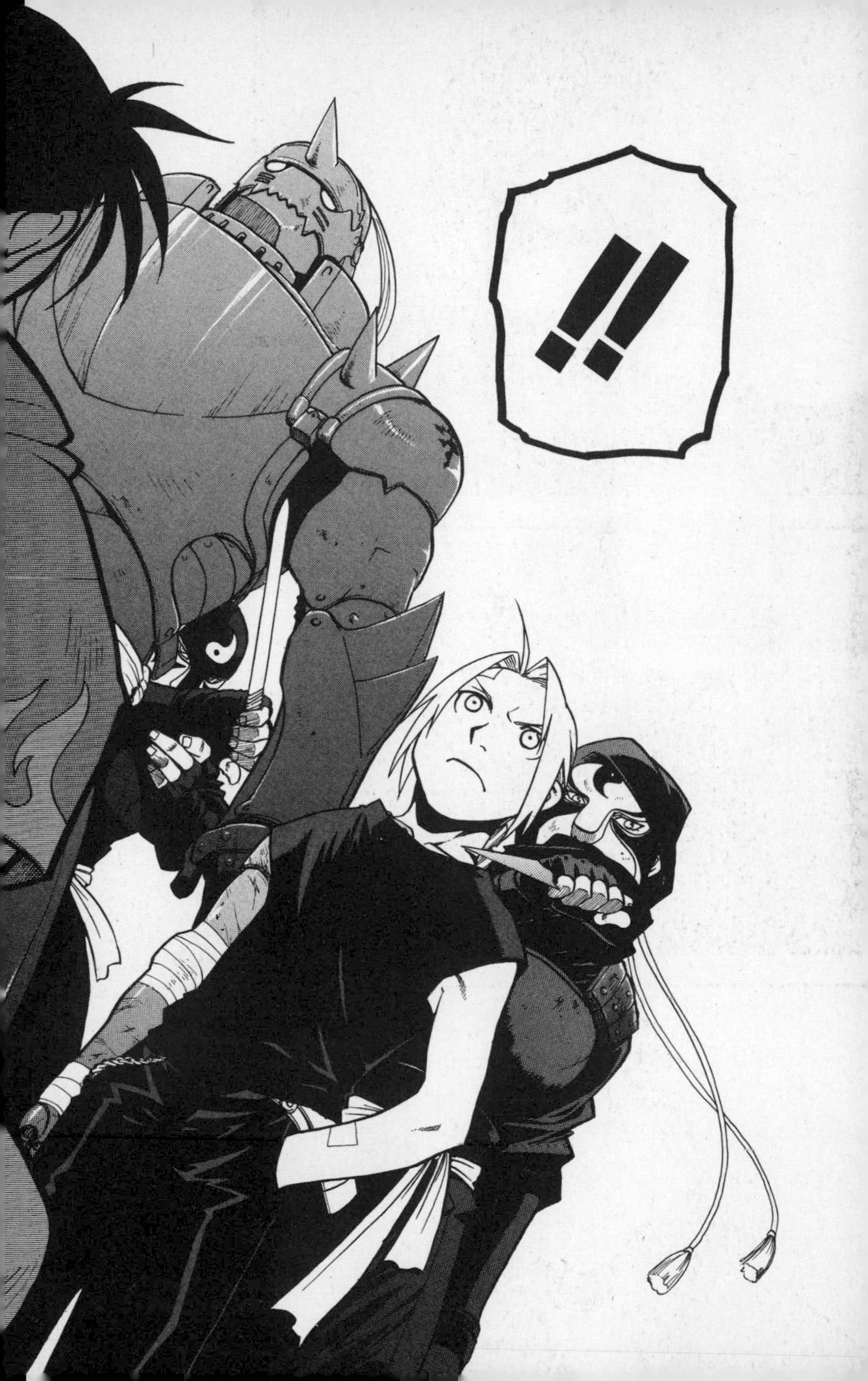
!!

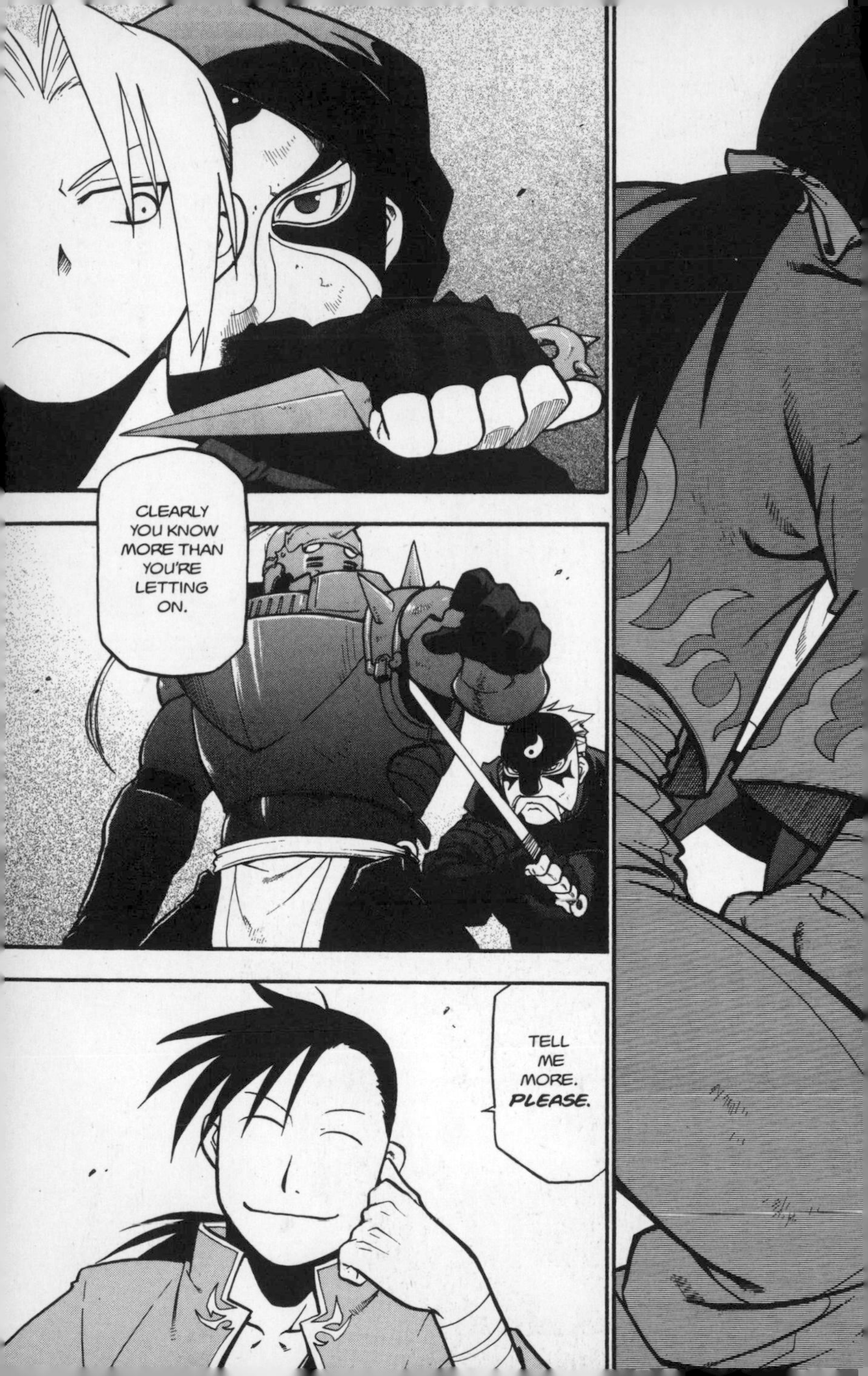
CLEARLY YOU KNOW MORE THAN YOU'RE LETTING ON.
TELL ME MORE. *PLEASE.*

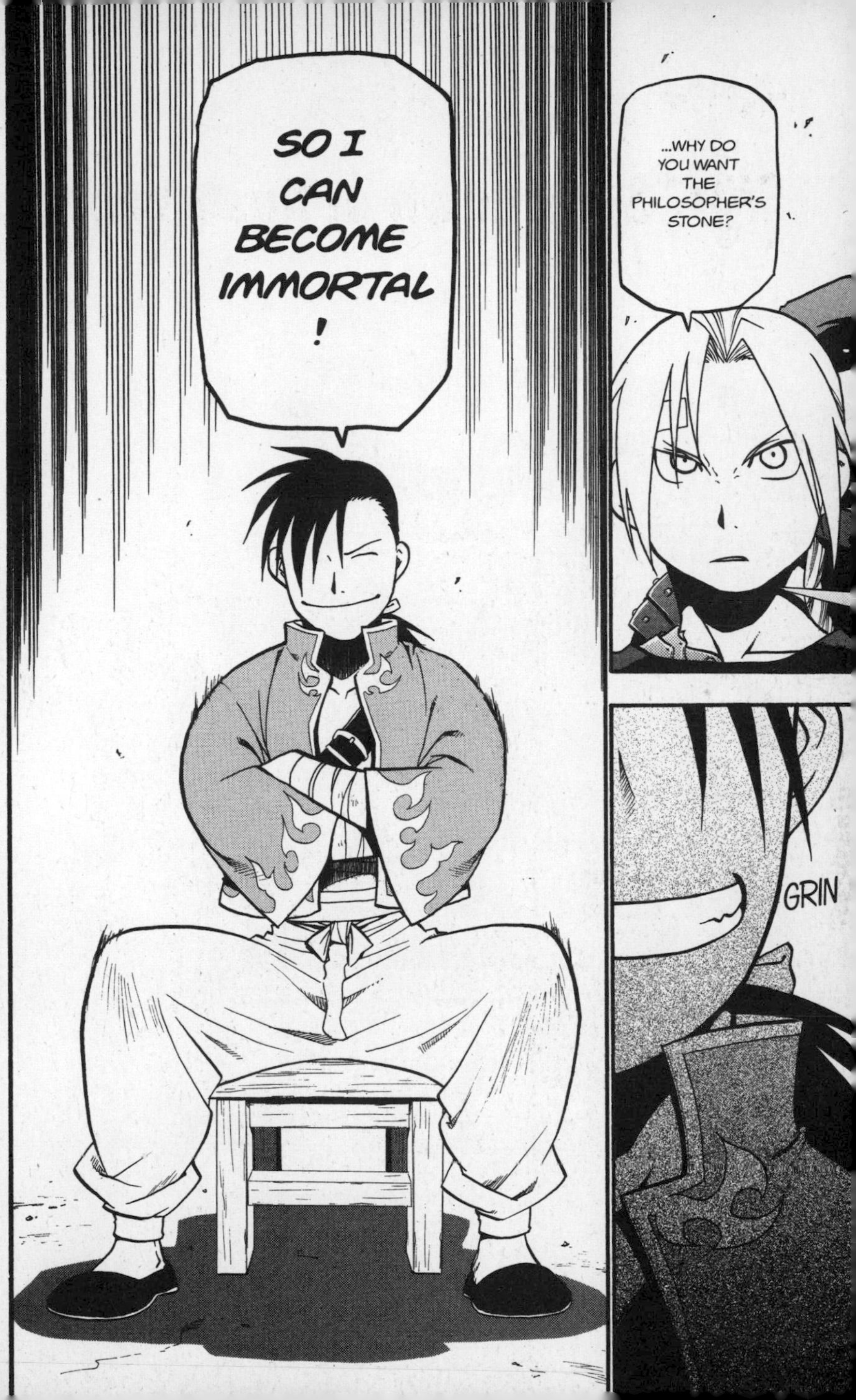
...WHY DO YOU WANT THE PHILOSOPHER'S STONE?
GRIN
SO I CAN BECOME IMMORTAL!

Chapter 33: Showdown in Rush Valley

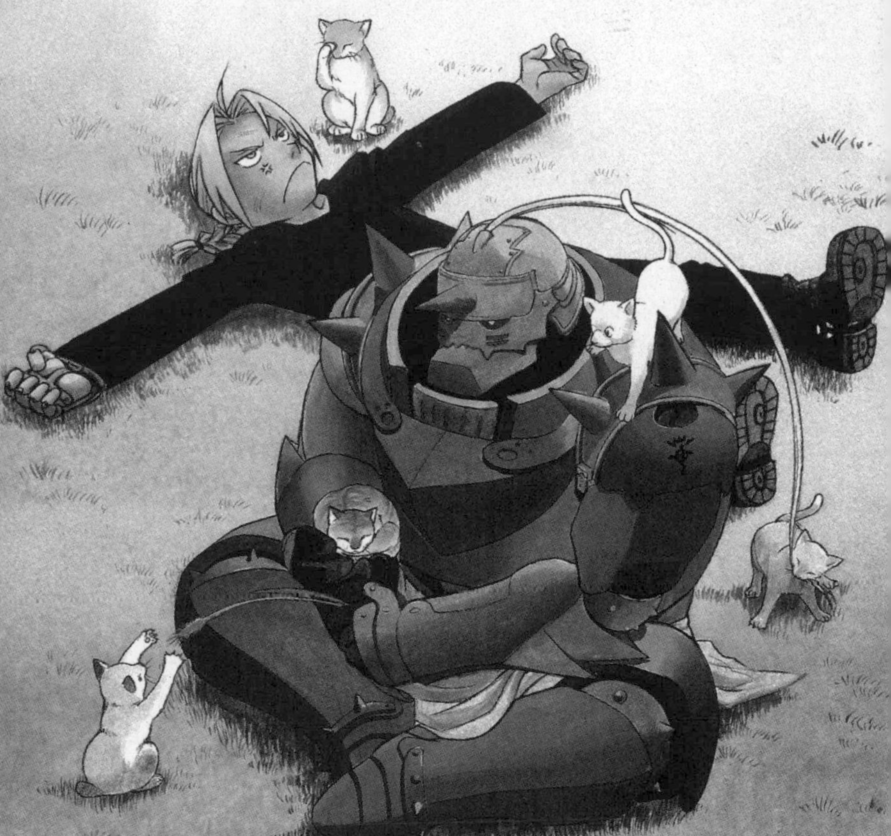

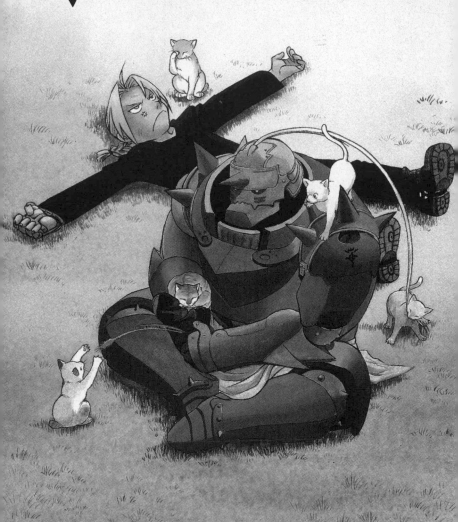

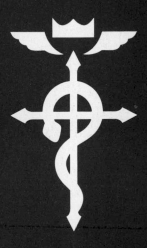

FULLMETAL
ALCHEMIST

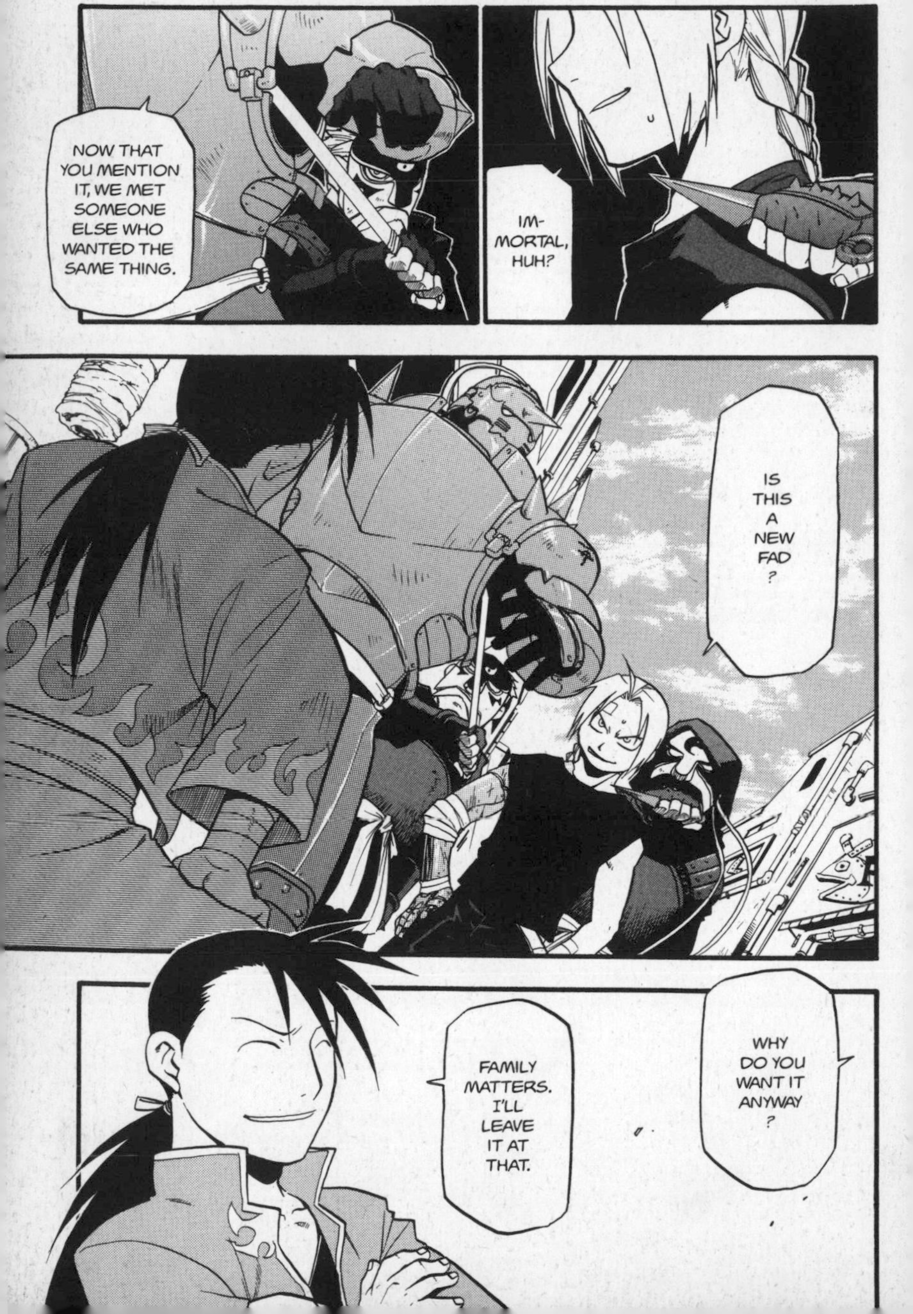
IM-MORTAL, HUH?
NOW THAT YOU MENTION IT, WE MET SOMEONE ELSE WHO WANTED THE SAME THING.
IS THIS A NEW FAD?
WHY DO YOU WANT IT ANYWAY?
FAMILY MATTERS. I'LL LEAVE IT AT THAT.

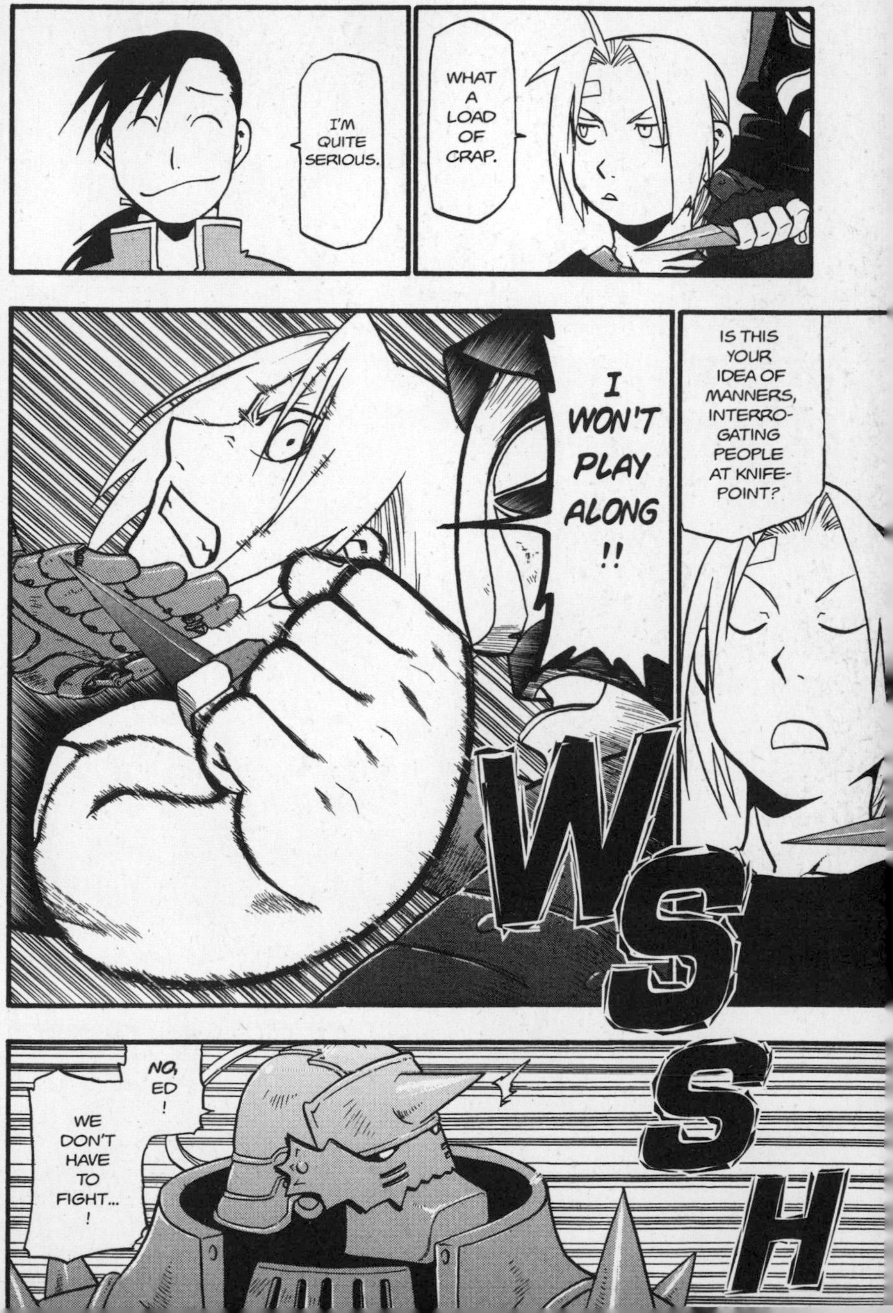
WHAT A LOAD OF CRAP.
I'M QUITE SERIOUS.
IS THIS YOUR IDEA OF MANNERS, INTERRO-GATING PEOPLE AT KNIFE-POINT?
I WON'T PLAY ALONG!!
WSSH
NO, ED!
WE DON'T HAVE TO FIGHT...!

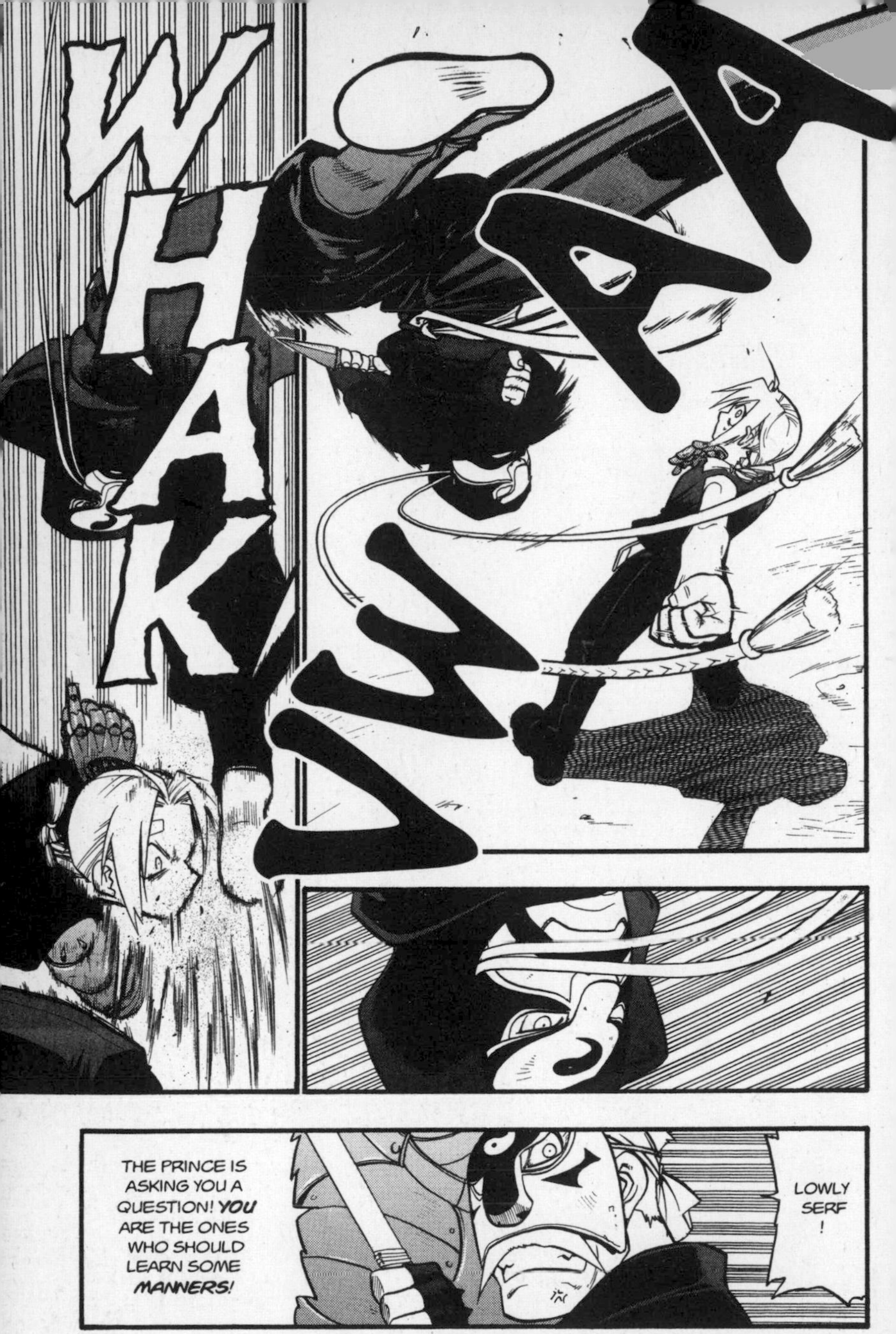
WHAK
LOWLY SERF!
THE PRINCE IS ASKING YOU A QUESTION! ***YOU*** ARE THE ONES WHO SHOULD LEARN SOME ***MANNERS!***

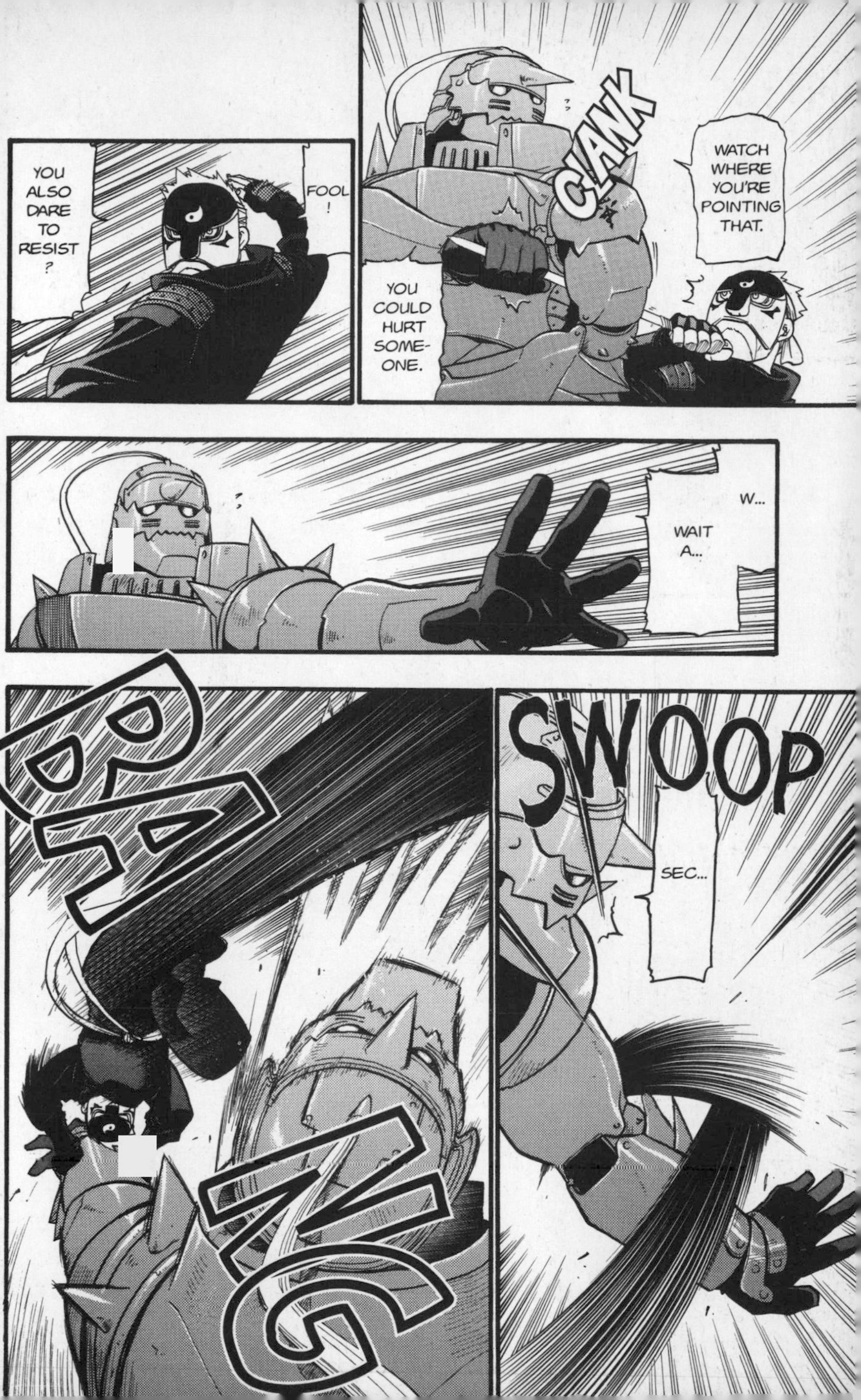
CLANK
WATCH WHERE YOU'RE POINTING THAT.
YOU COULD HURT SOME-ONE.
FOOL!
YOU ALSO DARE TO RESIST?
W...
WAIT A...
SWOOP
SEC...
BANG

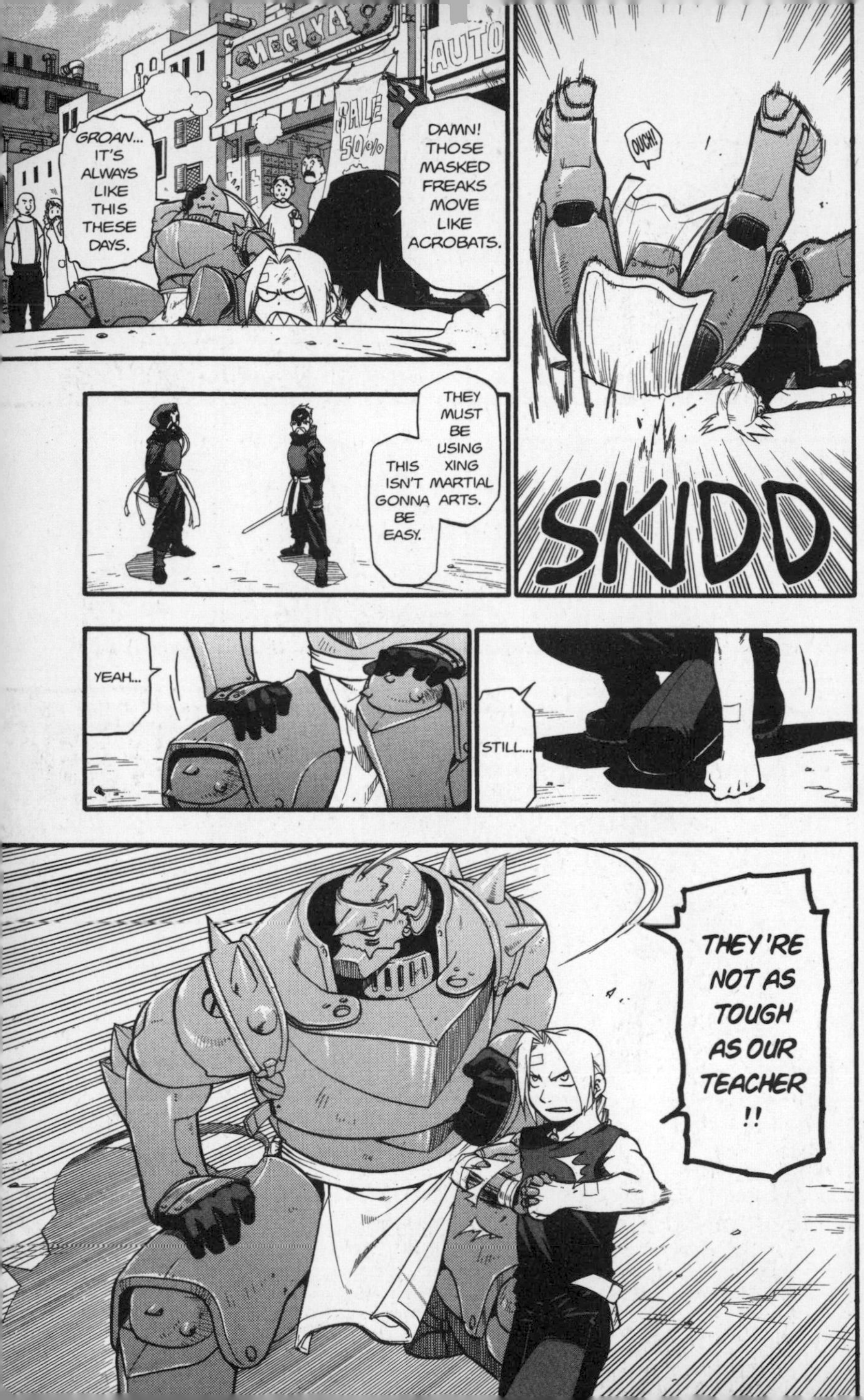
OUCH!
SKIDD
AUTO
SALE 50%
DAMN! THOSE MASKED FREAKS MOVE LIKE ACROBATS.
GROAN... IT'S ALWAYS LIKE THIS THESE DAYS.
THEY MUST BE USING XING MARTIAL ARTS.
THIS ISN'T GONNA BE EASY.
STILL...
YEAH...
THEY'RE NOT AS TOUGH AS OUR TEACHER!!

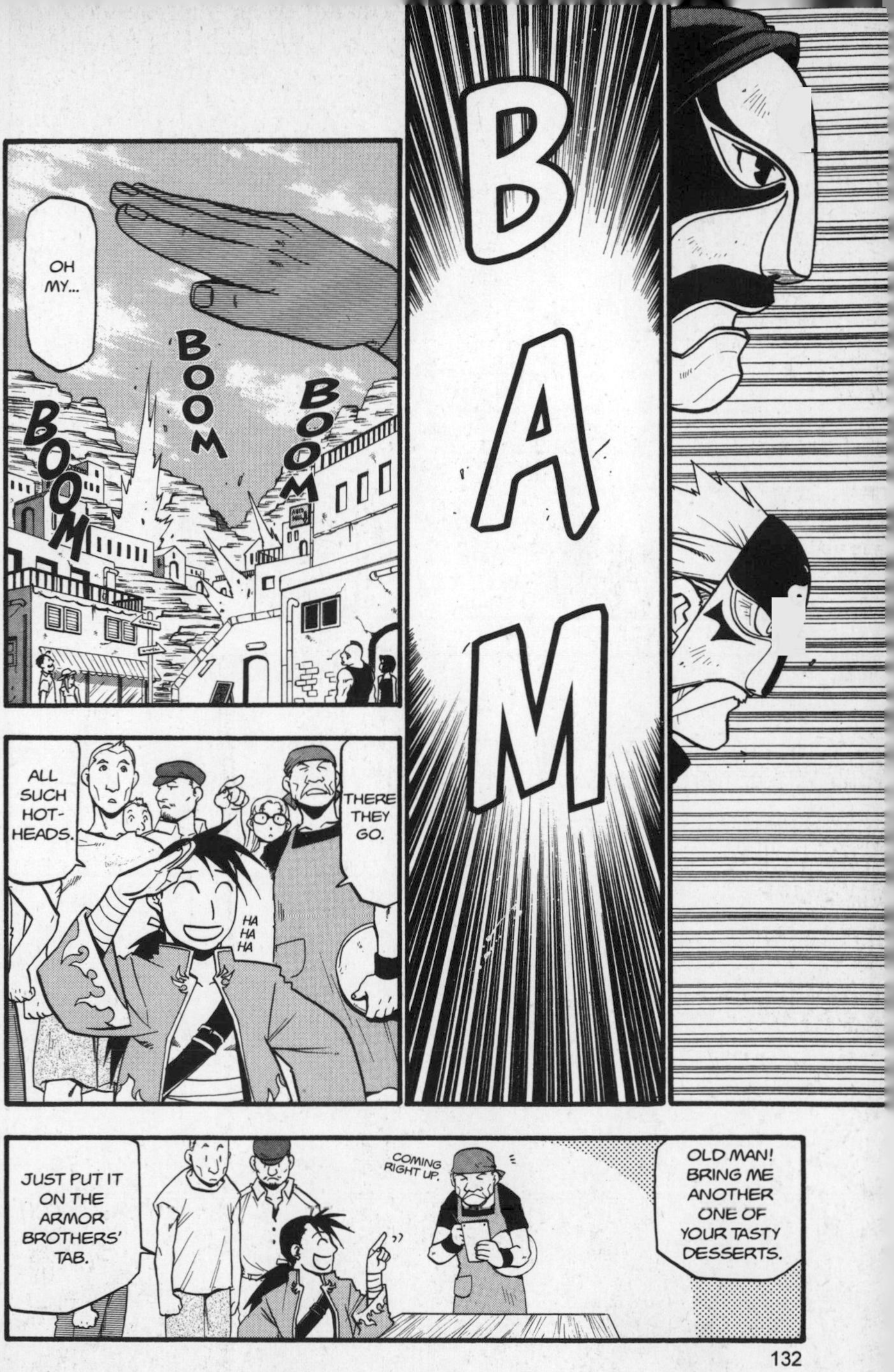
BAM
OH MY...
BOOM
BOOM
BOOM
THERE THEY GO.
ALL SUCH HOT-HEADS.
HA HA HA
OLD MAN! BRING ME ANOTHER ONE OF YOUR TASTY DESSERTS.
COMING RIGHT UP.
JUST PUT IT ON THE ARMOR BROTHERS' TAB.

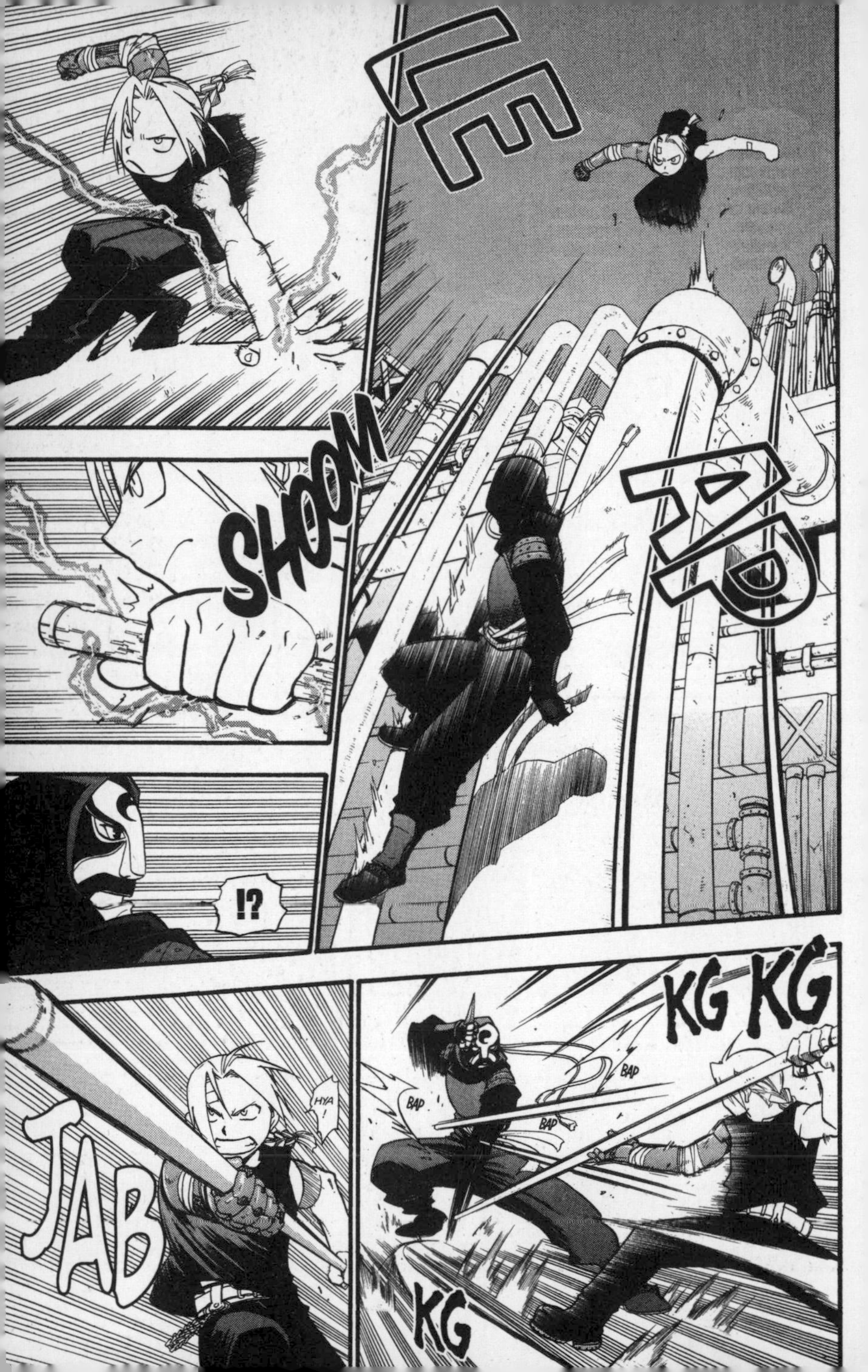
LE
AP
SHOOM
!?
KG KG
BAP
BAP
BAP
KG
HYA!
JAB

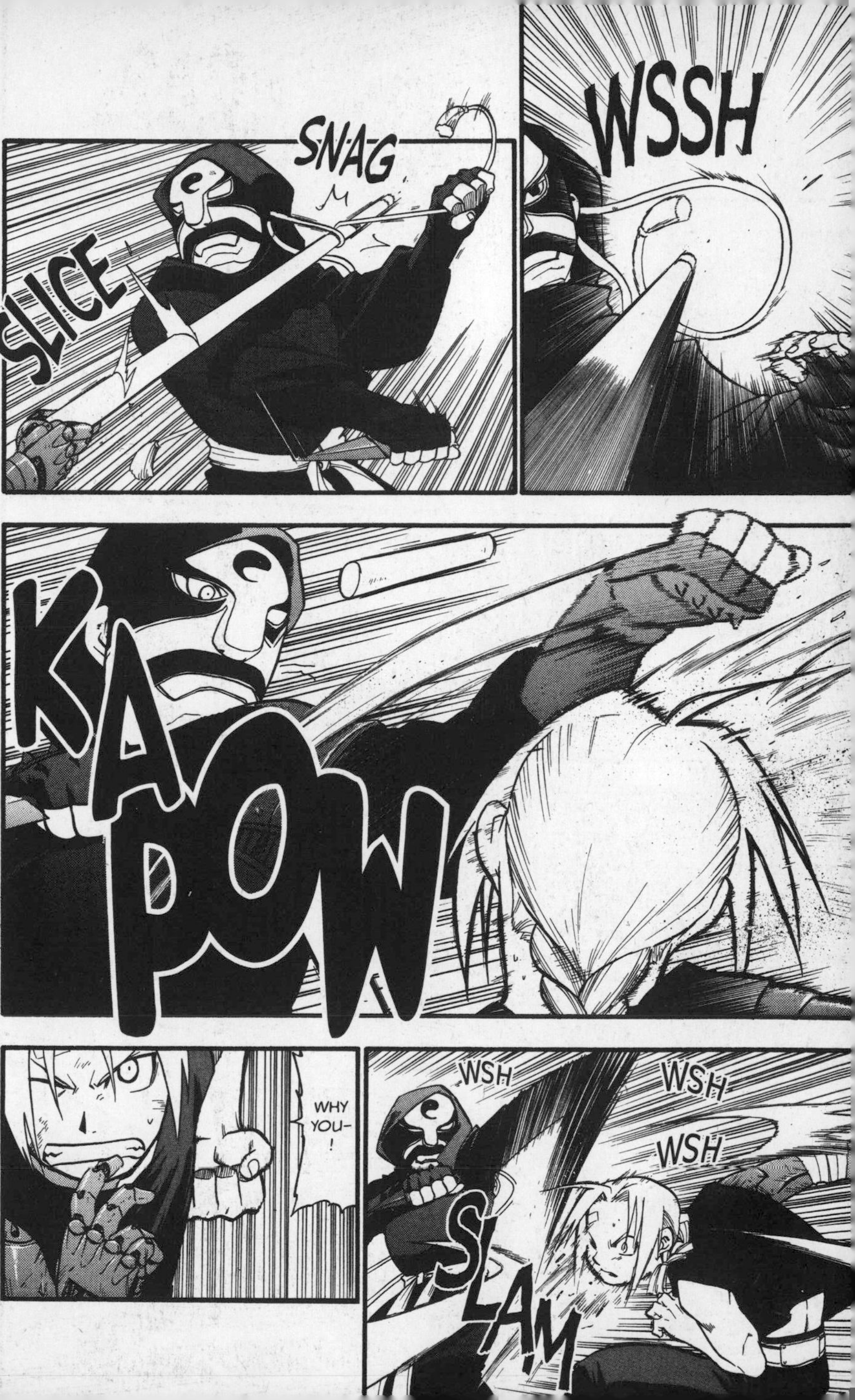
WSSH
SNAG
SLICE
KA POW
WSH
WSH
WSH
SLAM
WHY YOU-!

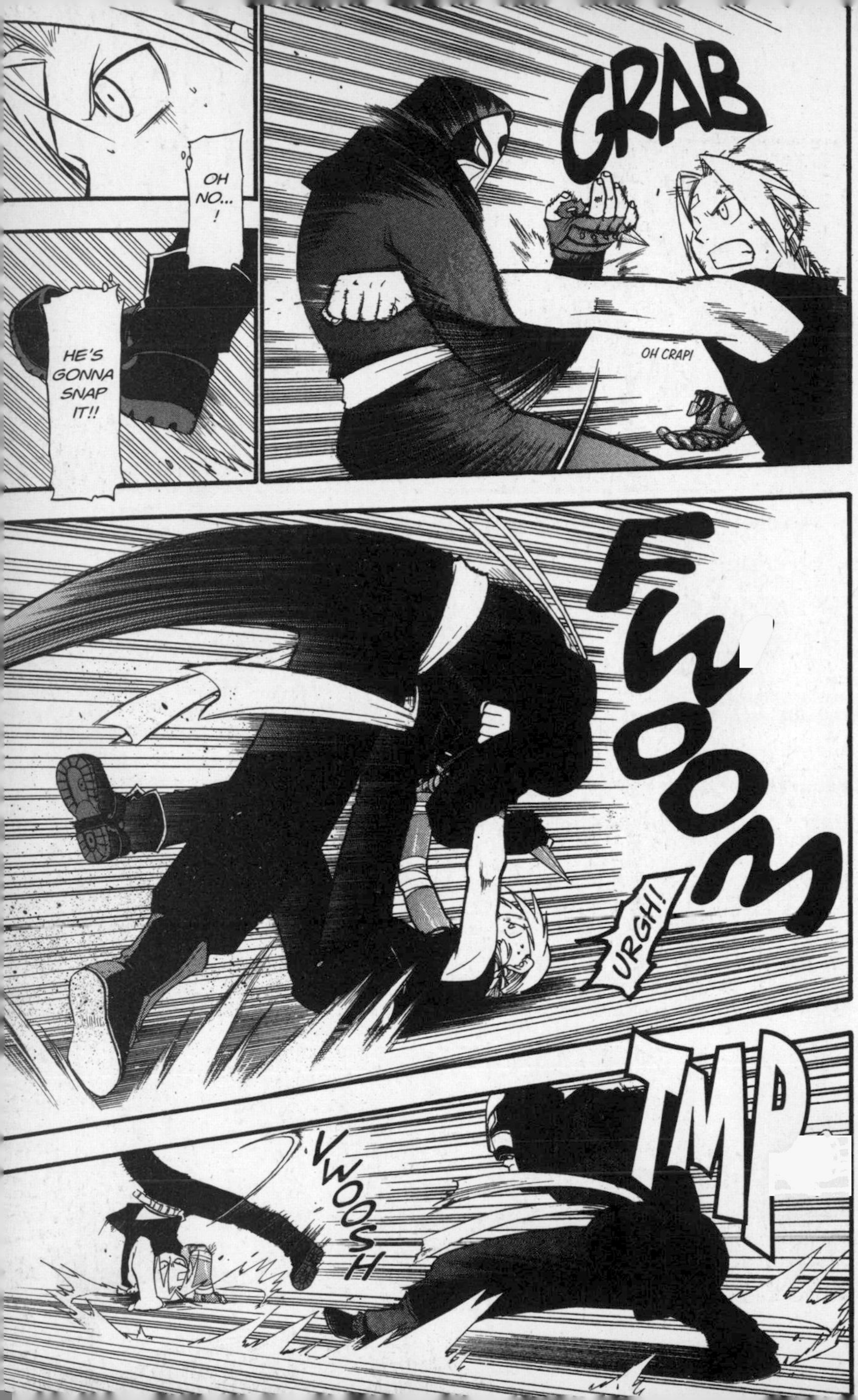
GRAB
OH CRAP!
OH NO... !
HE'S GONNA SNAP IT!!
FWOOM
URGH!
TMP
VWOOSH

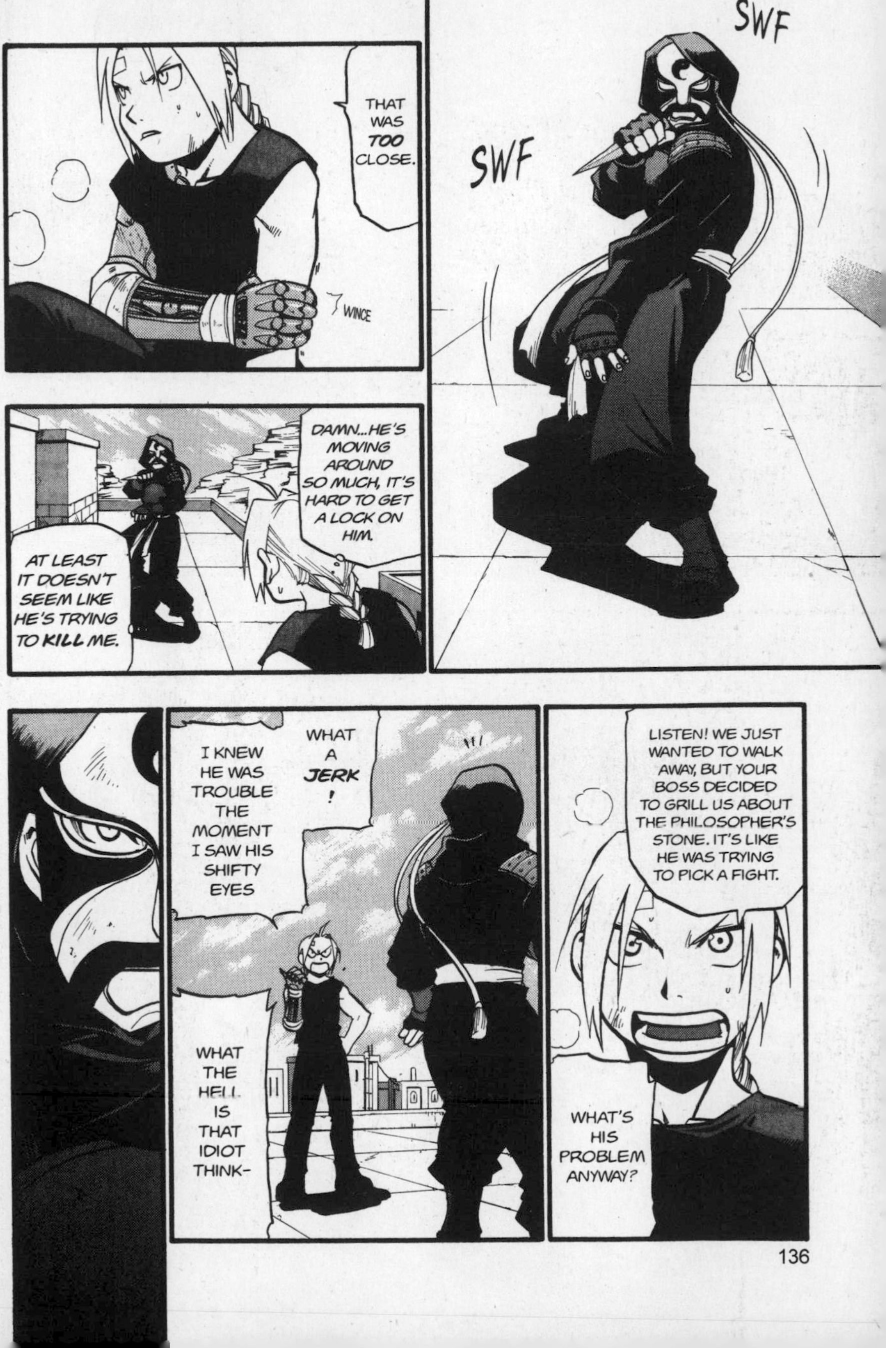
SWF
SWF
THAT WAS TOO CLOSE.
WINCE
DAMN...HE'S MOVING AROUND SO MUCH, IT'S HARD TO GET A LOCK ON HIM.
AT LEAST IT DOESN'T SEEM LIKE HE'S TRYING TO KILL ME.
LISTEN! WE JUST WANTED TO WALK AWAY, BUT YOUR BOSS DECIDED TO GRILL US ABOUT THE PHILOSOPHER'S STONE. IT'S LIKE HE WAS TRYING TO PICK A FIGHT.
WHAT'S HIS PROBLEM ANYWAY?
WHAT A JERK!
I KNEW HE WAS TROUBLE THE MOMENT I SAW HIS SHIFTY EYES
WHAT THE HELL IS THAT IDIOT THINK-

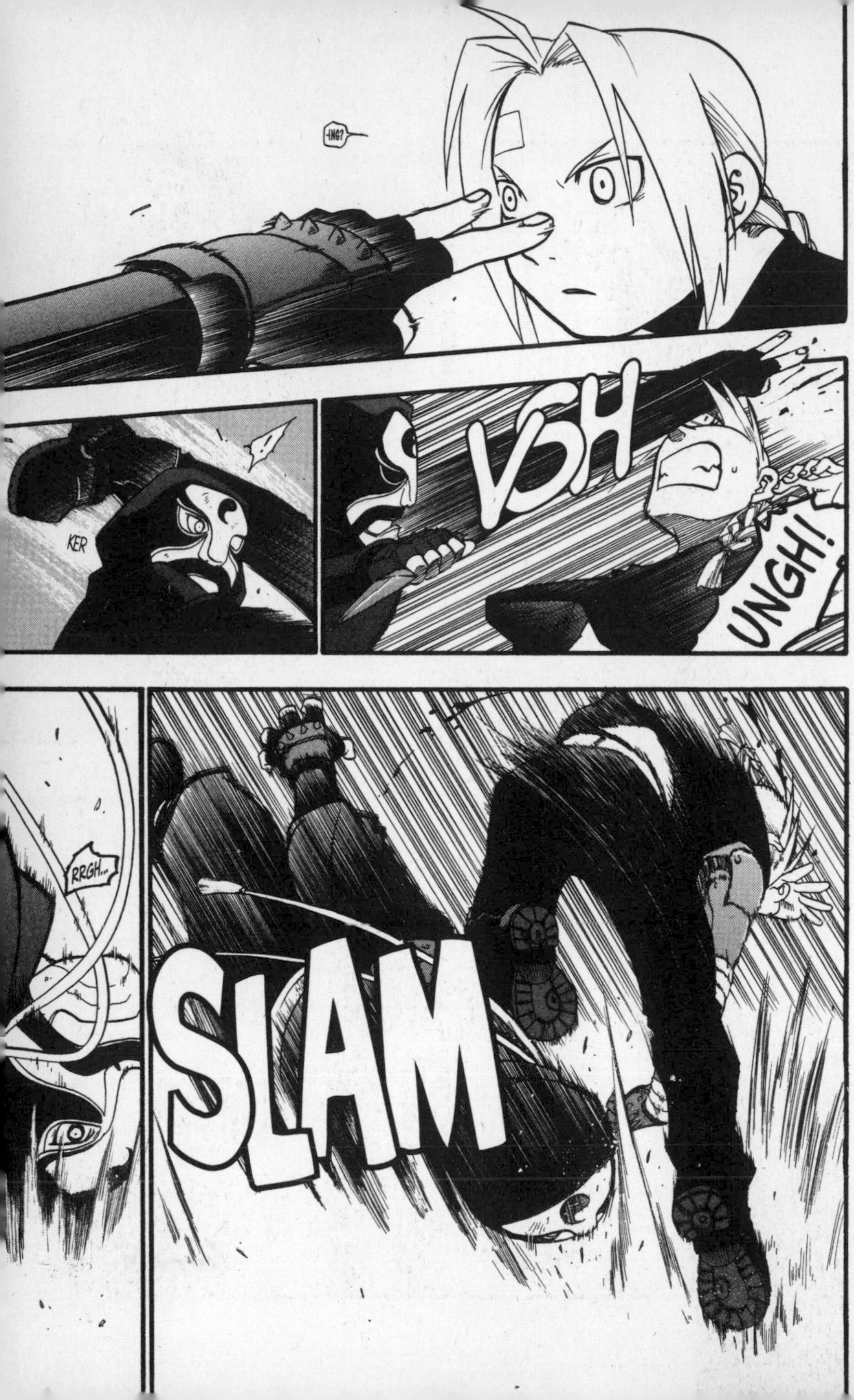
-ING?
VSH
UNGH!
KER
SLAM
RRGH...

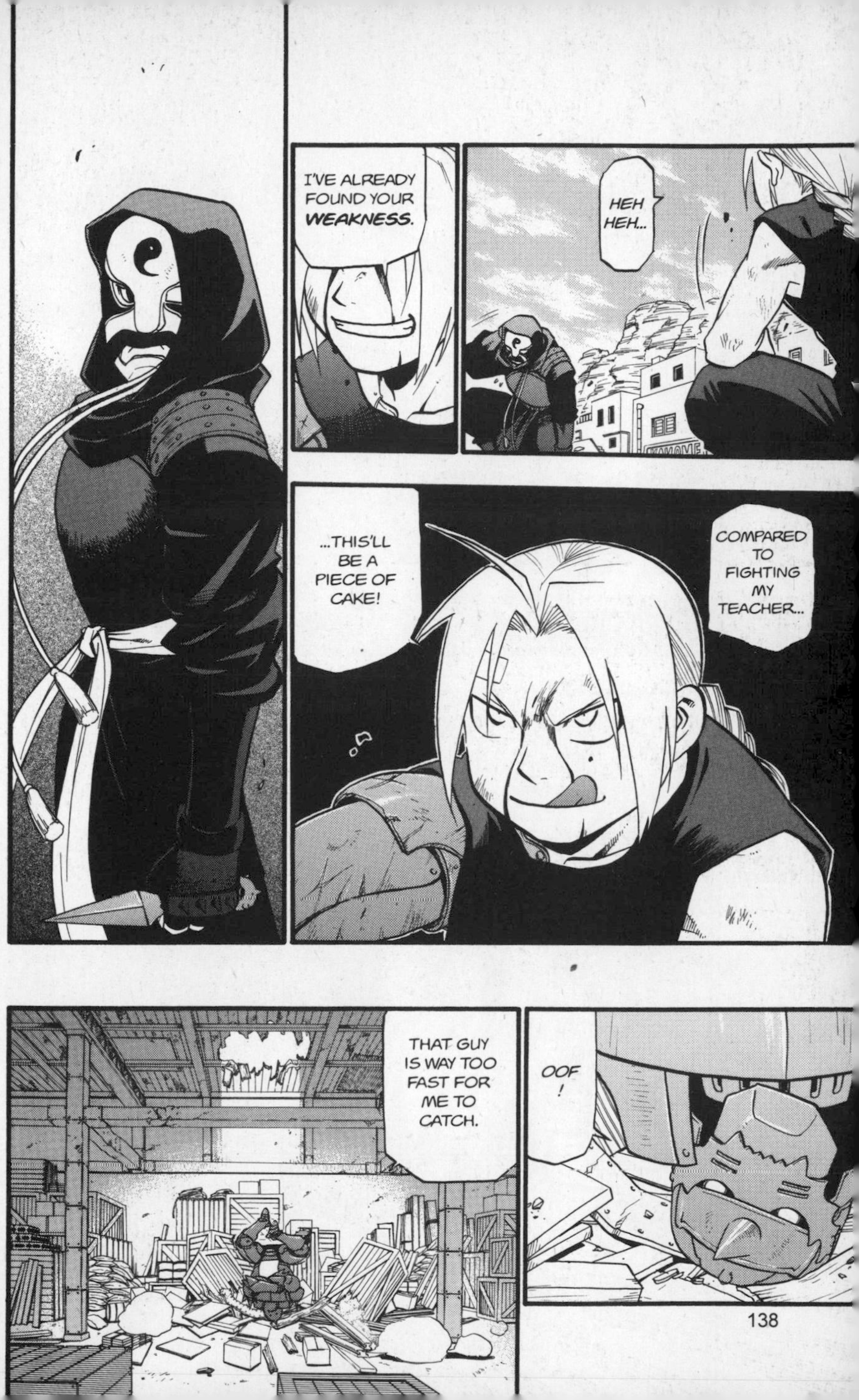
HEH HEH...
I'VE ALREADY FOUND YOUR **WEAKNESS**.
COMPARED TO FIGHTING MY TEACHER...
...THIS'LL BE A PIECE OF CAKE!
OOF!
THAT GUY IS WAY TOO FAST FOR ME TO CATCH.

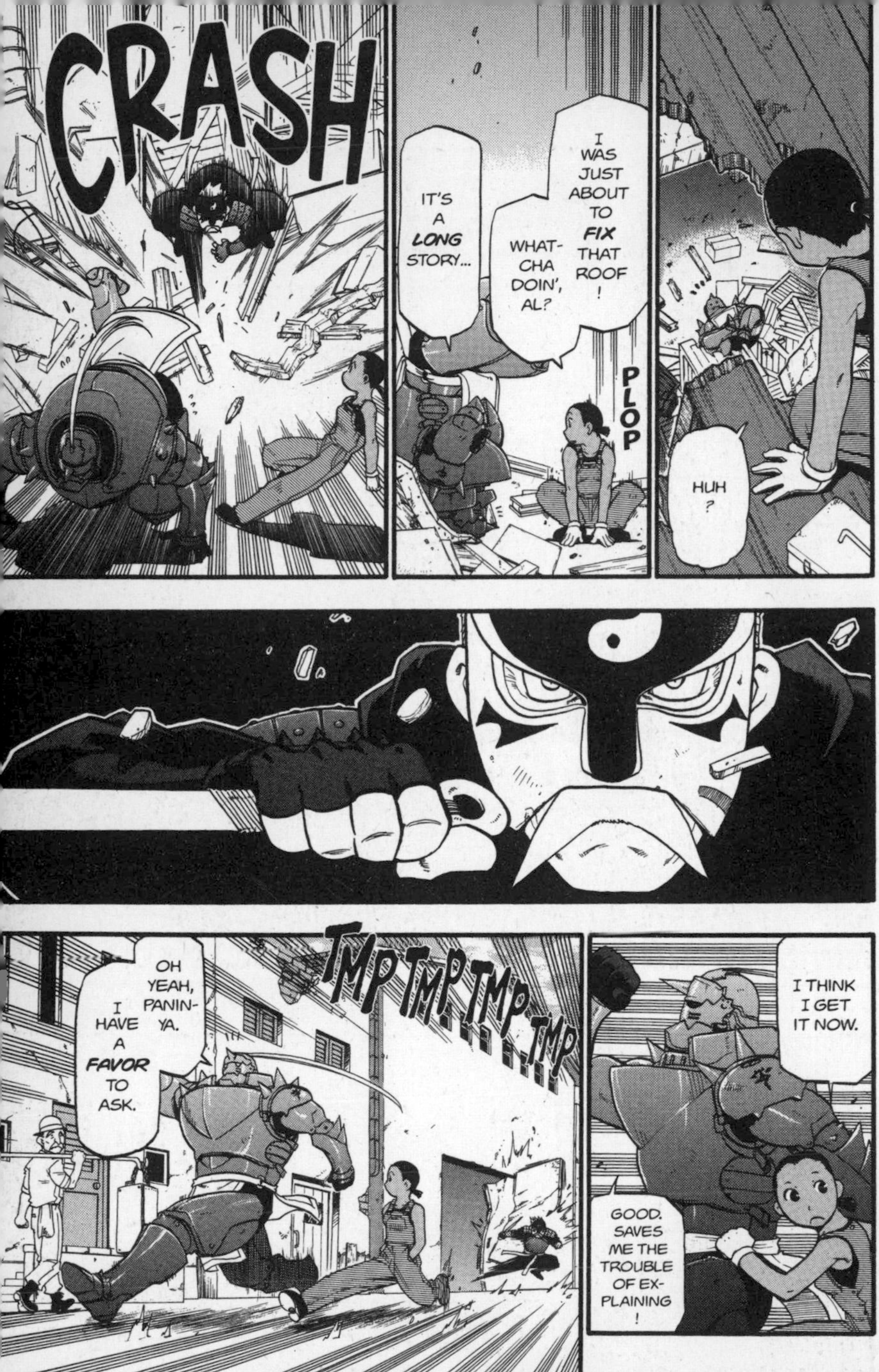
HUH ?
I WAS JUST ABOUT TO FIX THAT ROOF !
WHAT-CHA DOIN', AL?
IT'S A LONG STORY...
PLOP
CRASH
I THINK I GET IT NOW.
GOOD. SAVES ME THE TROUBLE OF EX-PLAINING !
TMP TMP TMP TMP TMP
OH YEAH, PANIN-YA.
I HAVE A FAVOR TO ASK.

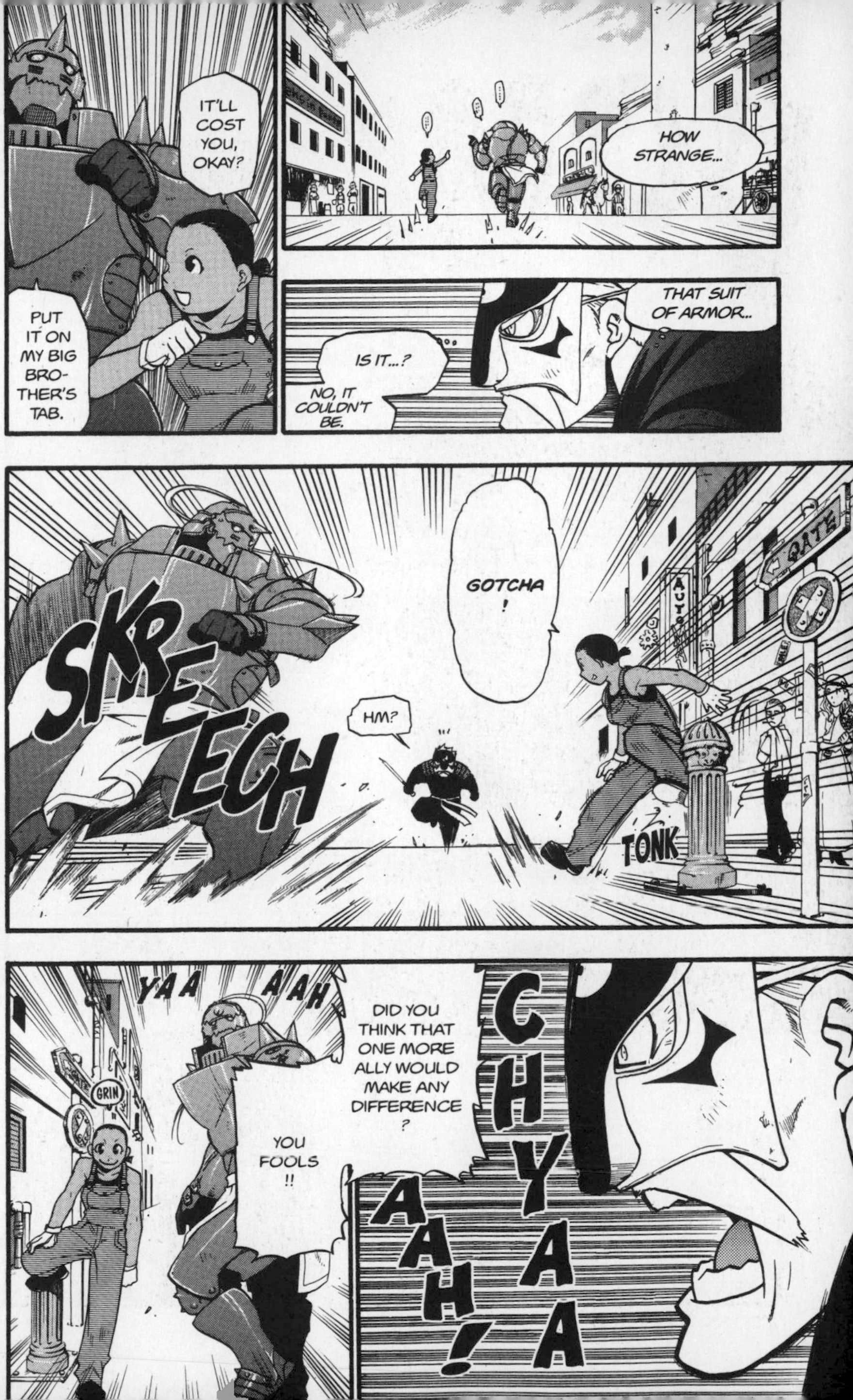
HOW STRANGE...
THAT SUIT OF ARMOR..
IS IT...?
NO, IT COULDN'T BE.
IT'LL COST YOU, OKAY?
PUT IT ON MY BIG BRO-THER'S TAB.
GOTCHA!
TONK
HM?
SKREECH
CHYAAA
AAH!
DID YOU THINK THAT ONE MORE ALLY WOULD MAKE ANY DIFFERENCE?
YOU FOOLS!!
YAA AAH
GRIN

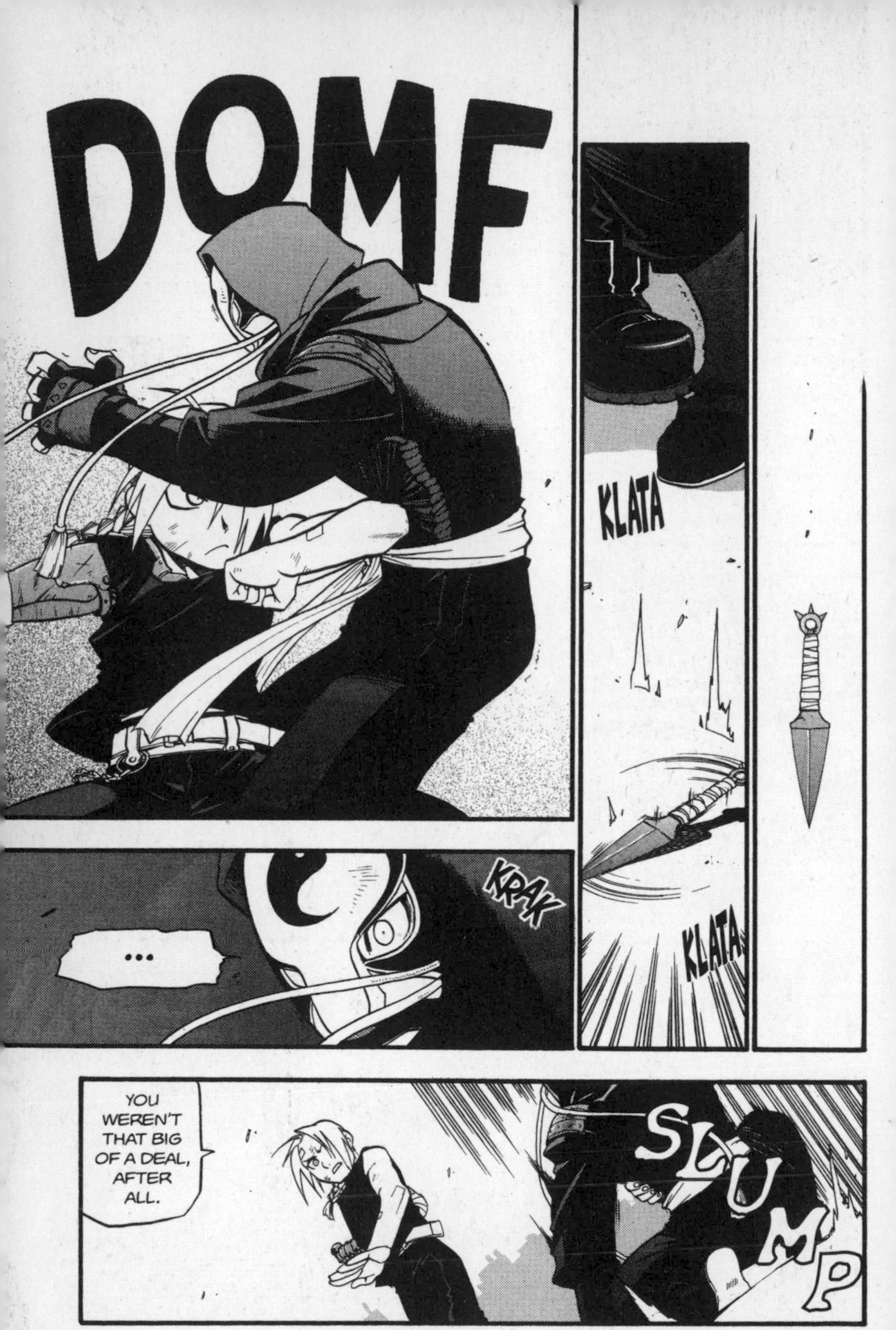
KLATA
KLATA
DOMF
KRAK
...
SLUMP
YOU WEREN'T THAT BIG OF A DEAL, AFTER ALL.

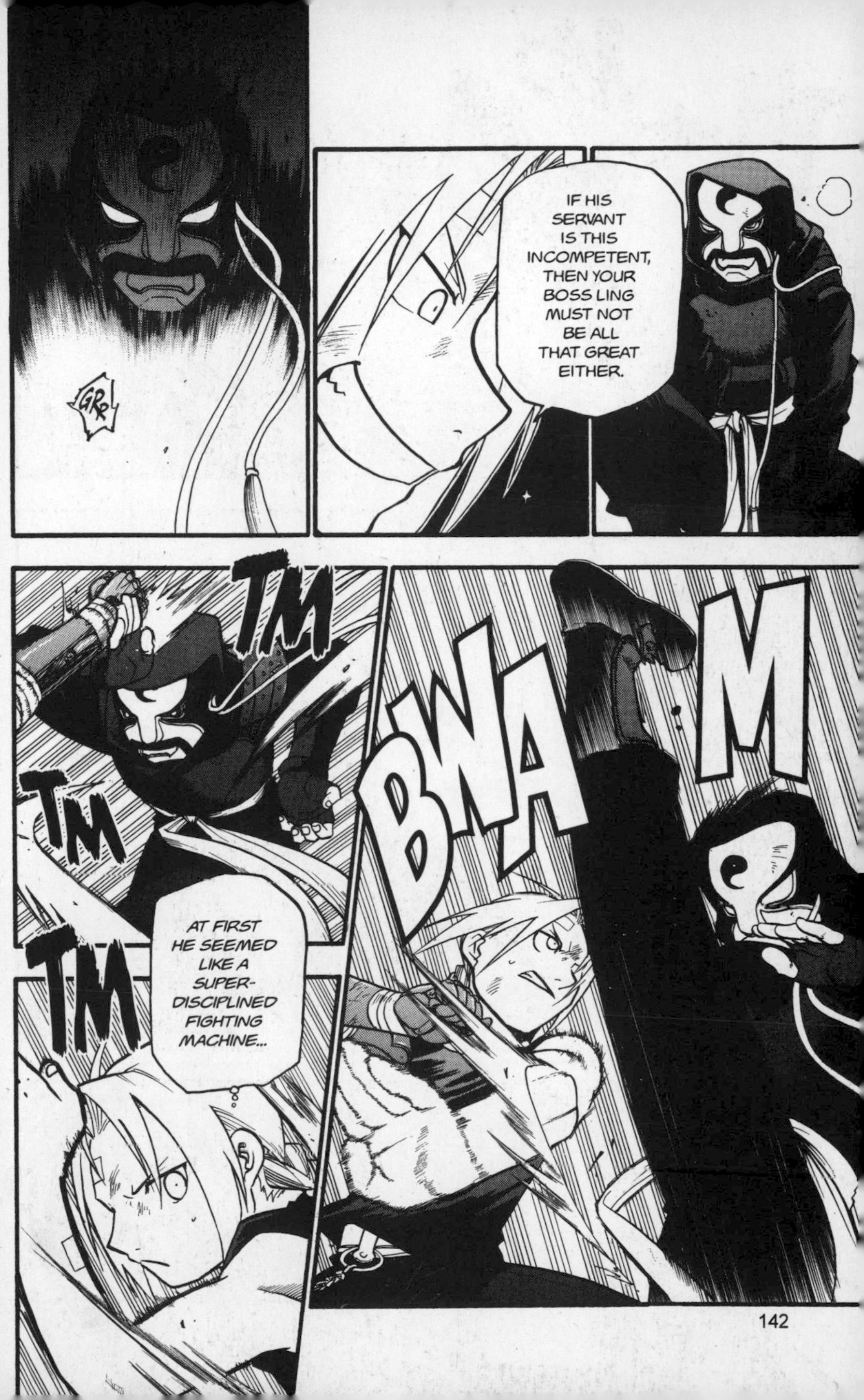
IF HIS SERVANT IS THIS INCOMPETENT, THEN YOUR BOSS LING MUST NOT BE ALL THAT GREAT EITHER.
GRR
BWAM
TM
TM
TM
AT FIRST HE SEEMED LIKE A SUPER-DISCIPLINED FIGHTING MACHINE...

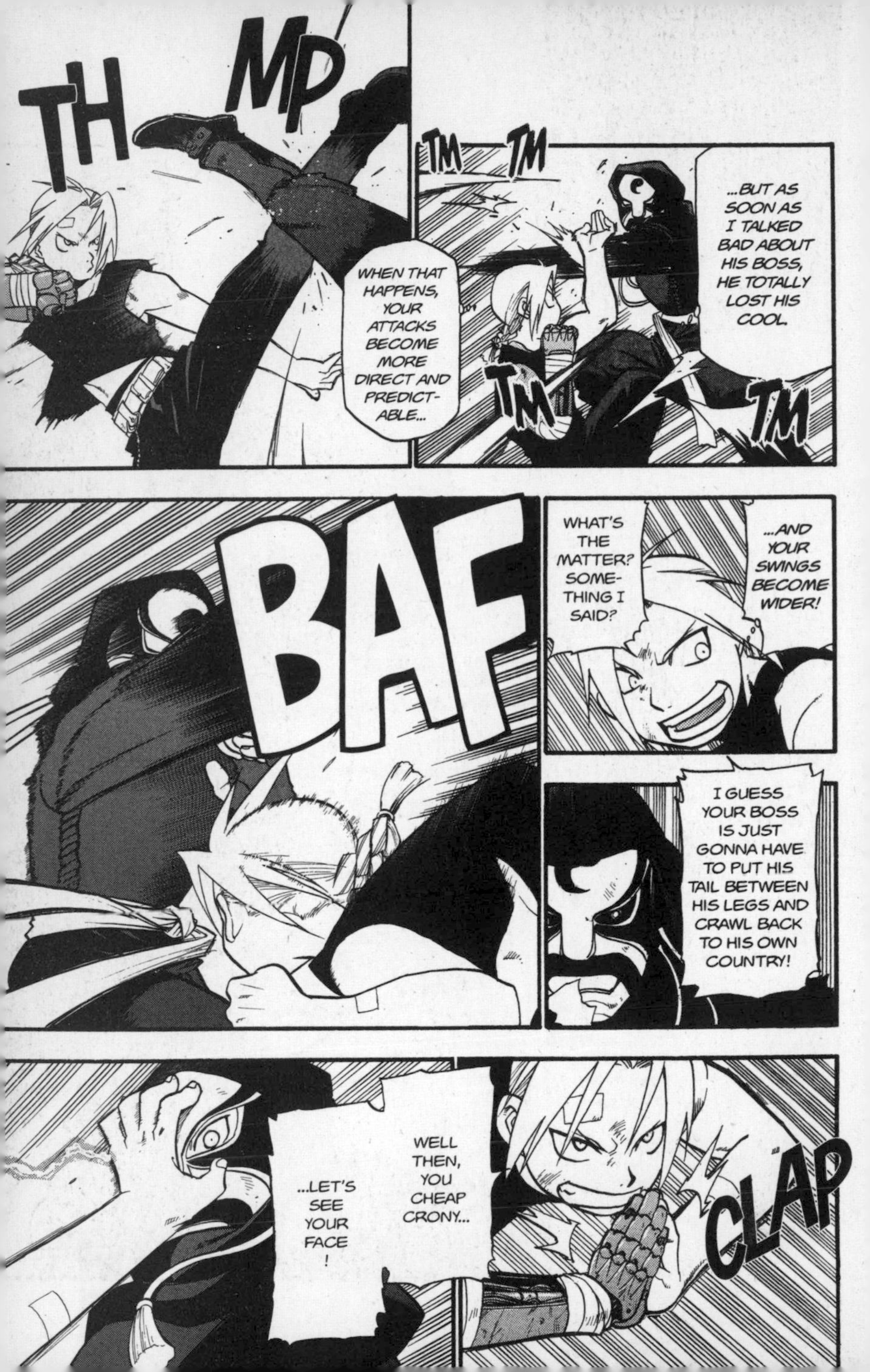
TM TM
...BUT AS SOON AS I TALKED BAD ABOUT HIS BOSS, HE TOTALLY LOST HIS COOL.
TM
TM
WHEN THAT HAPPENS, YOUR ATTACKS BECOME MORE DIRECT AND PREDICT-ABLE...
THMP
...AND YOUR SWINGS BECOME WIDER!
WHAT'S THE MATTER? SOME-THING I SAID?
I GUESS YOUR BOSS IS JUST GONNA HAVE TO PUT HIS TAIL BETWEEN HIS LEGS AND CRAWL BACK TO HIS OWN COUNTRY!
BAF
CLAP
WELL THEN, YOU CHEAP CRONY...
...LET'S SEE YOUR FACE!

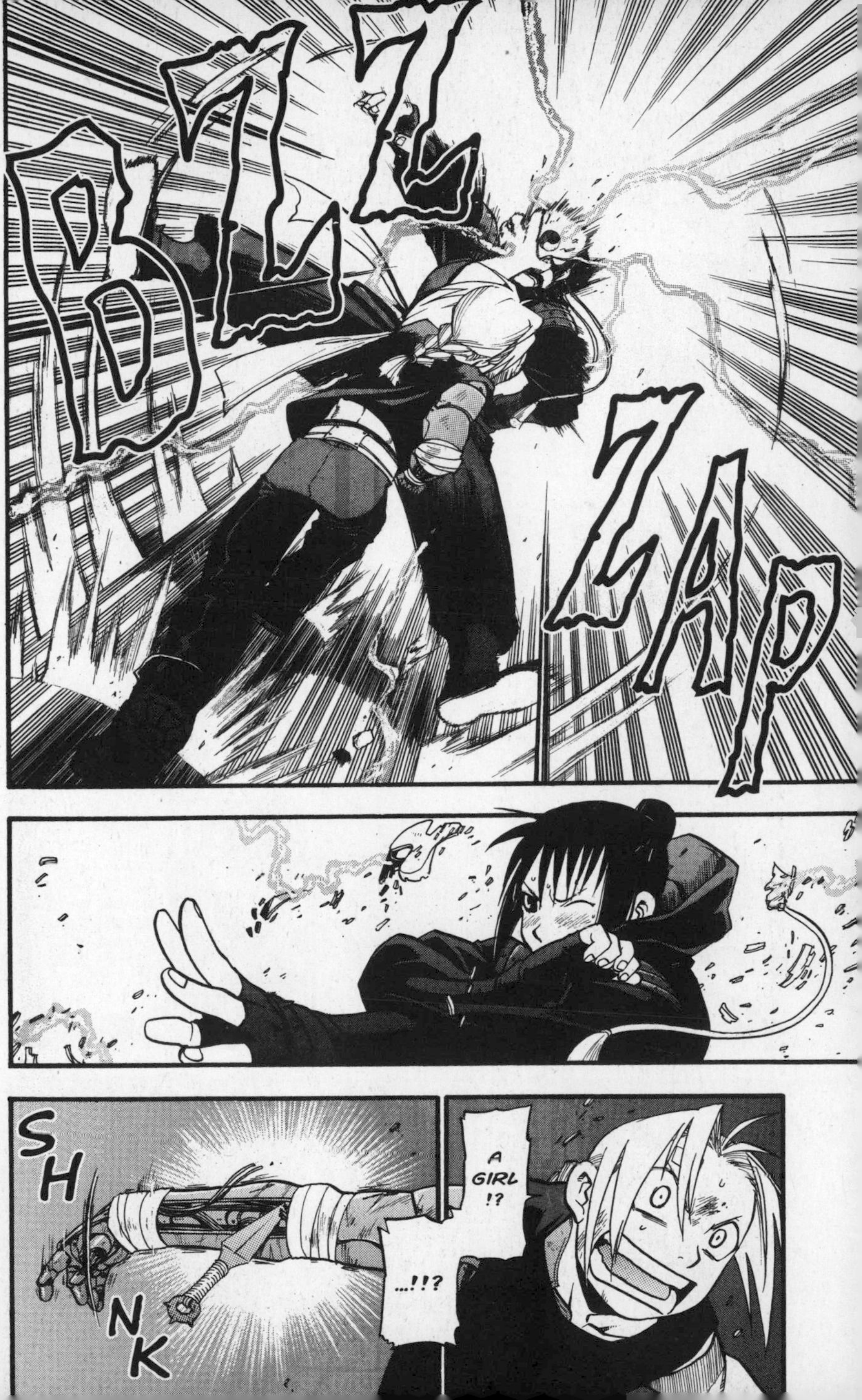
ZAP
A GIRL !?
...!!?
SHNK

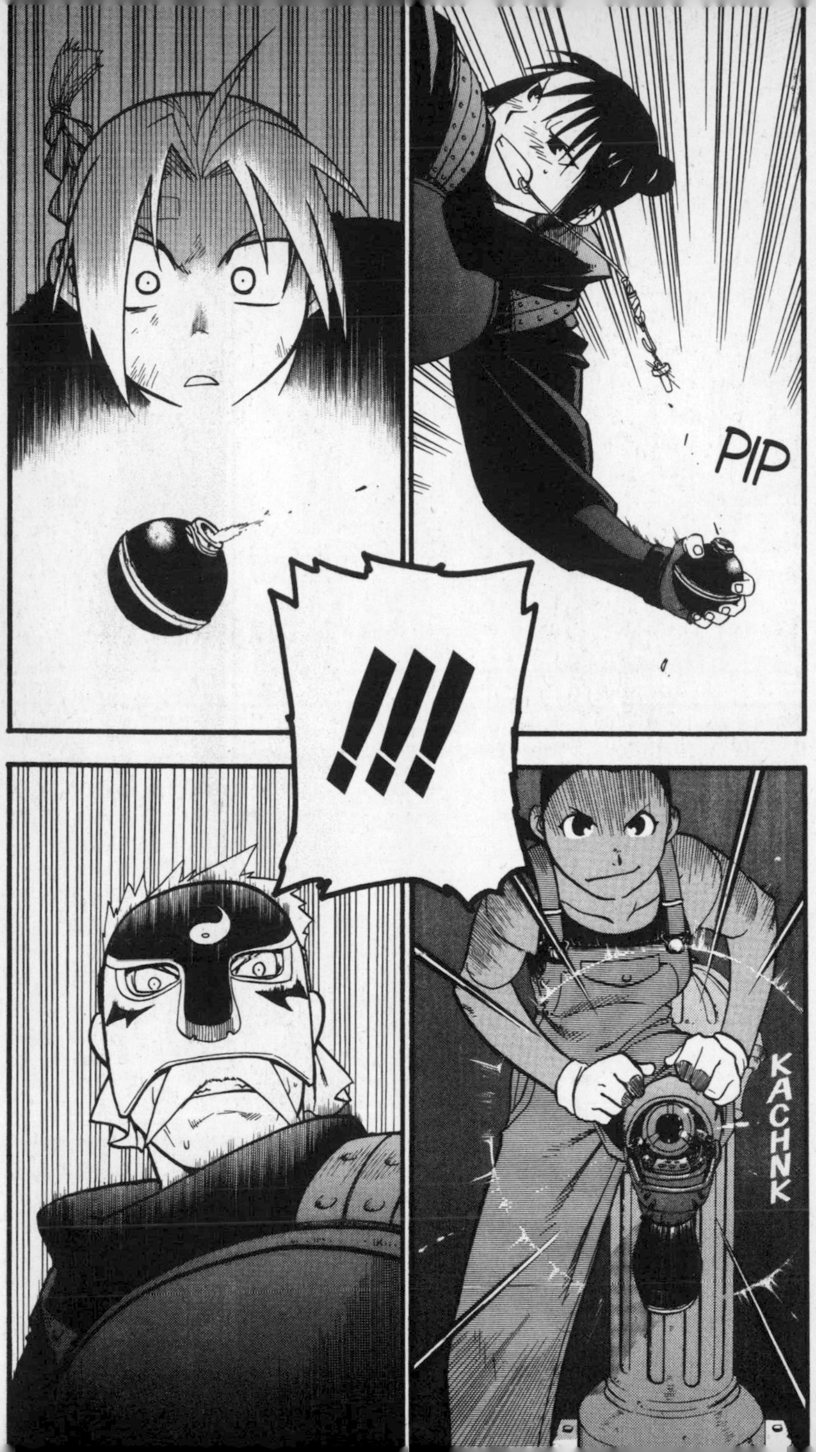
PIP
!!!
KACHNK

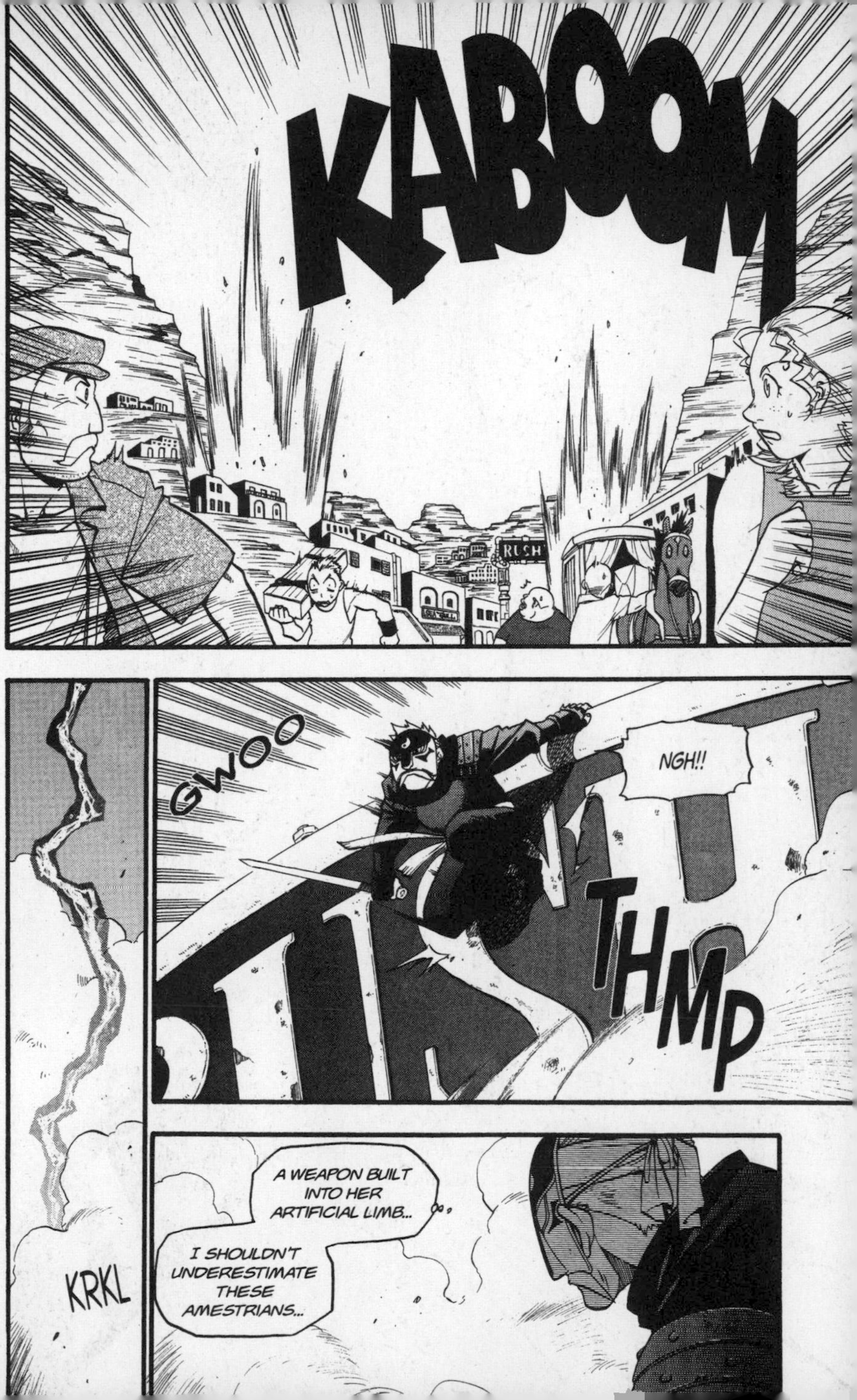
KABOOM
RUSH
NGH!!
GWOO
THMP
A WEAPON BUILT INTO HER ARTIFICIAL LIMB...
I SHOULDN'T UNDERESTIMATE THESE AMESTRIANS...
KRKL

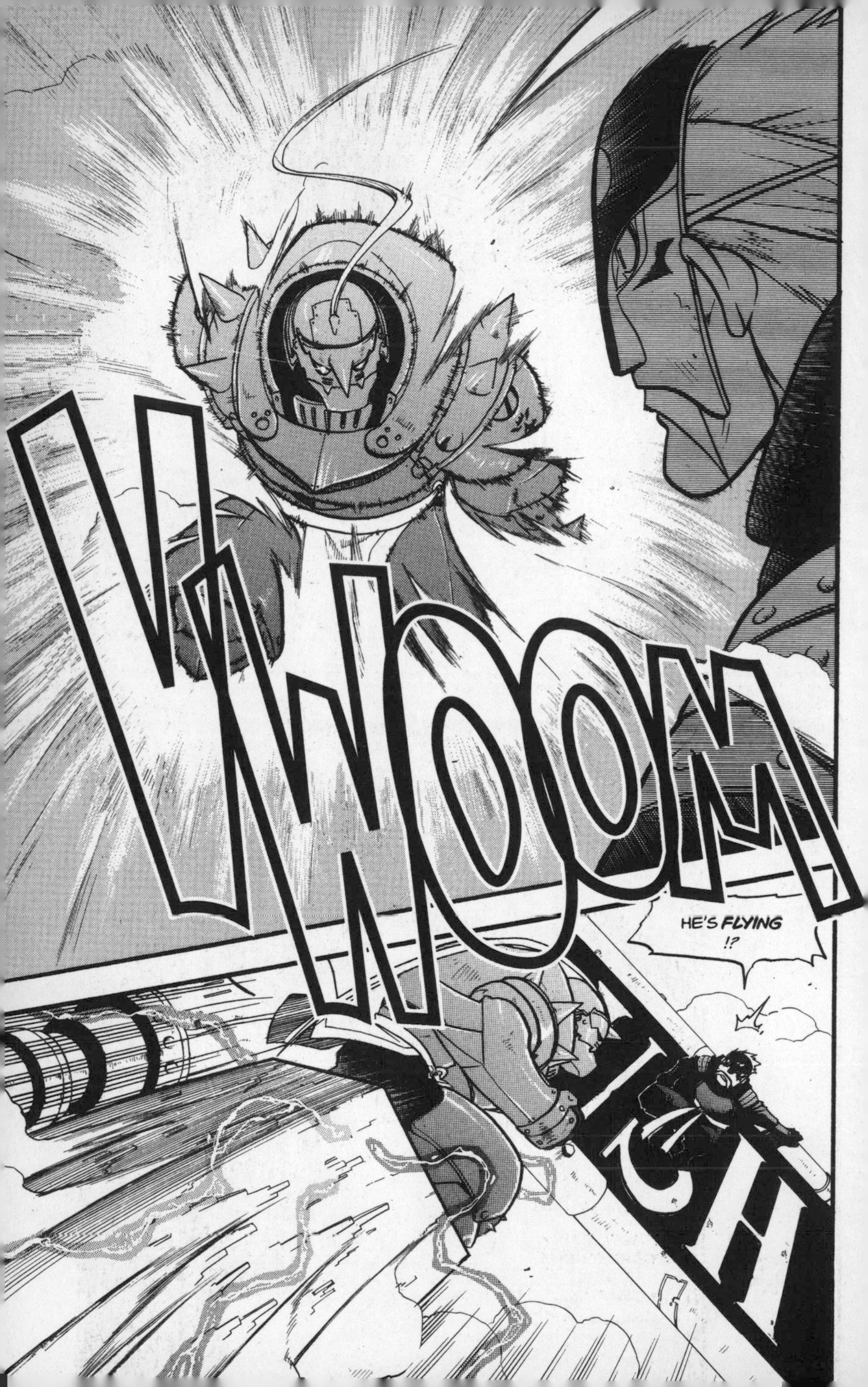
VWOOM
HE'S FLYING !?

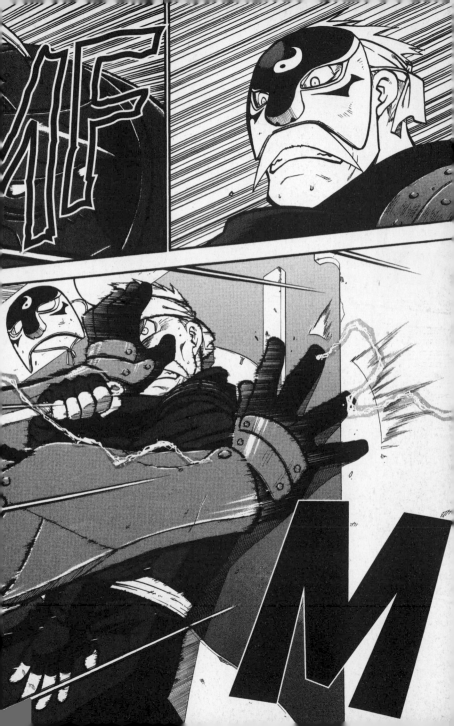

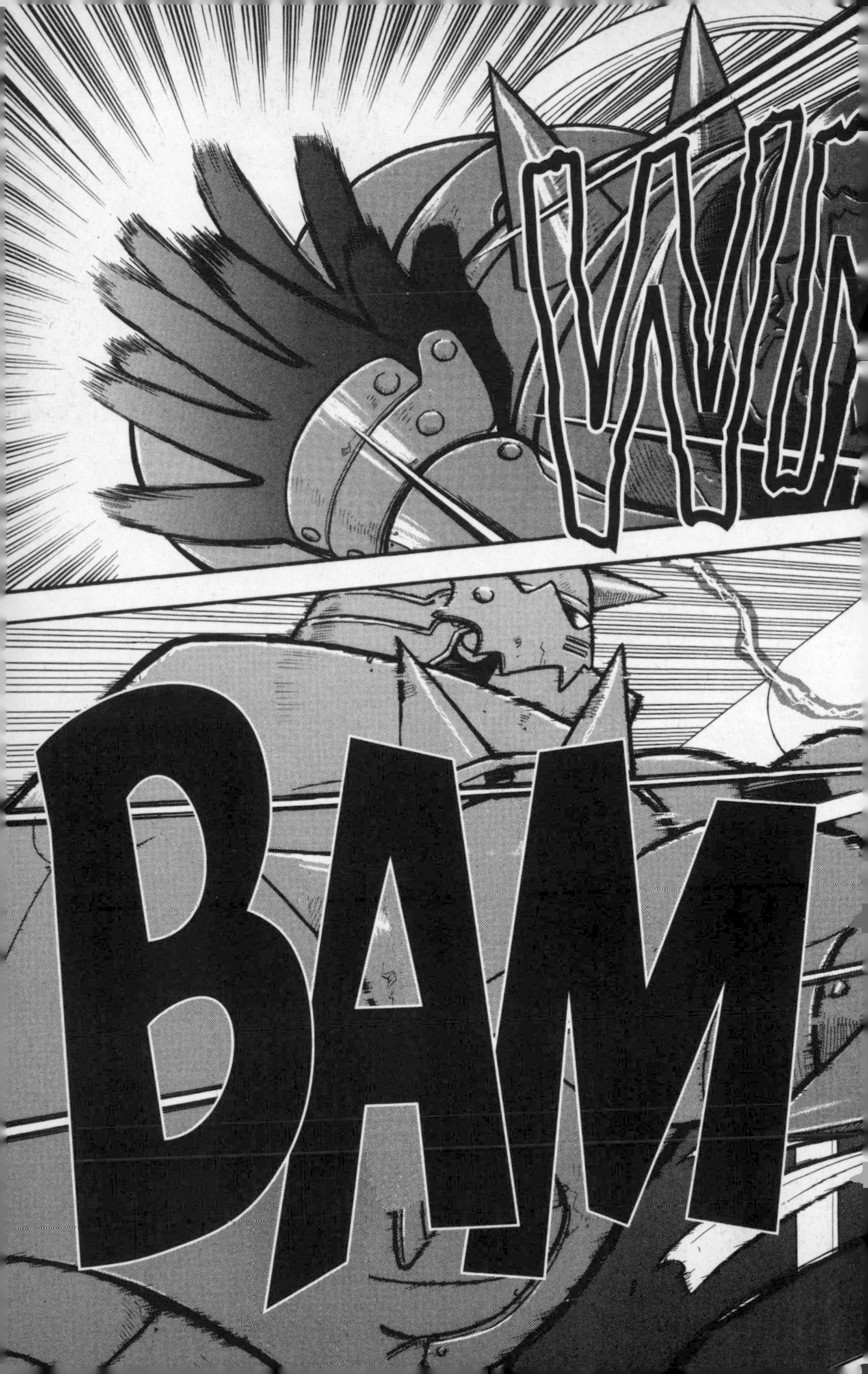
BAM

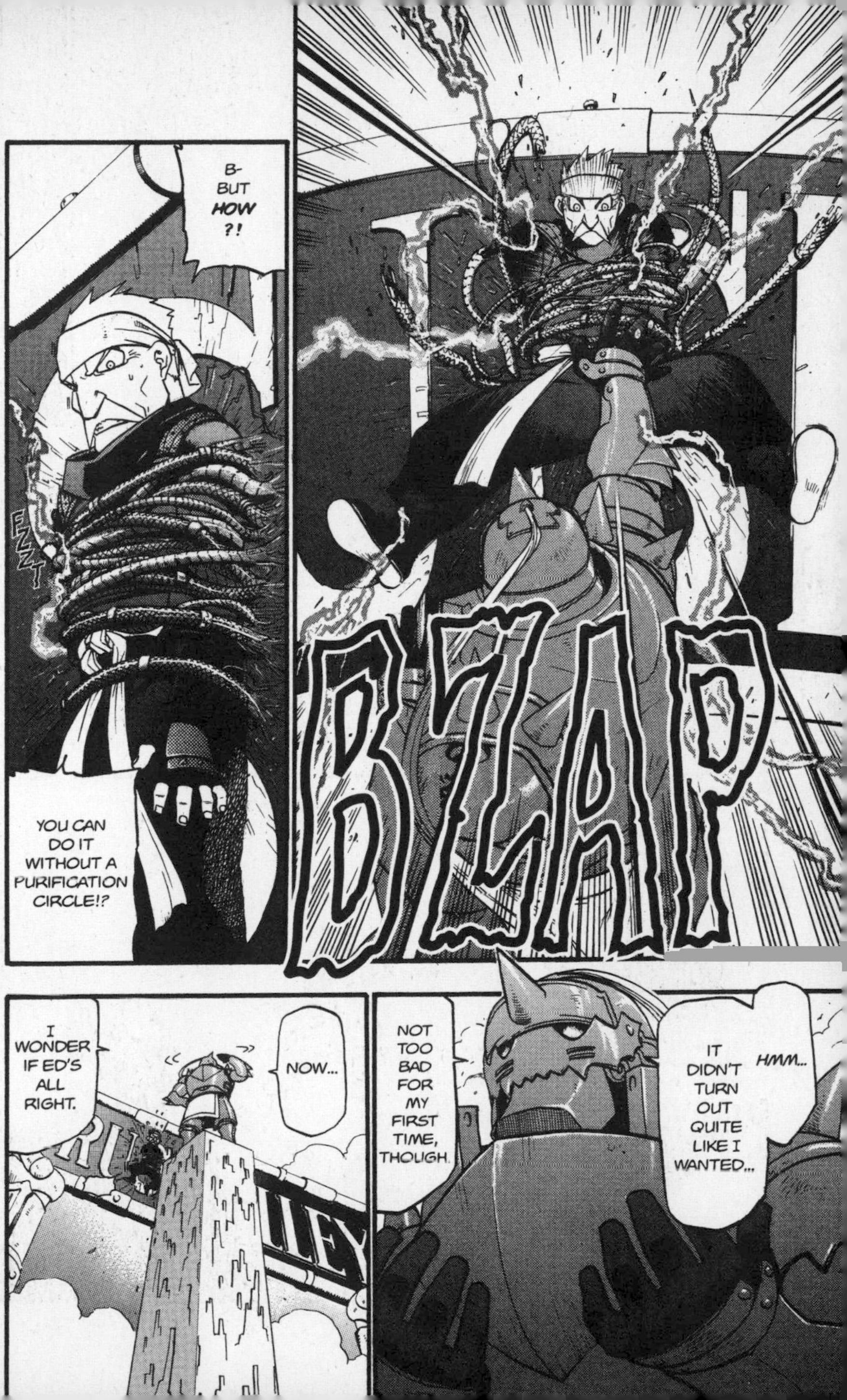
BZZAP
B-BUT HOW?!
FZZT
YOU CAN DO IT WITHOUT A PURIFICATION CIRCLE!?
HMM...
IT DIDN'T TURN OUT QUITE LIKE I WANTED...
NOT TOO BAD FOR MY FIRST TIME, THOUGH.
NOW...
I WONDER IF ED'S ALL RIGHT.

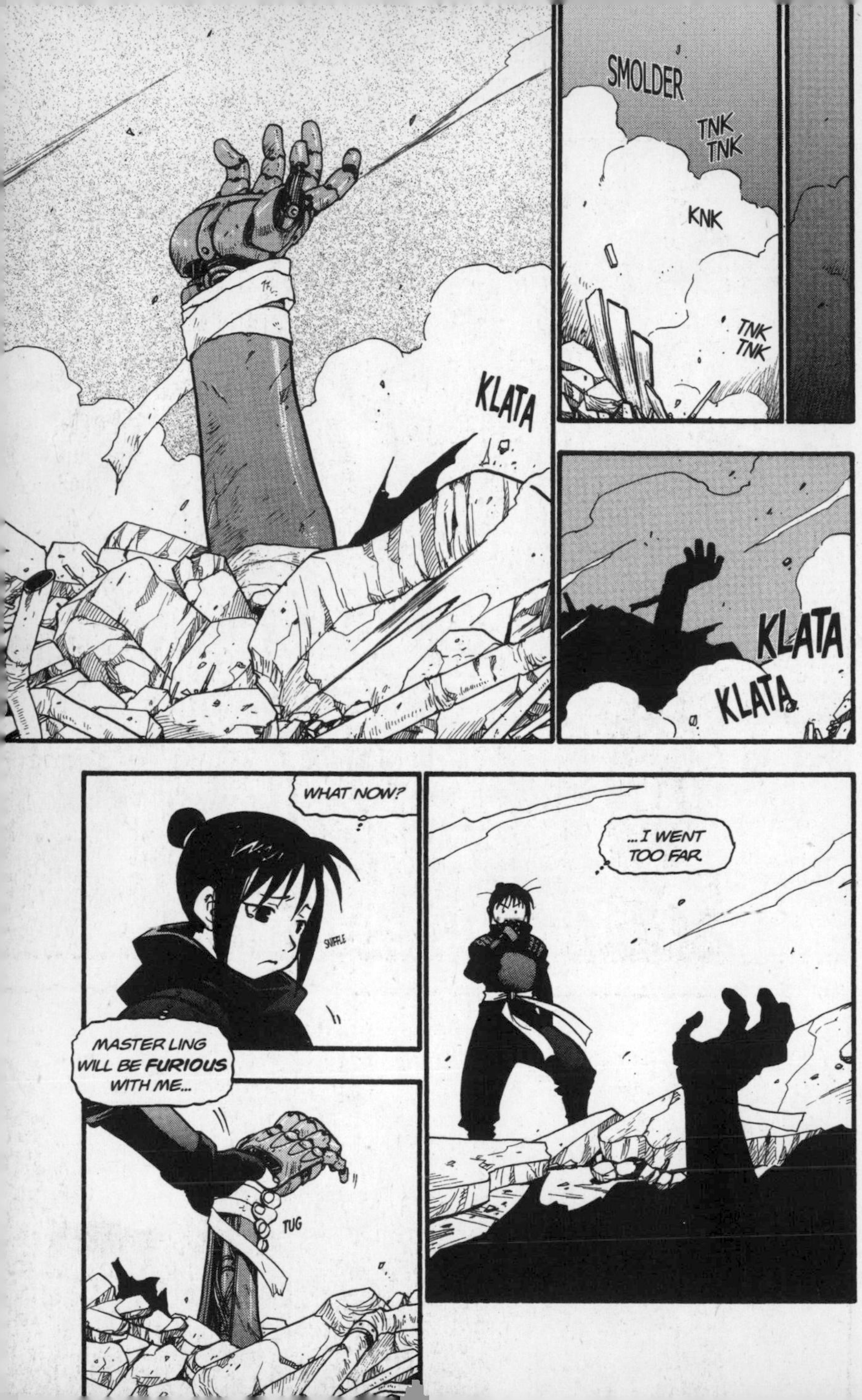
SMOLDER
TNK TNK
KNK
TNK TNK
KLATA
KLATA
KLATA
...I WENT TOO FAR
WHAT NOW?
SNIFFLE
MASTER LING WILL BE FURIOUS WITH ME...
TUG

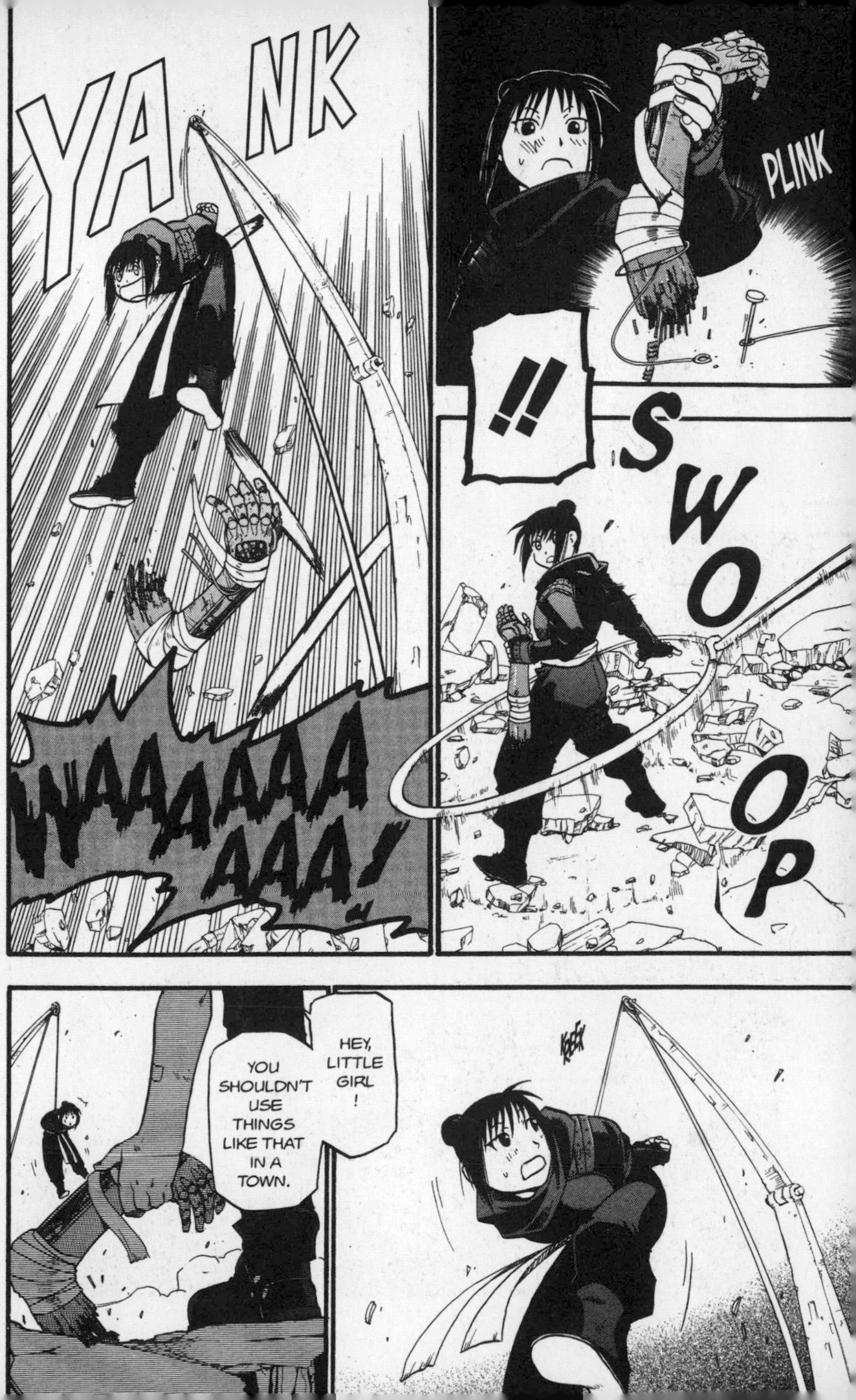
PLINK
!!
SWOOP
YANK
WAAAAAAAAA!
HEY, LITTLE GIRL!
YOU SHOULDN'T USE THINGS LIKE THAT IN A TOWN.

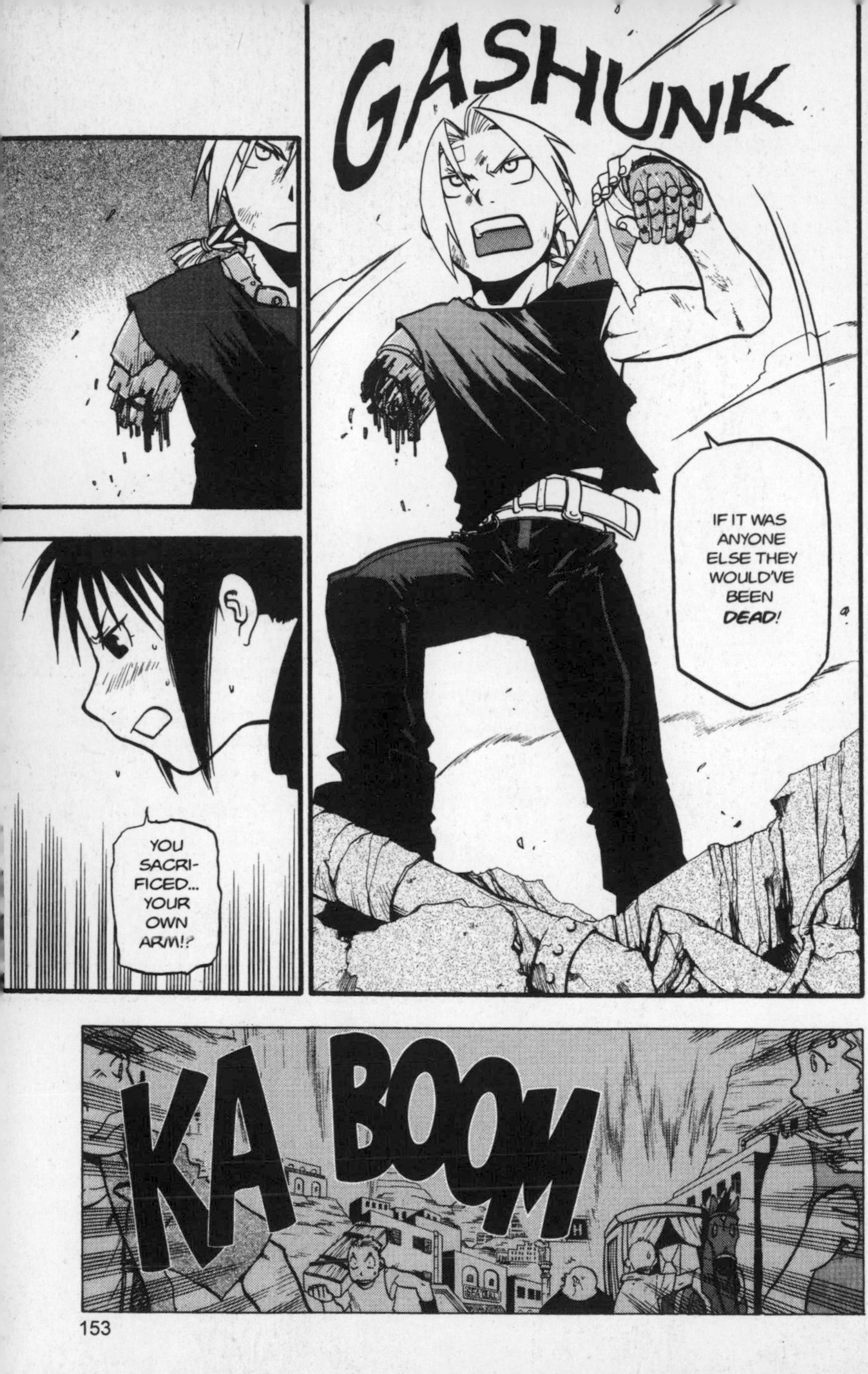
GASHUNK
IF IT WAS ANYONE ELSE THEY WOULD'VE BEEN DEAD!
YOU SACRIFICED... YOUR OWN ARM!?
KA BOOM

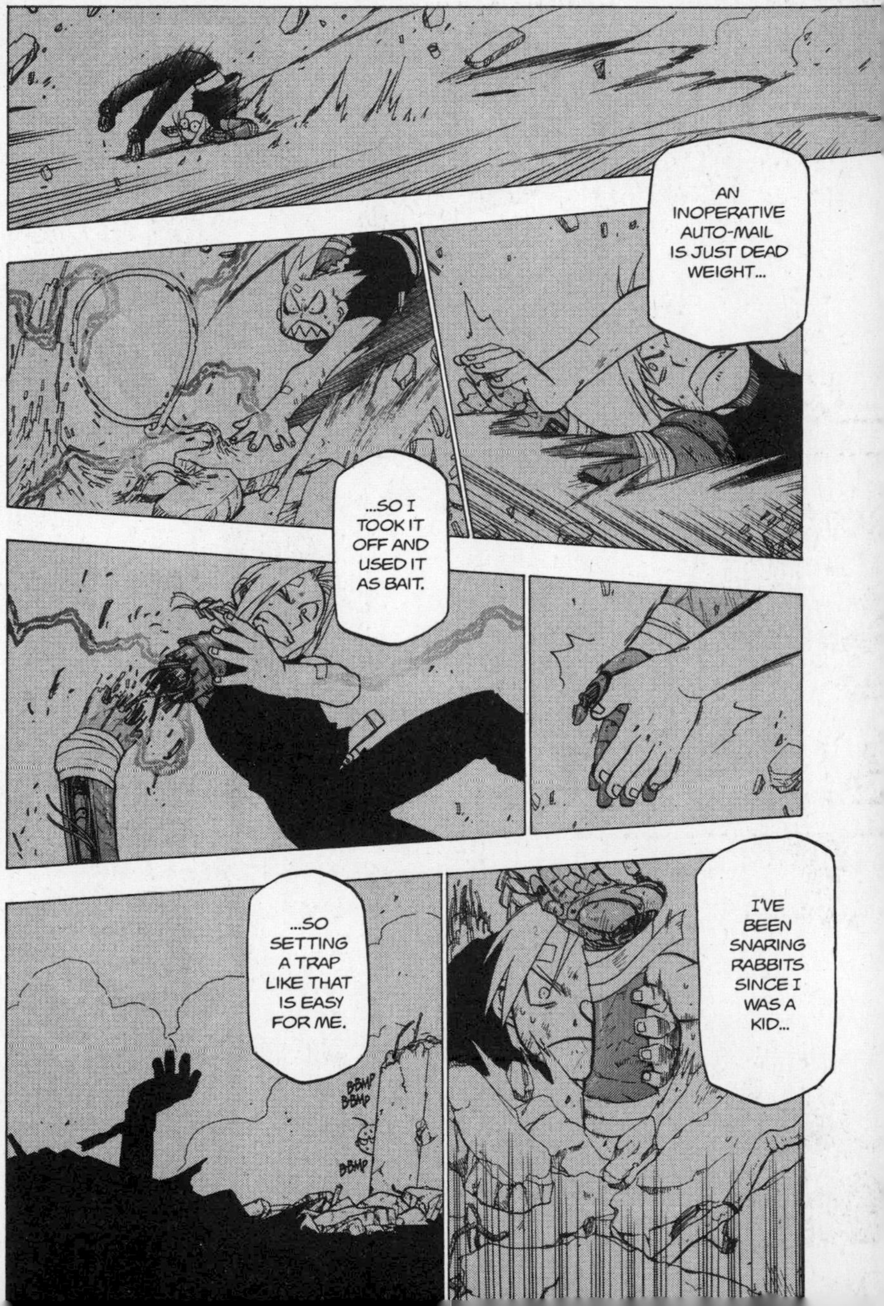
AN INOPERATIVE AUTO-MAIL IS JUST DEAD WEIGHT...
...SO I TOOK IT OFF AND USED IT AS BAIT.
I'VE BEEN SNARING RABBITS SINCE I WAS A KID...
...SO SETTING A TRAP LIKE THAT IS EASY FOR ME.
BBMP
BBMP
BBMP

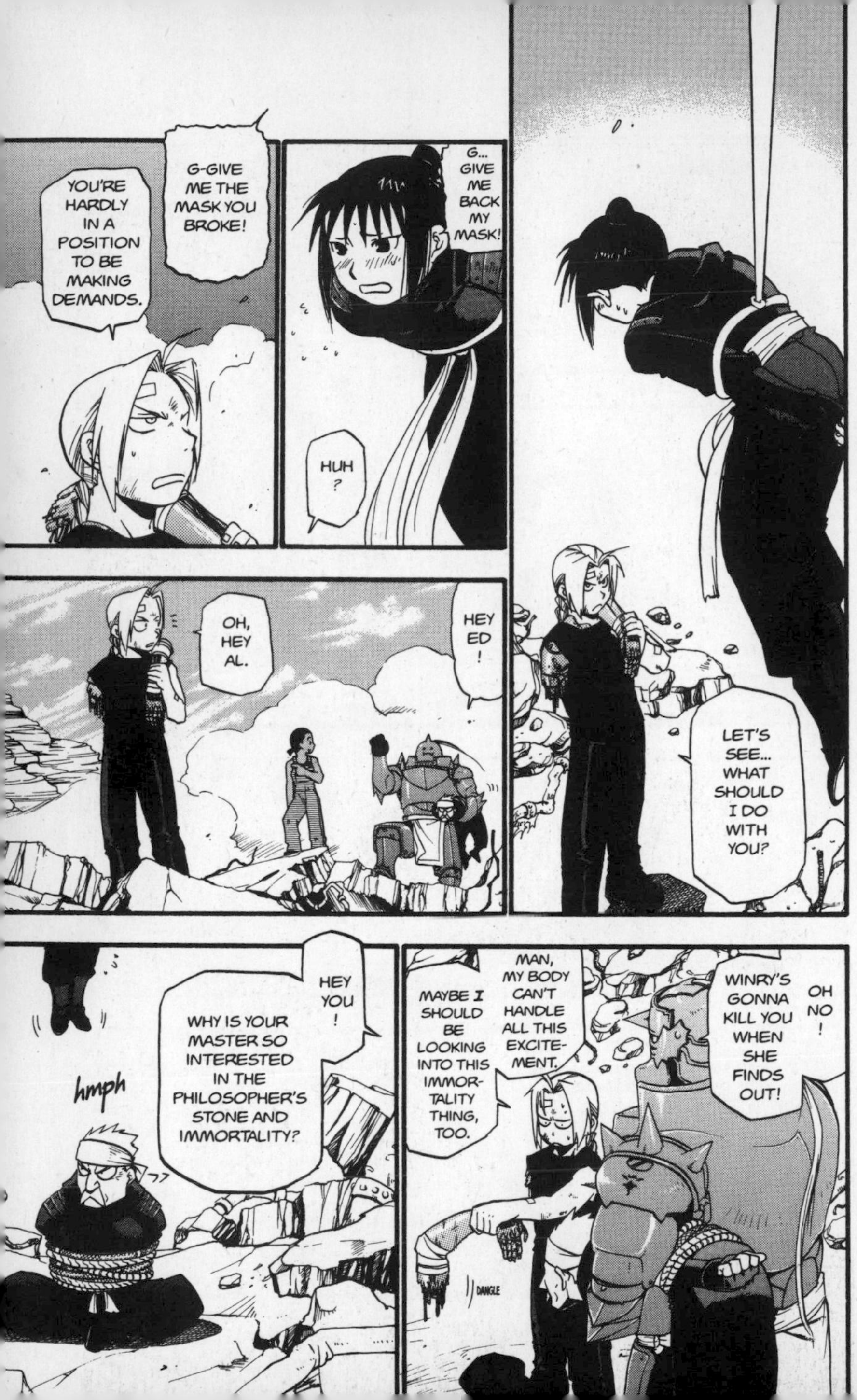
LET'S SEE... WHAT SHOULD I DO WITH YOU?
G... GIVE ME BACK MY MASK!
HUH?
G-GIVE ME THE MASK YOU BROKE!
YOU'RE HARDLY IN A POSITION TO BE MAKING DEMANDS.
HEY ED!
OH, HEY AL.
OH NO!
WINRY'S GONNA KILL YOU WHEN SHE FINDS OUT!
MAN, MY BODY CAN'T HANDLE ALL THIS EXCITEMENT.
MAYBE I SHOULD BE LOOKING INTO THIS IMMORTALITY THING, TOO.
DANGLE
HEY YOU!
WHY IS YOUR MASTER SO INTERESTED IN THE PHILOSOPHER'S STONE AND IMMORTALITY?
hmph

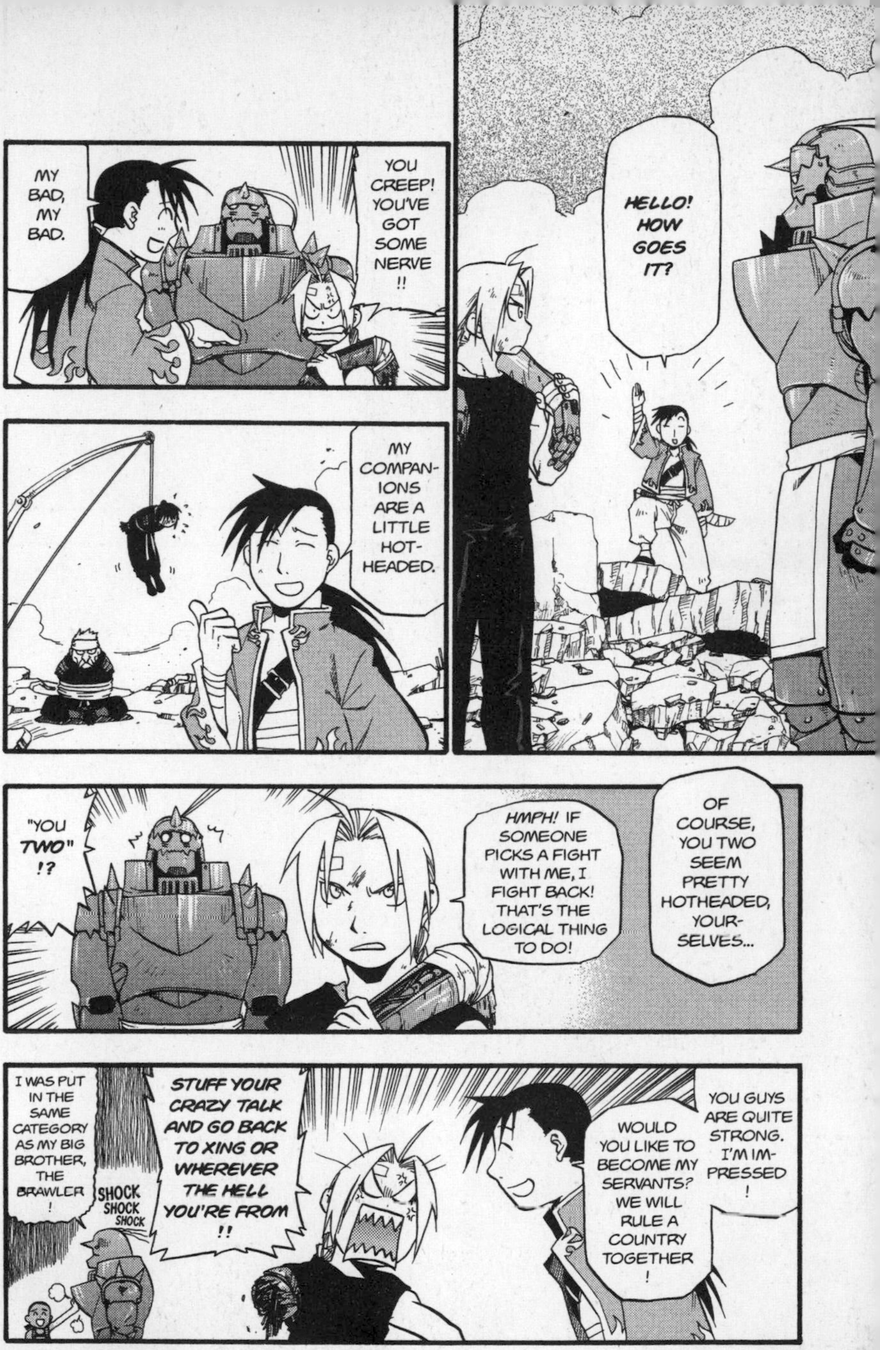
HELLO! HOW GOES IT?
YOU CREEP! YOU'VE GOT SOME NERVE!!
MY BAD, MY BAD.
MY COMPANIONS ARE A LITTLE HOT-HEADED.
OF COURSE, YOU TWO SEEM PRETTY HOTHEADED, YOURSELVES...
HMPH! IF SOMEONE PICKS A FIGHT WITH ME, I FIGHT BACK! THAT'S THE LOGICAL THING TO DO!
"YOU TWO" !?
YOU GUYS ARE QUITE STRONG. I'M IMPRESSED!
WOULD YOU LIKE TO BECOME MY SERVANTS? WE WILL RULE A COUNTRY TOGETHER!
STUFF YOUR CRAZY TALK AND GO BACK TO XING OR WHEREVER THE HELL YOU'RE FROM!!
SHOCK SHOCK SHOCK
I WAS PUT IN THE SAME CATEGORY AS MY BIG BROTHER, THE BRAWLER!

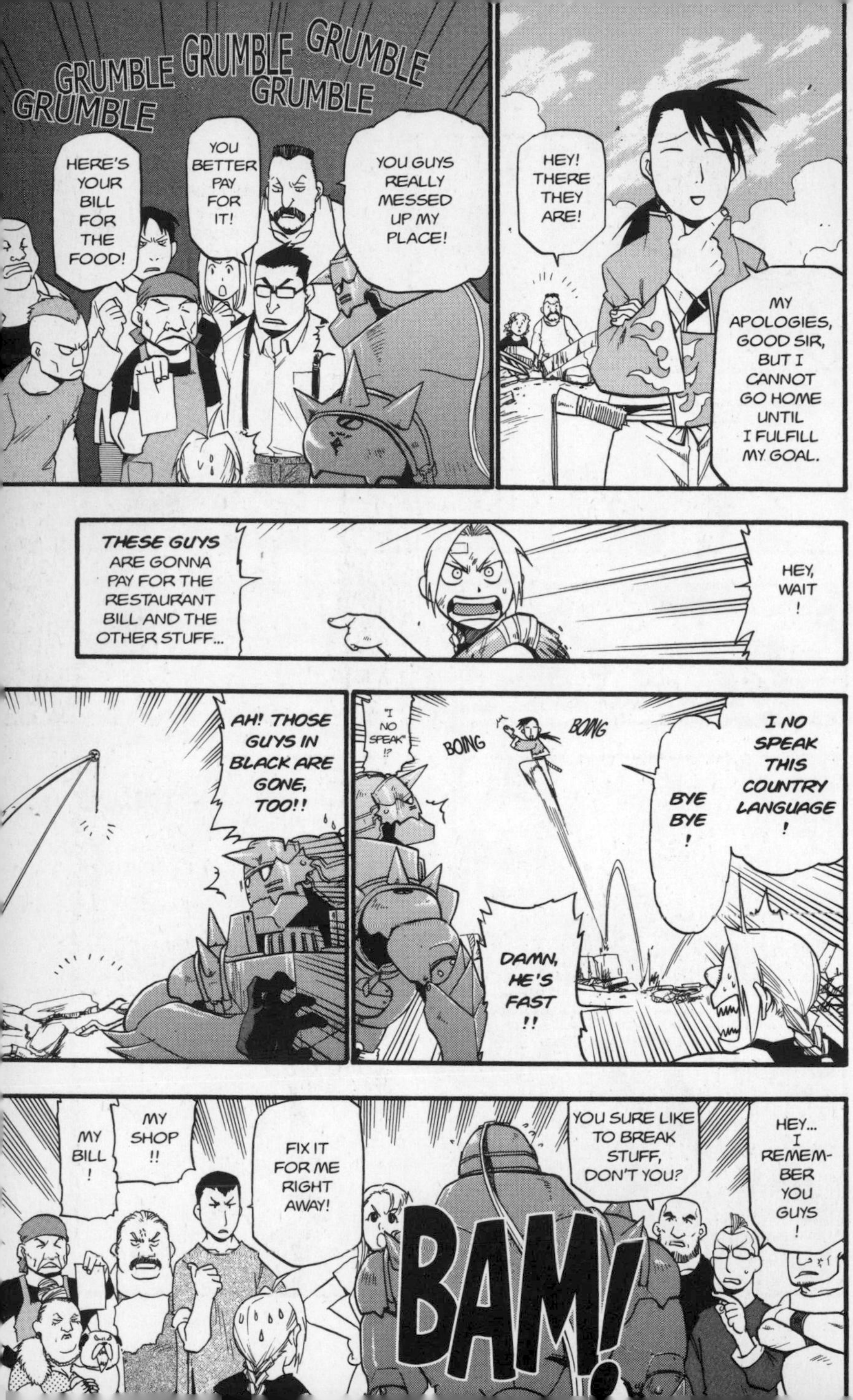
HEY! THERE THEY ARE!
MY APOLOGIES, GOOD SIR, BUT I CANNOT GO HOME UNTIL I FULFILL MY GOAL.
GRUMBLE GRUMBLE GRUMBLE GRUMBLE
YOU GUYS REALLY MESSED UP MY PLACE!
YOU BETTER PAY FOR IT!
HERE'S YOUR BILL FOR THE FOOD!
HEY, WAIT!
THESE GUYS ARE GONNA PAY FOR THE RESTAURANT BILL AND THE OTHER STUFF...
I NO SPEAK THIS COUNTRY LANGUAGE!
BYE BYE!
BOING
BOING
"I NO SPEAK"!?
DAMN, HE'S FAST!!
AH! THOSE GUYS IN BLACK ARE GONE, TOO!!
HEY... I REMEMBER YOU GUYS!
YOU SURE LIKE TO BREAK STUFF, DON'T YOU?
BAM!
FIX IT FOR ME RIGHT AWAY!
MY SHOP!!
MY BILL!

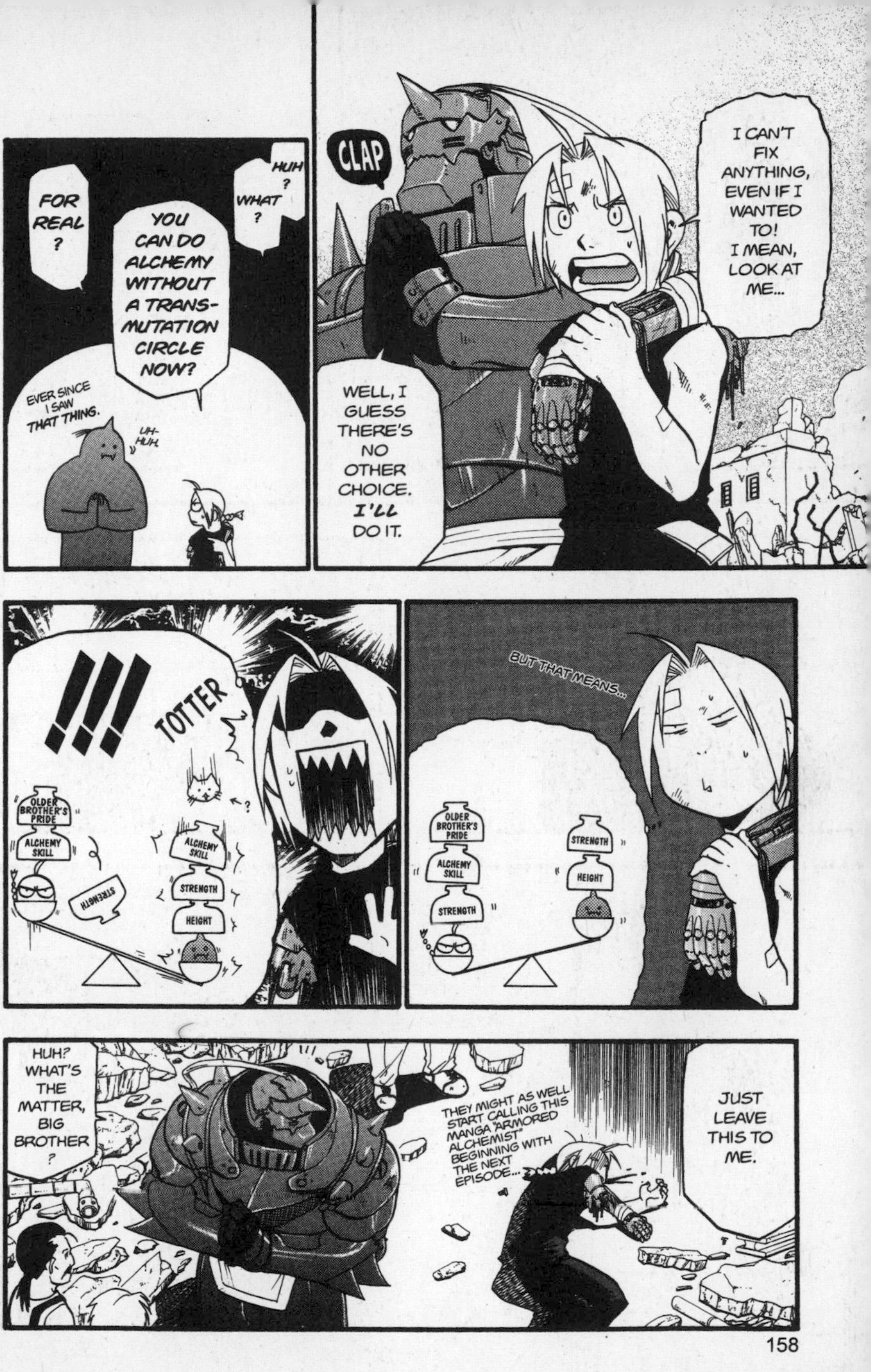
I CAN'T FIX ANYTHING, EVEN IF I WANTED TO! I MEAN, LOOK AT ME...
CLAP
WELL, I GUESS THERE'S NO OTHER CHOICE. I'LL DO IT.
HUH? WHAT?
YOU CAN DO ALCHEMY WITHOUT A TRANS-MUTATION CIRCLE NOW?
FOR REAL?
EVER SINCE I SAW THAT THING.
UH-HUH.
BUT THAT MEANS...
OLDER BROTHER'S PRIDE
ALCHEMY SKILL
STRENGTH
STRENGTH
HEIGHT
!!!
TOTTER
OLDER BROTHER'S PRIDE
ALCHEMY SKILL
STRENGTH
ALCHEMY SKILL
STRENGTH
HEIGHT
JUST LEAVE THIS TO ME.
THEY MIGHT AS WELL START CALLING THIS MANGA "ARMORED ALCHEMIST" BEGINNING WITH THE NEXT EPISODE...
HUH? WHAT'S THE MATTER, BIG BROTHER?

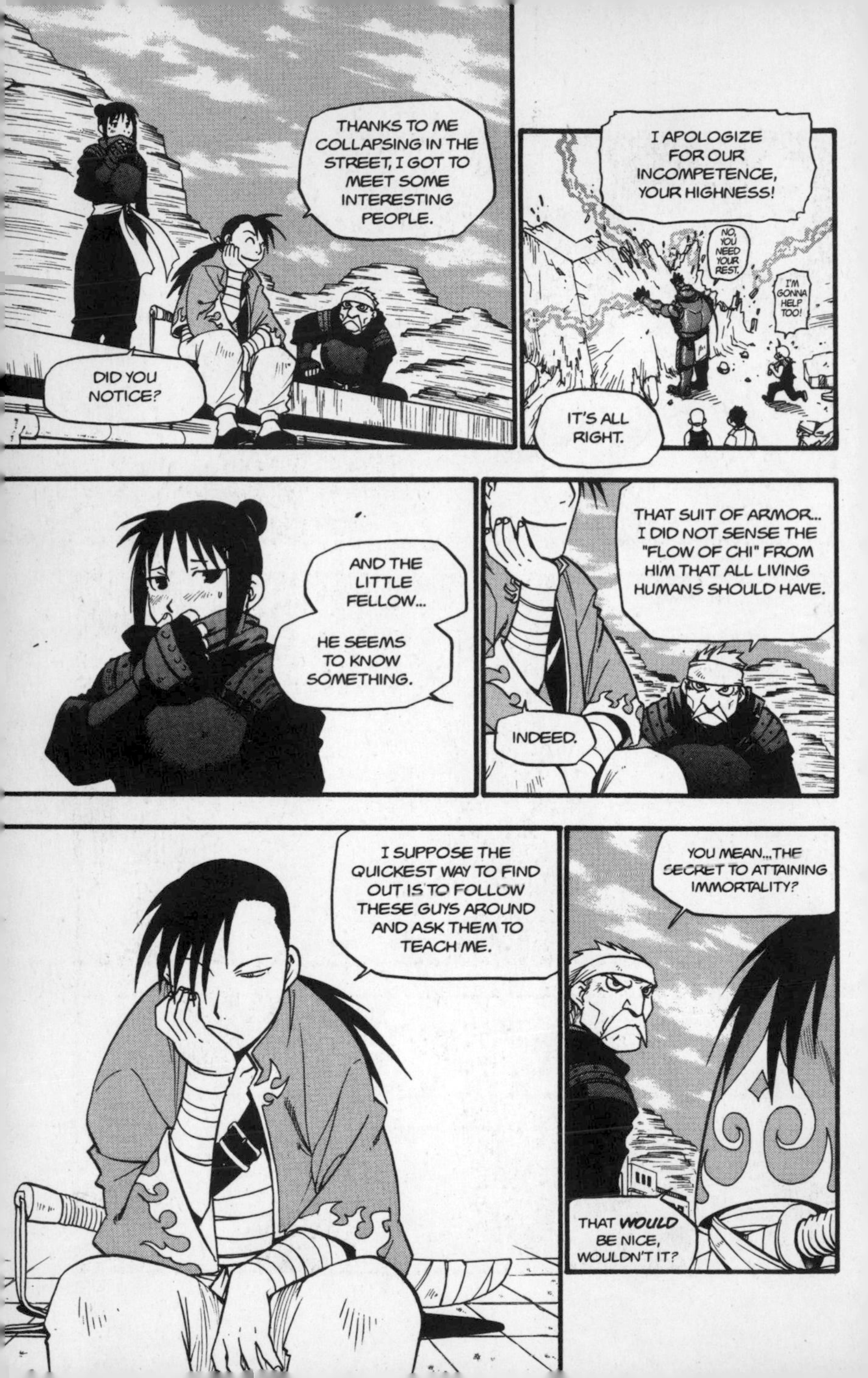
I APOLOGIZE FOR OUR INCOMPETENCE, YOUR HIGHNESS!
NO, YOU NEED YOUR REST.
I'M GONNA HELP TOO!
IT'S ALL RIGHT.
THANKS TO ME COLLAPSING IN THE STREET, I GOT TO MEET SOME INTERESTING PEOPLE.
DID YOU NOTICE?
THAT SUIT OF ARMOR... I DID NOT SENSE THE "FLOW OF CHI" FROM HIM THAT ALL LIVING HUMANS SHOULD HAVE.
INDEED.
AND THE LITTLE FELLOW...
HE SEEMS TO KNOW SOMETHING.
YOU MEAN...THE SECRET TO ATTAINING IMMORTALITY?
THAT **WOULD** BE NICE, WOULDN'T IT?
I SUPPOSE THE QUICKEST WAY TO FIND OUT IS TO FOLLOW THESE GUYS AROUND AND ASK THEM TO TEACH ME.

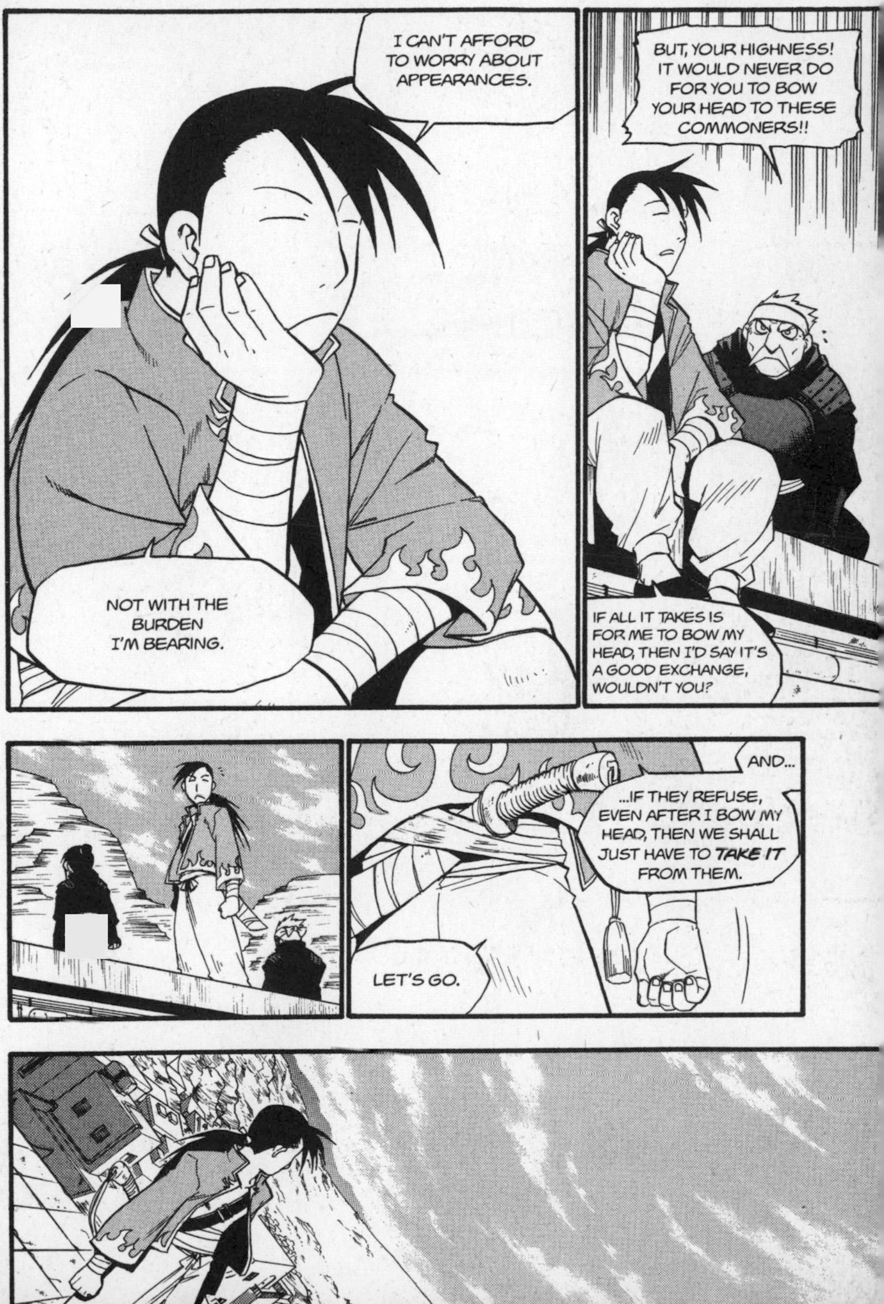
BUT, YOUR HIGHNESS! IT WOULD NEVER DO FOR YOU TO BOW YOUR HEAD TO THESE COMMONERS!!
IF ALL IT TAKES IS FOR ME TO BOW MY HEAD, THEN I'D SAY IT'S A GOOD EXCHANGE, WOULDN'T YOU?
I CAN'T AFFORD TO WORRY ABOUT APPEARANCES.
NOT WITH THE BURDEN I'M BEARING.
AND...
...IF THEY REFUSE, EVEN AFTER I BOW MY HEAD, THEN WE SHALL JUST HAVE TO *TAKE IT* FROM THEM.
LET'S GO.

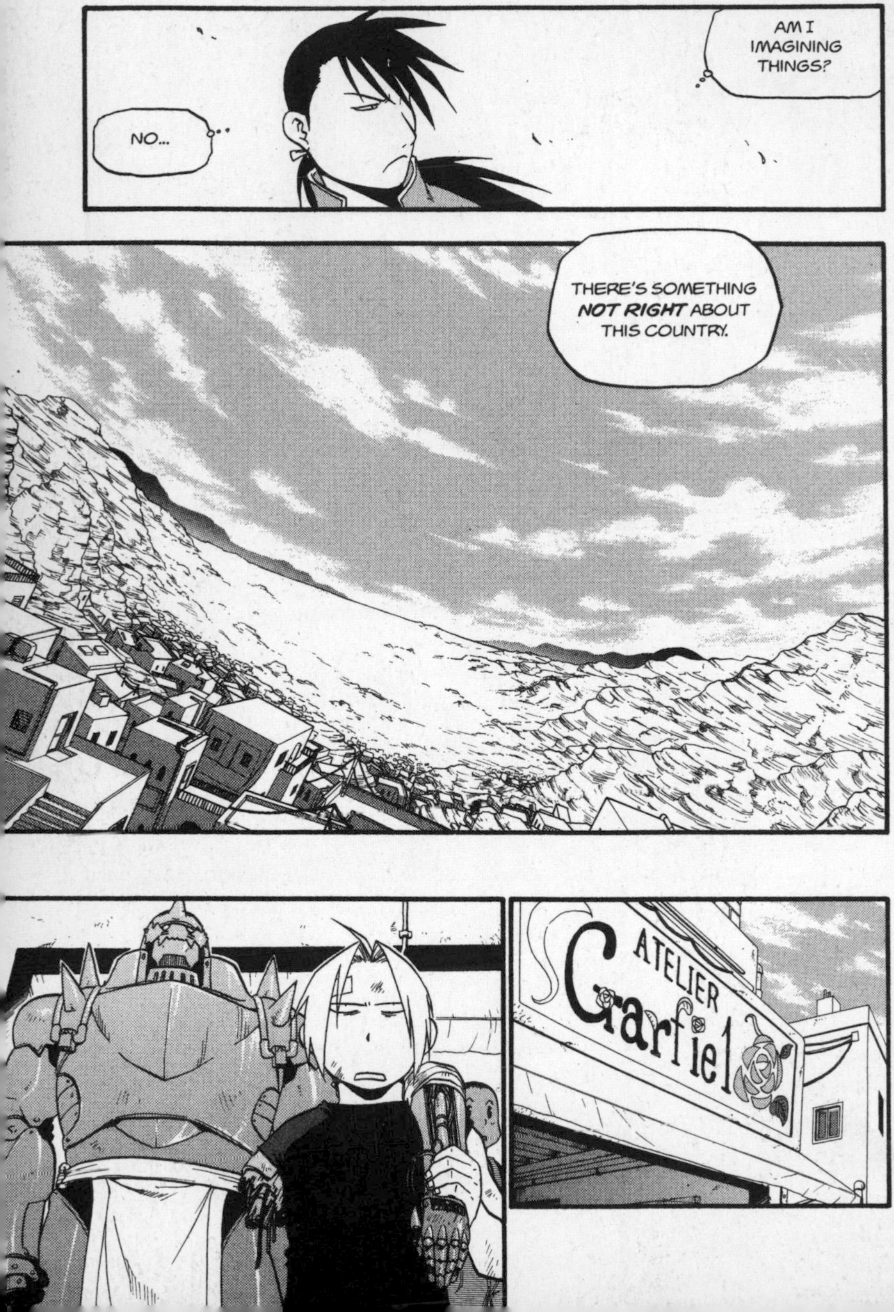
AM I IMAGINING THINGS?
NO...
THERE'S SOMETHING **NOT RIGHT** ABOUT THIS COUNTRY.
ATELIER
Garfiel

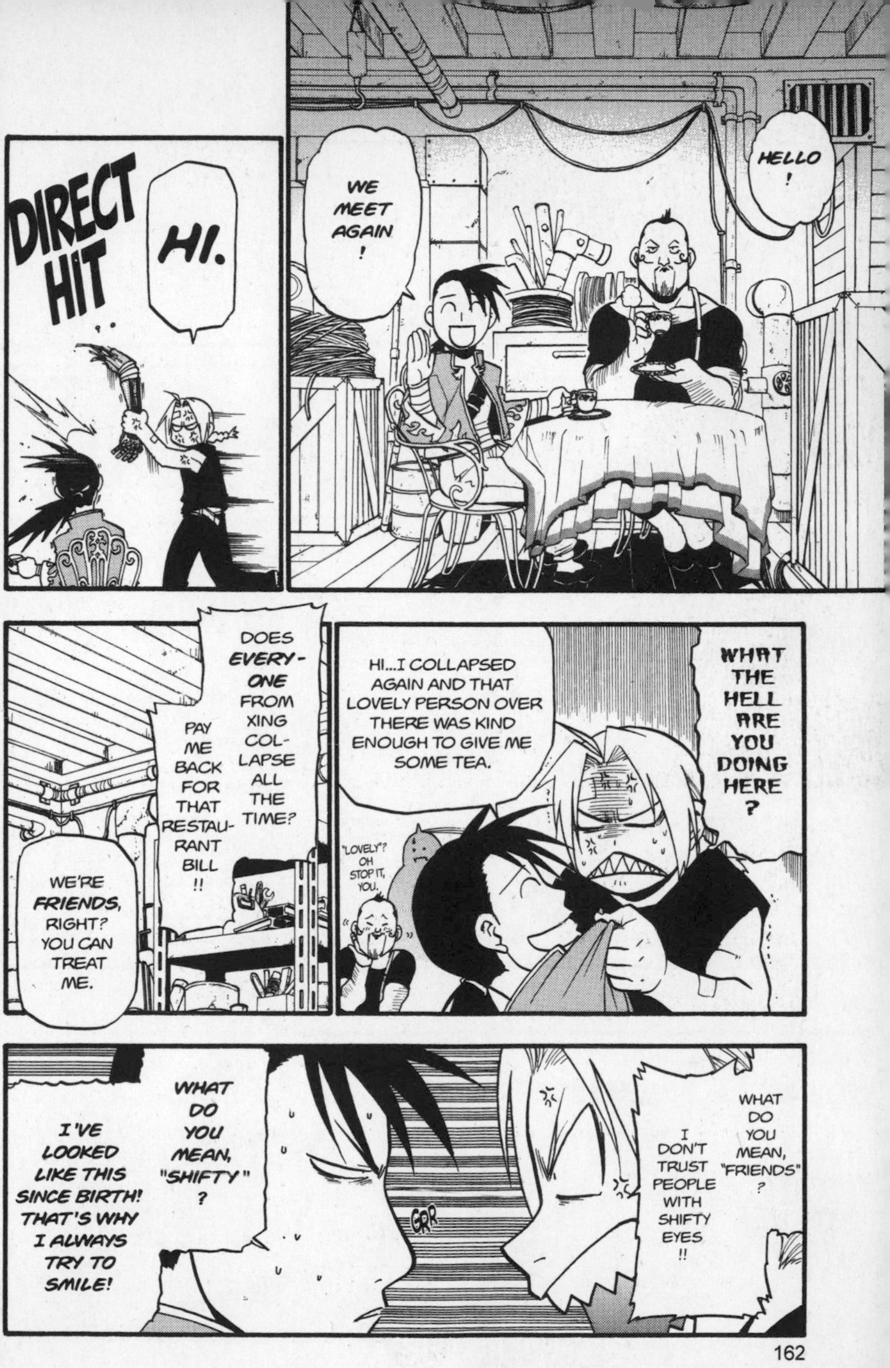
HELLO!
WE MEET AGAIN!
HI.
DIRECT HIT
WHAT THE HELL ARE YOU DOING HERE?
HI...I COLLAPSED AGAIN AND THAT LOVELY PERSON OVER THERE WAS KIND ENOUGH TO GIVE ME SOME TEA.
"LOVELY"? OH STOP IT, YOU.
DOES EVERYONE FROM XING COLLAPSE ALL THE TIME?
PAY ME BACK FOR THAT RESTAURANT BILL!!
WE'RE FRIENDS, RIGHT? YOU CAN TREAT ME.
WHAT DO YOU MEAN, "FRIENDS"?
I DON'T TRUST PEOPLE WITH SHIFTY EYES!!
GRR
WHAT DO YOU MEAN, "SHIFTY"?
I'VE LOOKED LIKE THIS SINCE BIRTH! THAT'S WHY I ALWAYS TRY TO SMILE!

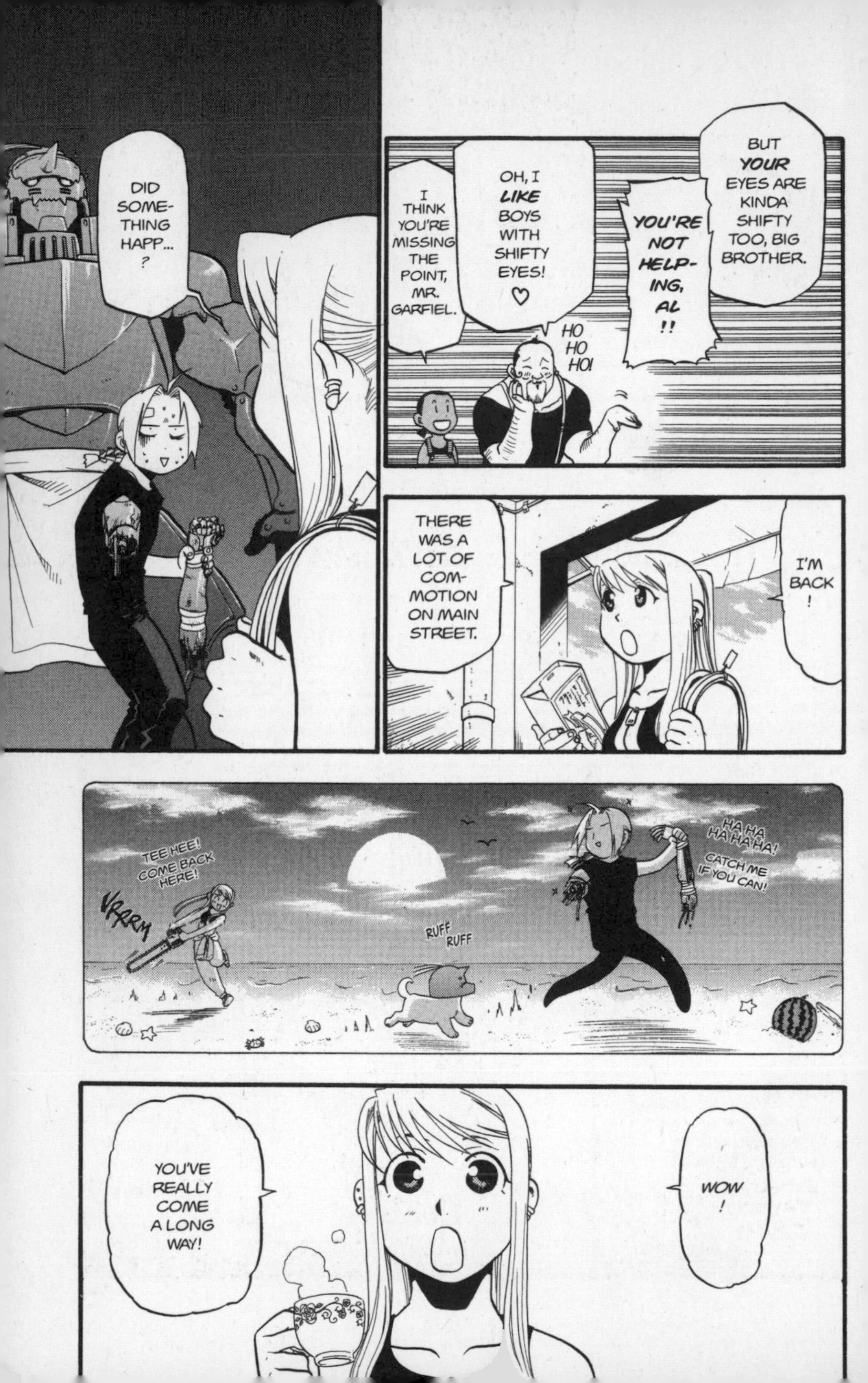
BUT YOUR EYES ARE KINDA SHIFTY TOO, BIG BROTHER.
YOU'RE NOT HELPING, AL!!
OH, I LIKE BOYS WITH SHIFTY EYES! ♡
I THINK YOU'RE MISSING THE POINT, MR. GARFIEL.
HO HO HO!
I'M BACK!
THERE WAS A LOT OF COMMOTION ON MAIN STREET.
DID SOMETHING HAPP...?
HA HA HA HA HA!
CATCH ME IF YOU CAN!
RUFF RUFF
TEE HEE! COME BACK HERE!
VRRRM
WOW!
YOU'VE REALLY COME A LONG WAY!

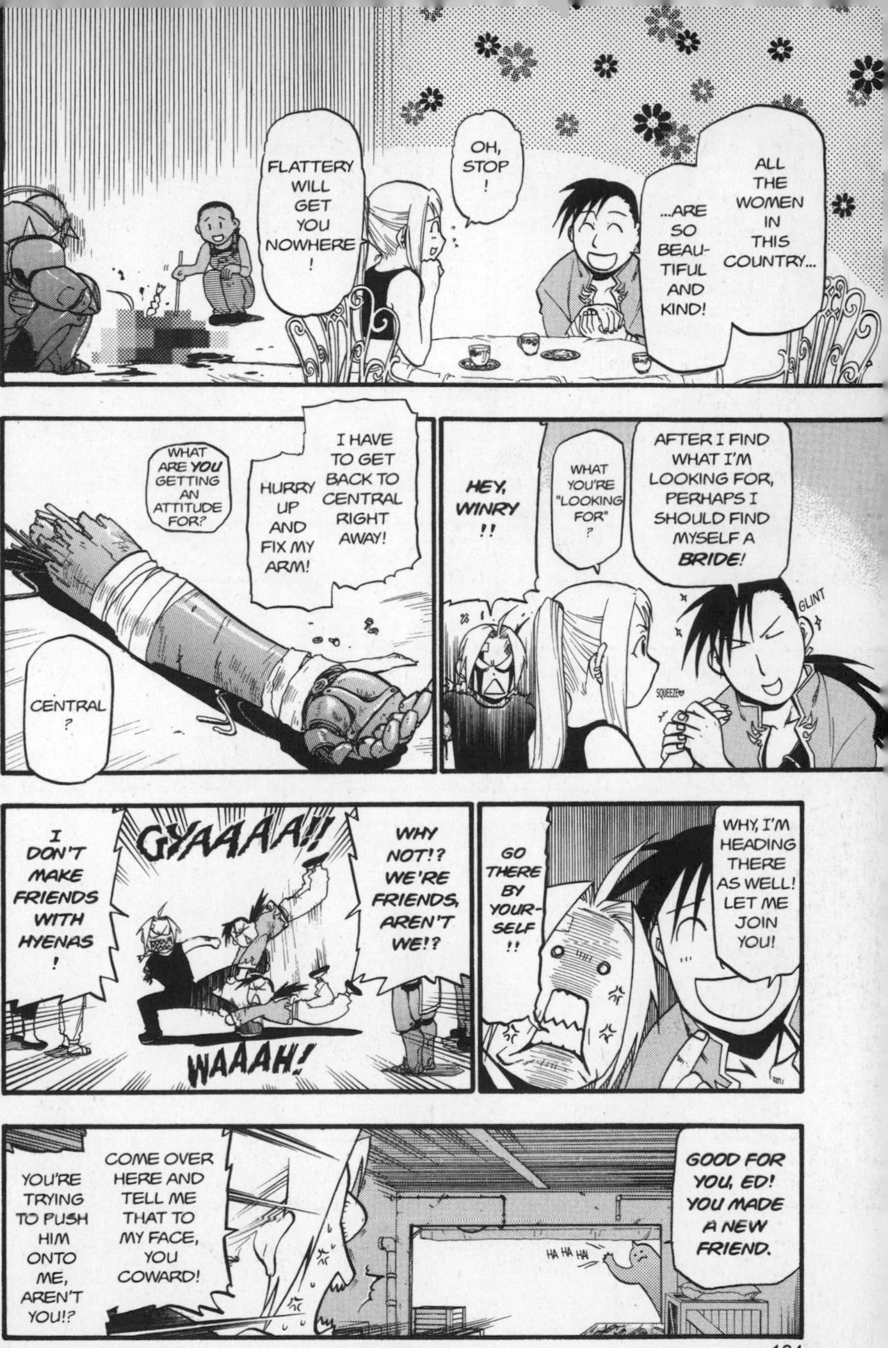
ALL THE WOMEN IN THIS COUNTRY...
...ARE SO BEAUTIFUL AND KIND!
OH, STOP!
FLATTERY WILL GET YOU NOWHERE!
AFTER I FIND WHAT I'M LOOKING FOR, PERHAPS I SHOULD FIND MYSELF A BRIDE!
GLINT
WHAT YOU'RE "LOOKING FOR"?
HEY, WINRY!!
SQUEEZE♥
I HAVE TO GET BACK TO CENTRAL RIGHT AWAY!
HURRY UP AND FIX MY ARM!
WHAT ARE YOU GETTING AN ATTITUDE FOR?
CENTRAL?
WHY, I'M HEADING THERE AS WELL! LET ME JOIN YOU!
GO THERE BY YOURSELF!!
WHY NOT!? WE'RE FRIENDS, AREN'T WE!?
GYAAAA!!
I DON'T MAKE FRIENDS WITH HYENAS!
WAAAH!
GOOD FOR YOU, ED! YOU MADE A NEW FRIEND.
HA HA HA!
COME OVER HERE AND TELL ME THAT TO MY FACE, YOU COWARD!
YOU'RE TRYING TO PUSH HIM ONTO ME, AREN'T YOU!?

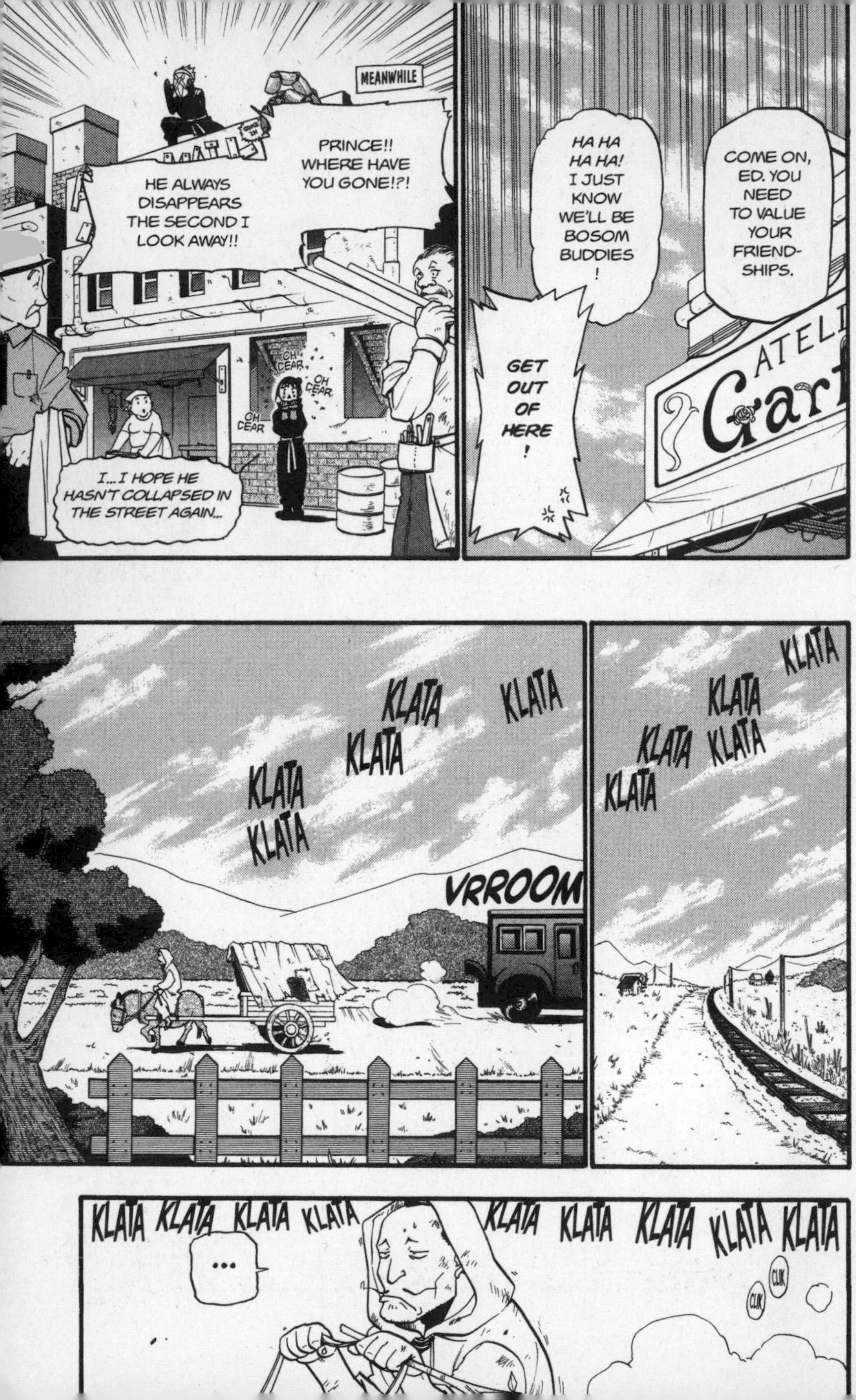
COME ON, ED. YOU NEED TO VALUE YOUR FRIENDSHIPS.
HA HA HA HA! I JUST KNOW WE'LL BE BOSOM BUDDIES!
GET OUT OF HERE!
MEANWHILE
PRINCE!! WHERE HAVE YOU GONE!?!
HE ALWAYS DISAPPEARS THE SECOND I LOOK AWAY!!
OH DEAR
OH DEAR
OH DEAR
I...I HOPE HE HASN'T COLLAPSED IN THE STREET AGAIN...
KLATA
KLATA KLATA
KLATA KLATA
KLATA
KLATA
KLATA
KLATA
KLATA KLATA
VRROOM
KLATA KLATA KLATA KLATA KLATA KLATA KLATA KLATA KLATA
...
CLIK
CLIK

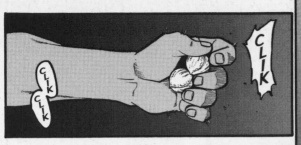

CLIK

CLIK CLIK

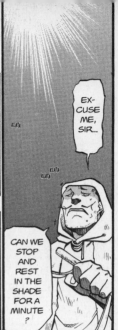

EX-CUSE ME, SIR...

KLATA

KLATA KLATA

CAN WE STOP AND REST IN THE SHADE FOR A MINUTE?

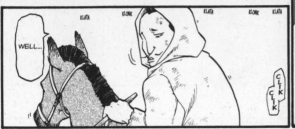

WELL...

KLATA KLONK KLATA KLONK KLATA

CLIK CLIK CLIK

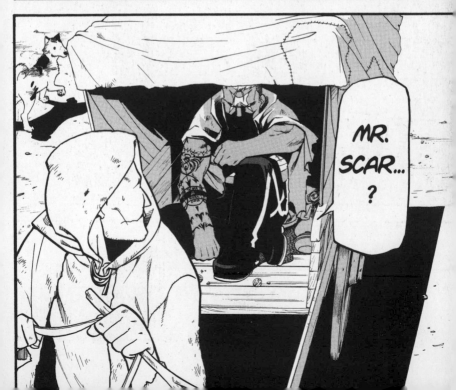

MR. SCAR...?

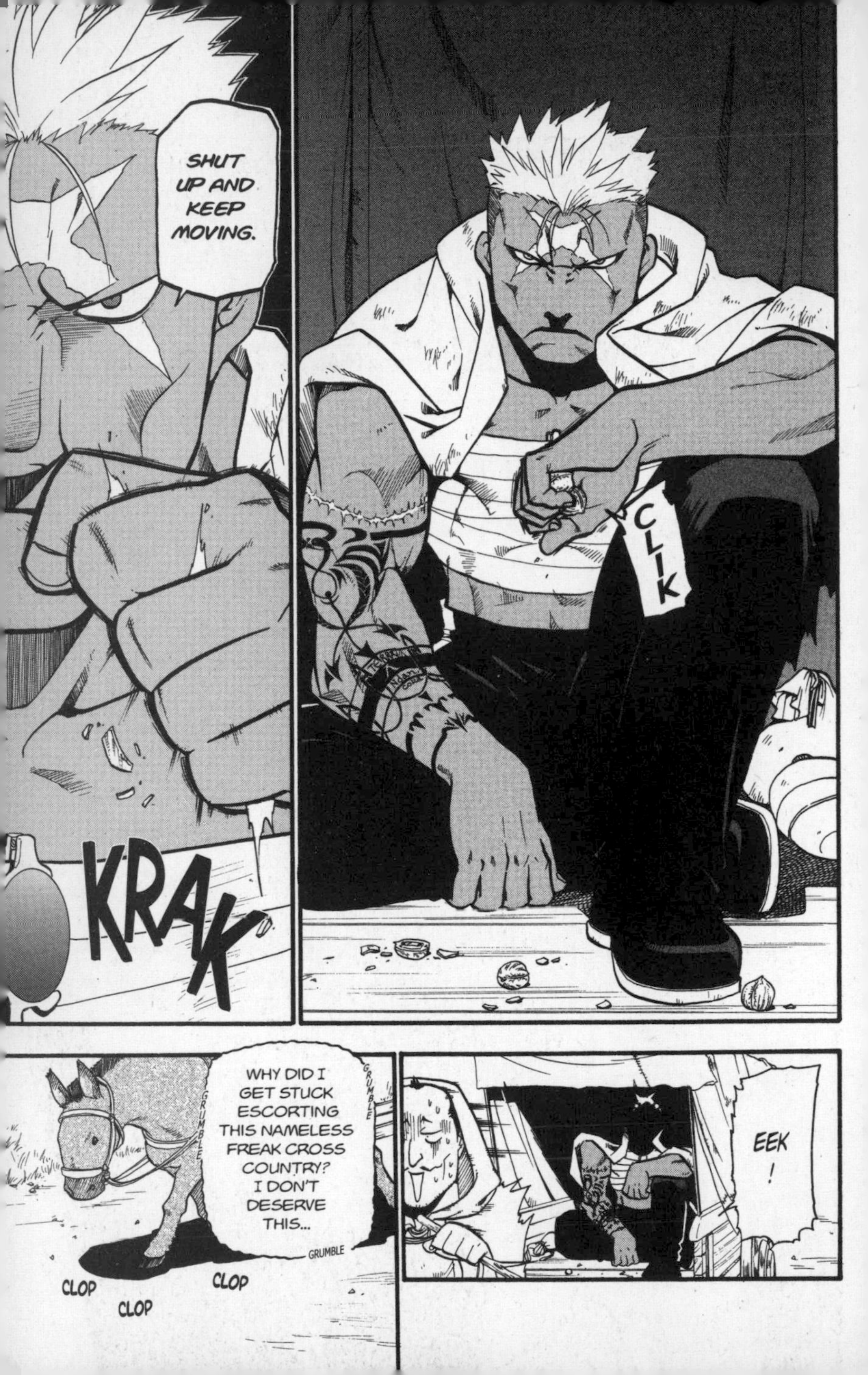
CLIK
SHUT UP AND KEEP MOVING.
KRAK
EEK!
WHY DID I GET STUCK ESCORTING THIS NAMELESS FREAK CROSS COUNTRY? I DON'T DESERVE THIS...
GRUMBLE
GRUMBLE
GRUMBLE
CLOP
CLOP
CLOP

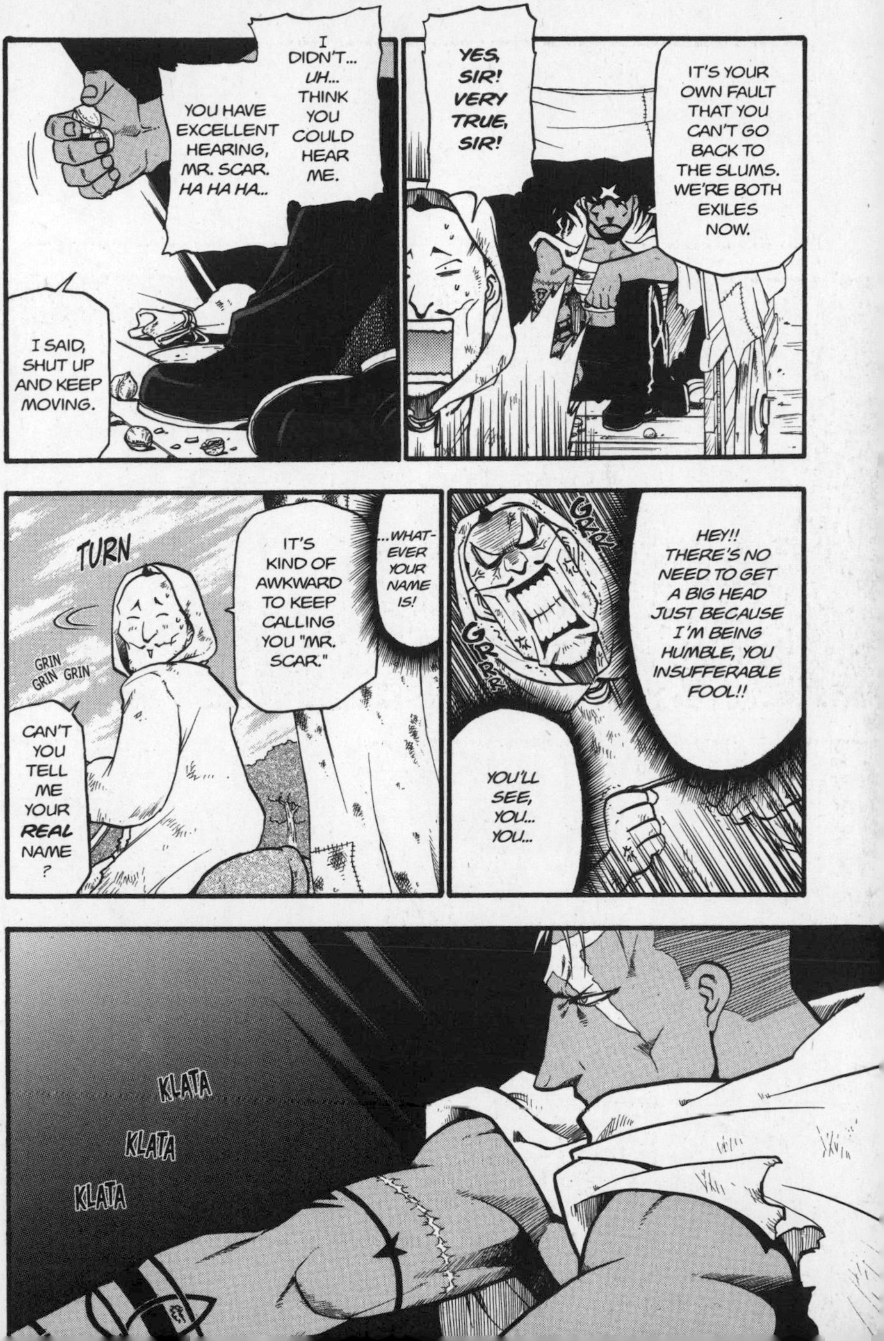
IT'S YOUR OWN FAULT THAT YOU CAN'T GO BACK TO THE SLUMS. WE'RE BOTH EXILES NOW.
YES, SIR! VERY TRUE, SIR!
I DIDN'T... UH... THINK YOU COULD HEAR ME.
YOU HAVE EXCELLENT HEARING, MR. SCAR. HA HA HA...
I SAID, SHUT UP AND KEEP MOVING.
GRRR
HEY!! THERE'S NO NEED TO GET A BIG HEAD JUST BECAUSE I'M BEING HUMBLE, YOU INSUFFERABLE FOOL!!
GRRR
YOU'LL SEE, YOU... YOU...
...WHATEVER YOUR NAME IS!
IT'S KIND OF AWKWARD TO KEEP CALLING YOU "MR. SCAR."
TURN
GRIN GRIN GRIN
CAN'T YOU TELL ME YOUR REAL NAME?
KLATA
KLATA
KLATA

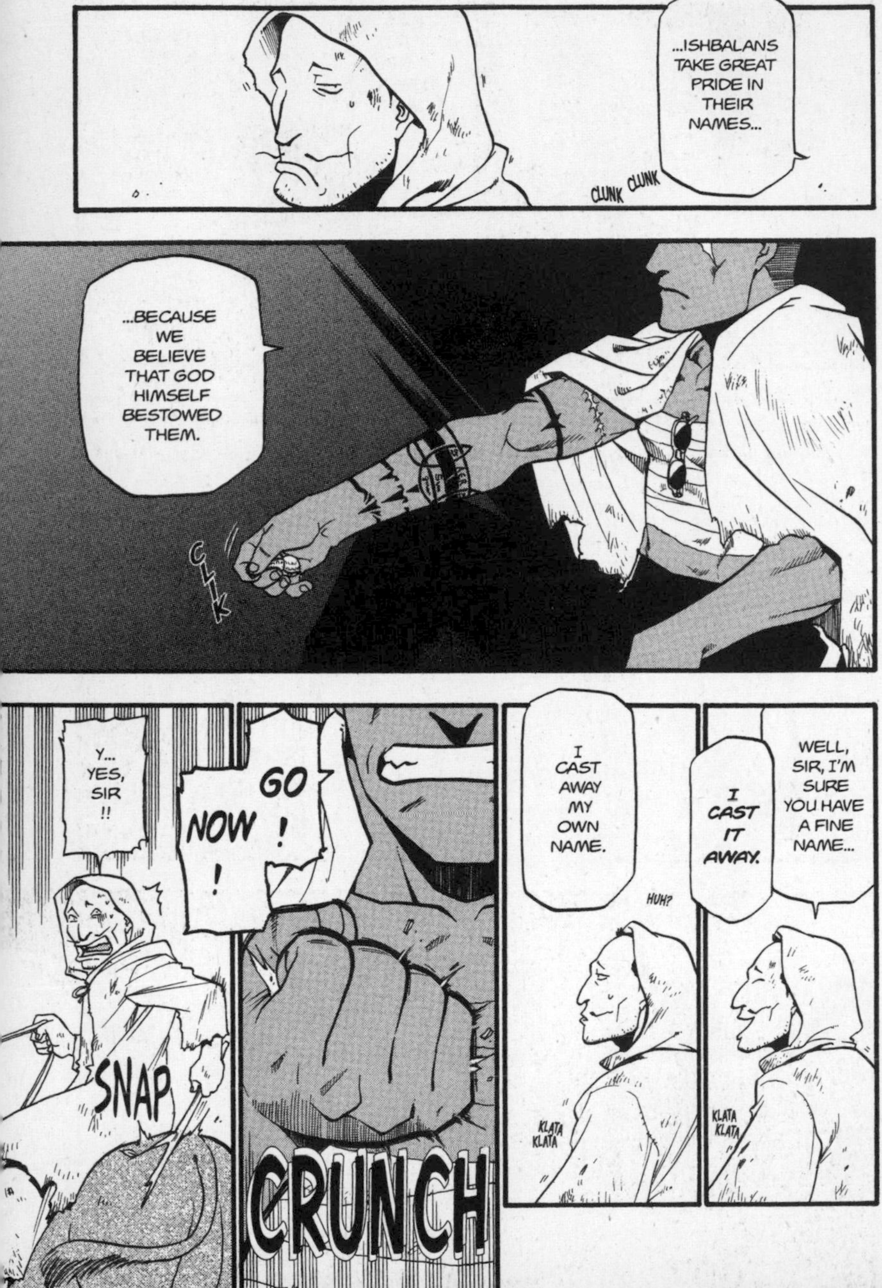
...ISHBALANS TAKE GREAT PRIDE IN THEIR NAMES...
CLUNK CLUNK
...BECAUSE WE BELIEVE THAT GOD HIMSELF BESTOWED THEM.
CLIK
WELL, SIR, I'M SURE YOU HAVE A FINE NAME...
I CAST IT AWAY.
HUH?
KLATA KLATA
I CAST AWAY MY OWN NAME.
KLATA KLATA
GO NOW!
CRUNCH
Y... YES, SIR!!
SNAP

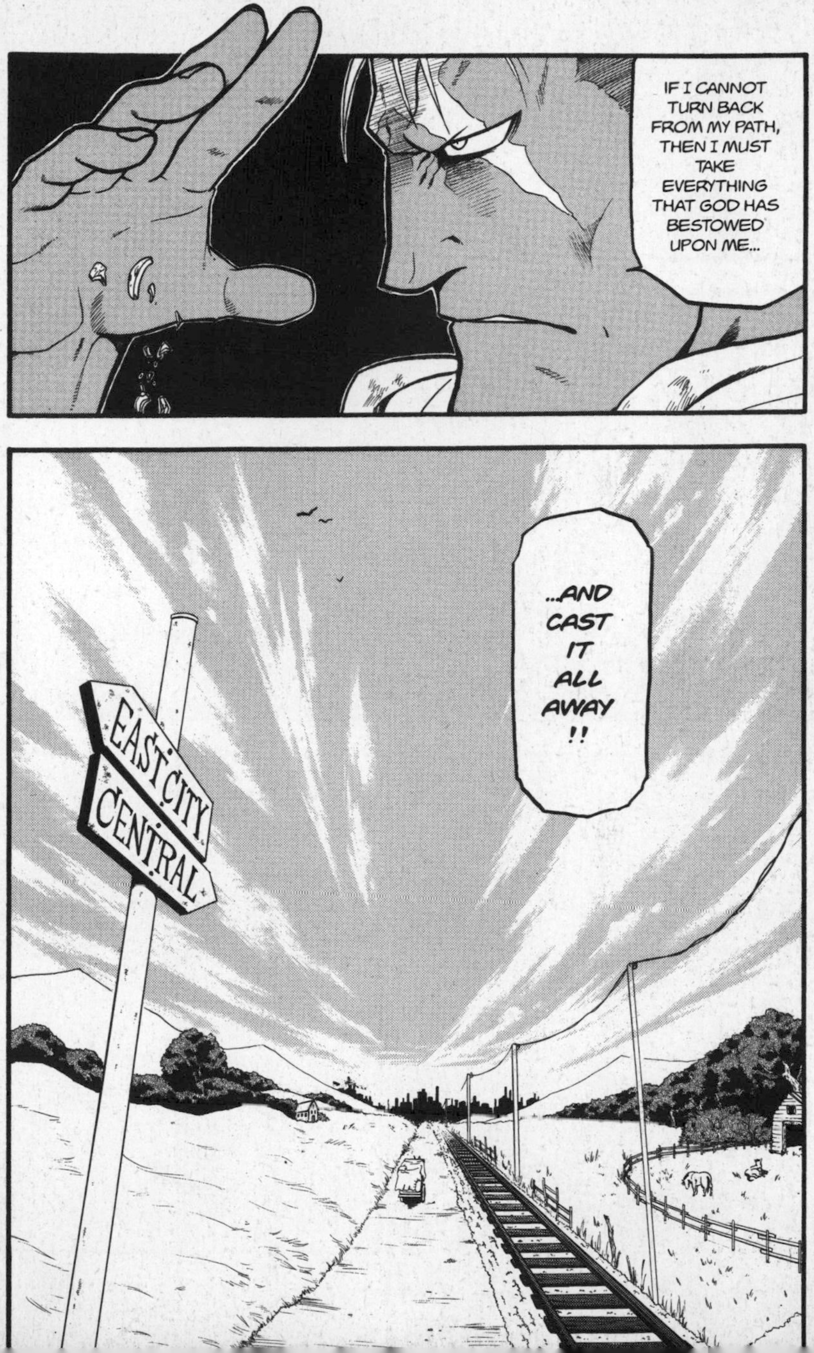
IF I CANNOT TURN BACK FROM MY PATH, THEN I MUST TAKE EVERYTHING THAT GOD HAS BESTOWED UPON ME...
...AND CAST IT ALL AWAY !!
EAST CITY
CENTRAL

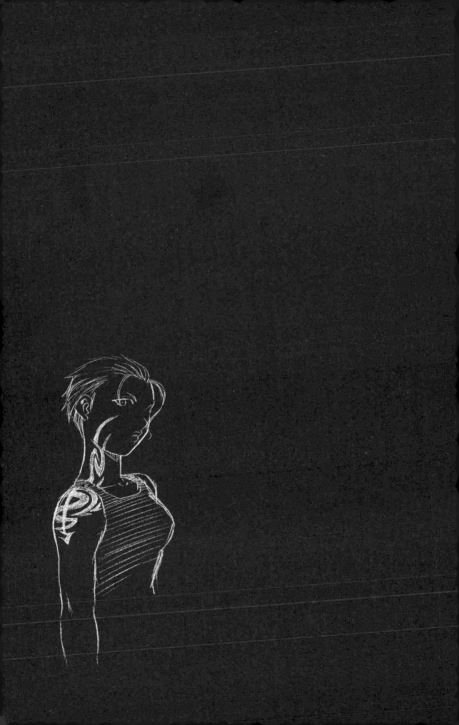

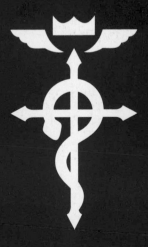

FULLMETAL
ALCHEMIST

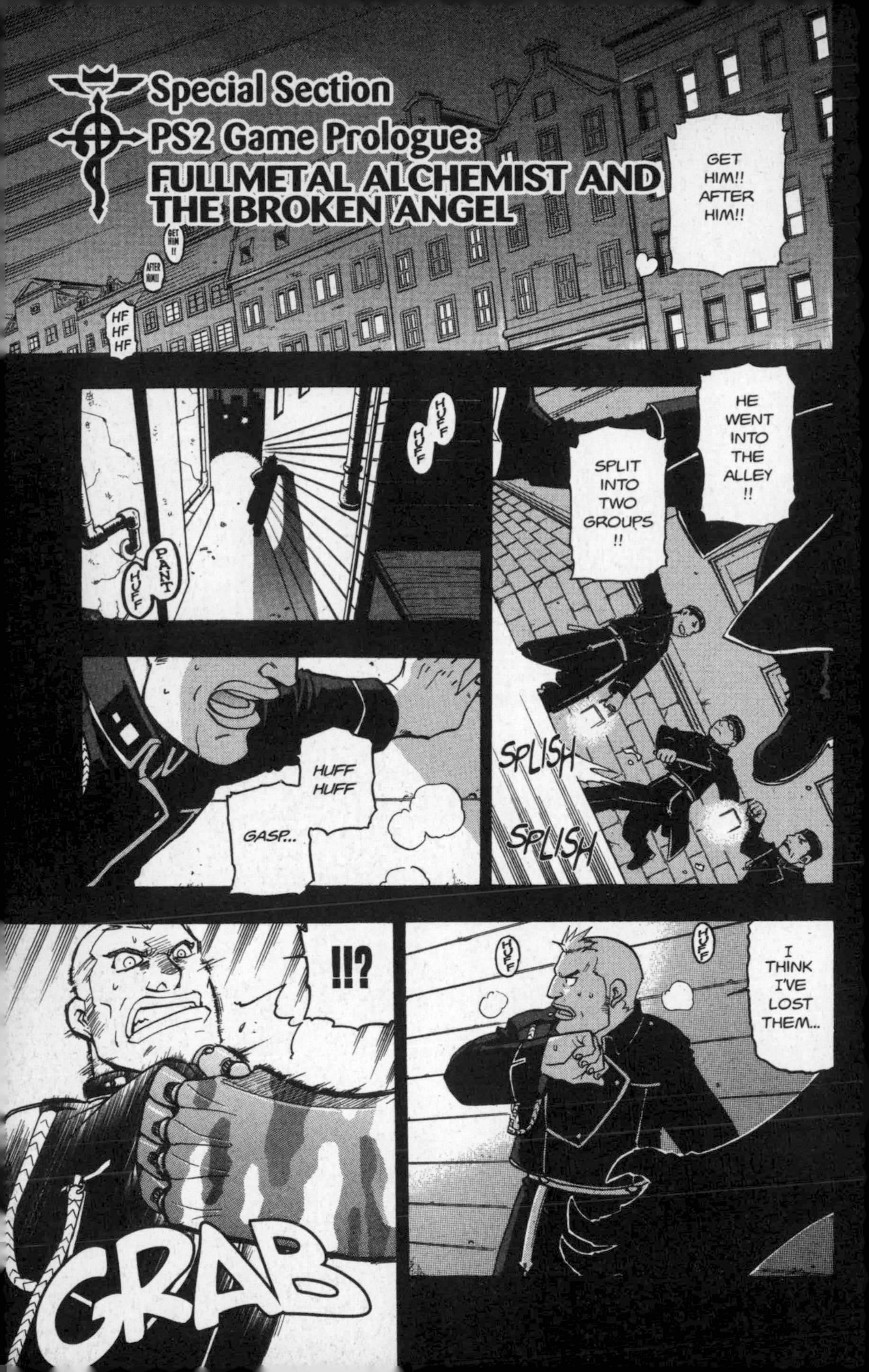
Special Section
PS2 Game Prologue:
FULLMETAL ALCHEMIST AND THE BROKEN ANGEL
GET HIM!! AFTER HIM!!
GET HIM !!
AFTER HIM!!
HF HF HF
HE WENT INTO THE ALLEY !!
SPLIT INTO TWO GROUPS !!
SPLISH
SPLISH
HUFF HUFF
PANT HUFF
HUFF HUFF
GASP...
HUFF
HUFF
I THINK I'VE LOST THEM...
!!?
GRAB

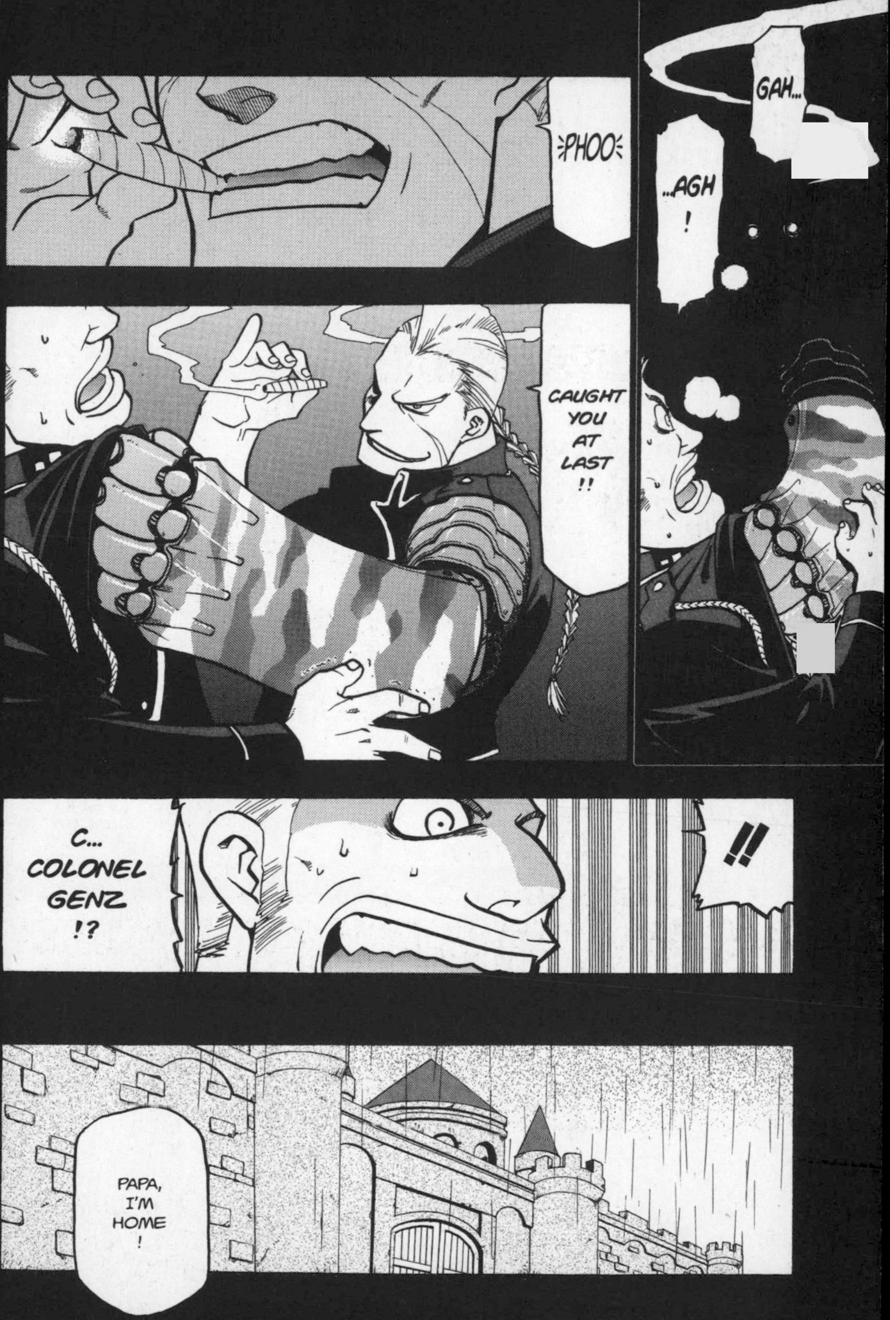
GAH...
...AGH !
PHOO
CAUGHT YOU AT LAST !!
!!
C... COLONEL GENZ !?
PAPA, I'M HOME !

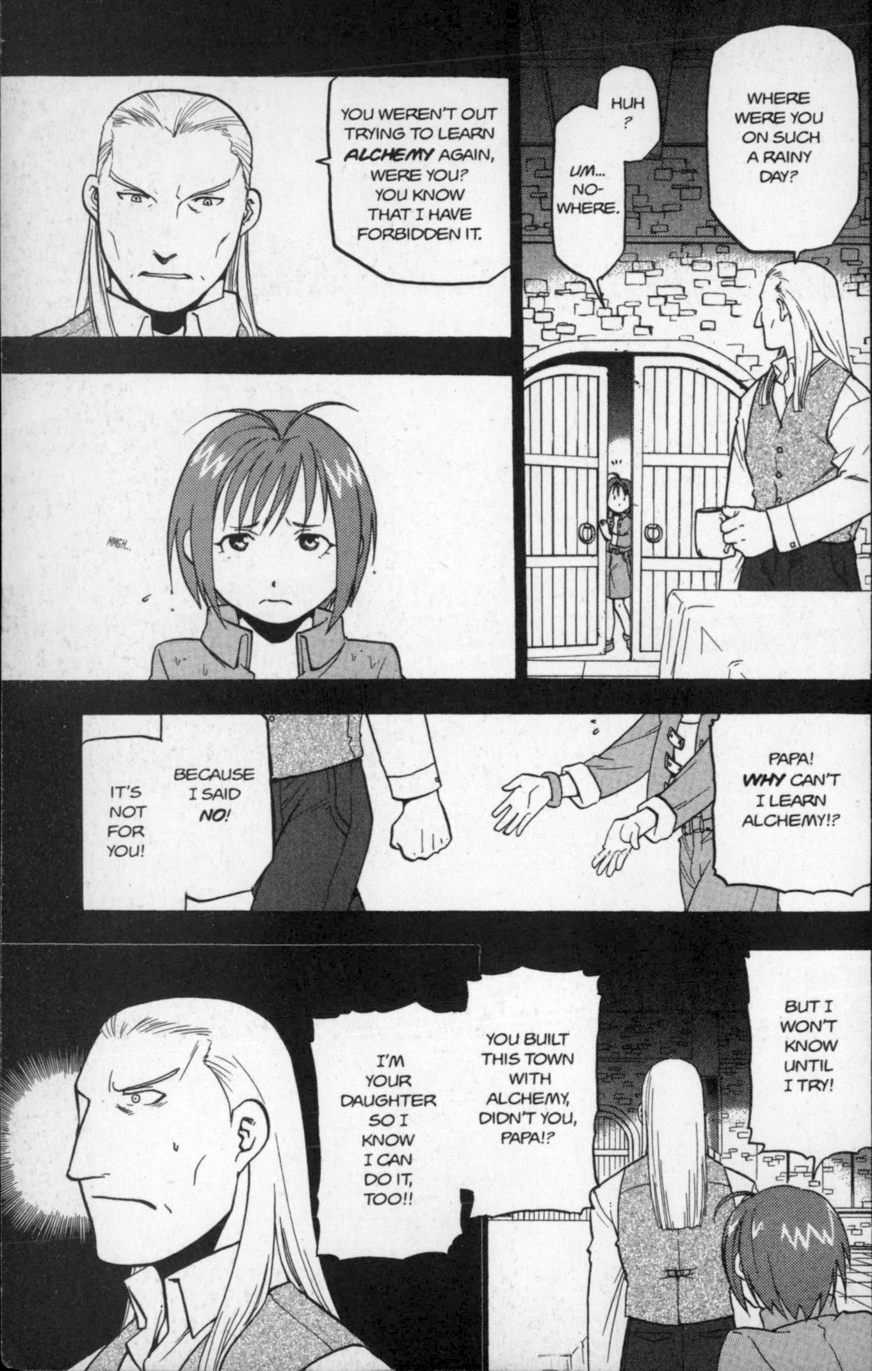
WHERE WERE YOU ON SUCH A RAINY DAY?
HUH?
UM... NO-WHERE.
YOU WEREN'T OUT TRYING TO LEARN ALCHEMY AGAIN, WERE YOU? YOU KNOW THAT I HAVE FORBIDDEN IT.
MMGH...
PAPA! WHY CAN'T I LEARN ALCHEMY!?
BECAUSE I SAID NO!
IT'S NOT FOR YOU!
BUT I WON'T KNOW UNTIL I TRY!
YOU BUILT THIS TOWN WITH ALCHEMY, DIDN'T YOU, PAPA!?
I'M YOUR DAUGHTER SO I KNOW I CAN DO IT, TOO!!

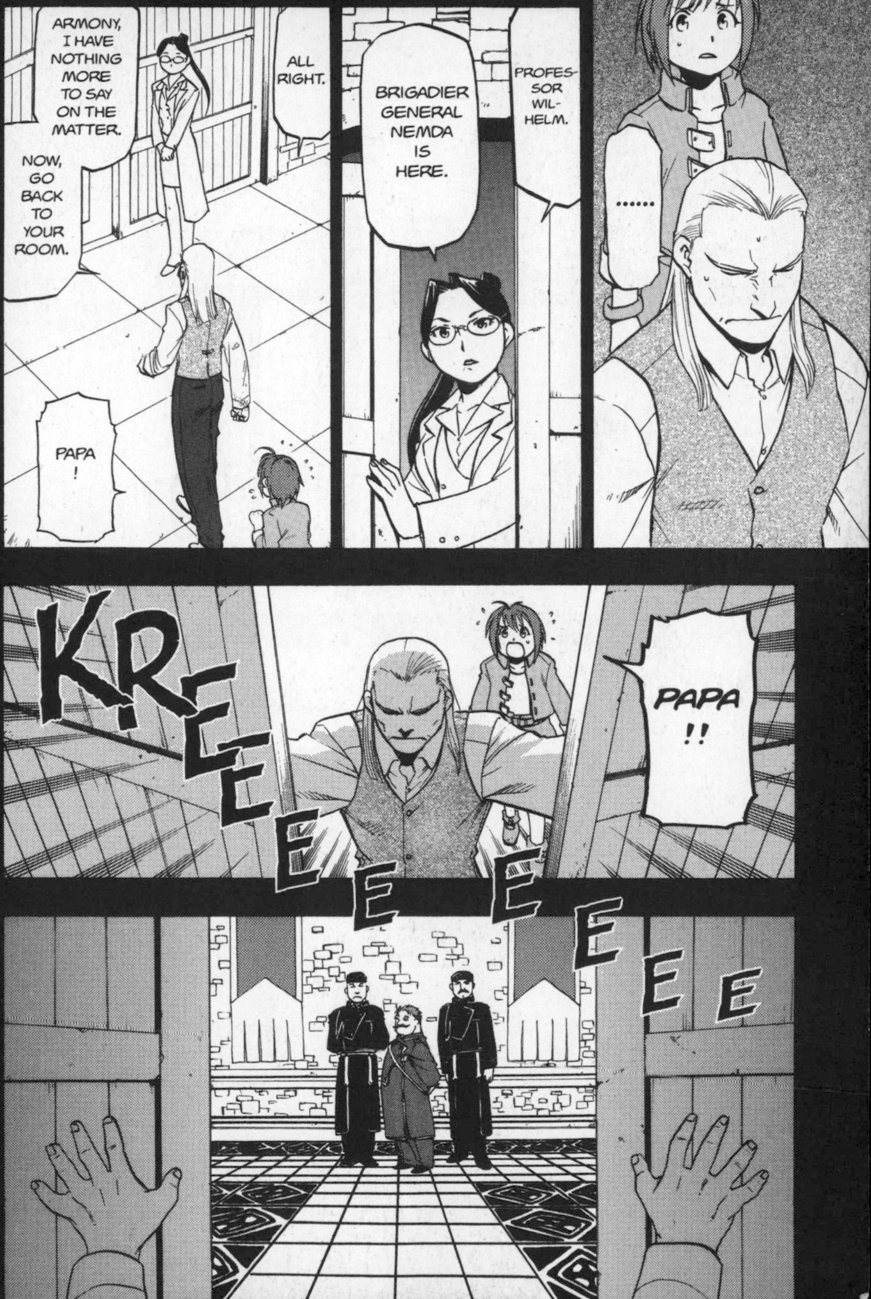
......
PROFESSOR WILHELM.
BRIGADIER GENERAL NEMDA IS HERE.
ALL RIGHT.
ARMONY, I HAVE NOTHING MORE TO SAY ON THE MATTER.
NOW, GO BACK TO YOUR ROOM.
PAPA!
PAPA!!
KREEEEEEEE

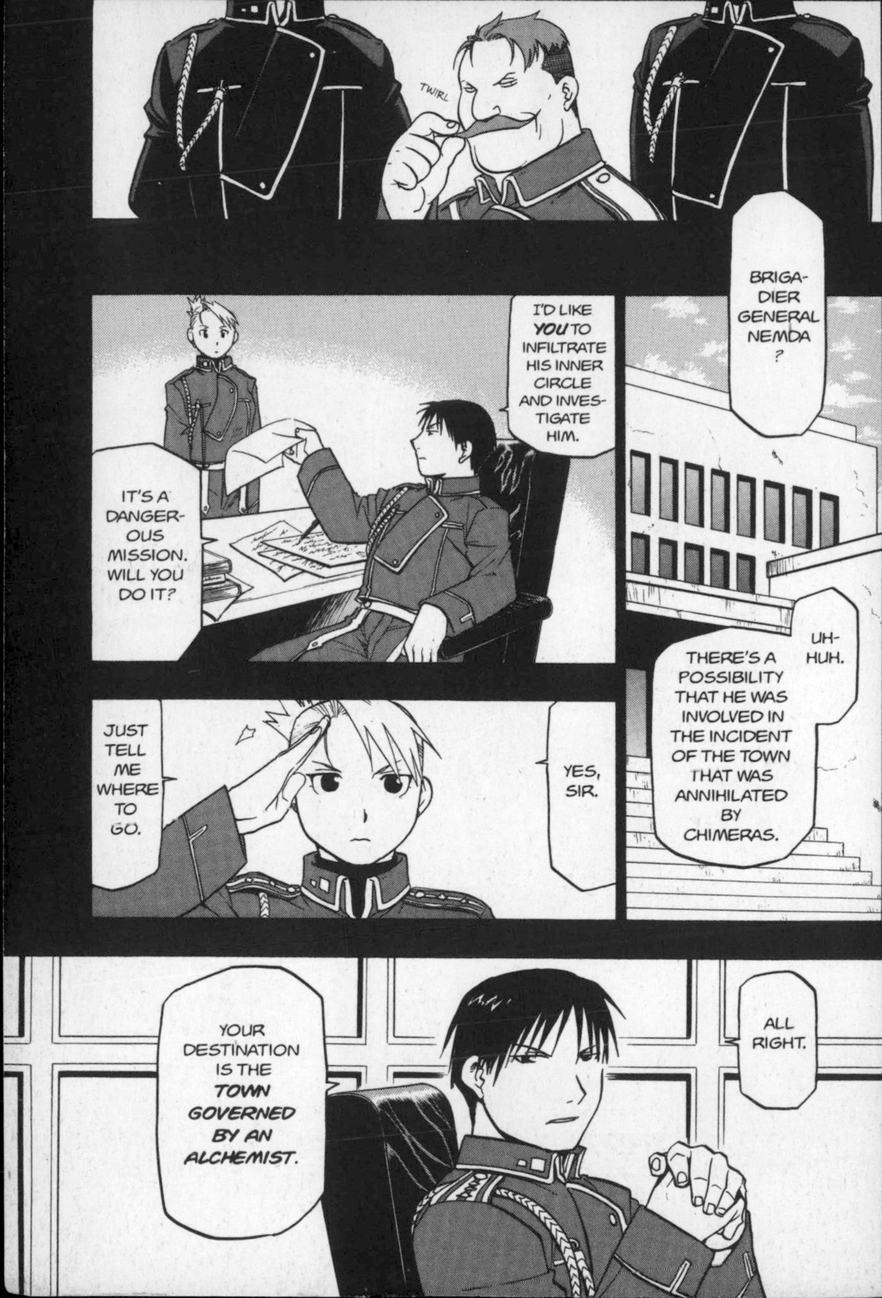
TWIRL
BRIGADIER GENERAL NEMDA?
UH-HUH.
THERE'S A POSSIBILITY THAT HE WAS INVOLVED IN THE INCIDENT OF THE TOWN THAT WAS ANNIHILATED BY CHIMERAS.
I'D LIKE *YOU* TO INFILTRATE HIS INNER CIRCLE AND INVESTIGATE HIM.
IT'S A DANGEROUS MISSION. WILL YOU DO IT?
YES, SIR.
JUST TELL ME WHERE TO GO.
ALL RIGHT.
YOUR DESTINATION IS THE *TOWN GOVERNED BY AN ALCHEMIST*.

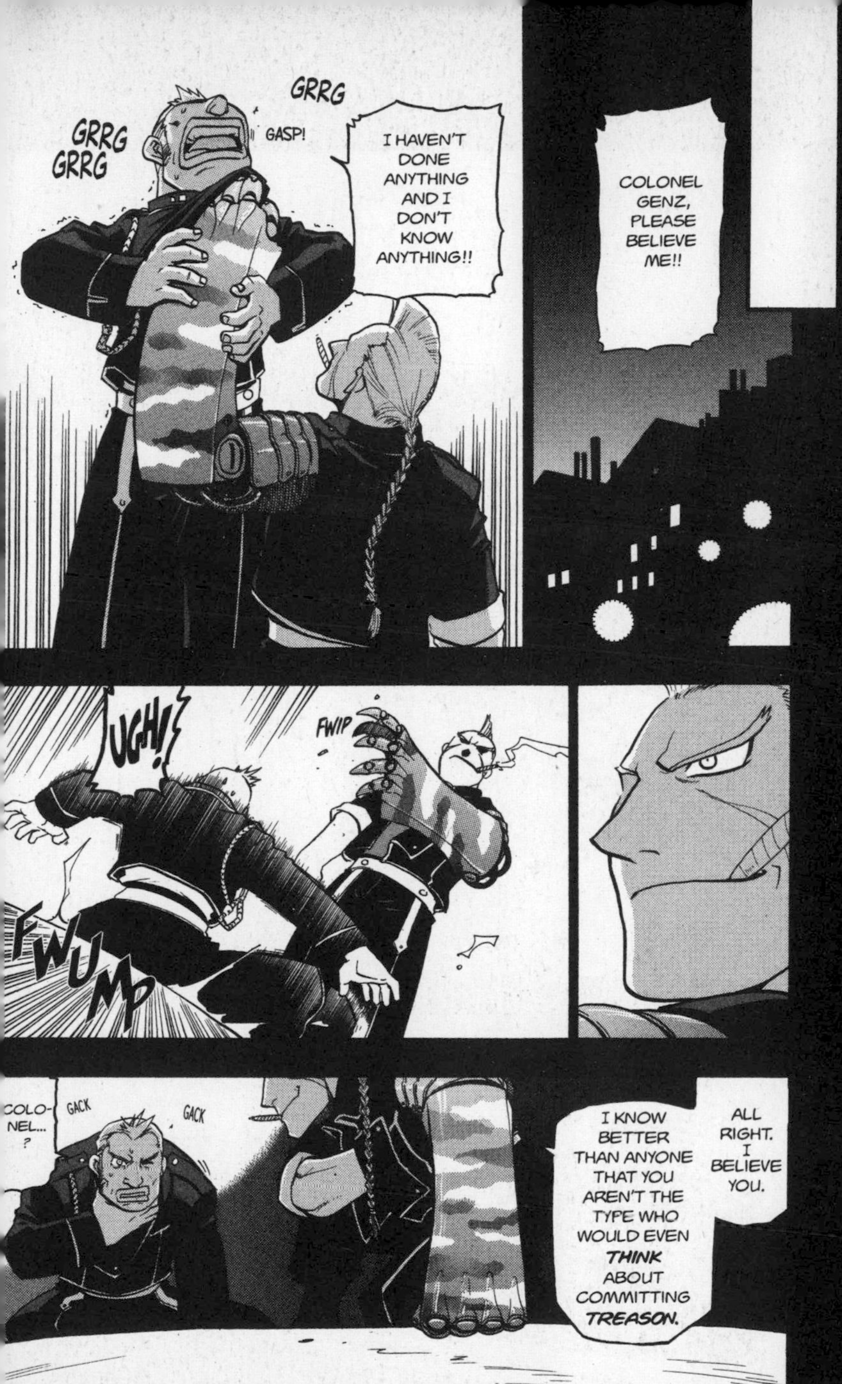
COLONEL GENZ, PLEASE BELIEVE ME!!
I HAVEN'T DONE ANYTHING AND I DON'T KNOW ANYTHING!!
GRRG
GASP!
GRRG GRRG
FWIP
UGH!
FWUMP
ALL RIGHT. I BELIEVE YOU.
I KNOW BETTER THAN ANYONE THAT YOU AREN'T THE TYPE WHO WOULD EVEN **THINK** ABOUT COMMITTING ***TREASON.***
GACK
GACK
COLONEL...?

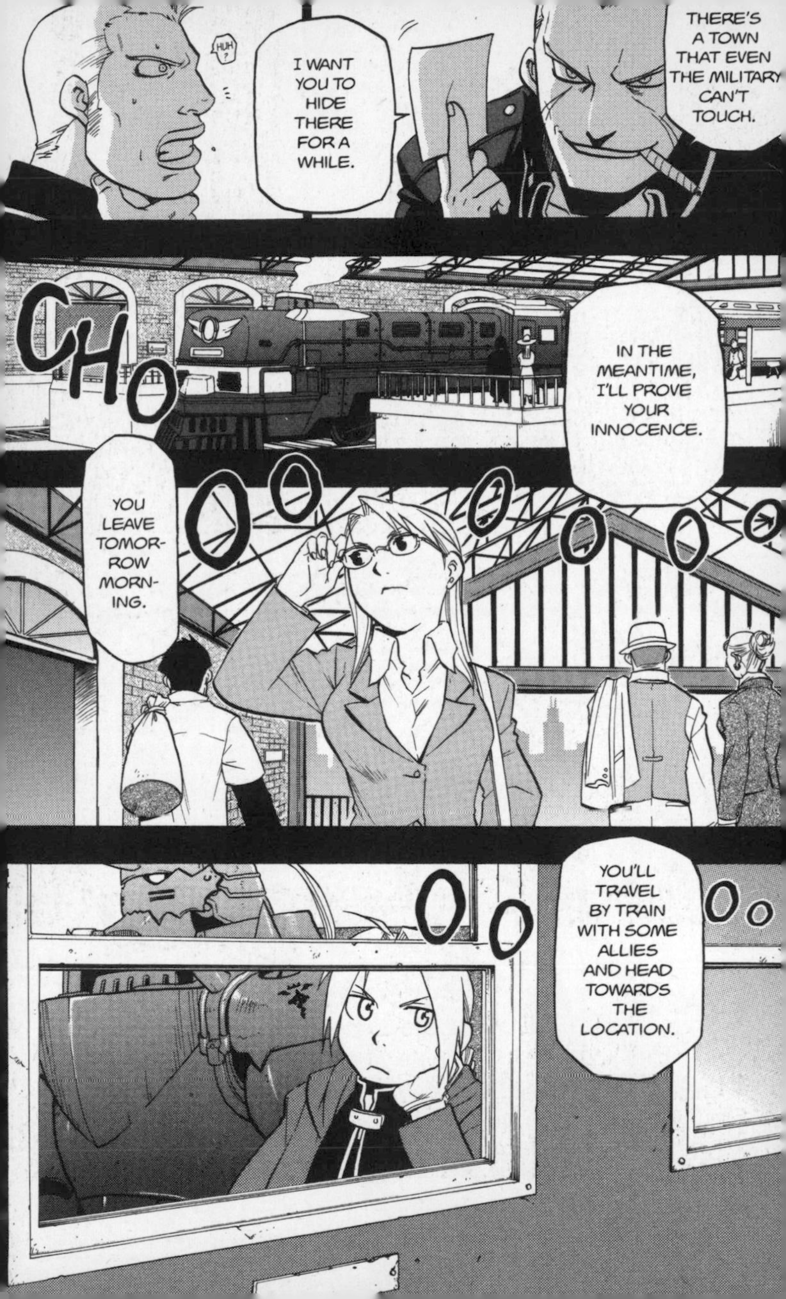
THERE'S A TOWN THAT EVEN THE MILITARY CAN'T TOUCH.
I WANT YOU TO HIDE THERE FOR A WHILE.
HUH?
IN THE MEANTIME, I'LL PROVE YOUR INNOCENCE.
CHOOOOOOOOOOO
YOU LEAVE TOMORROW MORNING.
YOU'LL TRAVEL BY TRAIN WITH SOME ALLIES AND HEAD TOWARDS THE LOCATION.

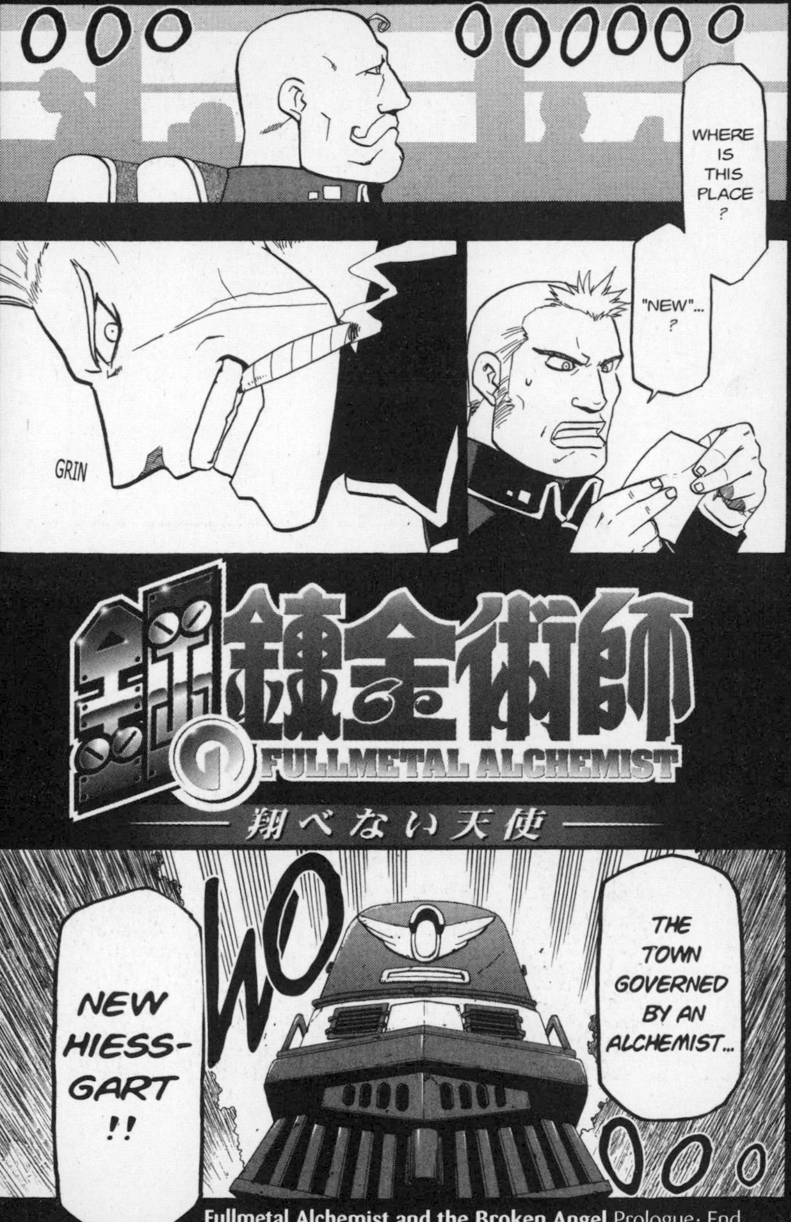
OOO OOOOOO
WHERE IS THIS PLACE?
"NEW"...?
GRIN
鋼の錬金術師
FULLMETAL ALCHEMIST
翔べない天使
THE TOWN GOVERNED BY AN ALCHEMIST...
NEW HIESS-GART!!
WO OOO

Fullmetal Alchemist and the Broken Angel Prologue: End

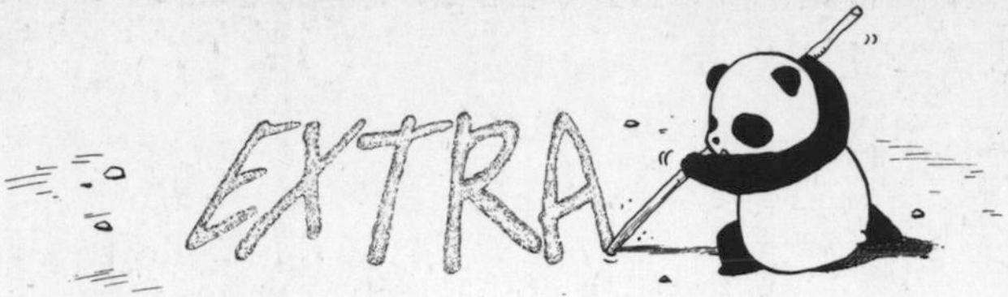
EXTRA

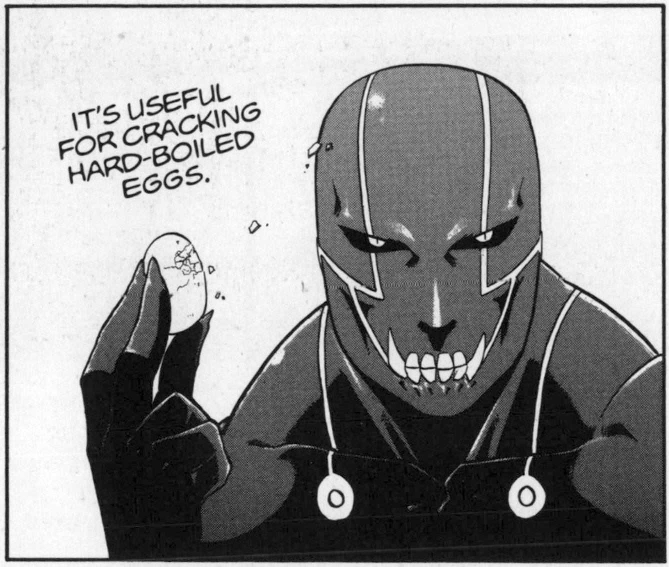
IT'S USEFUL FOR CRACKING HARD-BOILED EGGS.

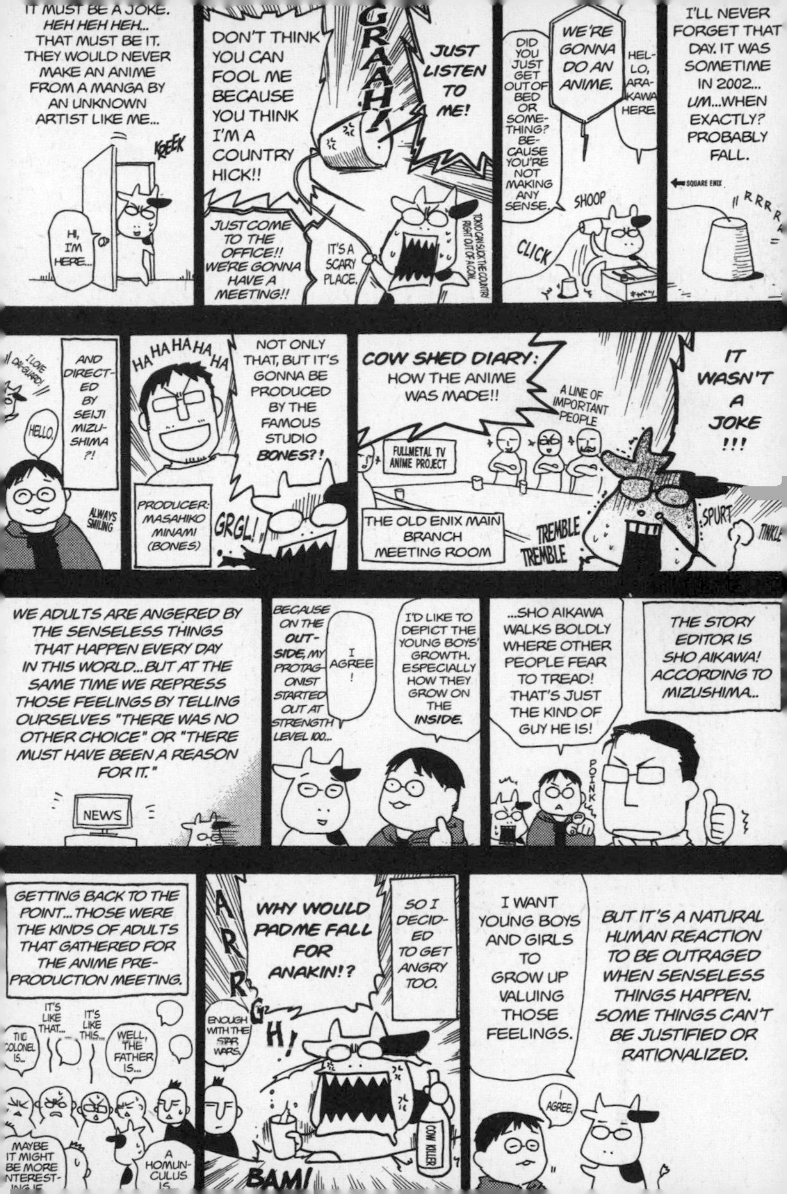

I'LL NEVER FORGET THAT DAY. IT WAS SOMETIME IN 2002... UM...WHEN EXACTLY? PROBABLY FALL.
SQUARE ENIX
RRRR
HEL-LO, ARA-KAWA HERE.
WE'RE GONNA DO AN ANIME.
DID YOU JUST GET OUT OF BED OR SOME-THING? BE-CAUSE YOU'RE NOT MAKING ANY SENSE.
SHOOP
CLICK
GRAAH!
JUST LISTEN TO ME!
DON'T THINK YOU CAN FOOL ME BECAUSE YOU THINK I'M A COUNTRY HICK!!
TOKYO CAN SUCK THE COUNTRY RIGHT OUT OF A COW.
JUST COME TO THE OFFICE!! WE'RE GONNA HAVE A MEETING!!
IT'S A SCARY PLACE.
IT MUST BE A JOKE. HEH HEH HEH... THAT MUST BE IT. THEY WOULD NEVER MAKE AN ANIME FROM A MANGA BY AN UNKNOWN ARTIST LIKE ME...
KREEK
HI, I'M HERE...
IT WASN'T A JOKE!!!
SPURT
TINKLE
TREMBLE TREMBLE
COW SHED DIARY: HOW THE ANIME WAS MADE!!
A LINE OF IMPORTANT PEOPLE
FULLMETAL TV ANIME PROJECT
THE OLD ENIX MAIN BRANCH MEETING ROOM
NOT ONLY THAT, BUT IT'S GONNA BE PRODUCED BY THE FAMOUS STUDIO BONES?!
HAHAHAHAHA
PRODUCER: MASAHIKO MINAMI (BONES)
GRGL!
AND DIRECT-ED BY SEIJI MIZU-SHIMA?!
I LOVE DAI-GUARD!
HELLO.
ALWAYS SMILING
THE STORY EDITOR IS SHO AIKAWA! ACCORDING TO MIZUSHIMA...
...SHO AIKAWA WALKS BOLDLY WHERE OTHER PEOPLE FEAR TO TREAD! THAT'S JUST THE KIND OF GUY HE IS!
POINK
I'D LIKE TO DEPICT THE YOUNG BOYS' GROWTH. ESPECIALLY HOW THEY GROW ON THE INSIDE.
BECAUSE ON THE OUT-SIDE, MY PROTAG-ONIST STARTED OUT AT STRENGTH LEVEL 100...
I AGREE!
WE ADULTS ARE ANGERED BY THE SENSELESS THINGS THAT HAPPEN EVERY DAY IN THIS WORLD...BUT AT THE SAME TIME WE REPRESS THOSE FEELINGS BY TELLING OURSELVES "THERE WAS NO OTHER CHOICE" OR "THERE MUST HAVE BEEN A REASON FOR IT."
NEWS
BUT IT'S A NATURAL HUMAN REACTION TO BE OUTRAGED WHEN SENSELESS THINGS HAPPEN. SOME THINGS CAN'T BE JUSTIFIED OR RATIONALIZED.
I WANT YOUNG BOYS AND GIRLS TO GROW UP VALUING THOSE FEELINGS.
I AGREE.
SO I DECID-ED TO GET ANGRY TOO.
WHY WOULD PADME FALL FOR ANAKIN!?
ARRGH!
ENOUGH WITH THE STAR WARS.
COW KILLER
BAM!
GETTING BACK TO THE POINT...THOSE WERE THE KINDS OF ADULTS THAT GATHERED FOR THE ANIME PRE-PRODUCTION MEETING.
IT'S LIKE THAT...
IT'S LIKE THIS...
WELL, THE FATHER IS...
THE COLONEL IS...
MAYBE IT MIGHT BE MORE INTEREST-
A HOMUN-CULUS

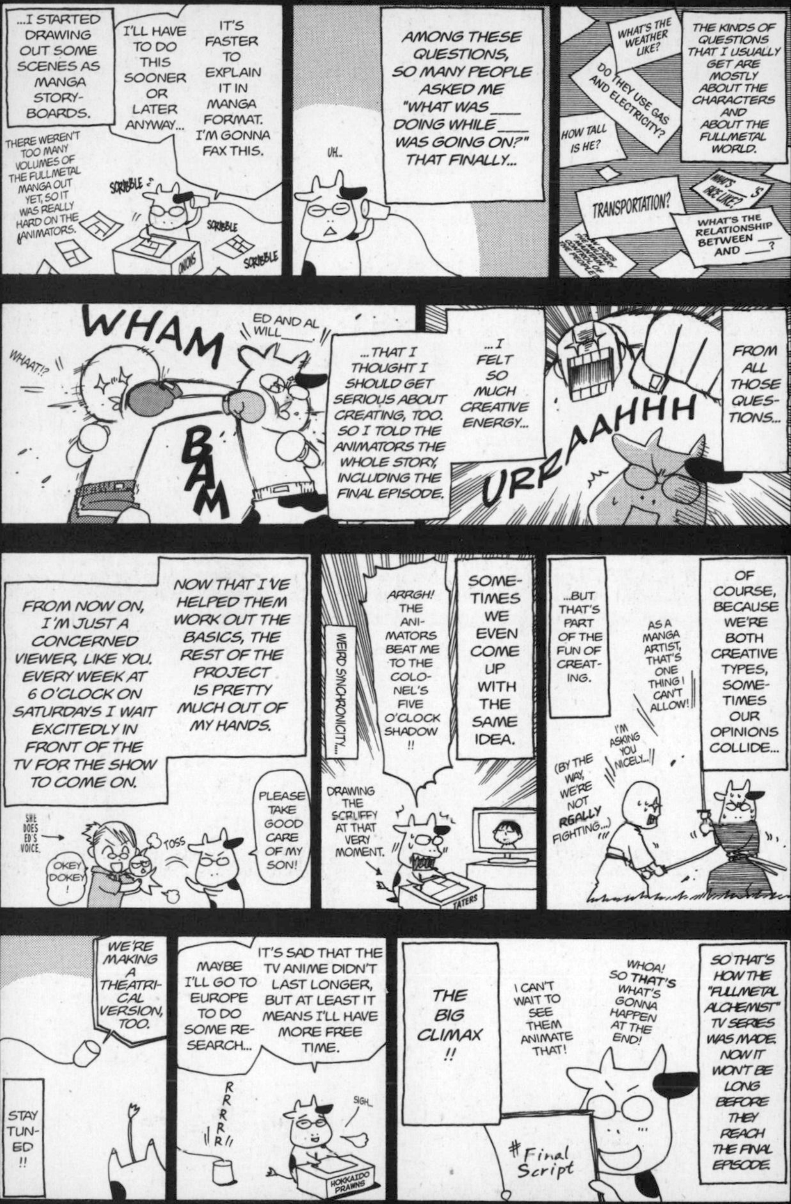
THE KINDS OF QUESTIONS THAT I USUALLY GET ARE MOSTLY ABOUT THE CHARACTERS AND ABOUT THE FULLMETAL WORLD.
WHAT'S THE WEATHER LIKE?
DO THEY USE GAS AND ELECTRICITY?
HOW TALL IS HE?
WHAT'S ___'S FACE LIKE?
TRANSPORTATION?
WHAT'S THE RELATIONSHIP BETWEEN ___ AND ___?
AMONG THESE QUESTIONS, SO MANY PEOPLE ASKED ME "WHAT WAS ___ DOING WHILE ___ WAS GOING ON?" THAT FINALLY...
UH..
...I STARTED DRAWING OUT SOME SCENES AS MANGA STORY-BOARDS.
I'LL HAVE TO DO THIS SOONER OR LATER ANYWAY...
IT'S FASTER TO EXPLAIN IT IN MANGA FORMAT. I'M GONNA FAX THIS.
THERE WEREN'T TOO MANY VOLUMES OF THE FULLMETAL MANGA OUT YET, SO IT WAS REALLY HARD ON THE ANIMATORS.
SCRIBBLE
SCRIBBLE
SCRIBBLE
ONIONS
FROM ALL THOSE QUES-TIONS...
URRAAHHH
...I FELT SO MUCH CREATIVE ENERGY...
...THAT I THOUGHT I SHOULD GET SERIOUS ABOUT CREATING, TOO. SO I TOLD THE ANIMATORS THE WHOLE STORY, INCLUDING THE FINAL EPISODE.
ED AND AL WILL____.
WHAM
WHAAT!?
BAM
OF COURSE, BECAUSE WE'RE BOTH CREATIVE TYPES, SOME-TIMES OUR OPINIONS COLLIDE...
AS A MANGA ARTIST, THAT'S ONE THING I CAN'T ALLOW!
...BUT THAT'S PART OF THE FUN OF CREAT-ING.
I'M ASKING YOU NICELY...
(BY THE WAY, WE'RE NOT REALLY FIGHTING...)
SOME-TIMES WE EVEN COME UP WITH THE SAME IDEA.
ARRGH! THE ANI-MATORS BEAT ME TO THE COLO-NEL'S FIVE O'CLOCK SHADOW!!
WEIRD SYNCHRONICITY...
DRAWING THE SCRUFFY AT THAT VERY MOMENT.
TATERS
NOW THAT I'VE HELPED THEM WORK OUT THE BASICS, THE REST OF THE PROJECT IS PRETTY MUCH OUT OF MY HANDS.
FROM NOW ON, I'M JUST A CONCERNED VIEWER, LIKE YOU. EVERY WEEK AT 6 O'CLOCK ON SATURDAYS I WAIT EXCITEDLY IN FRONT OF THE TV FOR THE SHOW TO COME ON.
PLEASE TAKE GOOD CARE OF MY SON!
TOSS
OKEY DOKEY!
SHE DOES ED'S VOICE.
SO THAT'S HOW THE "FULLMETAL ALCHEMIST" TV SERIES WAS MADE. NOW IT WON'T BE LONG BEFORE THEY REACH THE FINAL EPISODE.
WHOA! SO THAT'S WHAT'S GONNA HAPPEN AT THE END!
I CAN'T WAIT TO SEE THEM ANIMATE THAT!
THE BIG CLIMAX!!
#Final Script
IT'S SAD THAT THE TV ANIME DIDN'T LAST LONGER, BUT AT LEAST IT MEANS I'LL HAVE MORE FREE TIME.
MAYBE I'LL GO TO EUROPE TO DO SOME RE-SEARCH...
RRRRR
SIGH...
HOKKAIDO PRAWNS
WE'RE MAKING A THEATRI-CAL VERSION, TOO.
STAY TUN-ED!!

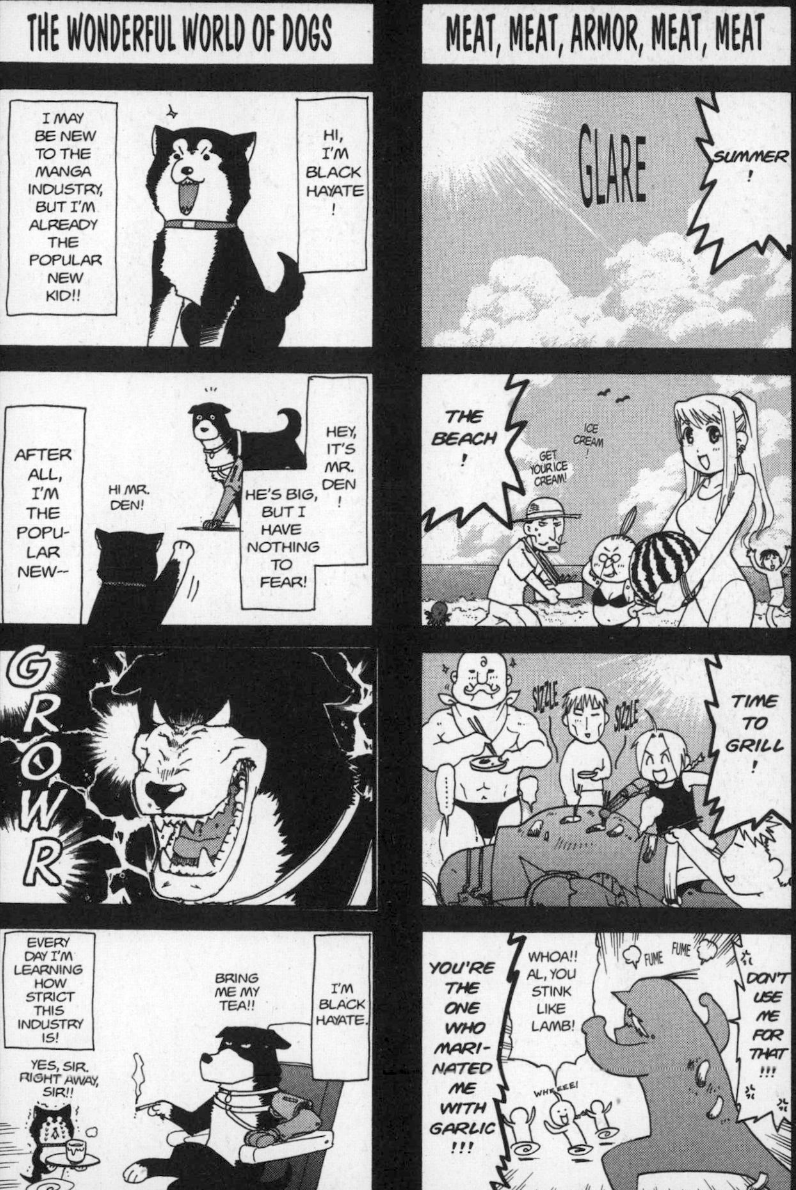
MEAT, MEAT, ARMOR, MEAT, MEAT
SUMMER!
GLARE
ICE CREAM!
THE BEACH!
GET YOUR ICE CREAM!
TIME TO GRILL!
SIZZLE
SIZZLE
DON'T USE ME FOR THAT!!!
FUME FUME
WHOA!! AL, YOU STINK LIKE LAMB!
YOU'RE THE ONE WHO MARINATED ME WITH GARLIC!!!
WHHEEE!
THE WONDERFUL WORLD OF DOGS
HI, I'M BLACK HAYATE!
I MAY BE NEW TO THE MANGA INDUSTRY, BUT I'M ALREADY THE POPULAR NEW KID!!
HEY, IT'S MR. DEN!
HE'S BIG, BUT I HAVE NOTHING TO FEAR!
HI MR. DEN!
AFTER ALL, I'M THE POPU-LAR NEW--
GROWR
I'M BLACK HAYATE.
BRING ME MY TEA!!
EVERY DAY I'M LEARNING HOW STRICT THIS INDUSTRY IS!
YES, SIR. RIGHT AWAY, SIR!!

DEATHTRAP

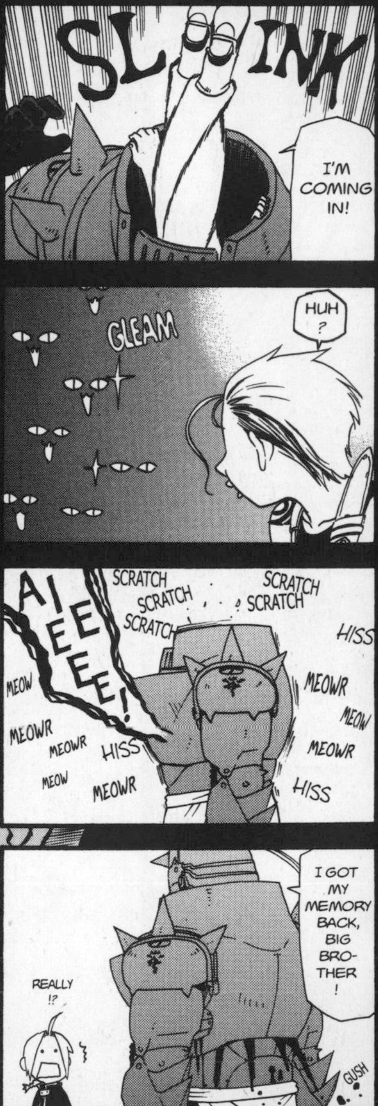
SL INK
I'M COMING IN!
HUH ?
GLEAM
AIEEEEE!
SCRATCH
SCRATCH
SCRATCH
SCRATCH
SCRATCH
HISS
MEOWR
MEOW
MEOWR
HISS
MEOW
MEOWR
MEOWR
MEOW
MEOWR
HISS
I GOT MY MEMORY BACK, BIG BROTHER!
REALLY !?
GUSH

FULLMETAL ALCHEMIST 8

SPECIAL THANKS TO...

KEISUI TAKAEDA-SAN
SANKICHI HINODEYA-SAN
MASANARI YUBEKA-SAN
JUNSHI BABA-SAN
AIYAABALL-SAN
JUN TOKO-SAN
YOICHI SHIMOMURA-SHI (MANAGER)
AND YOU !!

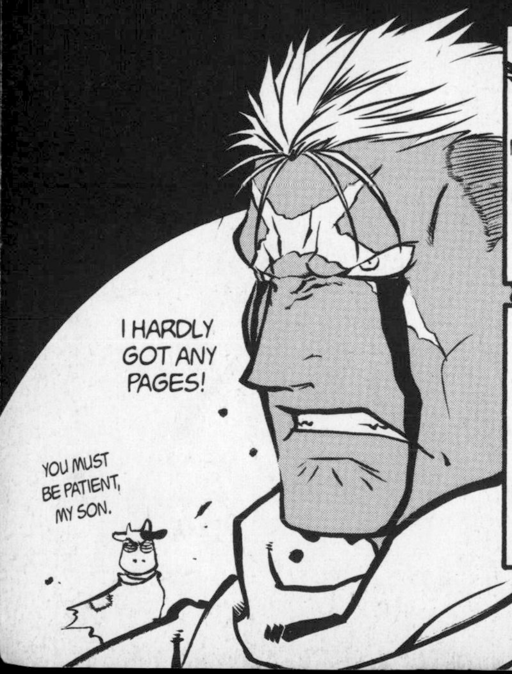
I HARDLY GOT ANY PAGES!
YOU MUST BE PATIENT, MY SON.

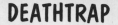

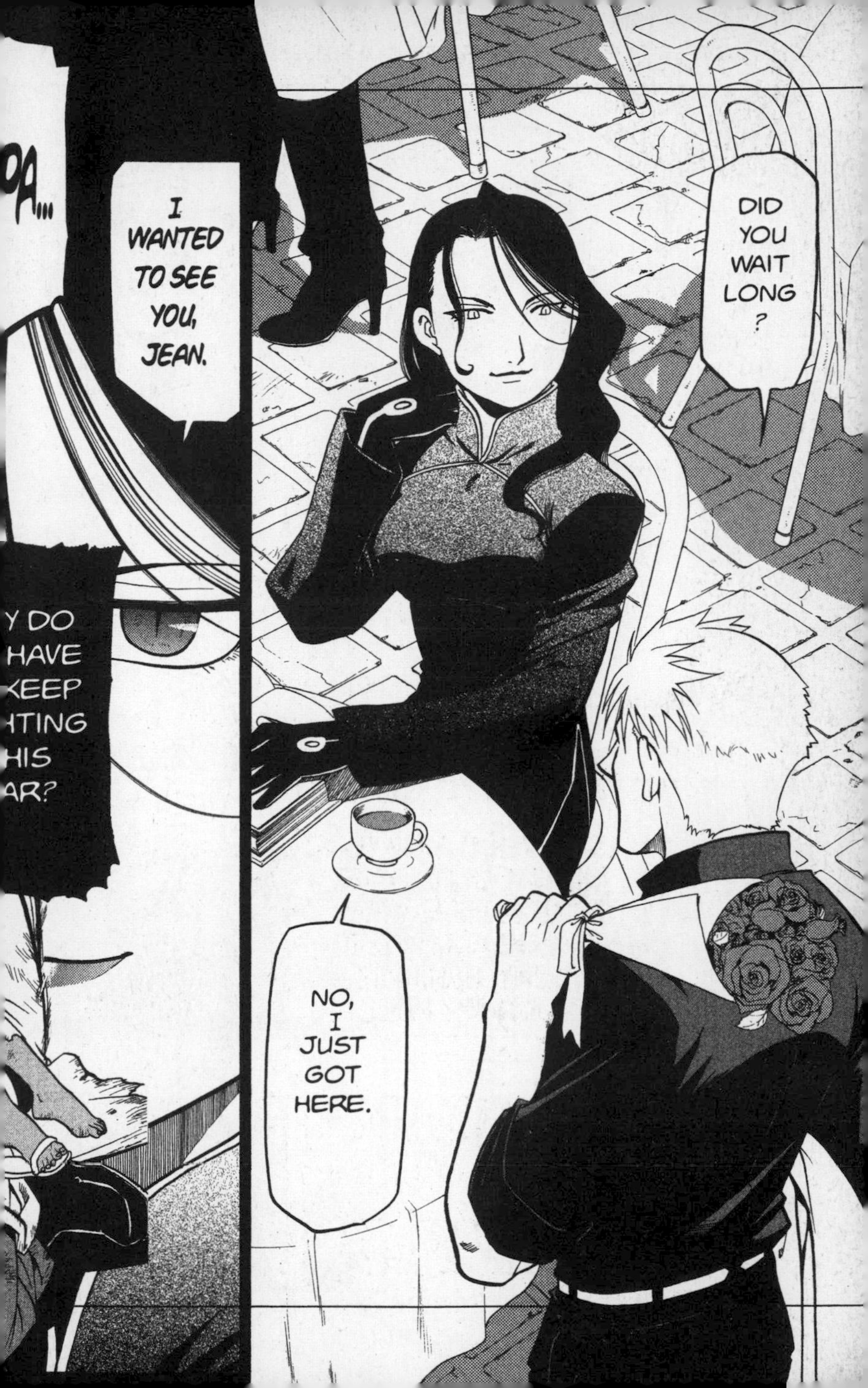
DID YOU WAIT LONG?
NO, I JUST GOT HERE.
OA...
I WANTED TO SEE YOU, JEAN.
Y DO HAVE KEEP HTING HIS AR?

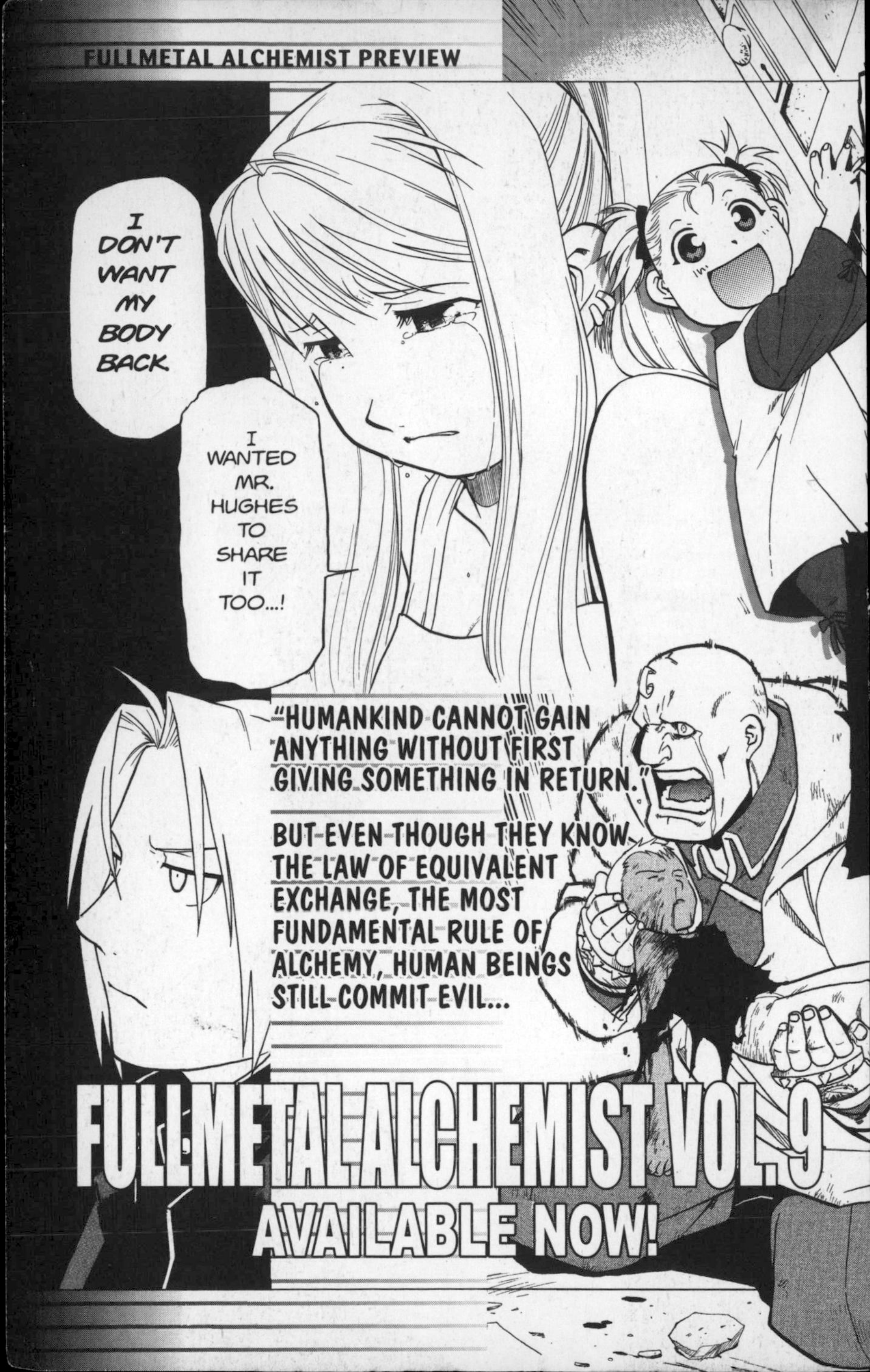
FULLMETAL ALCHEMIST PREVIEW
I DON'T WANT MY BODY BACK
I WANTED MR. HUGHES TO SHARE IT TOO...!
"HUMANKIND CANNOT GAIN ANYTHING WITHOUT FIRST GIVING SOMETHING IN RETURN."
BUT EVEN THOUGH THEY KNOW THE LAW OF EQUIVALENT EXCHANGE, THE MOST FUNDAMENTAL RULE OF ALCHEMY, HUMAN BEINGS STILL COMMIT EVIL...
FULLMETAL ALCHEMIST VOL.9
AVAILABLE NOW!

Image change

side
part

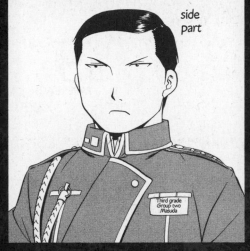
Third grade
Group two
Masuda

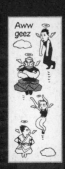
Aww
geez

In Memoriam

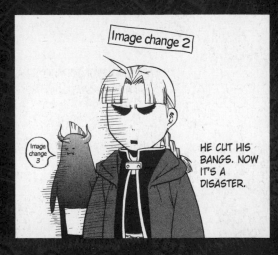
Image change 2

Image
change
3

HE CUT HIS
BANGS. NOW
IT'S A
DISASTER.

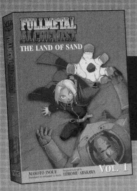
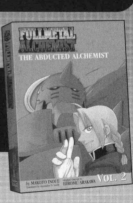
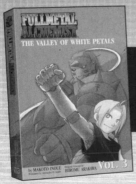

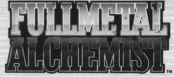

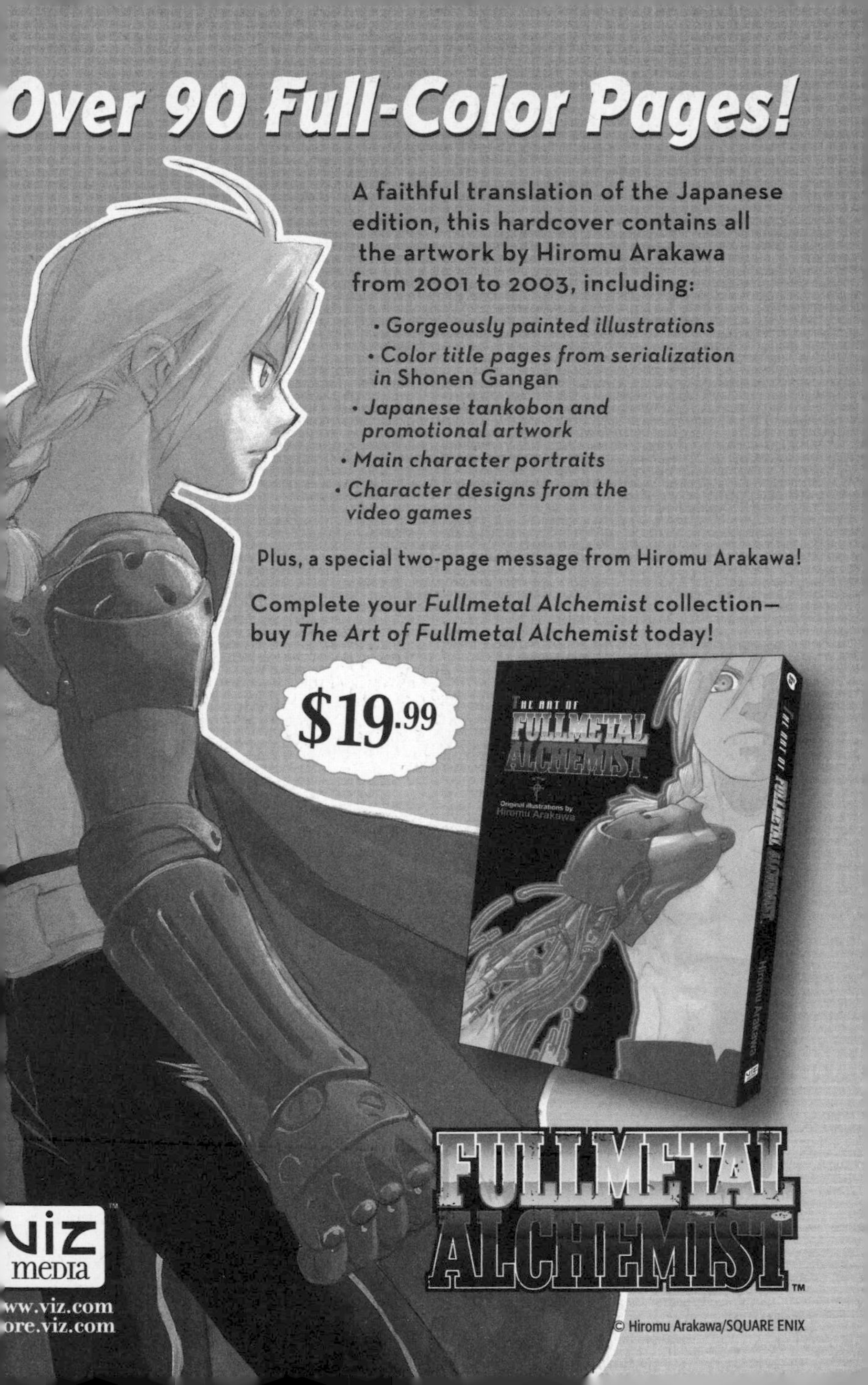
Over 90 Full-Color Pages!
A faithful translation of the Japanese edition, this hardcover contains all the artwork by Hiromu Arakawa from 2001 to 2003, including:
• Gorgeously painted illustrations
• Color title pages from serialization in Shonen Gangan
• Japanese tankobon and promotional artwork
• Main character portraits
• Character designs from the video games
Plus, a special two-page message from Hiromu Arakawa!
Complete your Fullmetal Alchemist collection—buy The Art of Fullmetal Alchemist today!
$19.99
The Art of Fullmetal Alchemist
Original illustrations by Hiromu Arakawa
FULLMETAL ALCHEMIST™
viz media™
www.viz.com
store.viz.com
© Hiromu Arakawa/SQUARE ENIX

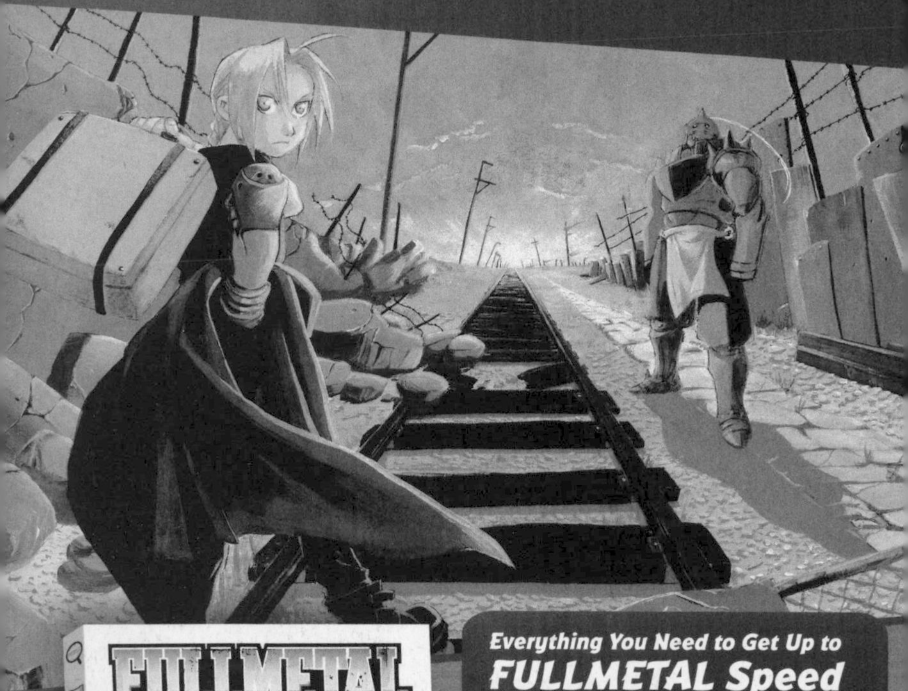

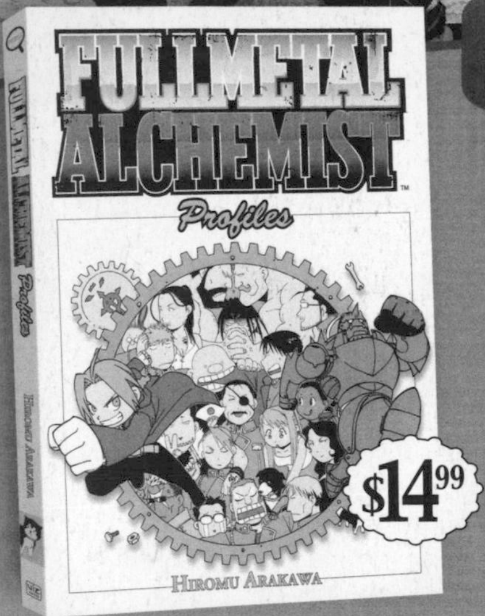
FULLMETAL ALCHEMIST
Profiles
HIROMU ARAKAWA
$14.99

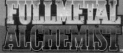

LOVE MA[...]

LET US KNOW WHAT YOU THINK!

OUR MANGA SURVEY IS NOW AVAILABLE ONLINE. PLEASE VISIT: VIZ.COM/MANGASURVEY

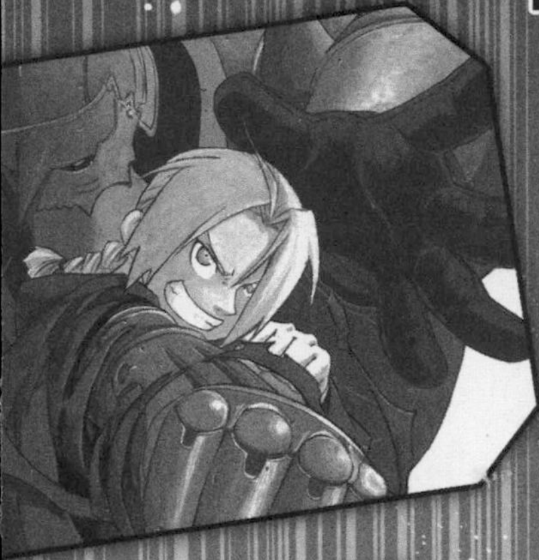

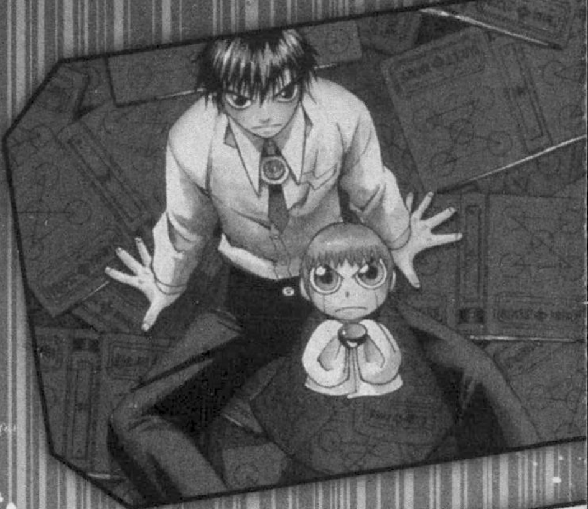

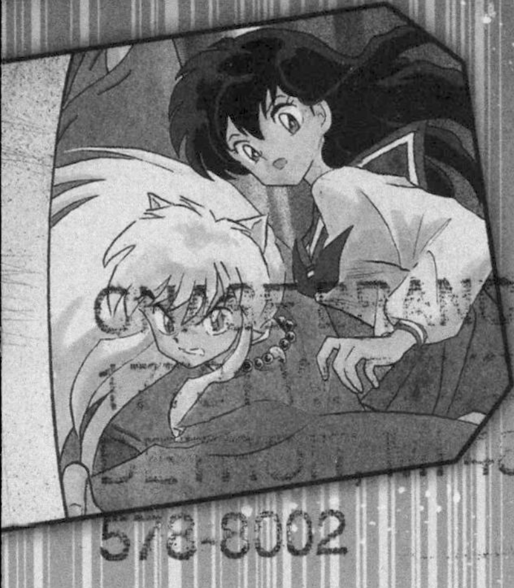

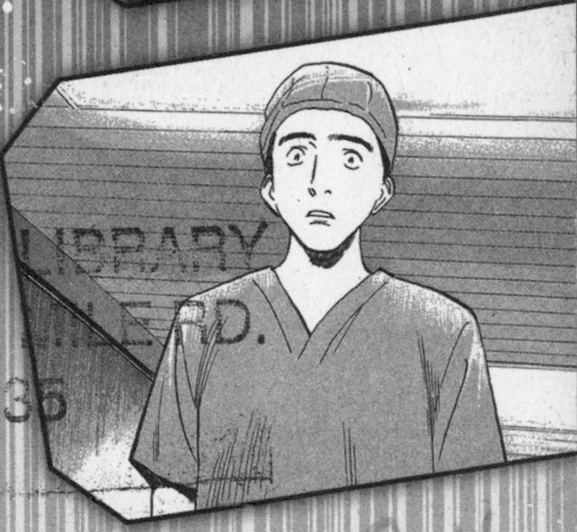

HELP US MAKE THE MANGA YOU LOVE BETTER!

VIZ media